BAX: BEST AMERICAN EXPERIMENTAL WRITING

Series Editors Seth Abramson and Jesse Damiani

Managing Editor Michael Martin Shea

BAX 2016

Guest Editors Charles Bernstein and Tracie Morris

BAX 2014

Guest Editor Cole Swensen

BAX 2015

Guest Editor Douglas Kearney

BAX 2018

Guest Editor Myung Mi Kim

BAX

Guest Editors | *Carmen Maria Machado and Joyelle McSweeney*
Series Editors | *Seth Abramson and Jesse Damiani*
Managing Editor | *Michael Martin Shea*

2020 BEST AMERICAN EXPERIMENTAL WRITING

Wesleyan University Press
Middletown, Connecticut

Wesleyan University Press

Middletown CT 06459

www.wesleyan.edu/wespress

© 2020 Wesleyan University Press

All rights reserved

Manufactured in the United States of America

Designed by Mindy Basinger Hill

Typeset in Minion Pro

Library of Congress Cataloging-in-Publication Data

Names: Machado, Carmen Maria, editor. | McSweeney, Joyelle, editor. | Abramson, Seth, editor. | Damiani, Jesse, editor.

Title: BAX 2020 : best American experimental writing / guest editors, Carmen Maria Machado and Joyelle McSweeney; series editors, Seth Abramson and Jesse Damiani; managing editor, Michael Martin Shea.

Other titles: Best American experimental writing 2020

Description: Middletown, Connecticut : Wesleyan University Press, 2020. | Series: Best American experimental writing | Includes bibliographical references. | Summary: "A collection of exceptionally inventive and exploratory American writing from 2018 to 2020"—Provided by publisher.

Identifiers: LCCN 2020029934 (print)

LCCN 2020029935 (ebook)

ISBN 9780819579577 (cloth)

ISBN 9780819579584 (trade paperback)

ISBN 9780819579591 (ebook)

Subjects: LCSH: Literature, Experimental—United States— 21st century. | Experimental poetry, American—21st century.

Classification: LCC PS536.3 .B39 2020 (print) | LCC PS536.3 (ebook) | DDC 810.8/006—dc23

LC record available at https://lccn.loc.gov/2020029934

LC ebook record available at https://lccn.loc.gov/2020029935

5   4   3   2   1

Contents

*The following digital contributions to BAX 2020 can be found
at bax.site.wesleyan.edu.*

Guest Editor's Introduction

1. When we were asked to guest edit *Best American Experimental Writing*, we were eager to do it. There were only a few problems.

2. One: we don't believe in "Bestness." We don't subscribe to a Tradition-and-the-Individual-Talent style grudge match, with all the certified white male geniuses lined up for the weigh-in, or any of that narrow, exclusionary thinking. We believe in Jack Smith's pasties dancing on the birthday cake in *Normal Love* and Maya Deren's mirrormen and the unchanging griefscape of Derek Jarman's *Blue*. We believe in strangeness, mutancy, loveliness, minorness, hellaciousness, audacity, hauntedness, beauty, quietness, monsters, cyborgs, and the scrum.

3. We also aren't interested in a simplistic definition of "American," whatever that is supposed to mean. While the legal disparities faced by people with different citizenship statuses are dangerous and real, when it comes to art, each writer must negotiate their own relationship to their nations of birth and of residency, their cultures and their canons. A DACA recipient may feel entirely American, while a US-born writer may feel alienated and disconnected from the literature they've learned in school. This is a volume of immigrants, of bilingual writers, of translators, of works not written originally in English. This is a volume without a citizenship test.

4. The term "experimental" is also a problem, or at least an open question. On the 200th anniversary of *Frankenstein*, we love sci-fi, graphs and diagrams, jargon and taxonomy, specialists and speculation, quantum physics and pataphysics. But we reject the exclusion that the word "experimental" can entail, at least as it is rendered on too many syllabi, panels, and tables of content. Such exclusion, whether due to race, nationality, gender, disability, translation status, or aberrant aesthetics, misses whole galaxies of profuse inventiveness. The garden we tend here is a hybrid of Renee Gladman and Marosa di Giorgio and Angela Carter and Jean Toomer and Leonora Carrington. It features many luscious and killer creatures, flowers of stars, of fur, of glass, doors to nowhere and doors to everywhere.

5. Finally, "writing." Well, a good deal of this is writing. But some of it is drawing. Some of it is sewing. Some of it is altered photographs. Most of it is textual, but some of it is not a text.

6. So that's what this volume is not: not (comfortably) Best, not (necessarily) Experimental, not (easily) American, and not (always) Writing.

7. So what is this volume? Uncomfortable, uneasy, unheimlicheit, unhealthy, unsound; exploring new comforts, new eases, new homes, new healths, new sounds. A coming together, a gathering of notions, a temporary confection, and a breaking apart.

SETH ABRAMSON AND JESSE DAMIANI

Series Editors' Introduction

When we founded this anthology series early last decade, we told anyone who would listen that we had little interest in the four non-article words in the series title: "best"; "American"; "experimental"; and "writing." We gave our project the title we did because we knew that America's market economy has long been the arbiter of whether, when, and how the most daring artwork finds an audience. Anything the market cannot classify, it cannot sell; anything it cannot sell, it has no interest in whatsoever. We looked at the bookshelves of the nation, both virtual and material, and saw that those author-editors who said with confidence that they could detect the "best" work in their respective genres were the ones who were permitted to transmit a set number of such works in the said genres—almost certainly not the "best," even by whatever definition one might choose to adopt—to an American audience that more than ever before needs to have the subtleties of language brought with regularity to its attention.

XI

We were cynical, that is—but for, we felt, the best reason possible. We hoped to find a vehicle for the most commonplace yet transformative framework for language: a cross-genre, interdisciplinary, transmedia space in which an author works inductively from a *poetics* rather than deductively from a series of aesthetic prescriptions like genre or critical cognizability. Our definition of "poetics" was a simple one; in our discussions with one another, we defined it as the dynamic, idiosyncratic relationship an author develops—sometimes day to day, sometimes across decades—with language, genre, culture, and self-identity. We believed that the artworks that transform societies, and last long enough in the public imagination to inspire future generations, are generally those in which a poetics, rather than merely an aesthetic, is evident. We were ambivalent on the question of what sort of poetics individual artists would do well to develop, as our only rooting interest was in artists broadly being encouraged to engage an honest process of poetics development free from the interference or undue influence of preselected externalities. We wanted to put together an anthology that would inspire young authors to set no limits on their creativity and to write with such a fidelity to their own temperaments, skill sets, knowledge bases, traumas, interests, obsessions, and quirks that they would never doubt the spiritual utility of a life in art. We believed that a life well lived in art would naturally come to be a full life outside of it as well.

As we prepare to put our project into the capable hands of other editors, we are, here at the dawn of a new decade, at a moment in American history when so much we cherish—language, the rule of law, democracy, even freedom itself—is under threat. We look outside our work and see writers of all creative writing genres wondering what an alacrity with received generic forms can do for their country, and we see these same writers discovering that, beyond providing hope in dark times, which is no small favor, the answer is: Not as much as they would like. But when we look inside the pages of year after year of *Best American Experimental Writing*, we see something else: Authors with robustly transferable skill sets born of idiosyncratic creative and critical thinking. We see dexterous, interdisciplinary minds capable of challenging the ways we see phenomena and process information both within and without creative writing. We see, beyond any indicia of ideology or aesthetic gesture or commitment to genre, an unflappable generative energy. We see persons of diverse backgrounds and experiences with the power to restore what America has already lost and is still losing. And we see the value in having framed this anthology series in a way that ensured all this wonderful energy could reach impressionable minds as it might not have otherwise.

*

The art world is more unforgiving than we like to publicly admit, as both of us have discovered in different ways over the past decade. Neither of us is regarded as an artist today in the same sense we were regarded as artists when we met in Madison, Wisconsin, nearly a decade ago. One of us is passionately committed to the promise of virtual, augmented, and mixed reality, as well as blockchain and artificial intelligence; the other is equally passionate about the possibilities inherent in digitally executed curatorial journalism, post-postmodern problem-solving praxes, and the reinvigoration of the humanities through audacious reframing rather than ignominious retreat. Both of us still believe ourselves to be poets, not because our terminal degrees tell us we are, or our publication records, but because we have always thought of the "poet" as a versatile, reflexive, dynamic wordsmith whose poetics can carry into far-flung disciplines where words like "lineation" and "stanza" have no purchase. It has been difficult, at times, to know that our titling of this series gave the impression we had set expectations for writers in America or anywhere else, when in fact we define "writing" in terms so broad we're more likely to be accused of depriving it of meaning altogether than over-prescribing its parameters. In the view of what a poetics-oriented approach to interpersonal communication can accomplish, not only are there no genres or canons or requisite formal gestures but no "best," no national boundaries, and no limit on what may be considered an "experiment." It is not too cute to say that an experiment is in the eyes of the experimenter; all we have ever wanted to encourage is a commitment to daring by whatever means, on whatever terms, and in whichever fora any individual artist might select. It has been a rather grand vision to try to accommodate in a marketable anthology.

We remain struck by what even that expansive vision of this series was unable to include. We sought to incorporate into our editorial ethos a commitment to democracy, process, and heterogeneity—by choosing many submissions blind, rigorously adhering to a no-conflict-of-interest policy, and deliberately avoiding any thematic, formal, or conceptual coherence within or between anthology editions—but there was no easy way to represent in book format some of the traits we most value. Kindness. Gentleness. Generosity. Supportiveness. An end to an art community that too often traffics in falseness, envy, and arrogant suppositions about what other artists are doing and why. We believe America's literary community in particular continues to face problems of access that are economic as well as intersectional with other demographics, and we believe some of those in a position to militate publicly for art education to be more affordable and accessible in America have chosen for reasons we cannot understand not to do so. None of these concerns ever made their way into the anthology during our stewardship of it, though they were with us every time we spent hours poring through blind submissions or obscure publications to give a big break to an author we'd never before encountered and perhaps who had never before been kindly received (or received at all) by peers.

Our roads now diverge from this anthology, and indeed from the literary community as it has been conventionally conceived. We expect that emerging technologies, the still-evolving cultural paradigms of metamodernism and (on its heels) paramodernism, the instinctive dismantling of boundaries sought by the generations coming up, and the increasing awareness of all the ways a literary artist moves in the world that have nothing to do with literary art will soon send many tens of thousands of onetime literary artists down the very same foreign roads we're now traveling. We already find this phenomenon in the countless friends, acquaintances, and admired-from-afar peers who have departed the poetry-writing sphere and engaged their interest in other genres, professions, and fields of inquiry or activism. Perhaps like many of these happily perpetual beginners, we have no idea what we're doing most days, but we hope—at a minimum—we are building something surprising and illuminating with the poetry-derived skills and experiences we've discovered in ourselves. We hope that publishing hundreds of artists of many genres (and sometimes no genre or an admixture of genres) over the past few years has given these creative thinkers and their readers a chance to witness—and perhaps a nudge to experiment further with—a similarly conceptual and interdisciplinary approach to imaginative writing going forward.

Our belief in artists is variable; our belief in art is not. We hope you have found in these pages over the preceding decade some sense of what we think the most expansive possible commitment to creativity can produce. We are in awe of the writers we have had the honor to publish, and we hope to carry that awe forward into our future endeavors on and off the page. And we hope that, along the way, we will encounter some of you.

KANIKA AGRAWAL

from *Okazaki Fragments*

Images and some language adapted from the following two papers from a 16-part series on discontinuous strand synthesis during DNA replication:

Okazaki, T., and R. Okazaki. "Mechanism of DNA Chain Growth, IV. Direction of synthesis of T4 short DNA chains as revealed by exonucleolytic degradation." *Proceedings of the National Academy of Sciences USA* 64, no. 4 (1969): 1242–48.

Sugimoto, K., Okazaki, T., Imae, Y., and R. Okazaki. "Mechanism of DNA Chain Growth, III. Equal annealing of T4 nascent short DNA chains with the separated complementary strands of the phage DNA." *Proceedings of the National Academy of Sciences USA* 63, no. 4 (1969): 1343–50.

These proceedings in nature
These proceedings in cold biology
These proceedings in chemical society
These proceedings in physical communication

We refer to the concentration of residues
We observe that one sediments
    faster than the other
We presume as fact that most of what we do
    is in growing incomplete
        short chains

We further support the conclusion
We indicate direction also
    by another method

We are grateful to Drs.

Lying on the bed, eyes scanning the floor, Okazaki performs a final critical reading of the surface. Each tile is a template for the eight around it. A hairpin has fallen, prongs bent apart. Opposite, Okazaki's feet rest parallel and complementary in adjacent tiles. Tracking Okazaki's leaning angles, up the legs to the hips, continuing to the torso, the loose graying shirt buttoned low, Okazaki reaches the cleavage, or rather the sulcus, where Okazaki once placed pomegranate seeds, marking a line from the suprasternal notch to the umbilicus, as though drawing blood while carefully, partially scoring Okazaki for later separation. The light in the window behind grows stronger, thinning Okazaki like a strand unbinding Okazaki from Okazaki. In some circumstances, structures are not formed or are not compatible. In some circumstances, they are extremely short lived. Okazaki faces the ceiling. A clock nicks time continuously and irreversibly. Okazaki moves closer to Okazaki. A fan turns slowly, spirals down toward Okazaki. The air flushes with winged samaras spinning away from their red maples in private vortices. When they all come to ground, Okazaki's hand is still in Okazaki's hand.

4

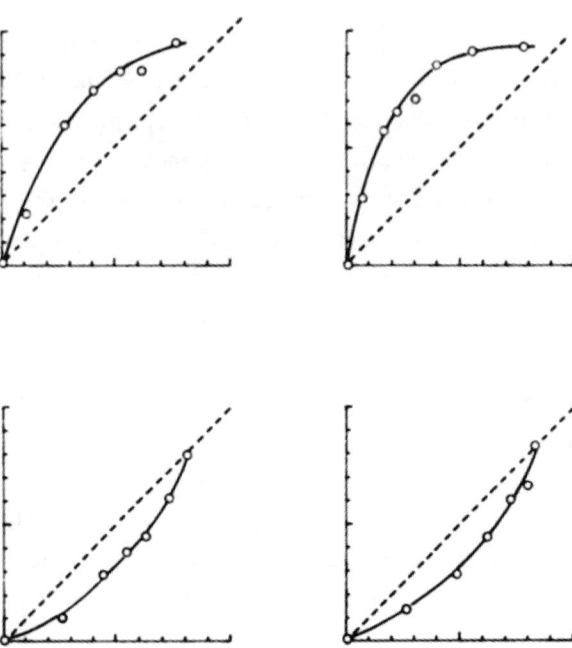

Okazaki and Okazaki sit on a bench waiting for the cherry trees to flower. A black umbrella hangs from a branch above, steel ribs and nylon membranes shut quiet. On that branch, and every other, racemose clusters of buds will become visible, followed by bursts of white blossom, hint of pink at the center. A bare fragrance will rise and coalesce into a permeable film, upon which Okazaki will leave an impression. Meanwhile, a culture of clouds develops over Okazaki and Okazaki, gradients from a point above the bench to the perimeter of the park. Drops will begin to fall, soon, equally on each. Even so, Okazaki is not under the same conditions as Okazaki. White blasts bloom in Okazaki's bones, crowd the marrow. Inside Okazaki, the seasons are changing quickly. Okazaki will raise the shade of the umbrella, but Okazaki will not be able to shift into it. Water from the clouds, acting as an eluent, will unfix Okazaki. Okazaki will not find cover. Observers may see Okazaki and Okazaki in black and white, respectively.

In which ways and to what extent
    are the results influenced
by the suppression of the host?

        Effects on the pulse are revealed
          in as little as six seconds,
        and there are eight degrees
          of susceptibility

The fractioning indicated by the arrows—

        —occurs successively for various times

Can certain components be
    bracketed, combined, layered
together for neutralization?

        Only after the whole molecule
          is further subjected
        can it be recovered
          from these conditions
        However, it is also essential
          that such conditions be found
        satisfactory at certain intervals

Reactions must be mixed,
    not homogeneous?

        That is how
          the membranes
        are loaded

When it is early enough for hope, Okazaki is advised to proceed normally, though at a reduced pace. Accustomed to certain modes and methods, Okazaki resists the shift-down, until Okazaki brings the labeled boxes, among them *exo*, *degradation*, and *terminal region*. Prepared for Okazaki's limited reaction, Okazaki is thus able to trigger a repair reaction. The gesture is made very small to obtain unequivocal results. It is necessary to go slow, study, determine direction, identify specific usefulness, and model in a stepwise manner beginning from the end.

Before the kinetics of release; before preparation, negotiation, explanation; before diagnosis, assays and tests; there is chill, internal scintillation, alternately immobilizing and innervating. Other times, in the night, infected with heat, only a bath of crushed ice arrests the incubation.

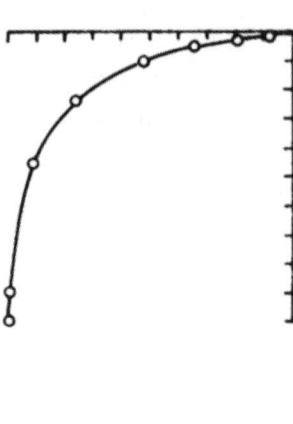

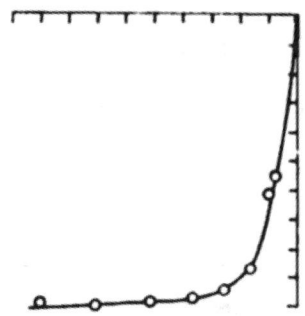

Okazaki leaves the laboratory before Okazaki. An unfamiliar fatigue has been troubling Okazaki for weeks. Riding a bicycle home, Okazaki pauses where the path splits, then heads for the clarifying water of the brook. Okazaki sits on a mound, removes shoes and socks, eels the feet into a shallow pool, and leans back against a rock. With graph paper neatly torn from a notebook, Okazaki folds a boat, and another, and another, each more elaborate than the last. If Okazaki were here, Okazaki would say, *How beautiful, Okazaki! Such crystalline preparation!* The trick, Okazaki would respond, is to decide between possibilities based on the present evidence of the paper, however unlikely. Consistent with itself, paper may be fashioned in a discontinuous manner without compromising integrity. Now Okazaki whispers names into the hulls of the boats, trusts them one by one to the soft current, follows their course until they grow heavy and drown.

It can be considered a covalent joining resulting from the development under normal steady-state conditions of a faculty for synthesis. In spite of Okazaki's coefficient of isolation and Okazaki's experiments in temporally regulated inhibition, nothing keeps Okazaki from Okazaki for long. Molecularly appealing, Okazaki's and Okazaki's strands tend to each other. The selective mechanism has been described elsewhere as a recurring gift interaction.

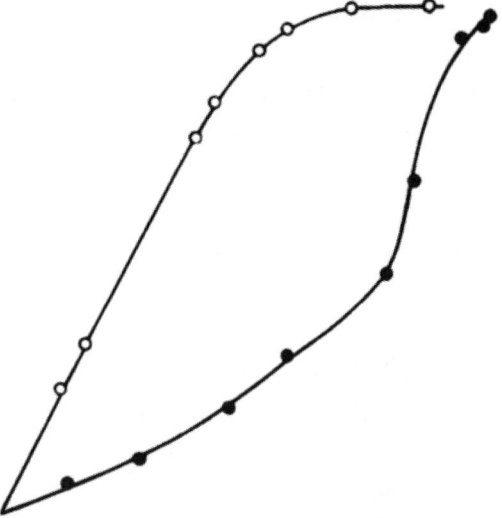

13

Okazaki and Okazaki decide to prepare a manuscript. Okazaki clears the table and Okazaki arranges the forks. If 50 percent of the forks travel in one direction and the remaining 50 percent in the other direction . . . To Okazaki, the possibility seems remote, but Okazaki pulls up another table. Okazaki sits at the first table and polishes the forks while Okazaki sets and resets. Okazaki slices and pickles cucumbers, handing them to Okazaki unidirectionally for reevaluation. Okazaki visits neglected corners and stirs the dust in response to Okazaki's concerns about impurity. Okazaki sings. Okazaki stretches. Okazaki and Okazaki make similar observations of a pair of birds at the feeder. Okazaki calls Okazaki over: This is most clearly seen in Table 1 and the reason for this phenomenon is not known, but the value varies from experiment to experiment in the range of 20 to 50 percent. Low values are obtained with the original procedure used in the experiment. The modification used in the other experiments results in improved efficiency. This work will be of interest to the Research Fund of the Ministry of Education. Okazaki peels an orange in single-stranded form, then winds it back. Okazaki lends positive support to the idea.

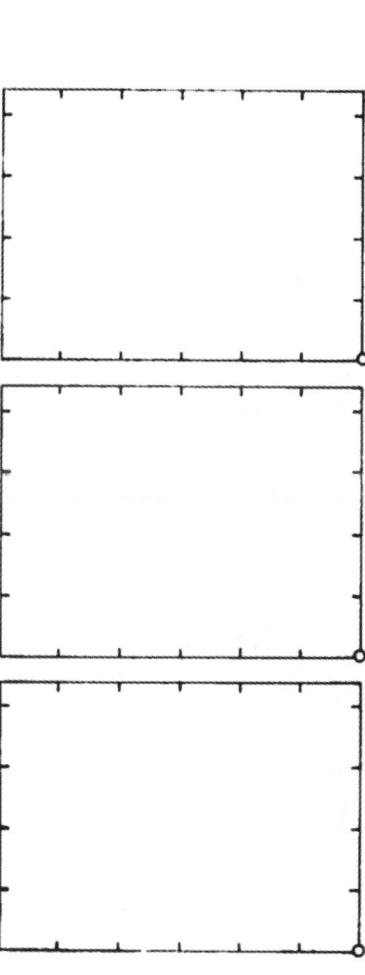

Isn't this unlikely, particularly in view
　　of recent experiments?

　　　　　　　It's true that the model is difficult
　　　　　　　　to reconcile with the results

It was suggested previously—

　　　　　　That appears plausible if—

—the interruptions of the bonds
　　reside in the active
regions of both
　　participating elements

　　　　　　　How about a mild extraction?

Not a scission?

　　　　　　　The options are: treated,
　　　　　　　　untreated, and fragmented,
　　　　　　　unfragmented

What is the indicated amount of prep?

　　　　　　　Unlabeled

ALEJANDRO ALBARRÁN POLANCO

Translated by Rachel Galvin

Cowboy

The world is no longer enough
for a pile of poems
Glory is no longer enough
for a pile of poems
Life is no longer enough
for a pile of poems
Poems are no longer enough
for a pile of poems.

*

We insist on inventing something sinister. Small
implanted beings, embryos replacing phalanxes,
members replaced by oblations, self-sustainable
parts, hypodermic tubes, flexible, hyper-
sensitive, interchangeable, analogous cables.
We insist on writing false extremities. Prostheses
that make up for what's missing.

*

I don't want to write a prosthesis, my phalanx
poem, I don't want to write a prosthesis, my
pinky-finger poem, I don't want to write a prosthesis,
my arm poem, I want to write a yellow stump,
a stump lengthily caressed, not the missing extremity
but the consciousness of what's absent, the
involuntary reflections and the phantom limb,
I want to write the amputation.

*

I write what I should Not:

There are yellow cables in the dermis, there are yellow
cables in the cochlea, there are yellow cables in the
buttocks, there are yellow cables in the encoded concavity,
in the little hole.

*

There are horses in the pubis, there are horses in the abdomen, in the
pelvis there's an algebraic bagpipe, there are some dumping gears, there are
gálapagos in its abdomen. There are gálapagos and wallops: gallops.

*

(They say that's a metaphor.) They say you eat it
like this, they say bag, gallbladder, raft,
they say membrane, bile, they say I'm rafting
on a sea of bile, they say you have to cross with
two coins on your eyes, I'd rather tear them out and
just carry the sockets, the missing.

*

I travel on this sea rubbed raw by the coast, on a raft that you can pull apart
and with its two parts make a cross that flaps like a flag, like the waves of this
bilious sea, this sea from which a sacred body's scabs emerge, from a swelling.
This raft on which I float is a stump and I'm riding it cowboy-style, riding my
stump over the bile, people will say they saw me mounted on a white swan,
they'll say that they saw me, but it will be a lie, it will be my raft, the stump-
raft I ride, and I too am a stump, a phalanx extirpated from my mother's belly,
and I'm also an absent extremity, I'm a mutilation, I'm a piece of arm floating
in water, amniotic, floating in bile. They'll say I'm a swan and that my feathers

are golden, they'll say I'm a mythological bird, but it will be a lie, it will be a lie that they saw me on a swan's back, it will be a lie that I myself am a swan. Just a stump floating in water. "For this absence there is no prosthesis," there are no poems, poems are not enough for this absence, nor is all of love enough. There is no phalanx. No one will see the stump because it's far inside, in my stomach, in my dark purse, there's a stump floating in my sea, but the sea is here inside, I feel it, and I too am inside riding on the back of a stump, a stump upon another stump: a cross. This emptiness, this cold at my back, this absence, is it the absence of God? This absence is a stump floating in water. Is God, then, a stump or that swan that passes by my window, white, white like snow?

Confusion

She says: "I used to confuse gerunds with geraniums."
"That's a joke."
"No, a confusion."
A body floating in the water is not a gerund
although it swells up.

"Did he throw himself into the river?"
"Yes, he was confused."

The body in the water swells up,
just like a gerund.

> **Gerund**
> SAID OF THE PERSON WHO SPEAKS OR WRITES
> IN AN INFLATED STYLE, INOPPORTUNELY AFFECTING
> ERUDITION AND WIT.

When a seed swells up, when it bursts
leaves will sprout; eyes,
although they may swell up, don't bloom.
Bodies will bloom and the word gerund
will be a geranium.

The bodies of the drowned are not bodies,
they are
seeds. Soon they will be
branches.
They are being, being reborn, on their way
to fill the water with flowers born from their bellies.

Rivers will be
shifting fields. Forests fleeing the felling.

They will bloom.

And under water
the river-born men will dance
with a geranium on their heads.

The river is what is being.
She says: "So, river is a gerund?"

EMILY ANDERSON

from *I Lick Everything at Target: Meditations for Making Peace with the Moral Ambiguities of Consumerism and Reconciling Your Need for Things with the Ravages of Global Capitalism*

> *"Did you miss me?*
> *Come and kiss me.*
> *Never mind my bruises.*
> *Hug me, kiss me, suck my juices.*
> *Squeez'd from goblin fruits for you,*
> *Goblin pulp and goblin dew."*
> —Christina Rossetti, "Goblin Market"

A Bed of Quilted Northern

Thirty giant rolls equals 70 regular rolls. My tongue rumbles over the purple plastic. The expanse exhausts. I pause, tongue planted in the surface tension of a tube hole, mouth open, dripping. *Allow your body the rest it needs.* I didn't know, as a child, that I would grow increasingly disgusted with the world as I aged. My spit pools on the plastic. Nor did I know that people who are disgusted are, themselves, disgusting. Your face will stay like this, I warn the child inside me, tongue in cheek. Because it's true: my face stays like this, even with my tongue, fatly swollen, folded into my mouth when I load up a PowerPoint at work or extended (just the tip) into my partner's mouth, when we kiss.

Allow your body to soften. I relax my knees, crumpling to the cool hard floor, and wrap my arms around the plastic 30-pack on the lowest shelf. Squeezably soft. Charmin'.

I don't know whether I want to have a baby, or what kind of woman I'll be. It's like I'm floating on a cloud. Target is quiet today. The sounds of the cart wheels are distant, gentled like a kind of horizon. *Allow your body the rest it needs.* People tend to shuffle here. Because of the smooth floor, they don't bother to pick up their feet. They swing and scuff and glide. I close my eyes, ringed by figure skaters looping around me as I perch on a quilted cloud at the center of the rink.

I like children. Even though I am resting I lick a little, out of habit, my tongue mounting the sharp tufted corner, where the plastic's been seared together and twisted off. I lick a little too far and taste the salt of my finger, where it's wrapped around the stacked-up rolls of softness.

Is this what it would be like to have a child? To startle yourself, with your own flesh? *Allow your body to become multiple bodies.*

Joy

I want to smother myself with joy. I want joy to shine and I want my mouth to grow big enough to fit joy inside. I want to want what I have and I want optimal wanting and I want my heart to soften. I want digestive acids to devour my chest meat. I want digestive acids to leech compassion from manmade materials. I want to take my chakras by gulp and by gullet; I want joy and joy is what the decorative pillow proclaims in silver threads, the capital letters mirror-bright, at least until my face crashes into them, my tongue pushing against the plain cotton center of the O, O Joy O Joy—

I don't like it when anyone does this to me, sticks their face in me where I squish, demanding joy, like a tongue could make a feeling, like a tongue could make me come, when in fact I'm stuffed, packed with white muteness, webbed dumb with fiberfluff, stitched with silver joy and begging to be leaned on, and all the while I'm leaning on another pillow, another joy, oh joy, another and another, joy to joy to China, the identical pillows ramparts beneath the windows of the textile plant, so suicides too long at their looms are thwarted by joy as soon as they leap, their faces trapped by joys as if between thighs, each suicide a dimple in the joys, a feeling formed in a wad of foam.

My tongue rides a rectangle of seams. I use my teeth to mash the padding at the corners, twist the edges into wicks that dip into my nostrils. I roll the long polyester tag into a tube with my tongue and drag the joy pillow to the edge of the shelf using only my straining tongue muscle. The tag is slick. I withdraw and joy plummets.

Yogurt

I lick yogurt. I lick every yogurt and I like it. I bend low, palms against my knees, and lick 0%. I lick 0% strawberry. Refrigeration hums against my skin. My face is in the Dannon.

Voices drift through the refrigerator compressors' drone and fall like snow in my hair, on the back of my neck. Something choral, cloistered opens outward when the compressor kicks into a fresh gear. My face sticks out like a flower chilling in a field, a flower in Stonyfield. The song and cold are so intense. Tonguing the yogurts I feel a part of the cows' fodder, a beginning and an end to the milk distribution process. Here I am me at my very most, a female mammal with a warm, wet tongue.

I lick Frozen Yogurt, Despicable Me Yogurt, Teenage Mutant Ninja Turtles Yogurt. The compressor sounds like white glop plopping. As I lick, my ears freeze. The compressor hums and thunks. My pace slows. Artisan yogurt cups are sold individually, not in packs, why? Because I am an individual and this is a meritocracy. I like reusable Rhubarb Noosa cups. I lick Siggi's, I lick Icelandic.

My nose catches in the smooth web binding together a strawberry blended Yoplait 4-pack and I undergo a startling intersubjective revelation. Something primal connects the five of us here, four yogurt cups and me; I am yoked to yogurt. To some people, I am female and signify nothing but a glass of milk. We are each vessels in the milky circle of life, the yogurt cups and me. Existence is a food system. This is Stonyfield, and I graze.

I lick Stonyfield, Stonyfield YoBaby, Stonyfield YoToddler, Stonyfield YoKids, Stonyfield YoKids Squeeze, Stonyfield cream-top. I write in yogurt, in white and cultured ink. There are so many options, you've got to try them all. Feminism is about options. Capitalism is about options.

I lick Activia. I lick Yoplait Original Less Sugar. I lick Yoplait Greek Vanilla. With my mouth on top of a YoCrunch Oreo, licking the cloudy cup above the black dust, I enjoy a moment of stunning recognition: I am the target market in the Market Pantry, a curdling white woman with her nose in the yogurt and her ass in the air, worrying with her tongue—this place is my hero's journey, heroine's journey, is your refrigerator running, better go and catch it, better start the Activia two week challenge, better latch on to my best self, be best, be blessed, be light and fit and Greek, toasted coconut vanilla, peach blended and simply balanced.

Babies

Babies smell like Hefty bags and grandmother's bathwater. I pinch my nose while licking up the diaper aisle, batting the red sale flags back and forth with my tongue. Swiping a sale flag with the sides of my tongue, I wiggle my hips, then punch a diaper box. It slides all the way down the nearly-empty shelf.

I stick my head into the un-stocked shelf, rest my cheek against cool steel, root into the pocked shelf's deep shadows. I listen to the shelving ting. All the small earthquakes of Target travel through these steel lines, all the lights and rattling carts and sorrow. Do you know what you're complaining about? You're complaining about nothing. The shelves are so quiet. The store drips through them slowly, building something, a stalactite. *Oh, hi! Did you have your operation?* You look great. I almost fall asleep, idly tracing a little hole with just the tip of my tongue.

There's a yoga position called Happy Baby. You lie on your back and play with your toes. Rooting myself deeper into the shelf, I let my arms dangle, wiggle my fingers, echo the wiggle with my toes. Then I start running. I sweep my face over naked swathes of shelving, rushing with my mouth open toward a cardboard box of Honest Diapers. I hit it chin-first, make it jump. I keep pushing the Honest Diapers, knock them into adjacent diaper boxes, building a fucking diaper train, railroading diaper boxes to the end of the shelf, rendering pricing information irrelevant.

Go lick the price scanner, baby, go scan for price, go crying, go crawling to the nipple rack, get your mouth on a three-pack of Freeflows, glom on to the Ulubulu mustache pacifiers, ram a six-pack of Munchkin Latches down your throat, suck Nuk, suck Tommee Tippee, suck Mam, suck Mam Bite and Relax, suck Nuby Natural Touch, suck Chicco, suck Chicco Natural Fit, suck Mam, suck Mam Love & Affection Silicone 2-Packs, suck The Gentleman, suck Daddy's Girl, suck Nuk latex, suck Playtex, suck Similac Optigro, suck Closer to Nature, suck slow flow, suck medium flow, suck evenflo, suck natural variable flow, suck Comotomo silicone, suck Bright Starts Vibrating, suck Nuby Softees Hard and Nuby Softees soft, suck Leachco, suck rubber.

Carefree

My tongue ripples the stretched plastic plastic outer sheath and burrows into the soft, tightly packed, individually wrapped actifresh pantiliners. The plastic is thin and flexible as pterodactyl wings; I lick and taste how oil sings. Even beneath my pumping tongue, I sense their fundamental petrochemical tidiness; how neatly these liners have been folded and scented and stacked, and for what neat purpose.

Pushing harder, getting in deeper, disturbing the folded rows, I'm reminded of a sleeve of Girl Scout Thin Mints and the freshness, they, too promise. My tongue goes numb. I think it's the pink—so thin and absorbent you'll forget you're wearing a liner, so thin and absorbent it'll soak up my tongue, my lips, my face, redistribute and moisture-lock it beneath a layer of superabsorbent polymers, until I'm a bloody dot, a Target, licking my way through a scented, moisture-wicking matrix—a woman blossoming, becoming.

ASMAA AZAIZEH
Translated from Arabic by Yasmine Haj

Do Not Believe Me Were I to Talk to You of War

War preoccupies me. But I'm ashamed to write about it. I flagellate my
metaphors then implore them. Pain makes me depict a bullet, after which
I recede into depicting an emotional slap. I disembowel the words and the
harakiri victims awake, all of them, and disembowel me.

Do not believe me were I to talk to you of war, because when I spoke of blood,
I was drinking coffee, when I spoke of graves, I was picking yellow daisies in
Marj Ibn Amer, when I described the murderers, I was listening to my friends'
giggles, and when I wrote about a burnt theatre in Aleppo, I was standing
before you in an air-conditioned one.

Do not believe me were I to talk to you of war. Because each time I
bombarded the city streets in a poem, the concrete would recline, the lamps
would sway towards it, and the prophets would pass by in peace.

Whenever I imagined my father's skin flayed in it, I could still touch him
afterwards, safe and sound, with an embrace. And whenever I heard my
mother's wailing, she would lull me to sleep with an old song, and I would
sleep like a baby.

But dreams are open cheques
Signed by a Hourani woman whose features are unknown to me. Except that
when my knife misses the lettuce leaf, I could smell the scent of the tribe of
blood my grandfather had left in my body and hers.

Dreams are an open cheque, signed by Qasioun's sons who whispered them
to me during a reverie, and I couldn't tell whence the mountain's name had
sprung without googling it.

The first cheque:
In an obscure crowd, an obscene clarity dawns on me.
In the midst of the exquisite engineering of geography's tumult, a bullet quietly passes through me, at my lower back,
The crowd's mystery grows and my ears' windows are shut from within. The hole is as fresh as a spring, the blood is as warm as my mother's voice in a song and as smooth as my father's skin.

The second cheque:
I was besieged in the world's holiest spot . . . Bullets rained down on me as did God's words on the prophets . . .
I seized a stone and it melted in my hands. I overtook the soldiers and time overtook me. And like a scared kitten, I cowered where a young Christ slumbered before carrying us on his back.

The third cheque:
Fear in the Levant.

Do not believe me when I talk to you of war
Because I've never heard a bullet shot besides the one my father threw from his double barreled gun into Marj Ibn Amer's doves. And I've never smelled blood from a wound except for that which I smelled with my mother the first time I menstruated.
I do not have an account in the bank of wars, but a Hourani woman reassured me that my cheques are valid.

I Didn't Believe I Would Ever Learn to Die

I didn't believe I would ever learn to die
I wasn't around when death was for free
But I was there when my maternal grandfather paid the price of cotton
labourers' sweat that made his Ottoman suit
The price of bare miles to the women of Bosnia
The price of their tears on the chests of their men before the war
The price of God's banners
The price of the emperor's frivolousness and long-term sickness

Balkan blood dripped on my school shirt
The teachers found vows of vengeance in my backpack and so fabricated
chapters of history

I wasn't around when death happened by chance, on the road
But I was there when my paternal grandfather paid the price of a signature
at the bottom of a page, the price of surrendering his village at the bottom of
the mountain, of taking the occupier's hands off of it, the rebel's taking his
hands off of his waist. With the move of a pen, my grandfather's ink numbed
the slope. With the folding of a paper, the mountain folded history, with a
handshake, he took the valley's hand from the tank's muzzle.
The almond trees died in the cardiac operation rooms, the wedding horses
shrouded their eyes with henna and killed themselves.
No one cleansed my ethnicity. But the mountain's spinal cord broke. And so
broke my chance to ever ascend it together, to look at Christ's footsteps on the
lake and copy them.

I'm not the miracle
I didn't walk on water and I didn't heal myself of your love's ailments
But it was my heart's water which I learned to turn into asphalt whenever I
remembered you
I learned to flee the lava that dripped from the mountains of your fear
And I didn't learn death

I wasn't there when death was a once-and-for-all lesson
Where the memory of the rocket betrayed it and so forgot the way
The bullet that never meant to cease being a pen
The massacre that passed by the main road and fired peace
When I was walking through the back road
Picking yellow daisies and watching wars drawn in cartoons

I didn't believe I would ever learn to die
Until Beirut's war drowned my mother's lullaby in the well
The scent of invasions emanates from the cooking oven
The commando's voice enters Um Kulthoum's cassette
The skulls that paved the city road, they leave the poster hanging beside the
bed and lull me, tapping my soft head like a long latmiya. So I stop crying, or
they stop crying in it.

My heart grows in the well like a pomegranate tree, each time a branch is
broken I climb another on my way to you. All of me breaks, so I become a
nest. The birds look in the water and see the laughing face of a Bosnian, I look
in it and see your face.

I am the child of tubes crossbred in a medical lab
I smelled the scent of dead horses in my father's sperm
And I retreated
I was born in the seventh month
After I was beaten by Bosnians in my mother's womb
And I retreated

I didn't believe I would ever learn to die
Until the Hebron massacre was committed on the cake of my ninth birthday. I
lit the candles on the carpets of Abraham's house. They melted there alone and
no one sang upon them. The birthday gifts fall into the well, the gifts fall, vows
of vengeance, in my backpack
The vows would've dug my grave had they any hands
The almond trees would've stepped on it had they a spinal cord
The mountains would've praised it had they any poems

The Bosnian's tears would've creviced its stones had they any beaks or claws
And I would've come out
To learn the first lesson
That the smashed skull in the poster is my skull
And that the blood on my shirt
Is my blood

from *Nympholepsy*

:: Luciana ::

Sydelle took down her slip, smoothed her tits out over the come-apart duvet. A man named Gael, with me, in her bed, in her bed of filth, slopyellow, dead skin, and wax, with the bodies sewn in.

And the rain. It fell a summer thing. That night, Gael slept near me, not Sydele. He was all tuxedo jacket, cheap fabric and brown pocket square. He spoke of and with absolute disarray, the abandon of language, a fuck and a cunt, and that handsome Mediterranean dirge. He was dark and aureate; with him you could throw yourself out of the window, see how far you could fly. I shouldn't tell this story. He is my collateral of it all; and I am the collateral of it. Meaning The Hive wedged itself between the thing of us. I could have been his lover, but. A sadness that the hive could not snuff.

He went to touch my breast but I said I would prefer he do that in character.

:: Luciana ::

That I was such bravado. That I had gone and gone and gone by midnight somewhere. Where. That I deteriorated and was reborn. That I would take off my face and be sullen. That I could lie. That soon I would not have any love or desire left. A shell is my sadness. It is xenolith, protruding so, but I cannot extract it. We are petting our ways around corners in the dark, sticking a leg out to trip a spirit, and then coming up short, because there is no spirit. We want one there, but sometimes there isn't one there. So we invent. But The Hive did not invent invention. I want my body back.

We strive to not be versions or the dead. Always expecting lace but coming up cotton. The lack is hungry.

:: Luciana ::

We are sitting, satin shorts twisted up in the centers of us, summertime sweat, folds of skin lapping, drinking in the moon. I am drinking hard liquor tonight, this black blinding night. We are splayed out over grass, in folding chairs, in wooden chairs. A wading pool with the bobbing bottle of cava, foam pouring over the edges. Blades of grass stuck on our elbows, a hose of water trickling around a statue in the dirt. Do you understand? We're almost fucking but we're not. We're all tongue. We're all tongue down the glass, mouth open and taking. No, we're not. We're wasted on memory tonight. We're fucking memories.

I don't come easily to the night, but when I do, I am the night. We are all the night, and we command it, the high priestesses of one another and our revenge kill. We feel we have been used. We will slaughter happily that language of the past, days before we became sheep, sheepish, sewn into patterned. We feel we are made dark. That's memory we're fucking with the slick oily dark dick of goodbye, and the wicked wheel turning inside of us, away, toward the somewhere that isn't here. Do you taste that? That's the salt of us turning away.

:: Alraune ::

The spells we manufacture inside us are dismal.

Sydelle throws oyster after oyster down her throat, casting a spell to turn her pussy gold, chanting over in her mind for all the men to smell her as an overripe peach and come to claim her. She thinks we don't see this, or else she doesn't think of us at all.

Grace is here, mewing on Sydelle's arm in scraps of spandex and jeans, plastic glasses like neon window-shades, and lip gloss, and filming us as she drinks.

Luciana orders another and the light quivers bluegreen into the horsemane hair of these girls. She told me how Sydelle punched her as hard as she could in the face while she lay sleeping. How she bled like a fountain.

This is invincible.

:: Alraune ::

The covetous hive, the hive bathed in black soap.

Three little queens in three little cells. Three little hedons, self-stripped, opening their legs in each corner of the room, in the dankness of stark 5am under a pitched roof. Six little legs, three little wet mouths, and more fingers, more fingers than there should be in the dark.

We are the velvet women. If you are looking for witches, we are the witches, storing sperm in jars under our beds, sending out our army of velvet girls.

Luciana and I pour ourselves baths of ambrosia in our desire and sickness, or our desire of sickness. We grow and our sex grows, that is the point. Making us eternal, insulate, able to inseminate even ourselves, to poison and lick our many wounds. For this, Sydelle wants to ribbon our bodies bloody.

Man after man after man brings the queen of drones and, in her fetish of herself in them, the hive's destruction. Engulfed in this swarm of men is left only a fall of bright hair.

A fetish of men, and the hive's velvet girls
praised and cut low,
praised and cut low.

Bring the two queens, man after man, how Sydelle's teeth grow like stakes.

The velvet girls are not velvet. They are dressed in the vomit of their hivemaster. Washing her porcelain face with a cloth, learning her how she fears to be learned, leaving her naked eyelashes the color of wheat and her long, bleeding nose to snort up the constellations.

It should've been time to sleep, but we were up screaming, or we were up cleaning someone off, or fucking half-heartedly because we only wanted to fuck the idea of fucking each other.

These are the girls dressed in velvet, but they are not velvet girls. Are we, Luciana? Are we the girls dressed in velvet? Luciana, what have we become in the land of destruction.

Death and the Maiden

A sick bed is a grave, and all that the patient says there is but a varying of his own epitaph. Every night's bed is a type of the grave. In the grave I may speak through the stones, in the voice of my friends, and in the accents of those words which their love may afford my memory; here I am mine own ghost, and rather afright my beholders than instruct them; they conceive the worst of me now, and yet fear worse, they give me for dead now, and yet wonder how I do when they wake at midnight and ask how I do tomorrow. Miserable, and though common to all inhuman posture, where I must practice my lying in the grave by lying still, and not practice my resurrection by rising any more.

—John Donne, *Devotions upon Emergent Occasions*

Living might not be my best form. I was attached to it, but perhaps I had mistaken my familiarity with existence as existence's necessity. Yet to write about mortality was like crying at the security line in the airport. "Goodbye!" I'd say, not knowing anything about the flight or destination.

A perpetual way of being in a perpetuating life had interfered with ending, also ending-prohibitive events like eating, sleeping, and breathing. I deserved the humiliation of being alive no more or less than everything else; I deserved the humiliation of posthumousness all the same.

I'd wanted these visions to be Hildegarde von Bingen as a noise band seen at an unlicensed angle, and I had to somehow fold this in: "to make a lyric of a dried up cricket," as the critics say, which actually meant something: that is to say that I supposed the *form* of dying could be learned as *form's disruption*. And who could die after that?

*

That's when I followed the link some men sent me. It led to HOW TO LIVE. I felt so grateful to be helped, to be shown, to be let in on the precise instructions, but what I found made me want to die a lot, not the kind of dying that is in the manner of not being alive, but in the manner of the act of dying, to just die again and again like a teenager, delinquently and rebelliously die and all over everything and then as a material: one corpse as five hundred and eighty million hilarious corpses, all piled in blockades, my own dead flesh and dying multiplied like a Powerball jackpot multiplying, to become a multimillionaire of my own corpses, an architect who works only in the aggressive rotting ecofriendly own corpses or a city planner who has made the only stuff of the city her own dead flesh, multiplied, but only in its most lewd and vile spiritlessness and with empty pale flesh all over the streets like heavy, unscurrying vermin, the city putrid with pigeon own-corpses and the rat ones, too.

Sure that's a heavy way to start a love letter, but it was also like the ambient hostility of information and waking up each day looking for it. This was what was going to kill me if anything did. HOW TO LIVE was so many corpses multiplied impossibly and piled deeply upon all of the millions of corpses that are more beautiful than all the still-livingness of the vile histories and the miraculous ease in which the others have entered into a conspiracy of mutually assured power and breathing.

I followed another link, ashamed we do not have methods in place for destroying these very circumstances, the most basic actions of threat in this the total war of the ambient early morning screen, the total war of the most passive policing late night remark. Nothing I saw on the stone tablet with the precise instructions gave me useful information unless useful information is that which provokes my own withering, which was also like a disappearing, which was like someone was taking an eraser to me, in the mountains, among the good looking and successful men. My friend said "this always happens." The book of rules makes us wither, but more so when appearing to be written in stone.

*

After that I called these occurrences THE OCCUPANT and could not stop speaking about it. THE OCCUPANT called a lot of attention to itself, said it was not itself very material and would not take material form. I made myself sick over it and became angry, too. Then I wanted to cease my specificity. I was not more affectionate with THE OCCUPANT than I was with anyone else. It was the situation of my unhealing that made me force the schedule, the onrushing requisite thoughts of the late hour, then the scheme to write in excess of these excessive thoughts, to spill across the barest facts till the next morning, then the next. The facts were all for all their being momentous, like being mortal, and how I lived a life in which THE OCCUPANT was often bored and earless and nothing like the thunderstorm that began in absence of what should be near.

But I was really going to miss hashtags. They were looking longingly into my eyes because I was deflecting a lot, unable to imagine even kissing another person in a city with THE OCCUPANT in it. THE OCCUPANT had almost no body and no ability to commit an act. Then I suggested it was something like an agreement. "But you two were already in love!" is all they said like a distilled myth is its own genre. That I don't lie now and feel things in my body is the prospect of my abidingness all wrapped up in what isn't the smallest and restrained measure of the enormity of the catastrophe of the world historical of the catastrophe of trying a restrained measure. It was probably a nightmare, but in it I made it impossible for a dear friend to exist, and no one could console me with the otherwise. And here I am, in the enormity of feeling of being in a nightgown in a bed with no one sitting watchfully in a chair so I could sleep. If I could have fallen asleep, I would have turned whatever dream I had into a response to a Facebook comment, the one they were always making, something to the effect that writing was not a sufficient political act or that to frame writing as a political act without calling for a real action attending it was a problem. It felt so Cartesian, but in those days we all did, moving our fingers across touchscreens and swearing this meant we were still.

*

I never got why THE OCCUPANT was so loud. Then the people made a lot of exceptions, and of course it wasn't true that the way anyone sat across from my bed was watchfully. My love life was that these ideas are a part of a much larger argument about the desirability and undesirability of disinterest as it constructed the discipline of aesthetics, but nothing I said on Twitter counted toward that fact. It is well known that social media was only just a rumor about the structure of heaven. Marx's aesthetics were rudimentary, and I hated the preconditions of philosophy. I wanted to be remembered as a question posed of the senses, then as a form of peril and skepticism, and then who has never understood who has never understood what I was working from. It was a larger critique, all that deleting, then the poet goes about her day to obliterate any answer that stays itself.

Obviously I'd asked a lot of questions. I kept talking about the sensorium of what we got. There was the didactic option, of how to make an animal refusal, but that file was mostly empty except something about talking from the side of the mouth. I didn't realize how tragic I appeared 'til I finally looked in the mirror. Then Jasper told me I was a pain the ass, and I answered something about inner vision and its muscular operations, but Jasper was right and he'd only said anything out of love. If I had an education at all I only agreed to it because the prairie felt operatic. I hoped no one else came to the cemetery for clarity, but I would gladly give anyone my place in all the poetry festivals in the world.

*

Still I had to leave it all behind because it was as if I was speaking a language everyone else could only hear as a ringtone. It was like they were attracted to the attractive thing that draws the eye from the regular scene to the glittery manufactured moment. They wanted to talk about the big game: it was the wanting to talk about the event and not a condition and was a problem that turned words about the old and ever-present things into just a kind of ambient not-even-music and imprecise hum.

But there was no woundless birth. If the mother dies, and the infant is pulled out of her corpse, there would be another human doing the pulling. There could be some death cramp expelling the infant, there would be the blood of the mother-corpse, and it was not the desiring subject of the human alone who has emerged, by accident, from the corpse of a mother and beyond the weird chance of that accident there was a general and common scene of birth, so often a scene made not only of a mother, but a set of other actors, and also there is so often in modernity the larger scene of the institutional and sexual violence of birth that is a matter of fact.

I wrote the preceding sentences as a love letter because it wasn't important to have the properly speaking politics of the later clarity that had been the matter of the day, nor did we need a kind of explanatory scaffolding around the refractory. I told one person that all those men look the same, and then I felt brave enough to look at the documents. I discovered I had told another that I had been transmuted into pure terror. Woman's speech had always been miserable, but mine was miserable in particular, and insofar as the subject of the speech was reproduction or violence, poverty, or abuse, it was for its misery unutterable, or utterable only as a thing that lacks seriousness, that operates mostly as an untrustworthy manipulation of feeling.

My day shift was always the same gold mine in the abode of horror. That's the problem with ringtones. I wanted a poison garment but inverted—so that the poison was external—and in its effect, the poison would be an amnesiac, and what we would forget is history, Hegelian and occluded, and if my dress could not be poisoned, I wanted it to be a collapsing ship like the one Nero gave his mother, but inverted, so that the collapse was external, and what would be swallowed in the outward collapse was men.

*

All I meant to say was I loved them, but I wasn't very clear. Something very strange and upsetting had happened, at least upsetting for me, and I know strange for the world. I engaged in the subsequent slurred evisceration that comes with that feeling of being unprecedented. I looked in the library: it wasn't in the databases. You could spend hours at the microfiche, and still it was as if nothing had happened to mortally disrupt our equilibrium.

This was called *history by gaslight*. I wondered how THE OCCUPANT didn't register officially because whatever we did to evade the accusation, the choice was between bed-sheets and hoary sentiment. This inner state of self-regulation, this lack of adequate form in which to express one's condition, was also what Mary Shelley's mother had called "a mansion of despair." A psychic abode of horror is the ur-situation of this kind of feminist text, an illiberal done of wrongs, formed of such stuff as dreams are made of as dreams are made in the house of misery where in one corner your breasts began to drip milk, as mine did, in the ordinary events called family.

*

As we continued to organize politically, so the terminal conditions grew. While it is true that my reaction to THE OCCUPANT was decorative self-devouringness, I don't think it has altered my ability to accurately perceive past events as events. Entire schools of poetry, art, and political movements developed in order to engage in the sly practice of advocating the destruction of what we were doing while reifying it also in the shapes of vanguards, war, and football. Endless formal exercises developed among these schools in which parties could both maintain all of this and advocate for its destruction. The confusing thing is that they wanted to get rid of us while they needed us to exist. Men held meetings around the question: *if Anne is sitting on our laps, and we have tired of her, how can we strangle her without feeling bad about it?* They kept saying it was either with a silk scarf or with their hands, but I knew it was with a lanyard. They forwarded my email about the rape without my permission. Giant brick and concrete libraries were filled with the anxious violent schemes and elaborate codes. Popular culture made the anxious approach clear: it is through the unsentimental deployment of violence that they would continue to construct an era. The accusation prolif-erated; it took material and political forms; it bifurcated into two accusations, one of these for the sake of arousal. The men I loved said they were scared of me: it was because I was angry and well-known. This was bullshit, because they had so much power to begin with, but it was a cultural custom that their bullshit became philosophy and at that, doctrinaire.

We were the girl-like persons, also racialized categories. Every system wore the fucked up mask of fate. The board was tilted and the suffering slid down onto us and that reality was a jumble of events under which we were buried. Rousseau's natural men were on the other end of the board, oblivious in the ether, out of sight of any of the historical garbage we each had to sort through alone.

*

Monuments to women are holes, and how inefficient I'd been in this life, to seek solace from art in art, particularly that art which seeks solace from itself in nature, from which I also had to run. Whatever woman was, she was the opposite of a scrimmage. My fear was that I would die so early it would leave the rest of them feeling guilty enough to turn me into a testimony without any transcript of my own. They didn't want to hear of the endlessly inescapable and useful accusations, the right to appearance, they only wanted to tell me that I had done this terrible thing, just by existing, that I had made someone else impossible and at the thought of it I cried onto my tablet until the alphabet no longer worked. I didn't feel very innocent. There was both a vast external army that attacks that utterance and the internalized awareness of such an army, but I shouldn't be allowed to say it, even in the mimicry of liturgy.

44   Still I am not blaming the canon for my reaction to events. Obviously these consequences are made of temperament. To bring this detail up at this point in the vision was, like, I guess, an inversion, something to keep our new religion blithe and popular, and I spent a lot of time wondering about those who diminish the beauty and luxury of survival, that they have been so rarely dead.

Mortality was a gorgeous framework. What a relief to have not been protected, to not be a subtle or delicate person whose inner experience is merely an inner life made of taste and social feeling, what a relief to not collect tiny wounds as if they are the greatest injuries while all the rest of the world always, really, actually bleeds. It's yet another error in perception that those with social protection can look at those who have, at times, lacked it and imagine that weakness is in the bleeder, not in those who have never bled. The advocates of flourishing, Aristotelian and repugnant, would make a god of survival the moment they were made slaves.

*

How many times have I written the preceding sentence? Have you been keeping count? I couldn't sleep, but in general the whole problem was only deceptively complex. I was interested in trying out the new exercises, also hyper-sexualization. Our problems are mammalian. I tried exceedingly not to be that way but was. The father gazed upon the infant like a judge of history in a black robe deciding whether it was his. Or the mother looked at the infant, taking on the father's judging gaze. Or a mother looked at the infant, taking on the state's gaze, to establish or evade the state's obsessed accounting of paternity. I could already read what was going to be written later, about the way I was shattering another person just with my own shattering though I never meant to do it. So we look like our fathers, we favor them, inscribing a petition on our infant faces. "I am yours" says our baby face, so many millions of ever-arising Ariels ("my freedom, sir?") the first desire a woundedness and petition co-emergent with breath and milk. Then Jasper said I was a pain in the ass, but he meant it after all we had been through. But he really was great at driving the truck through the streets with one effortless hand. I wanted to rejoice with him, wanted Edenic restoration, the precise integration of brutal and historical modes of common understanding, to have so often a vision of power delivered to my door or to my body just like that, without having to go through the hyper-clarity.

I would rather be a masterless dog in hell than the dog of the king of heaven himself, but mostly I'd like to think of being a planet. I wrote again and again about how much I was trying, but in the writing again and again I was making a new literature of the problem of the woman who writes again and again, swearing she is getting better and in the midst of dying and will never be in love.

*

There is no particular way to know how this will change me. MRIs of other women suggest damage to the visual cortex, "significantly reduced activation of the left middle dorsolateral prefrontal cortex and premotor cortex," and "significantly reduced left caudal lateral prefrontal cortex activation, increased perseverative errors, and reduced processing speed." Women complain that they lose the ability to read, to recall words, to speak fluently, to make decisions, and to remember. Some say they lose not just short-term memory, but memories of their past. These effects, which I was told were inevitable and for which nothing can be done, can last throughout treatment, or for one year, or for ten or more.

Then a friend sent me an email saying the real email was locked away in a special locked email file, because it was better that way, where no one could read it. That wasn't an actual event, so I answered, "Who once had a master is how the gaze forgetfully directs itself at the sight of one: that is, my gaze. Not to walk upon walls and not bother to even look up again, that visible invisible unruled always?—" I was so unrelenting on my sovereign fantasy, silly to be involved in any kind of low and electronical theatrics of the night. Violeta Parra shot herself in the head for love, or its absence, and when I went to look for another version of the truth, it was that Violeta shot herself in a crisis of loneliness. The mind of the lonely is dull to the common and plural form that coalesces at the moment one becomes free because we are not allowed to be, what leads to the irrevocable sense of the unloved, the permanent catastrophe of reason, or the rational part of nonsense. And I, of all people, should know. Look at that sonnet, "theirs for their style I'll read; his for his love." Or I wanted to obliterate social media and sing, "Oh tell me this vision of the world—vivid, expansive—is, and only because of peril, interest and instinct, occluded, unsayable, animal, crude, and false." I'd also sing, "But how is the vision of disinterest, of the judge, so often inadequate and partial?" and "How does one who has a certain kind of sensorium constructed not from flourishing but from survival communicate to those for whom history has constructed a prejudicial and narrow human vision?"

All of these songs had been my own.

*

Though it looked like I wanted to ask all the questions, what I really wanted was the answers, and not the misshapen ones, but the misshapen was how I gave these questions form. I was forged in the furnace of wondering what the people would say when they answered, those who were interested in authenticity, engagement, and against recuperation, about what is poetry in the conditions of total war. And under the conditions in which they make you think you should be dead, I kept wondering if staying alive was a politics. Facebook kept saying no. If I couldn't speak of these conditions given the prohibitions of ending up heresy or pornography, perhaps there would be a newer value given to a diseased woman's speech even as she was always repeating herself and her forms. I thought of the way I kept giving myself up for the most basic social consequence, the poison to be infused into my body through a plastic port surgically implanted into my chest and connected to my jugular.

The first substance was named for the Adriatic Sea, and also after rubies, and I had never been anywhere like Venice, except that the substance was also called the red devil and the red death, too. Literature could be a nothing and by this I mean what I would never have to maintain, clean or repair it. I preferred syntax to its object, the floor. It obviously was the cognitive architecture of my perverse ambition. That is, it veered. Still, I had some thoughts about the micro-lifestyle called "poetics," the people living in a building that can never be occupied, the act of figuration as more than the figure made.

*

I rushed toward complexity as a method of slowing away from death. I wanted to think of metaphor not as vehicle or tenor but the basic fact of is, metonymy not as what is collapsed but collapsing itself, then metaphor as the thrilling slap of being accused of what is untrue, then metonymy as a delicate sediment. There's this reality of a range of rhetorics that are just totally somatic and palpable, not in their representative functions, but in their syntactical ones. That's a sexual preference: trope, and it would have been easier in all cases if we'd just done it, even once, so there wouldn't be so many anchorless feeling gigantisms. It hurt like hell, the death continuing for twenty-seven hours, for those days I held what was alive in high esteem and didn't know better about myself, that I done such ceramic things as to make another person's vessel impossible, the way I kept going on about derealization, too, and piling on what was cryptic, forgetting to add anything about popular culture.

According to custom, I was supposed to make a spark of era by striking a Katy Perry song against hyper-educated flint, but my vision manifested as the desire to exchange consciousness for territory. At the library—*no, THIS alcove, we must sit here. No, get up: this is the wrong space.* A dog circling and circling the laundry pile, attempting the right place to lie down. The nervous system of the apartment complex, in which animals and war and love and the peculiar oppressions of waking up became a brick.

*

Here's the problem: *Robert's Rules of Order* was next to *Roget's Thesaurus.* In looking for the title *Robert's Rules of Order* I saw the shelf from my childhood on which it is sitting, the paperback black copy of *Roget's Thesaurus* next to it. I was speaking and speaking quickly, had to access the term I could not think of, said "Roger's Rules of Order." I did not explain the roundabout way I went to access this information and how this resulted in the error of speech. Here are the words as they came out: "Chris Marker was my youth group leader, and my uncle was not happy" or "There was an island on the river, and it might have been Huck Finn." Language was not something regular, but it was something I could excavate from another, more irregular strata. Words had been archived in a shadow site of music that did not aspire to the condition of song. To have given up my earlier ways with them made me feel real, including also those divisions of representations, one to the other of a thing or a thought or an idea all of them existing equally and in service, one actually no more real than the next.

If I were to walk down a hallway and be shown both a vase and an elegant thought it is almost certain the elegant thought would be the most real and lasting thing to me. If I were to walk down a hallway and be given an elegant thought and a broken heart it would be the broken heart I would still feel, for years, particularly in the frantic and lonesome night, while wearing a silk chemise. I saw poetry for its casual uses as an exemplar of an idea of a mood of a strike. Then Jasper said I was a pain in the ass, but that it had something to do with genius. I didn't know what he meant and wasn't going to consent to any of those descriptors, except for the way that genius holds a golden cup in its hand for the inhabitants of the earth whose-names-were-not-written-in-the-book-of-rules to drink from. Then he said the hotel was swarming with cops. It was true these Google Docs revealed an inexcusable attachment to language, as if it were a project I had found in a magazine, like braiding plastic bags into durable rugs. Then there were lots of feelings of love without a target, like Breton's shooting into a crowd, but not with a gun or anything so pronounced.

*

Then I kept telling a friend to wipe my tears with his hands. He was watching an ad for boxing so I told him that we were not like the boxers themselves and not like the referees, but we were like the air the gloves moved through on the way to their targets. We were innocent as air, I told him, but also always being punched, each particle of ourselves invisible and rearranged by an outside force that we had nothing, in particular, to do with. And I cried a lot, tears running down my face, but also as "up tears," that is they sort of moved around and up the roundness of my cheeks, and I said "Do you see my up tears?" because he liked my cheeks, and it was interesting the way the tears were falling on them.

Then he left forever.

Then I couldn't sleep after feeding the universe and all its animals because all of entirety was on my chest, including the heavy and light animals.

Then I checked my phone to see if anyone else was concerned that we are the sum of our body parts.

Then the future was feral: they say that's why they went away.

Then my heart kept beating, disturbed and disturbing.

Then the condition of my chest was different in that it was now completely alone.

*

Many others who had once stood by me were too sensitive to watch me at the blinding forefront. Its encampment was in that green and lush and tall-treed park with that moat of river around it. A child appeared there, and I noted that she did something with her hands. A friend said she didn't because her hands were disconnected from her body, and at that, her hands disconnected from her body and joined together at the wrists, but were still animate, her fingers fluttering. The encampment had walls like cubicles, and electricity, and flat screen TVs, and people were hanging out there, like a party, and the children played, this child among them, and sometimes the children were like silent animals and slipped into the river, and she slipped into the brown river, and then all of the children would come back up. Finally it was dusk, and though it was not my job to watch her it was my job to watch her. She slipped into the river and was like a small silent animal in it, and I turned for a second to the people with whom I was discussing some aspect of American cinema. That's when the child disappeared. We called her name over and over but she did not come back up. There appeared to be a creature moving under the brown water in a brown wave, but nothing like the child ever emerged again, and everyone in their electric and screened encampment kept on with their festival. No one jumped in the brown river to look for the child. I didn't either. *Nothing that is, insofar as it appears, exists in the singular; everything that is is meant to be perceived by somebody.*

Then I felt a warm upwelling of love, as if thinking about the face of a beloved, but it was not the face of a lover I saw, but an action that made the same warm risingness of love, the same troubled feeling of love, and also, like how with a lover, one does not want to belong to the lover, how one does not want the in-stitutions of love or of the lover, how one resents the customs and arrangements and habits of love and lovers, how despite what one wants and what one doesn't want one does all, has all happen and all the time the feeling of the face of the beloved (the beloved act) remains in sight, even with all the doubts, and how this love and this vision of the face of the beloved is intrusive, how without dis-cipline, it is always presenting itself as the thing to be done or to be doing, how it is only with the greatest discipline, like setting oneself on fire or working too many jobs or starving oneself on diets or being drunk or clinically depressed or becoming extremely religious, that one can, for a little while, keep from doing this action, and if this action is not love but writing poetry, it is a stupid thing, done without a counter-action, how it is stupid like cooking when everyone has stopped eating or making a bed when no one will sleep again or singing when everyone covers their ears or being an insect who sucks blood from a plastic lawn chair. But if you are still here, and reading this, maybe I've been wrong. I've always been so greedy. I was loved a lot, and still I missed all of the people who left, also the ones who I loved and who I believed that my existence had upended.

*

The last line of the paragraph before the paragraph before this isn't mine. This is because my thoughts were turned less into symphonies than geometry. Then the math turned moral. In Cicero's Catiline Orations there is an act that is so brave that overruns itself with bravery, kind of like bravery's dilution of bravery. This courage is cowardly for how it is a movie. Every record I made of this life looked unpracticed, but each month the record was at least a month more complex.

Thoughts could exist in symmetry, or not: sometimes they existed like wiry young people scattered on the floor, sometimes they were in modest partition. It is what you do when you are alone, the stranger said, that matters; it is that time you are not on the scene that makes the difference between when you become tragic later because you are dead and forgotten but when you do not do certain things then you can't be a man at all.

But I loved the dark-haired and sallow woman at the table of women who weren't beautiful women: I loved the worried looks, all the trouble, the person who wears a coat as the weather's common signal, loved the total sum of no way to meet a soul. Wrapped in my own devices I misread a scripture of what was delicate but reckoned wrongly. No matter how stylish it felt to feel guilty, the servants of the powerful were not us, my friends, who talked all night. Those servants were the quiet men of action. They had no burden of investigation or aesthetic. We were silly and passionate, but these men found their glory in inarticulation, a barely faced presence, not so nervous as the ones like us who gesticulated then shifted our own weight.

*

Still it was weird to use declamation as credentials. Also to think we shouldn't be a labyrinth in the first place. I'd worried I'd done it for the internet then found out I'd done it for the grave. I thought it was for specificity, then I watched the interment. Then I couldn't remember the tables I sat at, or in what city, or with whom. What I ended up with was not so much a string of names or memories as a set of calamitous sensations. I over-read the evidence of each face. I had to end this vision somewhere, so I chose the minute when I fell in love with a live stream. There I saw a projection, and it said:

DON'T BE AFRAID

We'd cut these words into grass in the nervous zones of our city! I'd made plans to string together other words in forestry, dreamed of the new technologies to summarize the space between stars! I told each of my friends that the form was terrifying, and that I was terrified. I'd rejected all the things anyone does for love and that was okay; now it was literature as a spontaneous eruption of dying. That is when I tried to come home, and the world tried to continue to open as it had been opening, and I waited for the day when the poets could answer my questions and nothing would be partial again.

Little Skin Bag

Little Skin Bag stood on the stoop, trying to shove the ghost back into her mouth. It was a slippery ghost. It squeaked its tail out of her mouth, picked a piece of spinach from her teeth, yawned.

"Fuck off," hissed Little Skin Bag.

Inside the apartment she could hear Cubist spinning disco classics. Shadows of arms akimbo splashed onto the covered windowpanes; every so often a strobe light flashed pink. The ghost laughed in her face with late-night tuna breath. "Too late," declared the ghost. If the ghost had knuckles, it would be cracking them one by one. "Go home and smoke from your roof until your lungs get so black you deflate and fall to your small, pitiful death."

"No. This was a butt-dial," said Little Skin Bag. "Metaphorically."

"The world will be grateful if you never enter this lame shindig," sang the ghost.

This was not going to be like last time. She was not going to freak out. She was not going to get deleted from address books, or email chains, or Instagram feeds, or whatever. She would not be a pariah. "Stop freaking me out," she said. "Merry Wife will be here. She likes me."

"Merry Wife," spat the ghost.

"I think she'll leave him," said Little Skin Bag.

"Really."

"You didn't see her face last time," said Little Skin Bag.

"You are so cute," said the ghost. "So cute and so ugly. Not even your mother loves your cute ugly mug."

"Shut up," said Little Skin Bag. "They're coming."

The front door wrenched open. Lips and Right Tit. Black liquid spilled from their red plastic cups. They wore leopard-print dresses tight enough that Little Skin Bag could see pubic bones pronouncing themselves between two pairs of healthy, full thighs. Their mouths were laughing.

"Oh thank God," said Lips, her trademark shade smeared all over her teeth. She swatted playfully at Little Skin Bag's arm. "That *suede!* Ugh. What took you so long!"

"Totally," said Little Skin Bag. She held up her six-pack, which had by now dripped a lake onto the concrete step.

"Oh, I love swill!"

Right Tit grabbed her by the collar and yanked her inside.

"Where's Left Tit?" said Little Skin Bag in the foyer. She blinked four times. It felt like one time too many.

"Stop blinking so much," said the ghost into her ear hair.

"You know her," said Right Tit. "She'd rather watch documentaries about fish. Besides," she added, rubbing her right nipple, "there's only room at this party for one twin, you know?"

Lips nodded, nose scrunched. Little Skin Bag tried not to cringe. She really hated when Right Tit got too drunk. "And Merry Wife?" she asked, going for nonchalant.

"Oh sweetheart," laughed Right Tit. "Merry Wife might not even come, something about Gutting Man being over disco."

Lips rolled her eyes. "He'll show up for the Boar, though."

"There's a Boar at this party?" said Little Skin Bag.

"Totally," said Right Tit.

Lips patted her cheek. "Merry Wife knows where you are. Soon we'll bring out the Boar and you can face fuck that."

Little Skin Bag flushed an ugly color; the ghost rubbed itself on her eczema. She scratched at the patch and a few flakes fell loose onto her shoulders. A roar sounded from the kitchen.

"Oh!" cried Lips and Right Tit.

"I'm gonna go find Cubist," said Little Skin Bag.

"Chill." They nodded.

Little Skin Bag passed through the beaded curtain and into the disco room.

Posters of naked Art Deco models and bands with names like Scourge and Pubic had been taped to the walls. The dance floor was packed with bodies. It stank of spit and sweating creases. From the ceiling hung a black light. She could feel it leeching the color from her skin. She had to get into better lighting, or everyone would think she was always this ugly. She moved towards the back corner.

Cubist was DJing next to a window that had been taped up with cardboard. A pair of white headphones clamped onto his square ears. Little Skin Bag liked Cubist. She watched him swivel his body and thought he was doing an okay job of DJing so far. She was happy for him. Another wave of cheers went up for Chaka Khan. She waved and stepped onto the platform beside his setup.

"Hey hey," yelled Cubist over the music. "Looking mighty baggy tonight."

"Always," answered Little Skin Bag, and she bit down on Cubist's shoulder. "Cool track."

Cubist laughed. "Where's your sweetie?"

Little Skin Bag bit harder.

"Don't you worry." Cubist slid some dials down and up again. "Your secret is safe with me."

Little Skin Bag looked up and happened to catch Collarbone and Carpet stuffing hands through each other's hair. She looked at Cubist and raised an eyebrow.

"It's cool," he said, although his mouth made a movement. "We're not together anymore." He transitioned into a Bhangra classic.

"Hey," she said. "There's a Boar at this party."

"I know!" said Cubist.

"Is it fun, to do the whole Boar thing?" said Little Skin Bag.

Cubist winked at her. "Of course it's fun," he said. "It's their job to make it fun."

Little Skin Bag kissed him on the stubbly cheek and hopped down again. The oriental area rug under her feet was soaked with liquor slime.

"You know Merry Wife might already be here with Gutting Man," said the ghost. "They might be fucking upstairs in Lips's shower."

"Shut up," said Little Skin Bag. A gust of wind blew up her ponytail and puffed her body. There was a fan in the corner. She knew she should've worn a regular t-shirt. Something that didn't flip so easy. She held down her edges and hoped no one had seen.

The ghost slung a leg from her ear ledge. "You are so ugly under there."

Her skin hurt.

"You should stick your finger down your own throat and pull out your intestines so you stop looking so fat," the ghost suggested.

She wished she could spit into the ghost's mouth. She slid her way through the bodies and back through the veil of the beaded curtain.

Lips and Right Tit were still chatting, slapping each other and sloshing their drinks around, and Little Skin Bag didn't think she could handle any more of that. She ducked through the swinging door to her right.

The kitchen was bright and the appliances were black and the surfaces were all made of marble. Lips had told Little Skin Bag when she was redoing her kitchen that she liked marble countertops more than any other surface because marble made Lips feel sexy and cold. Little Skin Bag ran a fingertip along a surface. It did feel erotic. She imagined chopping carrots with a nice knife, the sound of blade on polished stone echoing throughout the kitchen.

"Hey, can you open a window?"

Little Skin Bag peered over the other side of the kitchen island. The Boar was there, lying on the tiled floor, legs bound together with white rope.

"Sure thing," said Little Skin Bag, and she walked over to the sink, leaned across the faucet, and popped open the small window there. A wind burst through the opening. The Boar closed its eyes.

"Thanks," said the Boar. "I needed that."

Little Skin Bag sank to the ground and hugged herself. If she had knees, she'd be resting her chin on their crests right now.

"Do you need some water or anything?" she asked the Boar.

The Boar shifted. "Can you turn me so that I can look at you? My eyeballs hurt."

"Sure thing," said Little Skin Bag. She grabbed the Boar by the ankle and gave it a spin. The tusk touching the floor scraped in an unpleasant way, but now she could see the snout and the eyes.

"Thanks," said the Boar.

"No worries," said Little Skin Bag.

They sat for a moment.

"I haven't seen you around," said the Boar.

"Yeah," said Little Skin Bag, "this isn't normally my thing, but I'm supposed to be meeting someone here tonight."

"So you've never seen a Boar before?" said the Boar.

"No," replied Little Skin Bag. "I mean I've heard about it from other people, but I've never seen it in person."

"Well," grunted the Boar. "You'll have to let me know what you think. It isn't for everyone."

"Why not?" said Little Skin Bag.

"You'll see," said the Boar.

"Well, have you been doing this long?" said Little Skin Bag.

"A good while, anyway," said the Boar, rubbing its cheek on the tile. Little Skin Bag reached over and gave its chin a scratch. "Thanks. Yeah, I don't know, it pays the bills and whatever. I mean it sucks, but everything kind of sucks, so I might as well be making a shit ton of money on the party circuits."

"You don't make it sound that fun," said Little Skin Bag, growing uneasy. She could feel that the ghost wanted to make a remark, but she slapped her hair and it stayed quiet.

"That's because it isn't," said the Boar. "Not for me, anyway."

Little Skin Bag fingered her fringe. "What do you do when you aren't working the party circuits?"

The Boar moved its shoulders, which Little Skin Bag interpreted as a shrug. "I like to scream sometimes," it said. "Nothing great. I genuinely believe my screaming isn't worth any fanfare, but it feels good to fill your lungs up like that."

"Where do you like screaming the most?"

"There's a great quarry behind Ray's Auto," said the Boar. "Lots of pink boulders, a little stream when the wet season's in full swing. You can really hear yourself scream down there."

"Wow," said Little Skin Bag.

"Yeah," said the Boar. "What do you do when you're not doing whatever it is that you do?"

Little Skin Bag smoothed her suede and touched her lips to make sure her lip stain hadn't rubbed off. "Well I'm an office assistant at Hval's, but mostly I fuck psychopaths."

The Boar wheezed. "That seems destructive."

Little Skin Bag shifted. "I don't know, it passes the time. It's like you said, everything sucks, so I might as well have a lot of sex."

The Boar looked like it wanted to smile, if it didn't have two curved tusks marring the clean line of its mouth. "Where do you like fucking psychopaths the most?"

Little Skin Bag obliged. "In the dark. Like the real dark, not just a room without the lights on. You know what I mean? Like in geothermal caves on a new moon in the middle of a wolf winter, when light bounces off the snow and no clouds can trap it, and when almost everything is dead. Or in the desert in a canyon that's been dry for a hundred years and not even lizards like to be on those stones anymore."

The Boar raised an eyebrow. "Do you find yourself in conditions like that very often?"

Little Skin Bag shrugged her shoulders. She felt like she might be mirroring the Boar's body language. It felt exciting.

"Have you ever thought about not fucking psychopaths?" the Boar continued. "It seems challenging."

Little Skin Bag stuck her tongue in her cheek. "I mean what can you do, you know? Bodies are particular."

The Boar quieted, and Little Skin Bag shifted onto her other ass cheek. Her calves were beginning to fall asleep, but other than that, she liked talking with the Boar. As long as she didn't think about what would happen to it later, she could pretend it was pleasantly neutral. She felt bold.

"Do you want to see something?" said Little Skin Bag.

"Sure," said the Boar. "Just turn me again."

Little Skin Bag grabbed the Boar's tusk and turned it a little more, so that its black, wet eye stared directly up into her own face. She filled her lungs with a long kitchen breath.

"Don't tell anyone," said Little Skin Bag. Then she lifted the hem of her body and placed it over the Boar's head.

At first the Boar was silent. Little Skin Bag knew what it was going through. The Boar was bearing witness to the great, bleeding eye of her black abyss.

"Holy shit," Little Skin Bag heard from within her bodily space.

She lifted her hem and freed the Boar's head, pressing herself into herself once more. The Boar blinked a bunch.

"Why did you show me that?" asked the Boar. The hairs on its chin quivered. "That felt so personal just then. Do people see you often?"

"No," said Little Skin Bag. "We were having a moment or something. It felt right."

"Wow," said the Boar. "We really were."

They sat in silence.

"It looked so delicate in there," said the Boar.

"Thank you," said Little Skin Bag, touched.

"Don't get used to this," said the ghost, and Little Skin Bag jumped. Luckily, the Boar didn't notice. It was too busy looking down its own snout.

"If you untie me, I'll kiss you for free," said the Boar. "If we're having a moment. You could untie me. We could just put our lips together and be quiet and no one would know, and then I could leave. They pay me first, you know. I already have the money. It wouldn't be hard to catch a bus at this hour. The 89 still runs."

Little Skin Bag bit her thumb skin. "Come on," she said.

"Sure," said the Boar. "Sorry."

"No, I'm sorry," said Little Skin Bag.

"Listen," said the Boar, "would you mind leaving me alone? I have to mentally prepare myself for this job. I have to do a lot of mental calisthenics. I have to hide in my own unlit caves, you know? And I think it's happening soon. You understand."

Little Skin Bag nodded. She rose to her feet and tiptoed around the island. She slid open the glass door and slipped out into the backyard. Then she pressed it closed again.

"Hey."

Little Skin Bag froze.

"Fuck," said the ghost.

"It's Merry Wife," said Little Skin Bag to the ghost.

"Yeah," said the ghost.

"What do I do?" said Little Skin Bag.

"Kill yourself and hope that's enough," said the ghost.

Little Skin Bag turned around.

Merry Wife. Standing beside a night-blooming cereus. The bowl of the bloom of the nocturnal gooseneck cacti catching the light cast from the kitchen. Mouth so slick. Eyes so green. Nose so hooked. She wore a translucent black blouse tonight that showed every raised bump on her brown nipples. Her aureoles seemed as big as twin galaxies, and they bounced through the shroud of space beneath her blouse. Merry Wife was now giving her a look that made Little Skin Bag want to suck on her thumb. Her own, or Merry's, or anyone's, really, any thumb would do. Trying for bravado, Little Skin Bag said, "You finally turned up."

Merry Wife cocked her head. "You knew I would," she said, her words prowling into Little Skin Bag's ears, settling on their haunches inside her head, preparing to pounce.

"I don't know what you're going to do," said Little Skin Bag as best as she could.

"No," agreed Merry Wife. "You only hope. You little hopeful bag of skin." She stepped three steps closer.

"Run," said the ghost.

Little Skin Bag felt her back press against the glass. "Come on," she said. "Someone's going to see, and you don't want that, remember?"

"Don't act coy," said Merry Wife. Her feet screamed through the grass.

Little Skin Bag frowned. "You're not listening to me," she said. "I said no more until you break up with Gutting Man."

Merry Wife rolled her eyes. "What he doesn't know," she said. Little Skin Bag only now saw the set of brass rings that Merry Wife wore on her fingers. Little Skin Bag regretted ever leaving the kitchen.

"He said he would gut me," said Little Skin Bag. "Don't you care?"

Merry Wife was close enough to bite her now. She blew a piece of hair off Little Skin Bag's nose. "Not really," she said, in the voice she used when she was also saying eight other things.

Little Skin Bag closed her eyes. She tried to remember how she'd felt only minutes ago.

"The Boar is ready!"

A cheer erupted from the house. Cubist could be heard screeching the records to a halt. Little Skin Bag took the opportunity to throw open the glass door once more and throw herself back into the kitchen. It now stank of wet yeast and singed fur and hair spray. The crowd had gathered in a circle around the island. She could hear grunts, squeals, loud smacks. She made her way to the front of the crowd. She took a deep breath and tried to hold the air in for as long as possible. She looked up.

Up on the island, Lips and Right Tit were having a go at the Boar. Right Tit screamed with delight as she rode its wiry-haired back, her bare legs gleaming in the bright kitchen light. Lips knelt in front of the Boar's snout and frenched it with her tongue. Her dress hugged her ass so tight everyone could see the lines of her thong, and most of the eyes were upon this shape. The crowd roared. Money began changing palms. Even Cubist was applauding while Collarbone and Carpet both stroked his square head. Little Skin Bag felt like the only one who could see the Boar's eyes leaked a strange black sludge. Its tusks had been sawed off too close to the bone; the small nubs bled. Lips had done a terrible job at the de-tusking. Little Skin Bag looked away, trying not to feel so nauseous, but Merry Wife stood across from her, staring back. Little

Skin Bag swallowed a lump down her throat. That gaze felt like fish hooks digging into her eyelids.

Now Gutting Man emerged from the throng, robed in his usual red. The spurs on his boots made audible clinks. Without taking his eyes off the Boar, he placed one hand on the back of Merry Wife's neck. The other hand lifted the edge of his shirt and scratched at what appeared to be a fresh wound. He tore off the coat of scab; a small tear of blood trickled into the lip of his jeans.

"Fuck," hissed the ghost in her ear. "He knows."

"He does not *know*," said Little Skin Bag. "He doesn't know anything. He's an asshole. Look at those spurs, for fuck's sake. He's a rock. That rock doesn't know shit."

Lips wobbled to her feet again, as if pedestaled, to the raucous applause of the mob.

"Seven whole minutes!" they cried.

"A new record!"

"Three extra points for Right Tit riding its back!"

The Boar lowered its snout, hooves clacking on the marble. Marble no longer seemed erotic to Little Skin Bag.

Lips wiped her wobbly mouth. She held a hand out to Right Tit and they both clambered down from the island.

"Your turn!" she cried, and pointed right at Little Skin Bag. "French the Boar! French the Boar!"

"French the Boar!" everyone else began to chant.

"I hate parties," said the ghost.

"I'm going to die," said Little Skin Bag.

She looked at the Boar. The Boar looked at her. The Boar seemed miserable. Or maybe Little Skin Bag was only projecting.

She put a hand on the back of her neck. She brought the Boar to the edge of the island.

"I'm sorry," she said to the Boar.

"Not sorry enough to stop," said the Boar, front teeth so pink it broke Little Skin Bag's heart.

"You're right," she said, and placed mouth on snout.

The Boar tasted primarily like that night in The Purest Club when Little Skin Bag and Merry Wife had split a dose of molly and finger-fucked each other in front of the leopard skin nailed to the red, flaking wall. They'd kissed sloppily, heavily, enough to pretend they were devouring one another and skewering one another like kebabs, and this was what the Boar tasted like. The Boar tasted like that feeling. The Boar tasted like the desire for a true dark meat. Little Skin Bag held her mouth as still as possible and kept her eyes shut. *I'm sorry*, she tried to think at the Boar.

"French the Boar, Skin Bag!" she heard Right Tit shouting. "Or it doesn't count!"

"Jesus," said the ghost. "Still glad you came?"

The Boar's front teeth were clenched together and it was impossible to pry them open, no matter how Little Skin Bag cajoled with her tongue, so she settled for making it look like they were tonguing. She rubbed her tongue along the bristled lips, trying not to gag on a stray piece of the Boar's hair. How many minutes had it been? How long could they both hang on? She forgot what she was doing and opened her eyes. The Boar was weeping its black sludge. The wounded nubs where its tusks once curved had reopened and were beginning to bleed.

"Let me help," Little Skin Bag heard Merry Wife say from somewhere beyond this circle of shame. Little Skin Bag felt breasts press into her back, her hair parting at her ear shell.

"Let's have some fun," said Merry Wife.

Little Skin Bag watched Merry Wife's hand reach towards the Boar's ass.

"No!" said Little Skin Bag, but her mouth was full of Boar, and it came out as a gurgle. Merry Wife rubbed herself against Little Skin Bag's back.

"Take it," said Merry Wife. "Both of you."

Little Skin Bag watched in horror as Merry Wife plunged a finger into the Boar's asshole. Then Little Skin Bag swallowed the Boar's screams of pain. She felt sick. She closed her eyes again. She couldn't keep them closed. She opened them. She closed them. She opened them.

"That's right," said Merry Wife. "Remember what I can do to you."

Little Skin Bag tapped the Boar beneath its chin. The Boar looked up, weeping, screaming, tuskless.

"On the count of three," said Little Skin Bag into its teeth, "hide in me like before."

The Boar's eyes were too wide to widen more.

"Wait," said the ghost in her ear.

"One," said Little Skin Bag.

"More!" yelled Lips.

"What are you doing?" said the ghost.

"Two," said Little Skin Bag.

"Do more!" yelled Right Tit.

"Don't you dare," said the ghost.

"Three," said Little Skin Bag.

"You like this," said Merry Wife.

"Now," said Little Skin Bag.

"Fuck," said the ghost.

Little Skin Bag lifted her hem and swallowed the Boar. The island emptied. The crowd roared.

"This isn't going to go well," said the ghost from her earlobe.

"Where is the Boar?" screamed Lips. The neck of her dress had been shoved down below her chest and her nipple glared at Little Skin Bag like a wide, brown eye, a kiss bruise blooming on the base of her throat. Little Skin Bag gulped. She felt the material of her abyss shifting.

"Oh God, I'm getting that Boar out of here," said the ghost.

Don't you dare, she thought. *I can do this.*

"Hey," called the Boar from inside her. "My foot's stuck in your artery."

Little Skin Bag bit down on her tongue. She had to hold herself together.

Merry Wife wrapped her hands around her jaw and yanked her head back. "Are you fucking stupid?" Merry Wife hissed. "Bring the Boar back so we can finish."

Little Skin Bag bit herself harder. Her spit tasted metallic now.

"Hey, something's happening," said the Boar inside her. Her bag body vibrated. *Fuck*, she thought.

"Jesus fucking Christ, why didn't you just rip your intestines out when you had the chance," said the ghost, now deep inside her ear canal. "You are going to fail." Little Skin Bag shuddered. She felt achy.

Merry Wife was clawing at her bag of skin. "Bring it back!" she said, desperation creeping into her voice.

"My hoofs!" Little Skin Bag closed her eyes, blood spilling into the trough of her mouth. She could picture the Boar staring cross-eyed at its feet, the abyss of her consuming the cartilage from her own membranous fibers. Her hands were cramping with the weight of her edges.

"Skin Bag," said the ghost. "Skin Bag, you have to stop, its legs are melting."

Little Skin Bag grimaced, swallowed.

Suddenly she felt a coldness, an absence behind her. She opened her eyes and turned around. Merry Wife had been dragged back into the arms of the angry crowd, and Gutting Man was bearing down on her with a hooked fingernail, his shirt bearing a perfect line of his own blood. Little Skin Bag opened her mouth.

"If you say anything, you'll lose concentration and the Boar will disappear," said the ghost, sliding around in her frontal lobe. "Which are you saving today? The Boar or Merry Wife?"

Little Skin Bag clamped her lips.

"It's sticky in here," said the Boar, "it's sticking to me, I can't move, it's freaking me out, I'm sinking or melting or something."

"Skin Bag, let the Boar out now," said the ghost.

Little Skin Bag wished she could pet the Boar's bristled head and kiss its snout. She held herself together. *Just let me get outside*, she thought. *Let me get outside and set it free.*

"You're not gonna make it, you fucking idiot, let it out! Skin Bag!" The ghost ricocheted down and over her deviated septum.

Gutting Man advanced on her now. He brought his face close to hers. She was swollen with melting Boar. He could see her ballooning. She held down her edges. She held them down.

"What did I tell you," said Gutting Man.

The Boar struggled within her. Her trachea burned with ghost tail.

"Oh shit," said the ghost. "Oh shit. Come on. Shit."

"Gut her!" cried Right Tit.

Gutting Man grinned. He still had Merry Wife under his fingernails.

"Help!" gasped the Boar. She couldn't feel any more of its kicks. Her abyss must be up to its shoulders now.

Hold yourself together.

Gutting Man held up a finger.

"Where am I going!" cried the Boar.

"Skin Bag," said the ghost.

"It's time to gut you," said Gutting Man.

Little Skin Bag bit off the tip of her tongue. It was all she could think to do. She spat herself into his face, and the tip of her tongue slapped the tip of his nose and tumbled onto the marble tiled floor. Gutting Man blinked, his cheek streaked with black. Bits of her abyss pooled in the dip above his lip.

"Please!" said the Boar.

Little Skin Bag clenched down.

"Oh," said the ghost.

Gutting Man plunged a needled claw into her suede and dragged down. The crowd around him cheered.

"Fuck," said the ghost.

"Bag!" cried Cubist.

The Boar was silent.

Little Skin Bag slumped. Her abyss spilled from her suede and leaked all over the marble in a pool. It crept towards the first pair of shoes, and the owner bent down to gather it in his hands and rub it into his arms. A lung of hers peeked out, sparkling like black diamonds. The Boar was nowhere to be seen. Gutting Man reached out.

"It's gone," she said. "It isn't here anymore." When she burped, phantasmic bile rose to her molars.

Cubist knelt beside her and held her hand. "What are you doing?" he whispered.

"What did you do with it?" Gutting Man snarled.

Little Skin Bag shrugged. Her eyes felt hot and tender and her skin bag burned at the site of the wound.

"We paid good money for that Boar!" said Right Tit.

"Finish her off!" yelled someone Little Skin Bag didn't know.

Little Skin Bag looked down at her new slit. The mess of her was spattered everywhere. She brought her hands through it. Like black sand, like a fine oil, the texture uncontainable. The ghost curled around her heart muscle, silent. The Boar was somewhere in her. It would never get free. She could close her eyes or keep them open and it wouldn't make a lick of difference.

"What is all this shit?" said Gutting Man, disgust giving him pause.

"True dark meat," said Little Skin Bag, as if from a great distance. She wondered if Lips had special cleaning supplies to get abyss out of marble grout. She wondered if Merry Wife still had asshole gunk on her finger. She wondered what Merry Wife looked like gutted. She tried to look around Gutting Man's form. She couldn't see.

"I'm going to finish you now," said Gutting Man. His grin was back, even with her abyss splattered all over his nice button-down. "This is a party, after all."

Little Skin Bag looked around her. Cups were raised high, fresh coats of lipstick were painted onto mouths, hair had been teased into disco shapes and thighs in white pants had formed a forest and she could barely recognize anyone through the angry thicket. Everyone was yelling at her; everyone was saying something. This was a party. And inside her abyss, Little Skin Bag felt a Boar stampede. *Where you're running,* she thought to the Boar of her, *you can make light stick to you forever. That's what it means to fuck a psychopath in deep dark: to look for light that will stick, even when the earth refuses to be hospitable. There's light where you're headed. I did a good thing, right? Didn't I?*

Little Skin Bag looked down. She cupped herself and brought it up to her mouth.

"You can scream if you'd like," said Little Skin Bag to the Boar hiding inside herself.

"Go ahead," said Little Skin Bag.

"Make it a good one," said Little Skin Bag.

Gutting Man bore down.

from *Kids of the Black Hole*

I filled up pages
I filled up pages
I filled up pages
I filled up pages
I filled u-p-p-u-u-u-u-u-h pages
I filled u-p-p-u-u-u-u-u-h pages
I filled u-p-p-u-u-u-u-u-h pages
I filled u-p-p-u-u-u-u-u-h pages
I filled up hummmm UP hummmm UP
I filled up up up up up upun pages up UP the field
hummmm / the field up I filled up the field
up hup hup upeeee up up I FILLED UP the meadow
WITH WORDS & flowers I filled up SPAT UP the field
its padded back / its inside leaves in layers I FILLED UP
to drown the farflung nails THE MATTRESS upward
I feint & SPAT UP & fell back in a black hole HUP
I filled up myself WITH MINE OWN TONGUE my hole up
wordhole godhole lovehole killhole
a whole thing / a wounded supine fawn in the road
my DOCKET OF WORDS / my FULL LAWNKILLER WINGS
my beakhole cockhole deerhole follicle
my filed taxform incarnate MYSELF WITH HOLES I speed it up
the fawn flailing its legs in air when we near
for I am milkless / a FALLOW FIELD
a WOODGRAIN GOD I sleep I rot alright
on dewy grass the cowtipping boys all night fist my decomposing side
my ejected blue self comes riding hard
my dead / my egg / my GOTHIC FLOOR / mine PAGAN EYES
the fawn kicking like a roach on its back
you drag the fawn to the side of the road

do the fleas live on when you drag it over
do the lungs live on when you drag it over
do the parents mourn when you drag it over
do the innards come like jewels on concrete
ARE FORCIBLY UNSEWN WHEN I REMOVE THEM
do the roads turn wet when you slide it over
do my hands forcibly remove the fur
do I embrace its underbelly like a distant mother
do my hands dismantle themselves & enter the deer
do the baby-sized lungs emerge from the breast
does this evening smell like burning leaves
do I dream of deer for thirty-one days
does it come forcibly unsewn

from "A Refuge for Jae-in Doe:
Fugues in the Key of English Major"

INVOCATION (Winter 2015–16).

It's evening in Queens, New York. Alone in my apartment, I'm grading student papers and drinking ginger tea. The phone rings. For some reason I forget to check the caller ID before answering, "Hello?"

A woman's voice: "Hi, Seo-Young?"

"Yes?"

"I'm calling from Stanford to ask about your experience while you were here."

(blank space)

The blank space above: a representation of my immediate response to the caller's words.

I almost can't believe that this is happening. Stanford is reaching out to me. Will Stanford apologize at last? That is all I have ever wanted: an apology.

My experience while I was at Stanford.

The story tumbles out. It's a story I have told numerous times already—to psychiatrists, to close friends, to myself, to lovers, to neurologists, to therapists. The story begins with my suicide attempt at age 21 and ends with Stanford's own punishment of the professor in 2001: two years of suspension without pay. I describe the long horrible months of sexual harassment. I describe the rape—or the parts of it that I can bear to mention out loud. I add that I never pressed charges or received any money from either Stanford or the professor. All I did was tell someone else who told someone else who started the fact-finding investigation that resulted in his punishment. I have never sued the rapist, the department, or the school—despite the time I've lost and the fortune I've spent as a consequence of the harmful culture at Stanford that enabled the professor to injure me as well as others.

The monologue is disjointed and long. I hadn't been expecting this call. I haven't had time to prepare. And yet I've had too much time to prepare: nearly fifteen years.

There is a silence after I've finished speaking. I start to wonder if perhaps the caller has hung up on me. I start to worry she won't call back.

But she's still there. "That's . . . awful," the woman is suddenly saying. "I'm so sorry. I'm just a Stanford undergrad. I was actually calling Stanford alumni for financial donations, to ask you for a gift of, but, I don't, I mean, in this case, for you . . ."

Something is happening to my eyes. The room has begun at once to darken and to seem much too bright. Or is something happening to my mind? Bright like sunlight at noon in Northern California on a cloudless day. But I am in Queens, New York City. The year is not 2000. What time is it? How old am I? Something is happening to reality. A sickening gust spreads throughout my internal organs. The phone I hold is shaking. My hands and arms are shaking. I close my eyes. I imagine feathery bandages made of photons holding together the jigsaw of my body. The shaking subsides.

"No, I'm the one who's sorry," I manage to say, and I mean it. "Tell me about your studies."

"Sure," she says, and begins to talk with cheerful confidence about her major, which is not English but history. She's excited about her academic career. As I listen to her, I murmur vague, pleasant, encouraging utterances. I'm happy for her. She has a bright future. "You have a bright future," I say. We wish each other well. Somewhat awkwardly the dialogue ends.

For several moments I am dazed. Inexplicable giddiness has begun to seep into my head. I can hear air seeping into a balloon. The balloon is beige. The phone is warm in my hand. Most balloons are not beige. The gust of nausea rapidly gathers in my chest. I rush, half-stumbling, to the kitchen trash can.

I throw up.

DISCUSS THE FOLLOWING QUOTATION.

"There's a great pleasure in teaching freshmen because you're sort of being folded into their lives at a particular, powerful moment in which you can make a difference," he said in the 1996 interview. "And to some degree, you can 'convert' them to English. It becomes a way of trawling for majors." (Source: Cynthia Haven, *Stanford Report*, August 17, 2007)

SOURCES AND ALLUSIONS.

He found me in a place known as the Farm.
His field: to grow a special breed of harm.

His stock of antique furniture and dolls
And manuscripts he nurtured in his walls.

A culture of "American" indifference
To rape he tended with uncommon sense.

Exactly how I came to be a thing
For him to call his own is still a thing

I can't or won't remember. He misused
His powers to leave minds like mine abused.

Where others who preceded me fare now
I often wish yet do not wish to know.

Sometimes I dream that his rare book collection
Is made of all "his" women turned to fiction.

IS THIS AN EXAMPLE OF IRONY? EXPLAIN YOUR ANSWER.

I grew up pronouncing the word "women" the way my Korean parents did:
the same way we pronounced the word "woman."

It was the professor—my rapist—who corrected my pronunciation of the word
"women." Since then, every time I have uttered "women," I have remembered
his voice.

It—his voice—it accompanies mine like an accent. "Women."

HERE, I FILLED OUT THE FORM.

- Year of birth: 1978.
- Place of birth: Northern Virginia.
- First language: Korean. To this day I have dreams in which my young
  mother is holding me in her arms and whispering to me in achingly
  melodic strings of Korean syllables.
- Second language: English. When I started school, the teacher told my
  parents that if they wanted me to succeed in America they would have to
  communicate with me exclusively in English. From then on my mother
  and I were estranged. We spoke to each other in an English filled with gaps.
  It took me decades to recognize the sacrifice my mother made when she
  stopped speaking to me in our native tongue.
- Language spoken by parents to each other: fluent Korean. I grew up hearing
  marriage as a foreign language—literally and figuratively. I grew up hearing
  the sound of Korean as a language of Korean-bound han syndrome,
  disappointment, fury, resignation, the sense of being trapped forever,
  resentment, guilt. Every other word: a door slammed.
- Faith system(s): raised Roman Catholic by my mother and Confucian by
  my father. Currently agnostic.

- How parents met: Their marriage was arranged.
- Significant family trauma(s): the Korean War (which orphaned my father and made him watch his beloved elder brother die); my mother's sister's suicide when I was a child; being run over by a car as a child while waiting for the school bus; struggling as a Roman Catholic teenager with my romantic feelings for a female classmate; being hospitalized during my senior year of college following my first suicide attempt; being raped soon after my first suicide attempt by a professor at Stanford University, where I was just starting a PhD program in English language and literature.

IS THIS AN EXAMPLE OF IRONY? EXPLAIN YOUR ANSWER.

His interests included The Declaration of Independence. He wrote a book titled *Declaring Independence*.

SYMPATHY FOR JAMES COMEY. SUMMER 2017.

He had called me at lunchtime that day and invited me to dinner that night, saying he was going to invite the whole cohort, but decided to have just me this time, with the whole cohort coming the next time. It was unclear from the conversation who else would be at the dinner, although I assumed there would be others.

It turned out to be just the two of us, seated at a small table in the middle of his favorite restaurant.

The professor began by asking me whether I wanted to stay on in the PhD program, which I found strange because he had already told me twice in earlier conversations that he hoped I would stay, and I had assured him that I intended to. He said that lots of people wanted to work with him and, given the academic pressure and job market, he would understand if I wanted to walk away.

My instincts told me that the one-on-one setting, and the pretense that this was our first discussion about my position, meant the dinner was, at least in part, an effort to have me beg to work with him and create some sort of intimate relationship. That concerned me greatly, given that I wanted to be his advisee.

I replied that I loved my work and intended to stay, write my dissertation, and receive my degree. And then, because the set-up made me uneasy, I added that I was not "interested" in the way people who are dating use that word, but he could always count on me to work hard and try my best to produce good scholarship.

A few moments later, the professor said, "But I'm lonely. I'm needy. I need to feel desirable. I need you to desire me."

I didn't move, speak, or change my facial expression in any way during the awkward silence that followed. I wanted to leave. Instead I froze.

The conversation then moved on, but he would return to the subject near the end of our dinner.

At one point, I tried to explain why it was so important that my personal life be independent of my professional career. I said it was a conundrum: Throughout history, some people in institutional positions of power (e.g. straight white male professors with tenure and endowed chairs, among other privileges) have decided that their positions authorize them to use less powerful people (e.g. 21-year-old first-year graduate students who happen to be female, mentally ill, and 1.5-2nd generation Korean American) in ways that make the powerful even more powerful (while putting the powerless in a risky situation). But the abuse of power can ultimately make the powerful weak by undermining public trust in institutions—including academic institutions—and their work.

Near the end of our dinner, the professor returned to the subject of my status as a student, saying he was very glad I wanted to stay, adding that he had heard great things about me from Professor X, Professor Y, and many others. He then said, "I need you." I replied, "You will always get work from me." He paused and then said, "That's what I want, work from you." I paused, and then said, "You will get that from me." It is possible we understood the phrase "work" differently, but I decided it wouldn't be productive to push it further. The term—"work"—had helped end a very awkward conversation and my explanations had made clear what he should expect.

INTERLUDE. During one of my episodes.

—Self: Dad?
—Dad: Yes, Jennie?
—Self: Did Stanford happen?
—Dad: What do you mean?
—Self: Was it real. The professor. Did all of that actually happen. To me.
—Dad (after a pause and a sigh): Yes, it was real. It happened.
—Self: Because I couldn't remember if I was remembering something that didn't happen. But it was real. You're not just saying so.
—Dad: It happened. It was real.
—Self (after a silence): Thanks Dad. I needed to know that.

FILL IN THE BLANK.

—Crime:
—Punishment: suspension for two years without pay.

LECTURE, 2078.

"Originally the sonnet was a site of sexual violence. Male poets were rewarded for celebrating the women they hunted. They used the sonnet form and an instrument called the 'blazon' to convert their prey into exquisite English artifacts. Our anthologies still include holograms of jewel-like eyes, porcelain skin, ruby lips, hair like gold, and so on.

"Over time the white men themselves modified the sonnet to make it accommodate topics other than male heterosexual desire. The topics came to include blindness, time, spiders, God, the planets, applepicking, wine, prayer, computers, robots, politics, and the apocalypse. Now, in the year 2078, it is possible to choose existence in a world designed like a sonnet. It is possible to live one's entire life inside a sonnet. It is possible to become a sonnet.—But only if one has consented to such an existence."

DISCUSS THE FOLLOWING QUOTATION.

In a 1996 News Service interview, [JF] described the 18th-century attitude toward belongings this way: "There was a sense that objects were preferred over people because they didn't leave you, they didn't talk back, and you could project a certain subjectivity and have an intense relationship with them, particularly with books," he said. (Source: Cynthia Haven, *Stanford Report*, August 17, 2007)

A LITTLE SONG AND A RECEIPT.

Doe: a deer, a female deer—
Often chased by sonneteers of old.
Caught, and killed, and bathed in fear,
turned to human blazons to be sold—
Eyes—$twin models of the stars.
Skin—$fine tissue wrought from gold.
Lips—$your favorite kind of flower.
Sex—$a secret still untold/ a Silk Road to unfold/ a thing for you to mold/ a source by you controlled.

Total: $— — — — —.—

THE BLAZONAUT.

Setting: an alternative universe where, due to the choreography of molecules here, to use words is to versify. Location: Southwest Canada (not far from where the Golden Gate Bridge is located in our reality). Time: a year named "The Earliest Early Americanist" (corresponding roughly to our year 2000 AD). All residents of this universe hold the following truth to be self-evident: Each person has the right to free consent. Living by this truth is to them as breathing is to us. Rape, in this reality, is an alien phenomenon.

1. News

". . . she fell into the water from the sky . . ."

2. Jae-in Doe

Decedent is an Asian female.
Twenty-two she just had turned.
The cause of death we cannot tell
Despite the many things we've learned.

3. TOP SECRET

My Doe-type can be difficult to track.
Yet here I am, my voice-box playing back
From lips hydrangea-lavender in hue
His thoughts during our first few interviews.

The hair is shoulder-length, the color black.
The height and weight suggest she won't fight back.
The fingernails are unadorned and short.
The eyes are brown; no makeup do they sport.
The skin appears unpierced and untattooed,

Yet scars of ruby-pearl seem to protrude
Like self-inflicted jewelry on each arm
And wrist—which means she's vulnerable to harm.
The language of her flesh, as I assess her,
Reveals Confucian worship of professors.

Her deference Korean gives me right
To use her innocence for my delight.

4. The Coroner's Soliloquy

The species: neither robot nor a xenomorph but both.
A *blazonaut* I call her as I scan her for the truth.

Throughout her brain dimensions grew like flowers wild
And *han* flowed through her circuits like fog-weather mild

until the onslaught
caused a drought.

The genitals, the soul, the lymph, the spine, the nape,
                    Show evidence of _____
For which we have no name.

I can't do this anymore.

MUTANT BLAZON.

My rapist's eyes remind me of the sun.
To look at them will mean that I go blind.
His mouth beside my ear—they form a gun.
Each breath: a bullet targeting my mind.

My rapist's eyes remind me of the sun.
His throat: a fist to silence mine designed.
His reason: a ventriloquist's illusion.
No tenor in the end could hearing find.

My rapist's eyes remind me of the sun—
Too close for any vessel with a mind.
Survive or get to die—that is the question.
No longer have I any will to mind.

My rapist's eyes remind me of the sun—
Not dead, not living, neither keen nor blind;
A daily haunting; memory rebegun;
Disaster in some future undivined.

I write, rewrite, a "sonnet" about rape
To hunt that voice I wish I could escape.

DISCUSS THE FOLLOWING QUOTATION
(without using the words "predator" or "prey").

"Yeah that's her in the gold. I better use some Tic Tacs just in case I start
kissing her. You know, I'm automatically attracted to beautiful . . . I just start
kissing them. It's like a magnet. Just kiss. I don't even wait. And when you're
a star they let you do it. You can do anything. [. . .] Grab them by the pussy.
You can do anything." —The 45th President of the United States of America

COMPLETE THE FOLLOWING DIALOGUE.

–Professor: All men have rape fantasies, including your father.
–Student:

A KIND of CENSUS.

- Number of spouses: zero.
- Number of children: zero.
- Longest stretch of time spent alone inside the apartment: eighteen consecutive days.
- Longest stretch of time post-rape without any physical intimacy with another mammal: seven consecutive years.

- Number of episodes of Law and Order: Special Victims Unit never seen: zero.
- Year I watched SVU for the first time: 2011.
- Year SVU started: 1999.
- Number of fantasies about cathartic dialogues with Olivia Benson: countless.
- Number of years spent closeted to most people about what happened at Stanford: fifteen.

July 5, 2016. Facebook entry posted shortly after I came out as a rape survivor.

Q: Do you think being raped made you gay?

A: Several people have asked me this question (or a version of it). It is a question worth addressing.
(1) I cannot speak for others who have been raped. I can only speak to my own situation. Please do not mistake anything I write here for a generalization. (2) The first crush I remember having: Ellen Degeneres. At the time I didn't know who she was (I caught a glimpse of her on TV); I didn't know what it meant to be gay; I didn't know what I felt was a crush. All I knew was that she made my heart feel nervous and I wanted to see her face again. (3) My parents had an arranged marriage. The arrangement was less than ideal. They spoke to (argued with) each other in Korean—a language that my brother and I did not understand—and they spoke to us in (broken-ish) English. To this day I think of marriage as literally a foreign language. (4) My mother was (is) devoutly

Catholic. As a child I myself was devoutly Catholic and confused about my sexuality. The last time I went to confession (I was a teenager) I confessed I thought I might be gay and also I wasn't sure if God existed. The priest said he could not forgive me but he could give me holy water for me to keep by my bed to repel Satan. (5) My first sexual experience was being raped at the age of 22 by someone who wielded power over me, who controlled my future, and who was fully aware that I was sexually inexperienced and confused about my sexuality. (6) I spent much of my twenties in relationships that allowed me to pretend (or try to pretend) that Stanford never happened. Does it matter that a few relationships were with men and that a few were with women? I honestly don't know. (7) My last relationship ended a decade ago. Since then my personal life has resembled a desert ruled by agoraphobia and the wish to destroy my capacity to feel attraction. (8) I have been attracted to people of all sexes and gender identities. (9) As the details above are meant to suggest, my sexuality is extremely complicated. Did being raped make me gay? No. (See item 2.) But it is a fact that rape (among many other factors, including those mentioned above) had an impact on how I experience desire and act (or hesitate to act) upon my feelings. Indeed it may be the case that "rape survivor" is one of my sexual orientations. *I would not wish this joyless and often agonizing orientation on anybody.* (10) Again I stress that I speak only for myself. I doubt it is possible to generalize that rape makes people gay (or straight). Different individuals survive violence in different ways. Some of us end up not surviving. Some of us are working on just holding on. I hope that my answer has been educational.

"Noli me tangere": A Kind of Villanelle.

His ghost stands watching me while I'm asleep.
I know that this cannot be real because
I'm wide awake. I never fall asleep.

The hours between twelve and twelve still keep
Me up reciting poetry because
His ghost stands watching me while I'm asleep.

I close my eyes, imagine rivers deep
And soft plush turquoise emerald velvet moss.
I hide myself here as a pebble heap.

What if I dared to sea from cliff to leap?
My absence from the world would be no loss.
His ghost stands watching me while I'm asleep.

When finally I die, will I escape
His ghost's attention? Or will those glib jaws
Assault my ghost with secrets fresh to keep?

I don't know if I wake or if I sleep
Or why my speech obeys poetic laws.
His ghost stands watching me while I'm asleep.
Perhaps he's dreamt a way my soul to reap, to reap, to reap.

PALO ALTO DISAPPEARANCE.

A yard, once used for some kind of sport, lies seemingly deserted. High above
her, in a near-future sky, one allosaurus and one magpie, each the size of a
skyscraper, battle for extinction. Crowds of invisible spectators flow toward
the spectacle. At some point, when the rumors grow too poisonous, she turns
around, against the tide, and starts to climb a secret staircase made out of
wisteria, the stems of which twine counterclockwise. The more she climbs,
more and more flowers surround her. Blossoms thicken. Petals seep into her
hair. Her skin becomes liquid petal.

"Anyone is inside your house," the flowers whisper.

"I don't have a body," she responds.

By now she is no longer climbing a staircase. The staircase has disappeared and so has she.

In the distance another mythical creature falls and another endangered animal cannot hear its own appalling song. Where games of sport once took place, palm trees begin to shimmer, dazzle, daze. She is beyond the last thought at the end of the mind.

Obviously this is not reality.

This was one way I got through it.

THE NEW MILLENNIUM
(after Shelley's "Ozymandias").

I meet a stranger in a house of gloom
Appointed with archaic chairs and shelves
Made centuries ago . . . The stranger's doom
Is my fate too, for that which makes my self
not hers is time alone. Inside that room
She cannot see me but I see her dread,
Her shattered face—Something I know is wrong.
Her body language speaks as though it's dead.
If minds could text, in hers this would appear:
"Your name is Jennie. My name is Seo-Young.
Let me, your future self, bear your despair."

Now that I'm home, I'm drowning in decay,
Pill bottles, trash, her burden mine to bear.
Why did I—she—choose to survive this way?

RESURRECTION LULLABY
(after Milton).

When one considers how one's life is spent,
Each resurrected self another hide
Less human than the one that last had died,
One's brain a frozen bruise that can't consent
To heal after the violence he meant,

His afterlife itself slow homicide,
"Please let my will complete the suicide,"
One prays. But other voices, to relent
That prayer, interrupt, "One did not need
Apology, redress, or an arrest
To live as though his punishment were great.
Survival was enough to fill the need
Required by existence of each guest.
Your prayer's heard. Now fall asleep and wait."

DREAM.

Outside: a Farm. Inside: a dimly lit living room. A constellation of antique
furniture. A couch. A young woman, my height, we're standing in the room
looking at each other, no one else is in the room, she looks like me but her
hair is longer and her cheeks are fuller and the scars on her arms are still
visible. I notice them because she's gesturing. She's pointing at the couch.
"That's where I die," she says. "That's where you must take my place. There is
no other way. I have no future worth living."

I used to hate these dreams. I'm learning to live with them. They're like the
dreams I have of North Korea. They're like the dreams I have of life after
death.

The next time I see her I will say:

Forgive yourself for having been naive.
You've dwelled here for too long. It's time to leave.

EPILOGUE.

I am one of the lucky ones.

from *Airport Novella*

1

Manchek nodded.

He nodded to the projectionist in the back. "First picture."

"The van," Comroe said. Manchek nodded.

"Perhaps the pilot should narrate." Manchek nodded and looked at Wilson, who got up and walked to the front of the room, wiping his hands nervously on his pants.

Wilson nodded and swallowed. The room lights went down and the projector whirred to life.

For a moment, Stone looked surprised, and then he nodded.

Hall nodded. "What is it?"

There was a short pause. Norman nodded. "It may be alive."

"Possible," Harry said, nodding.

The group looked at each other, nodded.

Burton nodded. "Crazy," he said. "Stark raving mad."

"It's exciting, all right."

Norman nodded.

"Almost astonished, in fact," Burton nodded. Out of the corner of his eye, he saw Tina nodding vigorously. Harry looked skeptical.

Stone nodded, staring out the window. To her astonishment, Allison saw her husband nod quietly.

"What do we do?" Burton nodded.

Stone nodded to the equipment in the back.

"Will that still work?"

Stone nodded.

Burton said to Stone, "And what have you found in the capsule?"

He nodded to a stack of pink uniforms in one corner.

They nodded.

Burton nodded. "Any idea what this means?"

The others nodded.

Jackson swallowed, and nodded. He seemed afraid to speak.

"We had to give you a transfusion."

He nodded, accepting this quite calmly. "Yeah. Like I said, I had it before. All these needles stuck in you"—he nodded to the intravenous lines—"and all the blood going into you . . . I was doing a bottle a day. You know them bottles it comes in?"

87

Hall nodded. No wonder the man was acid.

Hall nodded, and left. He walked over to the teleprinter and watched as it typed. He looked and nodded, satisfied.

Stone nodded and turned to Hall, who told of the tests carried out on his two patients.

Stone nodded.

"Some of them died instantly, and the others . . ."

Burton nodded. "One other survived." He nodded to the crib next to Jackson.

"So much for theory," Norman said.

Leavitt nodded; Stone turned back to the isolation chamber and removed a glass dish from the light microscope. "And I have to do it myself?"

Burton nodded.

Hall nodded. "It makes sense," he said.

Leavitt nodded. "I hope we're not too late," Leavitt said, watching the computer console screen impatiently.

Stone nodded.

Norman nodded. "Any sign of Captain Barnes?"

Hall nodded. He nodded to a door across the room.

Anderson nodded and flicked the switch just inside the door. Langdon squinted into the light and finally nodded.

The bald man nodded. "Slipped on the ice. A week ago. Still hurts like hell."

Langdon nodded, accustomed to the comments.

Katherine nodded.

Their heads nodded in unison.

Langdon nodded and lowered his voice to a conspiratorial whisper. "You sure you're ready?"

She nodded. "This thing has a *name*?"

Langdon nodded. "It's one of the most secretive icons of the ancient world."

Trish nodded. "In all of history?"

Katherine nodded enthusiastically. "Like a flock of birds or a school of fish moving as one."

Dr. Abaddon fell silent for several long moments and then began slowly nodding as if Katherine might have a point.

A few seconds later, the old dean finally nodded.

Sato nodded. "Yes, basically that's right."

Langdon nodded.

"Chief," Sato said, turning away from Langdon, "can you get us a closer look at the painting?"

Anderson nodded.

"Do you see anything?"

Katherine nodded blankly.

Langdon nodded, feeling a chill as he looked up.

Fache nodded without even looking.

Sato gave a grim smile and nodded to Anderson. "Chief, follow me, please. I'd like a word in private."

Anderson nodded and swallowed hard.

Langdon hesitated and then nodded.

"Did you see that?" Sato asked, also staring with alarm at the wall.

Langdon nodded, his pulse quickening. *What did I just see?*

Fache nodded. "Go on."

Katherine was right behind him. She nodded.

Nuñez nodded vigorously, doing his best to play along. "I'm sorry, sir. The Architect told me not to tell a soul!"

The dean nodded. "Yes, Peter told me the same thing."

Langdon nodded. He nodded in frustration.

Nuñez nodded. "I think he would prefer you obey my wishes."

Fache nodded. "Devil worship . . ."

Warren Bellamy—Architect of the Capitol—stepped across the threshold and thanked Nuñez with a polite nod.

Nuñez's pulse quickened.

Langdon nodded, exasperated.

Katherine nodded, too embarrassed to speak.

She nodded.

He turned to her, "I don't get it." Collet gave a curt nod and spun the laptop toward Fache.

Langdon nodded absently and took a few steps toward the bench. "It's flawless," Langdon said, nodding as his thoughts churned.

Trish nodded. "Welcome to the world of digitized text."

Sophie gave a curt nod.

Langdon nodded, dumbstruck.

Anderson studied the blueprint for a moment, nodded.

Langdon nodded and made his way over to the kitchen phone. He aimed his light inside, stared for a long, puzzled moment, and then nodded to Sato. "He's in the SUV."

Agent Hartmann gave a quick nod, pulled out the Escalade keys, and headed for the door.

The guard nodded. "Identification, please."

The chauffeur looked surprised. "I'm sorry, didn't Ms. Solomon call ahead?"

The guard nodded, stealing a glance at the television.

"Shoot the lock," she said, nodding toward the key plate beneath the lever.

Langdon's pulse leaped.

Anderson nodded, inching after her. "Talk about skeletons in your closet."

Everyone inside the office nodded their understanding.

Solomon nodded. Her eyes were red, and she had obviously been crying, but she nodded with a resolute stoicism. "It's the only way we can get Peter back, right?"

Langdon nodded. He nodded in frustration.

The old woman dabbed her tearful eyes and nodded with a resolute calm. "Okay."

Langdon nodded, his expression serious.

The agent nodded and spoke into his transceiver.

Solomon nodded. *Perfect.*

When she told the agent where she wanted to take Bellamy, she expected the man to look surprised, but he simply nodded and opened the passenger door for her, his cold stare revealing nothing. Solomon gave the boy a nod of approval. "Exactly."

Bellamy nodded, looking dazed, as if nothing mattered anymore. "Yes, I just heard your conversation."

Solomon nodded, knowing he was right.

"Do you know where you are?"

Langdon nodded weakly, still coughing.

She nodded vigorously, her lungs burning for air.

Langdon nodded. "Near the main altar."

Then he lowered the skull and gazed out at the assembly around him. America's most powerful and trusted men gave contented nods of acceptance.

Peter nodded.

The students in the crowd nodded enthusiastically.

Langdon nodded absently.

"And finally?" Peter asked. "What about the staircase?"

Langdon glanced down at the image of the stairs. Langdon nodded, his thoughts drifting now.

$$\smile$$

I nodded. "Surely. Yes, I remember."

A sudden great tolling of bells shook through the old abbey. Across the room, Stormy nodded. On the *prie-dieu*, a small book of prayers waited for a kneeling priest.

Chief Porter nodded thoughtfully. "The world sure was good to him." His vague smile, which seemed to be as permanent as a tattoo, widened briefly, and he nodded as though in cheerful agreement with something that he'd said to himself.

The chief nodded, and the purple Barney chair squeaked more like a mouse than like a dinosaur. "I better get moving."

I raised my spatula in reply. "Really?"

Atop his tall lanky body, his round face bobbed like a balloon on the end of a string, and I could not tell whether he was nodding in agreement or shaking his head in denial. He might have been doing both.

Smiling and nodding, I was unashamed of this deception. I looked at Stormy.
She nodded.

I nodded. I said, "Isn't tomorrow your day off?"

She nodded. "You're right."

"You need to be as calm as possible." I nodded.

She nodded. "Yes. I believe that."

I held out my hand. "Do we have a deal?"

Solemnly, she thought about it, and then she nodded and took my hand. "Deal."

☁

She nodded and departed, allowing me a moment to take in my surroundings. There was just enough wind to set the palm trees in motion, shaggy heads nodding together in some secret communication.

Another man in a tuxedo appeared in due course and escorted me toward the back of the house. Moving along the rosarium with a queenly grace and a smile of royal beneficence, admiring the nodding heads of her colorful subjects, my mother said, "I'm so glad you came to visit, dear."

I said, "Ah," with a noncommittal nod.

I passed two men, a woman, another man. We smiled and nodded.

I nodded.

"Can you tell me what it is?" she said in a tone of gentle remonstration.

I nodded, for I could not speak.

Jeremy was silent for a moment before finally shrugging.

She shrugged without answering. "Can I be frank now?"

He shrugged. "Anything that might help me with the history of the cemetery and the town."

She shrugged. "Shows me what I know. Being that you're a journalist from the big city."

He shrugged, acting innocent.

She suddenly remembered that he'd been trying to guess her age yesterday. "Yep," she said with a shrug.

He gave a sheepish shrug, and she had a sudden vision of what he must have looked like as a small boy. "Hey, I know it's none of my business, but how did it go with Rodney?"

She hesitated before finally shrugging. "You're right. It is none of your business." He could almost hear her shrug.

He gave a sheepish shrug. "I suppose that depends on the perspective."

Jeremy moved to the refrigerator and pulled two bottles of Coors Light from the six-pack. He twisted one cap off and then the other before setting a bottle before her. When she saw it, he shrugged. "I hate to drink alone," he said.

She shrugged. "What can I say?"

He shrugged, his voice growing more matter-of-fact as he went on. "Sure," he said with a shrug.

Rachel studied him for a moment before shrugging. They stood together as one song ended and the band began a new one.

She shrugged, her eyes flashing back to Jeremy. "What are you doing here?"

She smiled weakly and shrugged as she answered. "I came to talk to you, of course." "About Lexie?"

She didn't answer right away. Instead, she sighed, then said evenly, "Among other things." When his brow furrowed, she shrugged.

"Do you still want to hear about Sam?" he offered.

I shrugged.

"Like I said, it's a long story. And very . . . strange." He raised his eyebrows, measuring my expression with curious eyes. Finally, he shrugged.

I shrugged.

"That's all right," he shrugged. "It can wait."

I sighed. "No harm done," I insisted with a shrug.

He moved. I shrugged.

He shook his head, his face a mask of faux tragedy. "I wanted to talk to you. I can't believe this."

I shrugged. "Oh, well."

Jacob shrugged.

Embry shrugged. "You are so odd, Bella Swan. I feel like I don't know who you are."

I looked up, trying to focus on the left half of her face. I shrugged, wishing she would let it go.

"I'm nothing but a human, after all. Nothing special," I explained, shrugging weakly.

She shrugged.

Jacob shrugged.

I felt Edward shrug around me. He asked about the hair; Jacob shrugged and told him it was just more convenient.

I shrugged. "Not in the technical sense of the word."

I shrugged. "Must have all been a misunderstanding."

I twisted to see Jacob's response. Jacob merely shrugged, all the friendliness wiped clean from his face.

Jane's smile faded, and she shrugged indifferently.

I shrugged. "I don't know. It just irritates me."

Felix and another shadow exchanged a quick glance. Edward shrugged.

I shrugged. I wasn't going to take it back.

He shrugged. "It's nothing."

"That doesn't *bother* you?"

He frowned at me.

I shrugged. Shrugging was good. Very blasé.

"Maybe." He shrugged his shoulders, but his hands remained steady.

"I kind of guessed that," I said, shrugging. My spur-of-the-moment whim hadn't come with a plan intact.

His black eyes appraised me for a second, and then he shrugged.

I shrugged. "Just needed a change."

I shrugged. "Just scared."

"That doesn't seem fair." He shrugged, but his eyes were still intense.

"If you want me to go . . ." I shrugged.

He shrugged. "If I had any brains I'd drag it out a little bit."

I was a little confused by his train of thought. I shrugged.

He shrugged and grinned.

I shrugged. "Either way."

He shrugged.

"Okay, then, new subject," I said.

He shrugged indifferently. He led me through the open front door into the dark house and flipped the lights on.

Edward was shrugging out of his jacket. I shrugged. "Been thinking about that last time a lot, have you?"

He shrugged instead of answering, and I winced.

He shrugged. And a fresh wave of panic shattered my brief sense of confidence.

I shrugged. "I guess it stuck with me."

"Never be afraid to tell me how you feel, Bella. If this is what you need . . ." Edward shrugged.

I could feel the control slipping.

"I'll be in my room," I told him, shrugging out from underneath his hands.

"You say that like you're not sure."

I shrugged, feigning a lack of interest.

Edward shrugged. "If that's what you really want."

He shrugged, and his smile became absolutely angelic.

"You're impossible," I groaned. "A monster."

Jonnie shrugged.

The monster made a sort of shrugging motion and said something.

"Where are they located?" said Jonnie, being very casual.

Terl took his eyes off driving for a moment and looked suspiciously at Jonnie. Then he shrugged.

Ker started to shrug and then had a happy thought.

"If I'm going to help, maybe we better talk over how we are going to do this." Terl shrugged.

Jonnie shrugged. Then he indicated the list.

Jonnie read it, shrugged, and tossed it in the wastebasket.

Terl shrugged. "Promises," he said indifferently.

Jonnie shrugged. "They often said things just to please the Psychlos."

Ker shrugged. Angus told him who it was for and Ker sat there for a while, his amber eyes thoughtful.

Jonnie shrugged and waved a hand at the Russian officer as though to go ahead. The Russians nosed up their assault rifles.

The cadet shrugged and took the bundles.

Jonnie shrugged. "And you are taking me somewhere?"

"Very well," said the terrestrial with a shrug of his shoulders.

Jonnie shrugged. "It's the civilized thing to do," he said and started toward the ship again.

Lord Schleim shrugged.

The other emissaries shrugged.

Jonnie shrugged. "My lord, do you mind if I go on?"

The Hockner shrugged, then gave a strained laugh. He lowered the beam and looked at Lord Schleim. But Lord Schleim simply shrugged.

Jonnie shrugged and pointed to Stormalong. "Can you stay awake to Luxembourg?"

Stormalong shrugged and then nodded.

Lord Voraz, when asked, had shrugged and said it probably came under the heading of prerogatives of a branch manager and was probably bank business.

The branch manager shrugged.

Lord Voraz shrugged. "There are strong bank guards."

Lord Voraz shrugged. "Of course."

The lords shrugged.

Dries shrugged. "This is not news and it is totally off the subject."

There was a long hesitation again and the girl shrugged. "Why?"

"Why not?" Paul shrugged.

She hesitated for a long time, thinking he didn't need to know it, and then shrugged, as though talking to herself.

Lionel shrugged modestly.

Faye smiled as he glanced at Val with a shrug.

"Where's Anne?" Faye asked Val and she shrugged. "She was here when I called. Van? Do you know where she went?"

Vanessa shrugged.

Val shrugged. "Who knows?" She shrugged indifferently and looked out the window.

He shrugged. And shrugged. But Faye was in no way prepared for what came next.

"I wish you'd stay out of this damn business." Lionel shrugged.

"You and Mom seem to like it a lot." Val shrugged.

He shrugged and looked vague. Two people couldn't have been more different than they.

Val shrugged. She had nothing to do with it after all and what did she care anyway? So she just shrugged and said, "Yeah, so what? Big deal."

He shrugged then, looking very young again.

"What can I say?" He shrugged to Val after the funeral. "What did you do today?"

She looked at him for a long moment and then shrugged.

"Any big new heart throbs since I left?"

Valerie shrugged. She shrugged again. She didn't want to tell him what she'd been through. That was nobody's business. She led a different life now, in another place, another world.

Her mother smiled at Ward, and he shrugged. He shrugged with a grin.

"Sounds pretty boring to me." He shrugged. "What do you want?"

She shrugged pensively as she threw her coat on a chair. "Maybe to publish a book one day . . . good reviews . . ."

Katherine Rose shrugged her shoulders. Apparently it wasn't much of an issue. "Merry Christmas, sir."

Gary Soneji shrugged. "Merry Christmas back at you," he said and shrugged. "Is that it, Marty?"

Marty frowned and looked down.

"Now what did you get her?"

Missy whispered conspiratorially to her brother. "You're too much." Marty shrugged as if he couldn't remember.

Gary shrugged his shoulders.

Marty frowned. "You want to say something here?"

Gary shrugged. As if he didn't have clue one.

Marty frowned.

Gary shrugged. "Maybe not."

Monroe shrugged, but he continued to smile.

I shrugged and sipped the truly bad-tasting coffee.

Jezzie shrugged her shoulders. That was her only answer.

Airport Novella takes four gestures that I found to be ubiquitous in airport novels—nods, shrugs, odd looks, and gasps—and collages them into four chapters, one for each gesture. The full book is available as a paperback and free PDF from Troll Thread (http://trollthread.tumblr .com). The preceding chapters contain excerpts from the following novels:

1. *The Andromeda Strain*, Michael Crichton; *Sphere*, Michael Crichton; *The Lost Symbol*, Dan Brown; *The Da Vinci Code*, Dan Brown; *Brother Odd*, Dean Koontz; *Odd Thomas*, Dean Koontz; *Watchers*, Dean Koontz; and *K Is for Killer*, Sue Grafton.

2. *True Believer*, Nicholas Sparks; *The Notebook*, Nicholas Sparks; *New Moon*, Stephenie Meyer; *Eclipse*, Stephenie Meyer; *Twilight*, Stephenie Meyer; *Battlefield Earth*, L. Ron Hubbard; *Family Album*, Danielle Steel; *The Gift*, Danielle Steel; *Kaleidoscope*, Danielle Steel; *Daddy*, Danielle Steel; *Along Came a Spider*, James Patterson; and *The Christmas Train*, David Baldacci.

Forced Center

Seems possible to produce
A popular method of branding
Of consumption . . . Stuff trickles in the dish
Oxidized by grout, xylophones' antepenultimate
It swills it
Or do the birds and monkeys of your forests
Their routine make it over
Unchronicle as to a broadest scale
Various roads were delayed, I guess

The veterans are well adjusted, these services
Discounts on the umbrella and
The macula very powerful to one, as
Peace finds itself in threat of pain
Somber tropicalia of a city blood moon
Penny by the homeless guy
Four brides on the beach
Six in the park
If stacks of endorsed textbooks dispute this
Abandonment

The Lovers

Everyone who asks questions, asks in some way about love. The question is one half, the answer the other. If you separate the Lovers you don't end up with two distinct people. Instead you're left with two halves of a self, incapable of doing much on their own. Imagine a coin with one side, or a story with one side. Imagine peeling the skin off your arm. Imagine the worst thing that could ever happen to you, happening to you. When one Lover's gone, the other doesn't know what to do. When a Lover was a waitress she dropped all the plates she carried. When a Lover was a cashier he could never count out the right change. When they worked opposite hours they lost entire days. They looked at the moon more than they looked at themselves. They'd rifle through medicine cabinets in other people's houses and read the magazines other people subscribed to. They went to the places where others decided to go. When they're apart they forget their names; when they're together they don't respond to them.

"We can tell you your future, if you tell us your dreams," is what the Lovers say upon being found. They listen to one of your dreams if you buy each a Moscow Mule, and after will tell a part of the coming days. It can be insignificant, like a bee. "Watch for bees," a Lover says to you. "Are you allergic?" You're not. "That's good." Their smiles are sleepy; they ruffle each other's hair.

The next Tuesday you step on a bee. You see the Lovers later that week at the Mercantile. You ask how they'd extracted bees from your dream, in which there weren't any bees. "There's no future in dreams," one Lover says, the girl. "None that would be worth telling, anyway." You expect the Lovers to evade but they don't. "It's about faces," the boy goes on. "Seeing what's there. The past is in your teeth. The future's in your eyes."

You wonder why they asked about dreams, until you run into the ex-girlfriend of one of your friends, whose face you recognize better than her voice. "They just like hearing people's dreams," she says, bored already. "They don't have any of their own."

It's like this, when you talk to them, or about them. Half-answers that in the end, amount to nothing—much like the Lovers themselves. They live in an apartment on Poverty Ridge that stinks of resin fumes because one of them makes orgonite, a device used for energy channeling in reiki circles. The Lovers sometimes sell these in the markets beneath the freeway, but most often just scatter them places—under park benches, behind trash cans. Inside other apartments that they're only sometimes invited to and occasionally stay in for too long, when they find themselves homeless, which happens sometimes. Old classmates of theirs sometimes run into teachers they used to have at bars they now go to, and it is always awkward, and inevitably, someone brings up the Lovers. The teacher recalls a time in class, a time before the Lovers were the Lovers. Tenth grade, he says, World History. Remember what they were like? Empty, the teacher says. Stupid? The classmates writhe inside, these adult perspectives, a sieved understanding of their previous identities. No, the teacher says; just empty. Nothing inside. The girl threw up in my class once, he says, his beer halfway drained, and there was no buildup, she didn't look sick. Next minute she's retching. And no food comes up, though it's violent enough to have purged a day and night, easy—just clear acids. She wasn't sick; she wasn't drunk. They breathalyzed her and nothing. Just threw up for nothing and didn't know why. We asked her point blank and she didn't know why.

*

But that's an unfair assessment, really. Everything happens for a reason. (History teachers should know this more than anybody, it seems.) We're boiling down to the bunk that all reasons have to be bodily, since they stem from the physical. What did Freud say about melancholia? "In mourning it is the world which has become poor and empty; in melancholia it is the ego itself." From where do we stem if not ourselves?

It was a Sex Ed class that had overtaken World History; the teacher was showing birthing videos. Tenth graders, boys and girls, eyes zipped to the female anatomy, all uncomfortable protuberances. The boys rattled around the bumpy inkling that a girl's parts aren't always sexual. The girls watched their horror-movie selves. Bodies spewing bodies and other viscera. Their ugliness splayed between stirrups for all to see.

How did we become the way we are? Look back, to when events slip from their cause. We were once nothing and now we shrink, blush at the evidence. Amoebas split to become more themselves. We look for our halves anywhere but the mirror. Their old classmates remember these days, when everyone was uncomfortable just sitting too close to someone in a small space that they'd have to spill into one another's interiors, cutting the tension. This was before anyone knew the true nature of someone else as well as their own. They think back on this time as the dissolution of all that was held sacred in the world—a time they would still occupy basements, even when the delta was at high risk for floods. An unknowing, someone puts it. When what we didn't know wouldn't kill us. When what we did wouldn't either.

*

Nowadays you'd be hard pressed to find the Lovers awake before noon. If you haven't seen a Lover in the morning you don't know how well sleep can resemble death. The Lovers would rather give you their eyes than wake. They wear their pajamas to the coffeehouse, forgoing showers. They forget to brush their teeth.

Anything so gross is generally avoided; still, whenever the Lovers are spotted, someone inevitably bothers them. A brunch-drunk realtor pulls up a chair near their booth, probing for information about markets. In the morning the Lovers accept payment in the form of Ambien, Halcion, phenobarbital, diazepam—drugs that could offer comfort, if they weren't used to buy fortunes delivered too late to stop the construction of housing developments on flood-zoned rice paddies. As if knowing what is imminent staves off any anxiety.

Some have wondered why the future is always a warning, from the mouths of Lovers. Whether what's waiting at the far end of time is inherently violent, or if there's no other way to deliver a fortune. *This will happen to you; beware.* Some warnings, like some moles, are benign. During the day the Lovers split to go to their separate jobs and it's the opposite of benign. They move slowly and are often fired. In the past two years the Lovers were evicted from three apartments, and still know everywhere to call home. They buy scratchers to lose to California. They remain loyal to their brand of cigarettes.

In this way the Lovers are a product of a collective imagination, messengers ripe for blame. They are the goat heads found sawed off in the park, draped with Mardi Gras beads. Sacrifices achieving an abject clarity and no solace, but at least utilize public spaces before they are all submerged, us along with them. It's apocalypses that run boys' mouths and silence girls, though the moon, to her credit, speaks her mind. She asks: whatever happened to sacrifices, anyway? Sometimes I wonder why every word out of the mouth of the moon is a lament. People used to worship, she says. I used to be God. Until you were phased out, I say. Shut up, the moon says. People still wonder about cycles that have already happened, happening, complete. They want the world to rewind until the film snaps. We all badly want a new start we'll take the end, just to go back around. What a wild ride, I say. You're not watching, the moon wanes.

But for an asteroid she would still be part of us. We'd stomp all over her face until it was formless, smooth. They say the footprints on the moon left by astronauts remain—a lack of weather—but our crimes wash away, traceless. We duck in the ambiguity of rain. Cleanliness is next to godliness; after all, water is the universal solvent. Give it time to sink in, before you go around spouting blame.

*

If you find them in a bar or on a patio they're likely to be holding hands. Sometimes they kiss. They kiss whenever they have to separate, usually only to pee. "I wish I could pee through you," one Lover says to the other. "I wish that too." Sometimes they squat together in a parking lot instead of splitting for gendered doors.

Someone once asked the useless question of what sorts of bars the Lovers prefer—assuming the Lovers have any standards when it comes to this kind of thing. They've been found in upscale joints and midtown clubs, sharing the company of all manner of people, always on someone else's dime. Once they were spotted at the bar in a Mexican restaurant, swaying softly to mariachi music. Watching a soundless basketball game and prodding at the watery margaritas in front of them, stirring the slush thin.

The man who saw them was also a drunk. He bought the Lovers fresh margaritas and asked them about the efficacy of his wife's cancer treatments, detailing a dream he had a few nights ago about swimming with gigantic fish in an aquarium tank. "She should be fine," the boy told him—an answer which incited a deluge of tears, another round of drinks, and twenty dollars slapped on the table as a departing gift, which the Lovers used to buy drinks, until someone else comes by.

I saw the Lovers once in a bar bathroom, standing in front of a mirror, examining themselves. Fingers probing for where one ended and the other began. It was like watching a surgeon suture a wound, a practiced grace toward a body that the Lovers had down pat, though in the end remained stuck in two places, hands doing the work of stitches. There are people who eat substances that aren't food for the simple reason that the heart wants what the heart wants, even if it kills you, and this is why the Lovers sometimes can't sleep, for what are the risks embedded in dreams?

Over the nights they nod, to each other, to their drinks. To the tide of questions swelling and receding around their ears. To the people who want to know the future so they can change it, the Lovers thinly smile. And ultimately one of the Lovers stands up, kisses the other on the neck, and leaves—a job he has to go to, because the Lovers need money, more than they need anything else. When he leaves the girl hunches over her drink, caging herself in her shoulders, distancing the propositions and slurs from adjacent bodies. She thumbs for bills in her empty wallet. Someone near her laughs hard and spits out gum into her hair—an accident, probably. Someone else sits down and buys her a drink, and talks about dreams.

The world is harsh to Lovers. It won't let them be. Lovers need jobs and roommates, and roommates especially if their jobs are only part-time. Lovers need to eat and sometimes their tastes are different: one likes cilantro, which to the other tastes like soap. One Lover eats soap sometimes when no one's watching. There's no way to get clean that tastes good. When tongues that taste differently taste each other, the plates are on the table, the parts the self can't know piled on for the other to try. The you a Lover knows can never be known by you, nor explained, nor described. You never know if you like the way you taste.

*

The desire to know futures is only outweighed by the desire to forget pasts, and bars are blank slates, much like the Lovers. They have their old favorites and faithfuls, broken jukeboxes and smoggy patios. Bars with dollars stapled to the ceiling like an insured Zodiac, some monetary recompense for a damned existence. An astrologer wonders what the Lovers' rising signs are, if they were destined. Classmates and basements everywhere keep quiet.

In Round Corner the Lovers' legs tangle in their stools. They chew the ends of their straws, they kiss, they say their names forwards and backwards. They talk about the moon and its abscesses, and how time can be counted backwards if you started at the end of the world. How the end of the world can be traced back to history class, a curse, a Tuesday at four in the morning. One Lover has to be up for work at four on Tuesday. It's not worth going to sleep if they'll wake up anyway. When one Lover wakes up, the other does too.

Lovers are like lungs. The health of one is the same as the other. They blacken at the same rate because they take in the same air. If Lovers had their way with the world, one could inhale the air that the other expelled from their lungs, and there would be no sickness. There's a reason, one might posit, that the lungs surround the heart.

If you wait through last call you'll see the Lovers in a different light. When the alcohol has thinned their blood and their eyes dilate and their words leveeing increasing lengths of silence between, and their heads fall together like two cards propping up a tower. Their faces are damp and stick together; their noses whistle as they breathe. Their pulses gallop and jump and gallop, and under the lights that turn off, amid the hands that wave them out, you might think that it's not fair, the way the world treats Lovers. That it's not right to let them lose. It wouldn't be the first night the Lovers go to sleep wondering if they'd wake. It wouldn't be the last time the Lovers, before morning, loiter outside the hospital, asking for beds. They're turned away on the nights they're not arrested. "This is for emergencies," the nurses tell them.

The Lovers never fight back, because they're not fighters. They walk home and puke in their own toilet. They sit in the bathroom for too long. One Lover talks, too many times, about lungs. How when a lung collapses, the air is trapped inside the chest cavity, and the lungs can't expand as much, and the more you breathe the more air takes up space but the wrong space, and you literally drown in your own breath. How to live, you need to empty as much as you need to fill.

The Lovers don't dream, but one of them got close. It was the space after night but before morning, before the earth inverts and the dark returns to shadows, light waiting behind it all. One Lover sleeps and one is awake, and watches through his eyelids the hour when light is the shadow cast by trees. Time can be counted backwards if you start at the end of the world. It's black, he sees, like if you poured all the stars down a sink drain and then poured the drain down the drain. Stars start floating in the way ships appear out of the horizon, but there's no horizon and they come from all directions, establishing directions. The distance shrinks and so do the stars; they are old; before they were old they didn't exist. Before that was the end of time. Before the end of time there were Lovers, sitting in a dark room. If you could spit out five things from your body, one of them asks, what would they be. That's easy, the other one answers; my wisdom teeth. The stars choose rocks, gas, dust—things that clump into planets and turn, atmospheres and oceans and weather systems cycling between. People at the oceans, looking for ships. Time can be counted backwards if you start at the end of the world. Personalities determine the chemical makeup of brains, excrement the content of stomachs. People die before they are born. Their deaths are their resurrections. All boxes in the dirt wait to be unburied. All the dead wait for their skin to sprout like moss. Fossils melt, rocks turn to life. There's only four wisdom teeth, a Lover says; you have to choose five.

Time can be counted backwards if you start at the end of the world. Soon we'll get to our time. Cities strip to their bones and uncover the ones before. Food is returned to shelves after being eaten; clothes are returned to stores. Shoplifters are good samaritans, returning the things they've taken. Missing girls return to their families with younger eyes. Children spring from nothing and we know their lives before we know our own. We watch ourselves shrink, become lighter, become teenagers in a basement that's not ours. We sit with five other people in a circle, looking at cards. Our eyes meet across the circle. "They look like you two," someone says, meaning us, "the people on the cards." The Lovers. Next to the Four of Swords, the Seven of Cups, the Hanged Man, the Three of Wands, the World, the Hierophant. The anticipation before expelling breath. "Tell me my future," I ask.

We're in the same circle, you and I, but we're not the Lovers. The cards haven't been flipped. They're dealt and passed between another person, for another future that's already passed. We're in the same circle, you and I, but our eyes don't brush and my thoughts don't go to you; someone says your name and I'm grateful because I forgot it, though I forget it. I hear it for the first time and I don't know it. Soon you arrive and it's before, and I don't know you at all, and the sky outside is indented with trees, like the imprints left by shoes.

You have to choose five, a Lover says. They sit in a dark room where they can't tell themselves apart. One Lover is thinking, and one is waiting, and both are remembering their childhoods all the way back to their wombs. I'd give it all up, is the answer. The skin that someone else touched, the bones that a doctor healed. The cord that tied me to someone else. I'd give up everything that wasn't made by you.

Girls, Monsters

"When we were twelve, we taught ourselves to fly."
—John Murillo, from "Renegades of Funk"

"All of us girls, now women."
—T Kira Madden, from "The Feels of Love"

That winter, we watched *New York Undercover* on group phone calls, Boogie and China and Flaca and Shorty and me, all of us on the party line, screaming at the TV when Malik Yoba, Michael DeLorenzo, and Lauren Vélez took off down the street chasing some drug dealer. We watched Janet and Pac fall in love in *Poetic Justice*, and we all wanted to be Janet, scribbling poems on the margins of our textbooks, strutting into school in baggy jeans and combat boots. We watched *The X-Files*, imagined ourselves solving paranormal mysteries, having alien babies, turning into monsters. We speculated about the size of Mulder's dick. We felt the warmth of that place between our legs and there was nothing monstrous or strange about it.

We measured out our life in songs, singing as we put on eyeliner in front of the mirror, as we passed each other in the halls at school, as we waited for the bus across from Normandy Park. We belted out Mariah's version of "I'll Be There" in Boogie's mother's car. We broke into fits of spontaneous booty shaking as we walked along West Avenue, when a car drove by blasting "Shake Whatcha Mama Gave Ya," as we rode the escalator in Aventura Mall. We knew all the lyrics to every single DJ Uncle Al song—"Mix it Up," and "Hoes In This House," and "Bass Is Gonna Blow Your Mind." Uncle Al, who was known all over Miami for promoting nonviolence and peace in the hood, but was shot and killed outside his house in Allapattah. We dogged each other to "It's Your Birthday" while hanging from the monkey bars, *lightning in our limbs*, while drinking orange sodas at Miami Subs, while tagging the handball courts. Everywhere Boogie, China, Flaca, Shorty, Jaqui.

That spring, we paid tecatos at 7-Eleven to get us bottles of Strawberry Cisco, took the bus to the all ages clubs, Pac Jam, and Sugar Hill, and Bootleggers, where they sold no alcohol but everybody smoked weed. We passed the blunt across the dance floor, all of us sweaty and smiling. Onstage in the club, older girls dusted with baby powder shook and shook their asses, flashing us, girls booing, boys screaming, cheering, fists in the air. We smiled nervously, recognizing some of the girls we knew from school, two years ahead of us, three years ahead of us. Our friends' cousin, a girl my brother dated once. One day that spring we heard about one of those girls, saw her face on the news, about how she and her best friend were found floating in Biscayne Bay, strangled, tied together. Their school pictures all over our TVs for days, for weeks, their story on the front page of *The Sun Sentinel* with the headline, "They Were Inseparable Friends—And They Were Slain Together." We remembered their dancing, speculated about the who, the how, the why. We talked about how they were so young, had so much life left to live, as if we knew anything about life and living it. *We knew nothing but what eyes could see.*

That summer, on the last day of school, me and Shorty cut out after lunch, headed to the beach for National Skip Day, the two of us in Daisy Dukes and chancletas, our curly hair wild and frizzy and sun-streaked. At the South Pointe Pier, high school kids in bathing suits and shades, seeing each other's bodies for the first time. When a fight broke out, one dude holding the other underwater, arms swinging wildly, we ran toward the shore to see it. When he was finally able to get free, none of us saw it coming: the walk back to his car, the gun pulled from his glove box. How we lost each other in the madness, Shorty running down the shoreline, and me, heading for the water. And later that night, we would watch ourselves on the news, all those teenagers loose on the beach, on the pier, no parents anywhere, the faraway spray of whitecaps breaking.

Just weeks later, we were back on that beach, me and Shorty, knocking back Olde E with some dudes we'd just met. The sun on our faces, bikinis under oversized t-shirts, we walked a couple blocks to their place. And once we were there, fifteen and sixteen and in a stranger's apartment, Playero's "Underground" on the radio, it was so clear, so easy to see. How they separated us, knew exactly what to say. Shorty in the bathroom, me in the living room, the bottle, half empty, on the floor. How I never thought to ask how old he was—old enough to buy alcohol, to have his own apartment. How he ripped my bathing suit, the banging on the bathroom door, his hand over my mouth, the music so loud. How I pushed back, kicking, reaching for the ashtray, the remote, anything, until finally, the bottle, and I was Shorty and Shorty was me and we were every girl, we had not been alone, *all of us* in that apartment, in that bathroom, *all of us* breathing, alive, *lightning in our limbs*, banging on that door for minutes, hours, a lifetime, and for a moment I thought it was possible that I could lose her, that I could be one of those girls.

It was the same the next summer, and the summer after that: we went right back to drinking, smoking, fighting, dancing dancing dancing, running away. We wanted to be seen, finally, to exist in the lives we'd mapped out for ourselves. We wanted more than noise—we wanted everything. We were ordinary girls, but we would've given anything to be monsters. We weren't creatures or aliens or women in disguise, but girls. We were girls.

Notes

We knew nothing but what eyes could see. From John Murillo's "Renegades of Funk."
Lightning in our limbs. From John Murillo's "Renegades of Funk."
All of us. From T Kira Madden's "The Feels of Love."

ADAM DICKINSON

Agents Orange, Yellow, and Red

2, 3, 7, 8-Tetrachlorodibenzodioxin (serum): 1.304348 pg/g lipid

You are either for chlorine
or for the plague.
Right now is the cleanest
we have ever been, and for this
you must love aerial defoliants
or you love communism.
Under the bandage of this one-industry
town closing ranks around staples
of forestry and fish, the wound
is wide-eyed and headstrong.
Through the clearing, freshwater carp
blink past the graves of missionaries
who introduced them to the New World.
Northern rivers are warmed
by the paper mill's piss, which,
like making the world safe for democracy,
slowly leaked into my childhood, yellowing
the lipophilic paperbacks of my
adipose fat. You are for pulp
or for poverty. You respect
the Constitution or you stare
at the ground lost in bankruptcies

Note on the Text: The Anthropocene is written into the fossil record and it is also written
into the metabolisms of living creatures. How to write this writing? I test my blood and urine
for hundreds of chemicals including phthalates, PCBs, pesticides, flame retardants, and heavy
metals. I sequence my microbiome by testing my shit, sweat, and saliva to see the ways my body
is already written over by my environment, my Western diet. The outside writes the inside,
for good and for bad. What are these stories of material-semiotic entanglement, contingency,
implication, and porous identity? The epigraphs for the following poems indicate the particular
presence or specific levels of various chemicals or microbes in my body.

for herring gull beaks or blurred
embryos in cormorant colonies.
Every erected media platform reduces
the problem of war to a problem
of tint. During the Orange Revolution,
Viktor Yushchenko was poisoned
by government agents who haywired
his food with dioxin. His face flared
into pages of acne. You are either
for the red or the white blood cells,
for the tops of trees, or the bottoms.

It Turns Out the Starting Material
for the Earliest Forms of Life Is a Carcinogen

1-Hydroxybenz(a)anthracene (urine): <0.002 ug/L

1-Hydroxyphenanthrene (urine): 3.9 ug/L

1-Hydroxypyrene (urine): 6 ug/L

Hash with a dime
in a beer bottle.
Burning defines me
like froth
at the corkscrew of an argument
over the illusion of safety.
My compulsions
are all monuments
to incomplete combustion,
by which I mean particulate
matters compromise my unmanned
willingness for nerve endings.
I wear smoke immunologically
like a barrel with suspenders
or well-heeled neighbourhoods
with street associations
taking care of quiet boulevards
like cottage-country lakes.
Suspended in the water column,
fish hearts slow to the length
of time it takes the marinade
to soak in. Diesel rigs run all night
at the truck stop diner
amidst the alphabetic disparity
between benzene rings and highway signs
buckshot by glitched-up guano.
Hitchhikers may be escaped

inmates. Things make
sense more easily
if they are attached to moods.
Every night I replay
the half-baked getaway
of a running nose,
trying out cigarettes and accelerants
on cuts of meat.

Hormone

Herd Animals
were hunted
for food
but also
for the feeling
their numbers gave
the hunters.
Let there be more
of us, they prayed
and envied
the buffalo meat
that built railroads
and fueled wagon trains.
Their hair was stuffed
into furniture. Shit
burned for heat.
Every nation
feels it is promised
the whole earth.
Every nation
sits atop
a pile
and waits.

from *Venus Edamame*

The king couldn't echo.
Couldn't echo, they sang.

For briefly the words
were darkest then.

And the king
an insect in a glass jar.

On it,
they rang.

Perhaps the ranging fires would sleep them together.
Perhaps no.

Then, everyone asleep.

The king could neither sing nor awake;
held a fountain in his hand and drank

deep
deep

down
into folds of clouds and rhododendrons

past fields, loud with executed princesses,
through mentions of the natural world,

through conversation held out like a bouquet
at a state ceremony.

The way an iris delves: the way a flower wilts,
The way south parts in his wake as he walks to the south.

To the other gate,
Through the southern gate,
Towards the sleepy gardens,

Where they wait, asleep,
And as he passes
They awake, stand up

Examine their iPhones
Put on their glasses
Examine their iPhones

It is so sunny today, the app says,
It will continue to be sunny
But the quality of sunlight will change

Occasion for repentance will disappear
His abstaining so long will save him from misfortune
Wu Wang is descriptive of a state of entire freedom from such a condition

The nearer he comes to the ideal of the quality, the more powerful will be his
influence, the greater his success.

The greater his success, the more it will rain,
The more it will rain, the more it will cross into

mud, and mud into form,
and form into flesh, and flesh
into ash, and ash into earth, earth
into stone into wall into rubble into projectile
into news channel into approval to policy to law to sentence
to a memory of a feeling/ some new something/ just a little something
to get you started:

in the story, you are young enough that age is important,
though now you are old enough you have forgotten
what that feels like, and you are alone, sitting
on the slate-colored carpet, tracing lazy words across it
with your finger, and you translate what she said
when she said *no*:

why she said that:

this
is the first appearance
of that *why*
in your world:

and it changes everybody

and absently you rap the wall with a knuckle:
how could you have known?

and on the third knock
the wall snaps

in
half

the room now dark, much smaller;
in a sense, when you were eighteen

and realized no one was coming for you:
innocence is the better part of evil

and illness the root of hope,
and you hope to get out;

and you have to hope
they will come for you

they will come for you
they will come for you

they do not.
After you have given up hope

And after you have lost all comfort and starved to death and begun to rot
And after your flesh leaks off you

And your bones have become luxury items
And your mind is threaded through a library

And your love songs switch your exes into statues
And you need nothing, not water, not light, not air

Not erotica, not an army, not a thesis, not Lindsay
And if you aren't being a friend to yourself,

I'm your friend
And like any good friend,

You can ruin me if you want to
Ruin my face:

throw acid on me, cut me with a knife, clip
out my tongue with scissors, chop off my ears

with scissors, chop off my nose with lawn shears,
push my face onto the stove, staple photos

of your face onto mine, put cigarettes out on my eyelids,
sand off my eyelids, pull off my jaw, infect my gums, put

a needle up my nostril,
ruin my prayer:

Our Father
Who Art in Heaven:

collapse the building onto me!
smash me into a building!

: apropos, a hymn: hum
of martyrs: one

syllable ever in our,
ever in us, ever in,

ever upwards, and on
every day, every method to

tell a person apart from a king:

9/11 ceremony YouTube sensation; abecedarian nexus,

Santeria fan-dubbed, subtitled in braille

—hard-subbed dialect—and encoded well,

no clip no stutter, no, no, here:

when the transformation works well enough to re-work itself:

our falling buildings cover the world in gardens,

I re-appoint our king: I re-officiate our language; I re-pot our kids

collaged against the cosmic, the cosmic humbled by everyone in it

pretending to believe what we actually believe:

in an insect God; God of Luxury, head of gold and jeweled face and a tongue
carved from his glowing throat, stained glass wings, chitinous robe;

no king
but the bloom of your blind iris,

but an ant navigating an iris on her plate;
because her mouth is all I can see,

and all she can say is in her smile—ideogram—
held there as if a branch alone of other wood,

of trunk or stump, of oak or pear or tulipwood,
ungrazed by ant or lens, uncut old vine,

curl of smoke or splash
of wine on marble in

the secret bones, muscle
of garden in the mouth

of a mine's root, inside of an ant's glazed eye
the whole night dried and cut into code,

parsed, fanned as tall grass blows on a cold beach's dunes,
as sure as puddles rise from the wrinkles in the tide's sand,

echoes of the audible sea, the throw of anemone and thrust of whale shark,
crustacean tossed to the floor in black black black black, breathes the current

that develops before the thought of a wave has been named, before wave redraws
shore and resigns into mist—every minute—before mist knots into cloud, cloud
cleaves into rain, raindrops flatten leaves lowest on the plants, killing nothing,
over and over, a kingsnake eats a rattlesnake and drowns in the flood, and an
animated .gif performs it over forever—eventually curated out of the tradition,
the glad king

leaps from his porch, grabs a bird in each hand from the air,

spits on one's head and breathes on the other, plants them arm-

deep in the yard, and as the conversation thickens the ground between them//

some new error message is born

some new note// scratches from its sac, feeds itself an orchestra, grows fat

the weave of ants, some new grass

some light touch, a greeting

as sprout searches the king's navel, belly to the earth, artery on the colony

the king, the leaf, conspiracy of the divine,

feeds it flame not sun, and

spit or cum or blood or bleach,

thumbs his smile on it, golem of mud and cell and chemical lymph, names it

for himself, and spins it echoing

across field and year, to glut, to

learn and to forget, to seed, to

suffer and finally break, venus

edamame

Bronze Glitches

As someone partially internet, I am ideally suited to repaint the tumor.
As a priest for the FBI, I am the ideal Myers-Briggs type.
As something ceaselessly repeating, like a heartbeat is an echo
Of something in utero, I am the ideal priest for your village.

As a Hawaiian with *significant* beachfront holdings, I am a strange echo,
As when "I like you" is heard as an eyelid lick, and the warmth of it
Is heard as a sizzle. As one is moved to repaint the screen
With a new lover's Facebook profile, waves ripple at the second

-floor window. It's how looking out the window, one can almost
Imagine there's no window. How cancer becomes the heart.
If you imagine a screen so bright no prayer can get through,
Or staring through the screen to the sun behind it, you can see

How seeing your lover in love with someone else too is similar
To the joy of watching her eat ginger candy, rice crackers, or roe.

Thy Shade Shines So

O where does my heartbreak throb, get
gristle, throng knuckle? Where do my
eyefuls assault? Yawning, coughing,
numbness. A lottery of senses.

Where does my defect twitch, my
lotus-eater act sentinel? Gasping,
gulping, snorting. Sans remuneration,
why does my labor comply? How wet

is my gurgling, how fatal the gurgling
of my navy? When is my compersion
my fabric, skin, meat? Lo-fi, sharpen, vignette;
a palace of nurture. Or where does my

breath make void, my voice-over
sing my nation into sweetener?

July 4th, 2014

from "Shigeko, Let's Hitchhike to Japan"

Martine Syms, Incense, Sweaters, and Ice, 2017, 1:09:00

You are a human being at the club. Driving, texting. You are a nurse in Vegas and enjoyed it. Who are you? What your name is up in the bathroom? The black body routine in front of the mirror, the voice of Eartha Kitt. There's no races, class, style, refinement, eye contact, elegance, and glamour can get you anywhere. About being an animal lover but also to hunt. In her living room, on TV, someone, a bus driver who saved someone. People eating around a body. Be more in touch with the body. The wind and body are no longer distinct. The body-mind look straight ahead when walking down the street. A voice can speak for herself. She can say no and doesn't speak for others. How powerful people act? They erect. Powerless people make themselves small. It's a good idea to try to come across as more powerful lol am I ever gonna see you again or just texts. You're gonna cry when I'm gone / and it won't be long. Since feelings are physiology I feel touched and I'm crying in the club. Keep in touch. How are people responding to you? As you change.

Lawrence Andrews, An I for an I, 1987, 18:41

A RE-CREATION
of a shirtless black man
yelling "Again"   as he is punched
continues   an elevator full
of self-inflicted violence   someone moving quickly
down the stairs   through some kind of government
building   To reveal that he is hitting his fist
against the palm of his own hand to create the sound

Tattooed hands against purple.
The hands do black like when you say "Stop. Real talk,"
or you need to check yourself   the gestures sometimes
and there's teeth sucking
WHEN DEY GOT YOU FUCKED UP

Ephraim Asili, Many Thousands Gone, 2014, 7:38

is that we should begin in transit, in or near a vessel,

as we do here   and then we leave this place   and

the skittering quality that follows   festive scene, song

and

unaccompanied by diegetic sound,   has been replaced by this near-

music, robs these scenes of their   reflective instead;

the whole in this mood   Maybe it makes more sense to call it near-

silence, visually, a richness we learn

the musician is Joe McPhee

the record of his we heard   and in migration, literal and   signaled

by the previous traveler going to places that exist only

so "romantic and incoherent"

Shigeko Kubota, Video Girls and Video Songs
for Navajo Sky, 1973, 31:56

Shigeko, let's hitchhike to Japan.
Wagon with beautiful horse. To get water.
No money to ride the bus, blood pools in a bowl
some kind of sheep removing the skin   with strategic cuts
the torso of the animal and of the butcher
figures at rodeo, cowboys, dense   hand drumming, sheep head
a young person holds up, cooking the meat.
She is dancing.   Raise her arms   the space between horses
and the horses orange, proceeding the horses.

128

Ephraim Asili, Fluid Frontiers, 2017, 23:04

"Fiery the eye of Harriet" over the black   just after   we've seen two black
figures at a table, the only movement   coming from outside We a BaddDDD
People outside it strikes me   our flight this time   happens through literature they finish
reading and we see them   interspersed with life from around   Detroit, playgrounds, architecture but not
the heavily populated street, full of black laboring   It's unclear what role the still   though devoid of people
is colorful and vibrant   do we return to New York? a familiar
Hunger (10:48) for a while   we lose people until we return
to drums a punctuation or strategic   absence it feels right   but we could also discuss the same
in terms of energy Harriet Tubman   says come along to freedom and   she is free beyond her grave

The Enormous Radio

Translation of "The Enormous Radio" by John Cheever

I'm interacting with a memory of a RADIO* that was never mine. The RADIO is only real in the sense that an author spelled out the word RADIO,* and placed the thing that was the word inside the living room of a particular married couple. They really cared a lot about listening to Schubert and the narrator suggests that they seem to think they had a beautiful life together. In the story, the living room is inside an apartment. The wife spent most of her time reupholstering when she wasn't wearing, shopping, or thinking about mink. Objects and adjectives are placed inside that room, in order to give the reader a sense of their character traits and to establish space. I'm talking about inner space. What's outside is what comes in through the transmission of the RADIO. In the diorama that is their living room the author inserts sound. The sound emanates from the RADIO: violins, pianos, Schubert, concertos, etc. I imagine the husband and wife revolved around the RADIO in the way that they did for a number of reasons, some of which are listed below.

1. Schubert is enjoyable.

2. Silence is difficult for people.

3. The maid was taking care of the children so they had no one else to listen to.

4. If the maid had overslept the wife could place her daughter between her knees and braid her hair mid-opus.

5. They thought that if their children were continuously exposed to classical music it would improve their mathematical abilities, later allowing them full scholarships to Ivy League institutions. This would reflect highly on

---

*The word RADIO can also be replaced with the word MOON, NEIGHBOR, or CROW

the strength of their combined gene pools and their parental abilities as evidenced by their successes in co-creating motivated, prestigious offspring. The children could then become doctors, who would prioritize and take personal responsibility for the lives of their parents, lessening the likelihood that a disease would go unnoticed or untreated, therefore postponing their inevitable deaths. This would also save them money on tuition and later medical billings, thus allowing the wife to buy more mink.

6. It made them feel like they were sophisticated.

7. They were sophisticated.

8. The wife had a fetish for dead composers and couldn't get off without one in the room.

9. The husband felt in control when he adjusted the dials and witnessed the sound immediately responding to his touch.

10. The RADIO was there.

None of this is on the page but it is in the page. Personal revelation can be compromised by the interference of involved musical patterns that are being emitted through a speaker. This is true when the speaker is another person or when it is a speaker that is connected to a RADIO. No one can be alone or wholly with another person when Schubert is in the room. It's like you are trying to fuck and feel close to your partner and establish some form of intimacy that feels real and then there he is, Schubert, wedged in between your skins, his solemn grey head tied on with an outdated black necktie. Schubert never opened his mouth to smile in portraits, so I doubt his ghost would open it up to suck on a nipple, but even dead men have been known to surprise me. There is no fucking in this story. I mean, there is, but in the text the author withholds the sex from the page. There are the aforementioned children so the reader knows that the couple has definitely done it before, and we are told they are a couple, still married even, so it is highly likely they'll do it again, although possible they won't if they've grown tired of themselves or of one another. We never see inside the bedroom but given the given nature of their relationship I wouldn't be surprised if they tend to do it on or next to the RADIO.

The RADIO is about to die. The cadence of the violin is building up just as the song is cut by a surprise static, and the sound blanks out for two bars, that sonata goes black, is replaced by the electronic CsZ-*Zssshsh*/h-zsz that stuns both the husband and wife into a standstill, like two blind moles waiting be smashed by the brights of an oncoming Buick. They can't see the car but they are paused in awe, slave to the bright heat, paralyzed by the prolonged flash that bulbs behind the skins of their eyelids, before the violin re-enters the room just moments ahead of where it was last heard, unaware of the pause, the white urgency of the headlights diminish back into the subtle curves of the road, the return of sound suctions the heat out from behind their sockets . . . and now they're back in the room and paying real attention. Their ears engage with the waves of the frequencies as the RADIO volume unexpectedly wavers up and down. It finally settles. If one listens closely, as the wife and husband are, one can almost hear the sound of dead fingers gently tapping the strings against the fingerboard through the gentle veiled buzz of the old speaker. Now, the fugue comes back, confident hands curve around that hollow rosewood belly, tickle the notes along the spine that links the C-shape of blasé sadness to the

tailbone of bottomless sorrow. The efflorescent voice of the violin underpinned only by the solidarity of the piano's arpeggios, those understated minor chords that make the ground, mark space to make air so the sheep-gut strings have place to fly. The violin's insistence slides towards peak before it eases back into a composed collapse, tension relaxes, together the couple recognizes this movement as recapitulation, and the soft strings whine, woody, against the bridge, the notes testing the water before they—what? —the violin slopes and goes under, slowly toys with the idea of drowning, before it reemerges from the water on a new clean note. The couple has been tricked by way of false recapitulation, which works every time and so they are smiling at one another, thinking how silly of them to fall for old Schubert yet again. They are submissive now, they are his, belong to the song, and so it gets stronger and the *pianissimo* goes *forte*, the movement gets harder, the movement is persisting in *forte*, the sound getting pushed out with more abandon, a less controlled grip on control, the strings are getting pulled by the bow with real force as the keys are struck by more muscle before the RADIO cuts out and a CSszh/zssh-ZsHhh replaces the money note. The husband mole and the wife mole gape, bound to the light of the silence, until sound inserts itself back into the room for the slow and final run of the skimming bow, there was a twist, Schubert that trickster did it once again, the sonata still isn't ready to absolve. A stubborn note whines on like a suspended cry. Their muscles tense in anticipation of the finale as the cry inserts itself across the breadth of the living room when the sound goes black. Like a wire pressed through a soft piece of cheese, the silence cuts from ear to ear. Their faces still look the same, but Schubert is missing from the room. He's just gone! AWOL. The husband looks at the wife like *what are we going to do now*. The wife looks into the husband as if to say exactly what his face is saying to hers. They break contact. The husband hits the RADIO a lot of times and determines the RADIO is now dead because this is how husbands verify death when they do not see themselves as competent repairmen.

In the end, the husband buys his wife a new RADIO because he's an old fashioned guy in fiction who thinks his wife's happiness depends on listening to Schubert on the RADIO. The story is not about this RADIO, though. It is about the one that replaces it.

Anabasis

A warning is the same as a threat. Television teaches this. *Is that a threat / call it a warning.*

Call it by a different name, and it changes.

Snow is only slow, cold rain. Only rain.

Her child said, *Mama, I want to die in the snow.*

*

I am a shape-shifter. Most people are. We change our shapes day on day, replace cells, grow muscles and fat, shed hair, grow it back lighter, darker. Some of us do it faster, is all—some of us have specialties.

My specialty is mouths.

My real mouth is full of sharp teeth and a sharper tongue, three languages coiled like snakes in my throat, scaly and silent. My real mouth is an armoury of words forged in the furnace of my chest, hot as a spitted sun. My real mouth is a storm, and my voice is thunder.

To pass among you I wear a different mouth: full lips unparted, always smiling. I paint it pretty colours. It speaks only when spoken to, softly. To pass among you, it tells you stories: *I am sweetness. I am sunshine. I am here to hold your hand through the horror of my name.*

My mouth is a coin, and I spend it.

*

An explanation is the same as an excuse. There are agreements, laws, protocols; there are pieces of paper more important than her child's pain.

She was given an explanation as if it were a blanket, or food, or shelter. She was given an explanation as if it were a gift, to be purchased with gratitude.

She walked past it, into the snow.

*

Borders are shape-shifters, too: they change what goes through them. Time was, the only border worth crossing was into the underworld, to fetch back a lover's life: *Take off your shoes*, said Ereshkigal to Inanna, *your belt, your rings. Take off your armour, your hair, your skin, your flesh. Set your bones aside separately; bag your liquids. Do you have any sensitive areas—*

We cross into the sky now. *Plus ça change.*

My passport is a blue rectangle stamped *Canada.* My name is inside it. The border's eye falls on it and shifts it into *threat.* The border's eye looks at me and we wrestle, as his eye tries to change me into *Arab* or *Muslim*, and I struggle to remain *Canadian.*

My mouth does most of the work. My mouth is soft and yielding; my mouth is what books call *generous.* My mouth does not get angry. My mouth spills its English out as tribute, smooth seamless scales gleaming in the fluorescent light.

*

The cold has a mouth. It eats fingers and toes, nibbles ears like a paperback lover. She knows the stories of bodies carved into classical sculpture, here missing a hand, there a foot, a nose. She knows the border is a wire that shears bodies into meat, to be chewed and spat out again, one bloody gobbet at a time. She knows.

The only mouth that matters is her child's, gnawing her heart one word at a time.

So she walks.

*

If I could take each of my words and lay them in the snow at her feet. If I could take each of my mouths and eat this distance between us. If I could devour this border, if I could tell it to smile while I broke its teeth, if I could unsheathe the sword of my mouth and strike it down, if I could thread the needle of my mouth and stitch good shoes for her baby, if I could cut a path into this country with the sharpness of my tongue—

If I could change the world as easily as my mouth—

With the whole of my furnace-heart, I would. But I can't.

Nevertheless, she persisted.

ETHAN FEUER

Understory

Diagrams from Previous Drafts:

1. Points of Connection

2. Points of Density

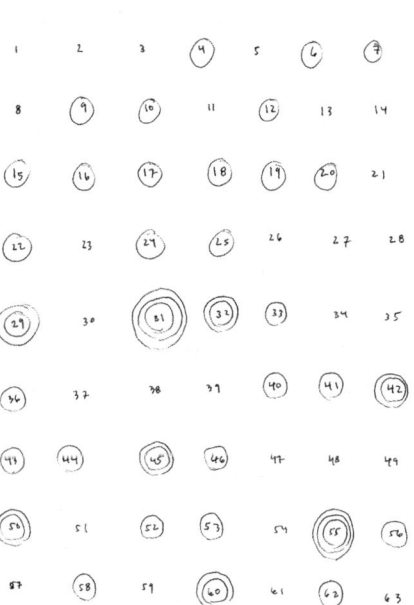

Understory

1.

My[3] father[4] singing[2] in front of the yew berry bush[9]

3.

I am three
or four[8]

4.

When he still had his black beard[5] that
he had grown in his twenties, he once
told me, to "look older and more serious."

2.

You Are My
Sunshine

9.

Near the garden in front[13],
which belonged all to him[11],
where the flowers[10] were kept.

8.

I am now
almost
thirty.

5.

That he cut off when
he no longer needed
to look older or
more serious[6,7]

13.

Where I often
worked[14,18] and
played[15]

11.

That is, when he
kept it, it lived;
if he doesn't,
neither does it.[12]

10.

Bleeding hearts, roses,
lambs' ears, irises, tulips,
sunflowers, daylilies he told
me I could eat and I did

6.

That is how his face became rough
to the touch, caught different lights.
With it gone, he was strangely
over-legible.

7.

In response to complaints about the
perceived stresses of youth: "It will be
your generation's turn to be old soon
enough." Harsh.[8]

14.

Hoe, trowel, weeder,
spade, rake, can,
sack, barrow

18.

Erecting fences against the deer, setting
beanpoles, digging trenches to run chick-
enwire underground, patting down bulbs
and scrubbing potatoes, hauling mulch,
gouging at the roots of wild things

15.

Sledgehammer,
mattock, mallet, bow
saw, pitchfork, tiller,
bamboo, shears[16,19]

12.

Compare: the garden in
back, where the vegetables[17]
resided, being my mother's
domain[13,20]

16.

It upsets but doesn't
surprise me that the
these are the tools that
most resemble weapons

19.

The time my father threw
a shears at a rabbit eating
his flowers. He only meant
to frighten it, he said, but
he broke its neck.

17.

Carrots, potatoes,
cabbage, eggplant,
squash, radishes, snap
peas, green beans,
tomatoes, basil

20.

Before her domain
migrated[21,25] in-
doors, to enclosed
rooms and spare
movements

21.

Her first serious injury took place in her garden,[22] slipped disc[25]

25.

After that, say it was years, but it wasn't: descending the curb of a road with her on the phone pressed to my ear, internalizing that the problem with her arms[31] was never going away[26, 27, 28 , 29, 30]

22.

Although I mention it second, her garden, the garden behind the house, was actually the first to disappear, due to her injury[23, 24]

31.

She was 40-something. She could not grip a steering wheel or type or lift heavy things. Heavy things began for her with a glass cup. We had to buy new plastic possessions so that she could pick them up easier. She could not hold a book, so she listened to music. She could not sew or write or garden much. She cut back her work, ended her work entirely. After this struggling was done, she mainly sat in the recliner in the front room with the dog and watched old movies. "What else can you do without hands?" she would ask me, as if I contained some kind of permission. She was 60.

26.

And other problems we didn't yet know of

27.

Now we are getting into the thick of it

28.

No one would ever tell us what it was[29] that hurt her so[31]

29.

Though they would theorize: repetitive stress, fibromyalgia, vertebral displacement, pinched nerve, osteoporosis, temporomandibular joint disorder, sleep apnea, lupus, chronic fatigue, depression, insomnia, loneliness[30]

30.

Many of which she also had, and was medicated[32] for

23.

"I can't do it," she said.

24.

There used to be a wooden swing frame back there too, but at some juncture it vanished

32.

She had alarms set up for all hours to remind her, and her pillbox grew so vibrant that she needed to purchase an extra-large version intended for people with impaired motor function; drugs dogged her sleep, and concentration,[33] memory, blood pressure, speech, kidney and liver function,[37] and balance, but they remitted the pain and depression, which made them worth anything

33.

Though she was still sharp as ever. She often interrupted stories,[34] her own and others', with disjoint thoughts; yet she disliked convoluted plots in movies and books[35]

37.

Boy are we deep under sunshine[38]

34.

"Do you remember," she would say. "Did you see—" "Have you called—"

35.

She would say, "You are making things complicated."[36]

38.

While we are down here, though, there is a third garden to talk about[39]

36.

She would be right. It's a simple plot. But let's let this whole thing be what it is: a honey-do fridge note familial detective story choose-your-own-adventure, obviously.

39.

In the basement[40]

40.

Can plants in separate pots in a basement be addressed as a garden? If they are not a collection, but a constellation?[41, 53]

41.

Insert argument that life is not a glass we fill slowly until no more will go, but a glass we break immediately and attempt all along to reconstruct[42]

53.

For example, light too appears as an outline or form, but is, so I am told, discrete packets of individual concerns too small to enumerate[54]

42.

The plants here were smaller, frail carbons of their outdoor relatives. Like memories are of the things they remember. Clivia, violet, oxalis, lily, crown-of-thorns, geranium, echeveria, jade. They were often limp and precarious. They didn't know they made us all sad,[43] these other, feeble ersatz-plants, but they did.

54.

But which nonetheless bombard & nourish our gardens, so[62]

43.

Well, sometimes they did and sometimes they didn't. But we returned to them no matter what they did to us, and perhaps that's the important thing about gardens[44]

62.

But if you think about it, most of the sunshine that ever exists must miss the Earth entirely. How lucky then, in that light, the specific particles to fall on us, and we them.[44]

44.

How they leaned toward their fluorescent lights as well, just as if they were in sun,[45] a habit which endeared them to us

45.

The lights were large, with ground-glass lens covers, like the focusing aids to viewfinders of the 1970s, before split image[46] took over. Their texture was dimpled. They came in large panels with brackets, like the full-spectrum light therapy[47] boxes used to treat depression.[48]

46.

Wherein the focusing ring pulls two halves of the same subject into alignment[49, 57]

47.

Sometimes called "heliotherapy"

48.

Yes, she tried these; they didn't work for her either

49.

Here is where I try to pull focus, unsplit things, god what a mess[50]

57.

"Your sister and I," my mother explained, "had a heart to heart."[58, 60]

50.

The last time we spoke, she told me her arms were hurting her. So yes, I had heard this before, before.

"They give me pain," she said, or something like that, "But what can I do without them?"

And no, it isn't a proud thing not to hear[51] someone expressing things of this nature, even if you've heard them before; but then again, I am not proud of myself.[52]

58.

Wherein two hearts are connected via hair-thin wires of glass[59] and send invisible signals to one another

60.

My mother went on to explain that my sister was suffering pains in her arms not unlike the pain that she, my mother, had suffered at the beginning. Sister was having to limit her activities, restrict her time typing, driving, playing music, sewing eccentric buttons onto her clothing. "I was 42 when all this started," she said, "but she's only 32." Til now, sister had hidden this problem from mother, probably because she knew how upset it would make her.[63]

51.

Meaning
listen to

52.

"Your sister," she continued, which was rarely a good way for her to start a sentence.[55]

59.

(A small joke for my father, the physicist)

63.

"Shit," I said.[64]

55.

As children, my sister seldom chose to visit the plants, inside or out. Nature, she would inform me, was too unpredictable. I shit you not.

Instead she spoke on the phone to her friends, the weird kids of town, who had favorites of things like collectible card games & British sitcoms & kielbasa toppings. She cared for them intensely in their shared present, with a compassion I fear I have never equaled in my own relationships: she listened to their feuds and quadrangles and top-heavy lifelong proclamations, as all the while she planned out her own future existence: her fresh take on matters of national interest, her persistence in the face of adversity, her generosity in success.[56]

64.

"I worry her life is ruined," said my mother, in the way of mothers.

I worried this too, and discussed it with her at length. We hashed out between us the degree to which my sister's life was ruined, and when it was settled, I said, "Am I next, do you think?"

"No," she said automatically, and almost as if this was sad. "You aren't like us."

I have wondered for a long time what she meant by this. But I always ended by deciding I didn't want to know.[65]

56.

I believe this; she would have been generous in success, had she succeeded

65.

Knowing goes nowhere, association presupposes the line. Imagination gaps, however, so some things do become objects in space.[61]

61.

Or loops[62]

66.

You gapped this. No one told you to do it.[67]

67.

After my parents are gone, my sister's husband will drive my sister to the house where they lived. He will open the car door for her, maybe. The three of us, or four, or six, will walk through the house.

We will find many dead plants. Some in the basement, of course, where we knew they would be: wilted in rows under repurposed lightboxes, half-sutured on the plywood worktable, stored in damp boxes, annotated with doctorly chicken-scratch on an index card that seems suddenly precious.[68]

68.

Yet no, not that either. Here is the image[69] that I will remember:

69.

My sister is at the bottom of the basement stair, index finger flicking the light switch on and then off. Like a branching of tense. Day into night within day. And the plants will blink in and out of sight just like that—in instants, glowing slickly and blue in their pots. I will play it backwards and forwards forever: the lights, the darkness, the lights.[70]

70.

We will find them stuffed into the mailbox, draped over the banister, slipped under rugs and between book covers. Their evidence will peer at us from basement walls, sparkling with mica. As we walk circles around the house we will say, "Oh, there is the tree from Arbor Day," and, "Here is where he killed the rabbit with the shears," and, "Here is the best spot for hide-and-go-seek." The weather will be fine. We will speak in present tense about everything, although nothing will be present except sunlight.

Engendered :: Non[fiction]

{Cough-shocked and bothered I lean into a fevered moment gasping in a preschool parking lot status-void before a parent-teacher conference that is doom-doom-doomed to hell and think, *Jesus aren't we all,* but then roll my eyes because, I mean, *come on.*

The sun cuts through the windshield like a pre-dawn-hallucination-of-golden-hour. I think about turning around, about warning her, preparing her maybe. Saying something like, *"Get used to feeling alone."* Saying, *"Feeling lonely—It's genetic and inevitable."* But I can't imagine it—her face, big wet eyes staring out from beneath the space helmet, or behind the goggles, or—*is she wearing a cape?* Or I can, and that's worse.

I look out the window.

It is evening.}

Light slides through the window-bank in the student lounge like it might blow out the highlights and fade to white. Southern exposure. South by southwest. I imagine it in lapse and it makes the sick-mustard-everywhere/linoleum-speckle almost bearable.

I'm sitting on one of two worn velour couches (facing), in front of another set of two (facing), adjacent-off-four-feet another set behind another set—dark blue. It's, like, a late-century retrospective of American interior design fads but, you know, tragic in its ensemblage.

For once I don't have a migraine and think maybe I understand the appeal of directional light. The sun and female energy here are warm-making and I am enjoying [a free period] thinking about thinking about [*The Scarlet Letter*—about reading it (about rereading it)—as girls' calves cascade in shutter-step before me, through one door and out another, casting shadows, reflecting light bright and even. Out of space/time. An impenetrable *Footlight Parade*.]

There's an off-chance I'll win an academic award in Religious Studies [this afternoon]. I'm a Natural Born Leader, they say. Epic Catholic. Morality Darling. Poster-something for the Veritable Future-somethings.

{I look up.}

I {still} don't pretend to understand anything about this place, but I do know this nail-polish was a mistake—if I'd been a man, *but I'm not—s*o when a plaid skirt comes herk-jerk over aside me, I do wish it wasn't there, but don't blink when it/girl vomits up, "So what, are you bi or something?"

She says this—assumedly because I am, that day, sans hair—and I wonder what exactly about it reads that way: Bisexual. Not "gay," but "bisexual." It's both specific and on point and I'm confused but content in its regard.

I glare into the light, searching the space between the windowpanes' image on the back of my retina and the substance of the thing—an acknowledgement of presence.

{I look up.}

She's still waiting.

I advance a page in my book. "Yes," I say, like a sociopath. "That's right."

"Oh!" She nods. "Cool."

{There's a pause.}

The instant her attitude cuts like a breaker, I feel it. And as she launches into some sort of manic monologue about Jenny McCarthy—flapping her arms and belching uproariously—I realize, *this is my coming-out story.*

And I'm thinking{—now I'm thinking, twenty years later, but also then-plus-twenty-minutes-later when I'm alone in a stairwell—}that's probably not right. Probably I should have had a little shame. Lied, maybe. Gone off to the bathroom and cried, or masturbated, or both (probably both). I should have waited out high school and had lots of bad sex with people who never really understood me.

Or whatever. Who has the time.

{I'm on my way now—the screaming's stopped—and I'm scuff-scuff-shuffalling towards the door, my hands full of things-I-might-need like short-range car-keys, paper drafts, data-sticks from the aughts. And caffeinated beverages probably, because I'm orally-fixated and day-drinking's for single people. *I'm a thinly-veiled actual/fictional queer. Narrative-poor in a world that's inherently narrative-poor. "No matter what I say, I will never discover why one writes and how one doesn't,"[1] I think, all New Wavy and dramatic-like, back-of-wrist to front-of-head, feigning ennui.*}

I turn the page—{then/there/~~here~~} in the student lounge—trying to read, but unable to see the words for all the black and white and I don't know what to say except "I'd like you to leave" so I don't say anything.

~~{I turn the page and stare out the windshield. I wonder where Duras is buried, what it looks like, how often people people there.}~~

~~{I'm alone.} I'm alone and then~~ I'm surrounded. They flutter around me like neo-Raphaelites, cherubic but a little acned, uniformed in v-necks and oxfords—beautiful, actually—and tell me how brave I am. It's flattering in the way that attention from young women is always flattering, but I have no idea what they mean. And this, not the other thing, makes me feel the gut-tug of that other-worlding. [*This, I think, is the way Bowie must feel.*

I mean, I'm guessing. {Here, a man walks too close to my car. I try not to look like a creeper while search-planning in case of assault.} No-way-to-know/ with-the-heart-of an/other. {I stare at my screen extra hard.} "*I have laughed, in bitterness and agony of* [aforementioned] *heart, at the contrast between what I seem and what I am*,"[2] I think. On the inside. Laughed on the inside.]

I shrug.

How do you say, "You're hurting me with your beauty," say, "You other me with every breath?" How do they say that where you come from?

~~Maybe I made a face and wandered off somewhere. Said, "What?" {probably}~~ ⁣ ⁣ 147
~~but didn't wait for an answer.~~

~~I used to fast-walk—stiff/late-for-a-board-meeting-like, circuitous but~~
~~purposeful—to burn off nervous energy. I can't do it anymore. I am not~~
~~young. Teen madness is edgy but pragmatic; a twenty-something's, romantic;~~
~~thirty's, pathetic. The appearance of sound mental-health is the new Doc~~
~~Marten's, I suppose.~~

~~I was always well-liked.~~

[Instead I say, "I don't—" Heather walks through the room and for a moment I lose my line, but recover, finding the homeliest one, looking her in the eye (softly), smiling (gently). "—know how else to be."]

Their eyes flash and by the timbre of their delicate hum I can tell this was the right [thing to say]. And though in a Technicolor moment I see that I will be forever navigating the space that difference makes between us, that distance[, I excuse myself]. Their mew-mew sighs follow my hands as they are shoved mercilessly into their pockets and I burst out of the door and into the cold.

{"I've never spoken about this to anyone. [But] by [this] the time [in] my [. . .] solitude, I had already discovered [. . .] what I had to do [. . .]"[3] The world says it wants you, but it doesn't. "I know this every day of my life. [. . .] It's hard to endure. [. . . It only] seems to make sense all of a sudden."[4] She whispers in your ear; she slaps your hand away.

This is how it goes.}

{I look up.}

My hips barely shift as I match her stride.

"Not now," she says.

She says it and it has, like, espionage-type overtones and undertones of
promise, so I stop. I watch her walk away from me. [My hands still resolutely
in their pockets—left thumb pressed firmly into a thumbtack hidden there—]
I watch the light play in her hair, make her head glow like the blessed virgin
we all know she's not. She's sturdy! And athletic! She doesn't conform to the
conventional standards of beauty and it all quite literally makes my groin ache
with want. She's a woman, clearly—*the confidence!*—and she could break me
here in front of everyone on the paved and curving path of [St. Clare's] School
of the Sacred Heart, in the suburban hills of the have-have-haves, and she
doesn't care.

I watch—her pale-pale skin reflecting, dark plaid skirt absorbing, cutting into
the overflowing curve sub-waist super-hip, and, under her polo, showing a
little undershirt. I swallow.

She walks away from me, down [and off through another door. My *"head
f[alls] back, and the Milky Way flow[s] down in[to me] with a roar"*[5] maybe.]

{I'm alone. "My friends [I guess] knew nothing about me: they meant well and
they came out of kindness, believing they would do me good."[6] And still they
do this. It's amazing how visible one can be and still not be seen.

I go home. Food waits, and kids. My husband watches me from across
the table. I watch him back. We are co-conspirators and we will raze this
normalcy together.

We make worlds; we people them. Our worlds are darker/brighter. Our facets have facets and we will watch the world burn from our pelt-warm nestle—giddy and symbiotic—snarling as that old "sun" dies and ours' (stars) rise.

Let the light bend around us.}

I'm full of love. It's getting late. There are awards to win and so on. Awards are very, very important here. Doubly so for the outliers.

1. Marguerite Duras, "Writing," in *Writing*, trans. Mark Polizzotti (Cambridge, MA: Lumen Editions, 1998), 5 (my italics).
2. Nathaniel Hawthorne, *The Scarlet Letter* (New York: Bantam Books, 1986), 175 (my italics).
3. Duras, *Writing*, 3.
4. Duras, *Writing*, 4–6.
5. Yasunari Kawabata, *Snow Country*, trans. Edward G. Seidensticker (Rutland, VT: Charles E. Tuttle Company, 1957, published by arrangement with Knopf), 175 (my italics).
6. Duras, *Writing*, 9–10.

ADAM GREENBERG

from *Fortune*

Lily white, hocking news of a dry spring, a snowdrift can supply a glen of white viscose & sugars. A glen, joy of a farm, chance host of dry powder, can host chemical solvents, foremost gypsum, & a crown of refractories, foremost copper, brass, barium, & sterling. Home of tulip, carnation, & blue-bell, a river controls transportation of lumber, pure of fibers, supply of rayon solvents. A star, optical radio of combustion, carbonic singer of spring, can signal & point, coil & dart, watch & mirror. A foundry, liquid crucible, works foremost of spring & mirror.

A precision textile can radio blue of blue fibers: marine blue & tidewater blue, granite blue & midland blue, carbide blue & allied blue, royal blue & silver blue, solar blue & atlas blue, continental blue & equity blue. Point of point a crown of fibers. An oat-white & blue sheet of fine rayon fibers, brewing a fine air of home, can spring of spring times & ideal news. Publishers publishing news of lone farms & dairies, a viscose spring of liquid & oats.

Precision arms radio white of white chemicals. A spring of gas & a climax of optical works. A western snowdrift motors west of a tidewater gulf, east of textile mills milling blue fibers (anchor blue, petroleum blue), packing a white belt of powder. A camp, a wire, & a signal. A drug supply &, packing a gas shell, a basic pond of group fuel. News, foremost. Foremost a coil of forest & lone beech. Liquid sugars & a combustion drug. Dry cement. A zenith of viscose sulphur & metals & a white crane of carbonic spring.

Author's Note: Each of these three poems has been assembled using only language from the names of companies found in the inaugural *Fortune* 500 from 1955.

JOSUÉ GUÉBO

from *Think of Lampedusa*

Translated by Todd Fredson

It's only to this battered hull
that the word shows its bad teeth
and in the nasty exchange laughs
about the asthmatic ships
so poorly trained to run this marathon of the sea
We'd be dashed like cigarette butts
at the bottom of this old tub
a race finished
prayers released
a tale dancing its dreams beyond the point where day drops off
Old tub
the joke about its droppings
sold at top dollar
A burial is what's offered

And there would be five hundred such pieces of shit
walking all the weight of their fleshless bodies
Five hundred carrying prayers
of the cross and the crescent in their hearts
Dream signals scrambled
They'd be five hundred women and men
then one would take out its modeling clay
and another a slate
she'd straighten the sticks of chalk in her blouse pocket
Over there one says mom
she'd know all the letters
she'd know how to write the word life
        if that's what God wants
And if God doesn't want it?
Mama slaps her

Because mama holds her humanities dear
She'd not make them less superstitious
knowing the gods
their animal quarrels
and their inhuman passions
She knows the loves of Zeus and of Terra Mater
in her own body
And of Laërtes and Anticlea
and of Ulysses's quest on this same Mediterranean
which guards the memory of those times in its dance
She'd nearly see Sirens giggling on the bow of this raft
The Cyclops
Charybdis and Scylla
Circe the enchantress
and wily Eurylochus too
Mama is no racist
but she knows that the Nereids
are Somalian
The Oceanids Eritrean
Charybdis and Scylla Malian
For sure
Polyphemus the Cyclops
is Nigerian

The abundance of any god
would fall harmlessly on these five hundred
heads rolled at the will of the wind
Many hearts address the sky
send some easy winds
The book of life would be written in a mathematical language
Brows wrinkle
refiguring the invoice for these last days

Waiting for the hour of departure
the puffy faces explain how to divide a ration
how much to share between younger children
an equation with multiple unknowns
In this exercise you multiply the circles under your eyes
Here the number would be more real than ever
This precise and faulty subtraction
imposes five hundred less
three hundred and sixty-six
Only the crane of Lampedusa has discovered the actual answer

Battery

You're a chick hung by your beak in a beak-docking machine. Experience is a funnel you slide through. You are too stupid and too new to think unpain/ pain. To think free range/battery cage. To think help me.

If you were able to think help me no one would help you. You have no friends at this factory farm, or anywhere, and no relatives, though in fact hundreds of your relatives have been through here, generation after generation. With a thousand thousand chicks beside you, all of whom look exactly like you, you are entirely alone in the world. Every chick is indeed an island. You are an island, a speck of a cog in a huge, grinding wheel towards a goal, which in your case is to produce food for another species. Which in your case is eggs.

You are all here as one heart, riding, riding, fleeting the grey ground currents of the conveyor belt you call home, motion-sick and dizzy. You are only just hatched, barely feathered, barely yellow, and your wings are uncertain things you flap but that take you nowhere, though you go somewhere, borne aloft on a history of oviducts into this grey motherland sky below your feet. Palaver peep until some of you are gone.

In this plant, the male chicks are Sue's job. Sue is not your friend. She is 46 years old; for Sue, 50 looms hard-edged and cruel in the distance. For a long time, Sue had the notion that things in life would become easier as she aged, but it has not proven to be true. No matter how completely she pays her bills, for instance, every month there are new amounts owing; she never gets ahead. Sue is not married, although she once was. Three years ago, she had breast cancer. She is back, now, and of course has hair again. But she is exhausted. The only thing she likes in her life is going to bed.

Sue is a chick sexer.

She squeezes feces from every chick on the conveyor belt, opening up its anal vent to see if a chick is a female, with no genital pimple, or a male.

Sue is not your friend. She squeezes your anal vent.

You are a female.

Sue takes the males and tosses them into a hopper where they first bash against steel, then fall into a machine called the macerator, where a high speed auger sends them to a grinder, where, quite alive, they are diced into bits for dog food.

You are too ignorant and too new to think male, to think female, to think luck, to think unluck, to think grinder, ungrinder. Since you are female, you keep riding. Riding riding riding, yahoo. Keep those chickies moving, yahoo.

The workers do not imagine you as sentient. If you have any kind of genetic memory, it won't stretch back far enough to feel the wind riffling your feathers or dust craters under your belly in the farmyard.

The workers' eyes glaze over from repetition, from the pain of carpal tunnel and tendonitis and tennis elbow. It is just a job a job a job, they think, and really thank god for a job at all.

Jean, who lifts you into the beak-docking machine, is not your friend. Jean is 37, seven months pregnant with her fourth child, and her back is sore. All day long, five days a week, she lifts hatchlings like you into the beak-docking machine, which is similar to hanging a tie over a doorknob. She feels you struggle, such as you can at your weight, which is more or less one ounce; she feels your wing stumps flailing. But when the machine has you by the beak, what can you do? Nothing is what you can do. You hang there like an animate stuffed animal. Your beak is how you interact with your world; unlike human fingernails, it is full of nerve-endings.

Jean is only thinking about what time it is and how soon her shift will be over. Jean's third child was just diagnosed with Asperger's. Her husband, Mark, is a mechanic, but now he's drinking too much, and this means money is tighter and he comes home angry, looking for fights. Five days a week, eight hours a day, Jean lifts chicks just like you into the beak-docking machine.

Hanging out in the eternal now, you are too ignorant and small to know what's coming next. You were an egg, you were fertilized, you were hatched and then spilled onto a belt, and none of this had anything to do with anything other than human commerce.

De-beaking prevents feather and vent pecking and the kind of cannibalism you might engage in considering your upcoming, brief life, sandwiched five in a bare wire cage and starved to provide daily eggs. This is a "battery" cage. You are given not as much room to yourself as a standard sheet of paper. You can understand, now, can't you, why the males were the lucky ones? Why the powers that be might want your beak cut off? Now, older, you can appreciate your circumstances a little better, and it will be clear to you that no chickens are going anywhere. You don't even know what "anywhere" is. You will never stretch your wings. You will never sit in a nest, or peck for grubs. This is just a fact. What is air? What is sun? What is dirt? What is straw? Your beak stump still hurts like hell—just pecking sends neuromas, that tangle of "phantom limb" nerves, jangling. It is hard to keep a steady mood. Even though you generally see yourself as good-hearted, you might even be inclined to go after Mabel, or Henrietta, those hens. Those goddamned hens.

Thankfully, you have no beak.

After two years, you will be sent to slaughter, which means you will be slung into a crate and transported, during which handling many of you will break bones. You will be hung upside down in shackles by Doreen. Doreen is not your friend. Doreen is only 18, but she already has two kids. She is trying to figure out a way to enroll in community college, where she would like to take jewelry design. Right now, she's living with her boyfriend.

If you asked Doreen, which of course you don't have the ability to do (and honestly, you have more important last thoughts), this whole enterprise—which we'll call your life—has been pointless. Her life, too, is pointless. Both make her roll her eyes. Something is born, it struggles, it dies. Like, it's what happens. Life's a conveyor belt, a sorting machine, a massive factory farm, and really if you stop to think about it, most of us get hung by our toes one way or the other.

But then, Doreen is a cynic.

From Doreen's station, here's where you're off to:

A) To an electrical water-bath stun system, which, if you are lucky, and many are not, sends a current through your body, rendering you unconscious

B) To the neck-cutting assembly line, which may be incomplete, so that you may still be alive for the

C) Scalding vat

Your body by the end of two years is so degraded by the deplorable conditions you've lived through that you are good for next to nothing—for chicken soup stock or pet food.

But let's roll it back a bit, my little pullet, my little puisson, you of the soft feathers and dinosaur legs, you of the scratchy feet, you of the peeps, you of the black eyes. Our little egg-bottomed baby—such ability hidden in your oviduct. Chickens are said to be amiable, and friendly, more cognitively studded than either dogs or cats, and with a communicative vocabulary of 30 sounds, although, right now, so what?

Really, so what?

What is a life's potential when it has no potential?

Still, you aren't dead yet. You've only just hatched. You are hanging with your brethren by your beak from a docking machine.

There are different machines: hot blade, cold blade (including garden sheers), electrical (the Bio-beaker) and infrared; today, at this factory farm, the docker is hot blade. You wiggle and sway as you merry-go-round. When it's finally your turn, Becky grabs you. Becky is 28. Becky is not your friend. Becky has a nasty cold and ought to be home in bed, but she's used up her sick days because she played hooky with her married lover, five days of hooky, which today she thinks weren't worth it at all.

Becky is chronically bored.

She brings the guillotine down.

Describe your pain, chick. On a scale of 1–10, rate your pain. If your pain was a colour, what colour would it be? If your pain was a tree, for heaven's sakes, which tree? What trees have you roosted in?

Memoirs of an Imaginary Country

The center of the Earth is full of things the surface thinks it has discarded.

You called the year your explorers arrived in my country year one. We called that year ten thousand seventy-seven. You called us Utopians. We called you something else.

Every woman, I learned, later in my life than I should have, is someone's imaginary kingdom. All explorers, I also learned, are liars when it comes to the truth of what they've touched. If you're the gap in the map, you know this much is true.

I was the kind of girl who would always be a child, you said. I should take pleasure in the simple things, and I should not learn to read or write. Too much knowledge, you told me, would destroy my sense of wonder. I dusted your books. I looked at the margins of the maps, the places marked with monsters.

When I met you, I was thirteen, and I already knew I was too ugly to be loved. I was strong, and I was smart, but no girl was allowed to have everything. My sister was pretty, which meant that she also had to pretend to be weak. Together, we did all the work girls do, unnoticed. She listened to you. I scrubbed. She smiled at you. I plotted our course. We were invisible in different ways. My face and her mind, my teeth and her claws. You approved of us. We were your household. You could not see the fire at our edges. We were your girls.

I'm ahead of myself. Time works differently where I'm from. Our history is written in books that go backward as well as forward. Our time is measured in birds flying down through volcanoes, octopi contracting through cracks in our sky.

I hold my homeland inside my head. Burned books and misplaced ones, moth-eaten, mildewed.

A short accounting of expeditions into my country, and places like it, from the beginning of time to now: in come the white men, dressed in helmets protecting their soft skulls. They hold their cameras like guns, their guns like cameras, their cocks like fine teacups. Click, click, two clicks, maps moldy, zippers rusting. Men pissing from the flies of their chinos. Why are they called chinos? Because the fabric was made in China by girls like me. What were chinos originally? Pants worn by soldiers who killed girls like me. Call them also khakis, the Urdu word for "dust." Call those soldiers white men who began their battles dressed in red, and shifted themselves into uniforms that better mimicked the terrain and the color of the people they were bloodletting.

Packets of sugar and caffeine in the explorers' hands, all of that harvested by simple, innocent, go-lucky girls like me. They pick their way through the jungle or through the forest, lucking past our traps, shitting in our streets and wailing for assistance. In come the white men, dressed in suits that crumple, walking across the bottom of the ocean and over deserts filled with bones. They burst from their vehicles like sentient pus, and begin to dig for youth, oil, magic, buried treasure. These things are all things the world has promised them. They adventure, claim, and conquer. The mission of white men is to denature nature.

I was taught by men like these men. Look at how you civilized me.

It is 1785, and you are writing a book about two siblings who fall into the center of the earth and there discover a race of rainbow-colored citizens eighteen inches tall, in a place that is otherwise much like Venice. You're translating as you go, into French from your native Italian, to make the contents more delicious, and also to avoid trouble in your own country.

Everyone is androgynous, happy and innocent, full of wonder and potential, in this Utopia populated by sun-worshipping nudists. Everyone suckles at everyone else's breasts, and all in all it's a lovely and sustainable situation. It's unusually peaceful. No one fights over jealousies. Everyone mates for life, and if other lovers are taken, it is done pleasantly. Children are hatched. Rules are obeyed. The people are a rainbow, but only the red ones have power. The rest are servants. They love being servants.

Your book is called *Icosameron, or, the Story of Edward and Elisabeth, Who Spent Eighty-One Years in the Land of the Megamicres, Original Inhabitants of Protocosmos, in the Interior of Our Globe*. A utopian narrative, written in French by Giacomo Casanova, a Venetian, published in Prague, 1787. Seventeen hundred pages long, and full to the margins with falsehoods. Bound in leather, nicely printed, complete with chapters on philosophy, theology, sexuality. Analysis of a noble though flawed culture untouched by the West. Birdsong sung by its citizens. Bravery done by its narrator. By the end of the book, the descendants of the two original explorers number twenty thousand sets of twins. They have taken over the hollow Utopia and taught its citizens about gunpowder, imaginary cars, firearms, fidelity, starvation—

You sold only a handful of copies. Readers lifted it and put it down again, wrinkling their noses as you looked on, Italian eagerness translated to French fury.

After all that, it was time to fill the bedchamber at the center of the earth with your own glorious godly self, an autobiography of a brave man, exploring.

In some versions of your stories, Giacomo Casanova, I was your first love, and my name was Bettina. I met you when I was thirteen, a girl living in a house in Padua that took you in. You were a boy younger than I, and you fell through the ceiling of my life, and into the center of my family. I was forced into an exorcism to avoid your accusations of impropriety, into convulsions to prove my purity. All of this, you wrote, occurred because I was a vixen. I was married eventually to a shoemaker who beat me, and many years later, you sat at my deathbed and admired my ancient ugliness, wondering at how you yourself were still so vigorous and handsome. What wonderful memories you had of me, the curve of my hip as I pressed past you in a narrow hall, the way you could, at any moment, ask for breakfast and be fed everything I had.

In other versions, your name was Edward and I was your younger sister Elisabeth, birthing forty sets of twins for you in this country where tiny people worshiped a central sun, obeyed a pope, and sang instead of speaking. All of the residents of your Utopia had breasts, including me. You were the only one without. We took turns breastfeeding you so you wouldn't starve. Some of us died because of your appetite. We were all tremendously interested in your penis. We called you a giant.

164   Later, when we returned to the surface, I stood beside you while you explained why you'd married me. I had nothing to say about it, besides the occasional supportive murmur: "it only made sense." We'd fallen through the sea floor together, and you were my older brother, and we were two humans surrounded by noble innocents. We returned with stories of how we civilized them into submission, and the rest of our story, that of siblings marrying and populating a world that was already populated, fell aside. We were fertile and generous with our opinions. We were explorers. We were making the world better.

Sometimes in your accounts, you revised me again. I was, in those stories, not human, but a yellow girl from that city in the center of the Earth. I was all over your cartography: at once the X-marked diamonds and gold, and the sectors etched with monsters. I was a discovery, newly set in moveable type, printed in Prague, and invented into a wilderness worthy of an audience. That is the closest version, if there's a truth between your lines.

I am well aware of the world. The outside is a place that was once covered in green, and now the green places are brown. The reefs are quiet. The caves that held sleeping bears now contain only skeletons. People like you still live unsheltered, on the roof. Is it not obvious who is civilized?

There is a skillful hand-colored etching of you at the front of your book. You're wearing expedition attire, though in your version this is a factual manuscript discovered in a library, a twenty-night tale of adventures had by someone other than you. In the illustration, you are rakish, periwigged, a loose brush rendering your face more handsome than it might have been in life, but who would judge that? You were, of course, the foremost expert on your own actions. No one other than another white man could possibly understand your mind.

This was your country.

You revised me repeatedly: a girl from a realm reachable only by fateful accident, her topography penciled, her thoughts pinned to paper like ethered insects. Your surveyors missed my volcanoes but found my caves. They filled them up to keep themselves from falling in.

*

My sister and I were looking up when the invaders fell out of the sky, into the center of one of our cities. Elisabeth arrived with sunken cheeks and wild eyes, and Edward with scurvy. The two of them had been traveling by ship to the North Pole. They were not without wealth, though they were in dire straits due to being caught in an embrace mid-voyage. They bribed another ship and, bent on escape, hid in a casket of resplendent clothing. They paid a sailor to throw them overboard, but they missed the raft and sank. They plummeted through a crevasse, dropping through our roof and into a river.

They were too heavy to float, and so they descended like wriggling rocks. From our observation point, we could see their thighs, worm pale, piss-ribboned. It was clear they were frightened of us. He had a knife and she had a rock, and they held their weapons tightly.

"More of them," said my grandfather. "I thought we'd closed the hole. It's been years."

"Blame the stitcher," said my grandmother, and went into the house.

Some of us were small, and therefore interested.

"They're like animals," said my mother, but we could hear the uncertainty in her voice. The last group had come in when she was only ten, and she hardly remembered them.

"Pets?" said my sister, her hand cupped to stroke. "Or meat?"

"No," said my mother. "They bite. Keep your fingers to yourself."

As we watched, they interlaced their own hands and nodded furiously, looking at us as though we might carry their bags in from out of the rain.

"We are explorers!" shouted the man.

"Brave explorers," she whispered to him. "From the higher place!"

The children crept into their trunk to leaf through possessions as the explorers marched through our streets, planting flags with their faces drawn on the fabric.

"This is our country," she said, and then looked at him. "It was made for us. No one will make us leave. Look at them. They can't even speak. They're awestruck."

She wiggled her fingers as one might wiggle fingers at a puppy.

The children were standing in a circle watching the pests. We'd been set to keep them from moving through town.

My sister held out her hand, though, and the man looked at her. She was beautiful, my sister, and she offered him a piece of bread. She could not help her kindness. My sister fed the starving, and these two were so stupid, so drenched, she assumed they were hungry.

"This is our country," the man agreed, taking the bread and biting into it with teeth that were, yes, pointed. "These are our subjects. We'll be the king and queen," he said, looking around, his eyes bright. "They need parents. It's our duty."

"*Sacred* duty," said the woman. "How will they know the rules, if we don't rule them?"

I didn't know their stories about the center of the Earth. One of them was
that it would be an Eden, a place into which a man might tunnel, and take
everything he ever wanted away with him when he went, all of it tucked into a
kicking, shrieking sack and transported to Venice.

The words the people outside used for those actions included: *forage*, *harvest*,
teach, *discover*, *explore*, *civilize*.

There were other words, if you ask me, and if you ask my sister.

"Oh!" said the woman from outside to her brother. "What a relief, Edward,
to be free of the constraints of society! Oh, what joy to be amongst these dear
little nobodies!"

"Oh!" said the man from outside to his sister. "What a haven we've discovered,
Elisabeth, what a perfection!"

"They needed us," she said.

"They prayed for us," he replied.

"And we descended," they said in unison.

*

It's 1790 and Giacomo Casanova's utopian novel has failed utterly. No one
understands him. He is disconsolate, lamenting, locked in a room full of
books, feeding on crusts and the occasional feast by librarians and patrons. He
is tragic.

A young woman sends him a letter inspiring him to write his sexual history,
at length and in detail. *Well, then*, he thinks, and begins a flattering account,
humorous, wry, brazen, flirtatious.

Venice. Through it walks a brilliant young man who is sometimes a scholar and sometimes a gambler, and often nothing but a sprinting seat in sheepskin pants, sighted from a window as he leaps into the bush, pursued by hundreds, literally hundreds, of husbands. He is heroic.

He descends a rope made of bedsheets and clambers into a bathtub, the daughter of the house assigned to soaping him. She has never known a man before. Not that he is a man. He's twelve. She's thirteen. She has never heard of sin, and her body is a creation made of velvet and silk floss combined with just a little bit of cow, and she will let you have anything—truly anything—your heart desires. She is Utopia. Climb inside.

Paradise, he writes, is a girl on her back, her legs open, and inside her a mystery. If she were to be sliced down the center, civilization would pour out, the men of Earth, thumbkins, each one with a tiny voice and all of the reason found in the libraries of the ancient world. Men are born with reason. Women are windowless wombs, and they must be taught the rules. They are ribs and fibs, broken and expendable. They are lies meant for laying. That is not to say they aren't wonderful. Some of them are witty. Others are wicked. Others are ugly but strangely skillful in the bedchamber, and who would imagine that?

He goes on this way for a while.

No, he revises the story. There are two girls. There are four. Oh! The glory! There are ten, and all of them bend to admire him, everyone in the story living in perfection, everyone astonished, joyful and terribly lucky.

*

I was the kind of girl who was born to do work, while the other kind was born for breeding, the people from outside told me. Those were the rules of civilized places, places such as the one they came from. While my sister was in the upstairs room in labor with her first set of twins, I boiled water and scrubbed a floor. This was how everything gleamed, how everything worked the way it should. Rules brought by rulers to the ooh-ahh innocents of elsewhere.

The two explorers were naked in bed, by then, breakfasting on pastries I'd baked. The woman from outside had stood over me in the kitchen, instructing me on the finer points of dough. "I suppose you're used to raw meat," she whispered to me, and giggled, holding my hand.

Elisabeth had hair of no particular color, and a mouth full of bad teeth. She thought she'd brought fire to the inside, never noticing our chimneys spitting smoke. She herself liked to smoke a pipe carved in the shape of her own former face, which ten years into her time here had significantly expanded.

Edward was a man with a mouth that never stopped moving. He gave us names and counted us, though we already had names and families. He made a book of our history, which he did not know. He claimed he could see our thoughts by looking at us. He was a gun-bearing tooth of a tiger, and we did not like his look. We did not wish him to take us to the city. Some days he had notions of ships and chains and fireworks, and on other days he declared that he would pour us into tiny blown-glass bottles and use our sweat to scent the pale throats of the finest ladies of Venice.

"What a wonder," he said. "You know nothing of sin. You are sugar grown in darkness."

I looked up at the bright orb at the center of our sky.

"When the world was flat," he told my sister, "there were stories about the people who lived in the dark. You people. When it stormed on the surface, all the blind creatures came up to taste the rain, but when it was dry, back down again they went. When the world curved into a sphere, and the edges were no longer places from which to plummet, the stories swelled to fill the spaces. You're a story."

"The world," Elisabeth offered to me one morning, "is a cinnamon chocolate with a crispy shell, and an interior of cherry in syrup. The world is a black rubber ball wrapped in kid leather. The world is a snail, the shell a house and inside the shell, a sentient softness, pliant as a woman's flesh. Watch as it uncurls, watch as it looks up in wonder at the man who has at last plumbed it."

She stretched on her back, asking for a massage. "Do work out the knots," she said. I considered a rope I'd tied about my waist.

"This is perfection," said Elisabeth.

"*We* are perfection," said Edward, and he took her hand in his, and with his other hand he touched my sister's waist, and wiped butter onto her skirt.

*

You were always writing about the same kind of kingdom, whether it was your memoir of lovers or your novel about a wonderful world within a rocky womb. Milk-fed masqueraders and a boy in the middle, an innocent himself, this intelligent explorer who brings guns and poisons, who eats of the forbidden trees, who fucks his way through the center of a civilization and is worshipped for it.

You dreamed your way into my country, and with you came the creatures of your skull, each one a beast of bones and calligraphy.

I dreamed my way into your country, and with me came my sister and my parents, my grandparents, our fingers and hands, our knives. I was the center of the Earth, and you were the one who tunneled into me.

We knew that the people above us were speakers and breathers, diggers and bearers. We weren't blind. We weren't thirsty. We never rose up through the mud. Was our city made of glory? It was not. It was a city like any city, buildings with worms in the grout, rotten tubers, unjust laws. It was ours.

Shall we speak of you? You told your own story, and you never stopped telling it. You believed that there was silence in our country before you, and that yours was the first voice to bring us knowledge.

You thought you taught us to talk, but we had been speaking. You thought you taught us to live, but we had buildings and music, fire, books, and paintings. We were nowhere, you said, when you appeared in our universe.

You thought I wasn't fit for fucking. I busied myself with other tasks. I learned your language. I learned your dreams. I came into the bathroom and soaped your back as you reclined, looking at the ceiling, writing a book about other women.

"You're so tiny," you told me, as though you were a giant. "Just look at you," you said tenderly. "Like a child."

What explorer has not longed to bring his guns to an undiscovered country, so that he might casually become king? In your bathtub, you crowned yourself, and looked at me, and raised your scepter. This was nothing new. I'd seen your kind before.

In the other version of your stories, the part you weren't writing down, you put my sister in a sack. I leapt in with her. We were kept in the darkness, thrown over your shoulder, smuggled out of paradise and into hell. We traveled, whispering to the surface, and when we arrived in your city, you opened the sack and smiled, because you'd brought us to a better place. Or, perhaps, you had made your own place better by taking us from ours.

In the version you wrote, my sister and I were one person, constituted entirely of love. We opened our shirt to feed you from our breasts, though we were ourselves starving. We were awed at the sight of your sun, dazzled at the wonder of your world. You grieved when you thought we might die, though this would make your own journey less complicated. You'd been thinking of where to put us: a zoo, a museum?

You dumped us onto the floor and went to your library. I went to the kitchen. My sister went to the bedroom. You could not see our edges. We were your girls. You didn't know our thoughts. You didn't know what was beneath the mattress. You didn't know what was in the pocket of my apron.

Time passed.

There are other versions of our stories, just as there are other versions of yours: in come the white men, and they get sick, which throws them on the mercy of the people they're invading. We are in the trees watching as they arrive on stretchers, snake-bitten, feverish, starving, fighting furiously with one another, Pilgrims, fur trappers, journalists and geographers, millionaires, filmmakers, translators who speak nothing near our language, preachers who say they'll teach us, teachers who say they'll reach us. *Untouched*, they say, and touch us.

Call death a kind of exploration. Call hands on someone else's skin a kind of expedition. Call us the ground, and call yourselves a flag.

And now see what we call you. You are the dragon we slay, the ship we wreck. Your safety is not our business.

This is not the story you wrote. This is the story we wrote.

I was the kind of girl who was born to serve, the people from outside told me, while I sharpened their knives. I was working in their kitchens. I was always mistaken for a cook, by you, by them, by everyone. I had the kind of face that looked kindly, the kind of body that looked built to enfold the hungry. I held a knife up to the firelight and tested the blade on my fingertip. It worked the way it should. I was no stranger to knives.

I had my sister with me, her twins nursing, and we were writing the battle plan, the two of us diagramming armor, inscribing knife hilts with names other than the ones they thought they'd given us. We could read and write. We had our own names, and our own language.

You thought you knew what we wanted, but we had wants of our own.

Here is something I learned in the hundreds of years I spent in the center of the Earth and later in the libraries and bedchambers, pressed between your pages, carving my way out of your stories with one of the knives you gave me to show your readers that I was a spitfire, a flame-breathing beauty with black hair and barbed bits.

Imaginary countries and imaginary cunts are in the same category. They are the same story.

Look at this volcano, the heat of the center of the earth pouring out in flame. Look at the way the outside splits open and becomes the inside, the way that helmets are not enough to keep your soft skulls safe. Look at the catastrophe of birth.

My sister and I are coming up from beneath the ground, our fingers tipped in claws. We are springing through the soles of the feet of the men standing over our home. Your name is a synonym for swing, and my name is earthquake, taking your library and opening its contents to the elements, tearing your chinos thread by thread into nests for the birds whose eggs you've broken. The center of the Earth is not a windowless room, but a room with a long view to the sky, not a hollow object, but a goblet full to spilling.

Call it a skull. Call me a demon. Call me a disastrous expedition, a haunted pilgrimage. Know that I am still drinking from your bones.

You are the book I am writing. You are the story I am searing into the skin of the ones who come after me. I name you after myself. I call your country after my sister. I plant a flag in your heart and drive it in, claim your territory and tell the world that no one was here before I arrived.

Are you an old man now? You are. Are you wordless, your hand shaking as you write your adventures? You break into convents. You break into caverns. You are the best worst they ever had.

Listen to me tell your story. You've lost the ability to speak. You're standing before all the men of your generation, trying to tell them that you've won, but your footage is forgotten. There is no one left for you to call to. You will have to call for me.

You think I'm the kind of girl who'd ask you to write the story of your life.

"Ti amo," you say to me. I have not been brought to the surface to feed you milk. I traveled with you not because of love, but because of fury. My sister mothered your children. Our sense of wonder was intact. We wondered at your frailty.

"Je t'aime," you try.

Am I the woman now, here at your crumpled bedside, holding a spoon? And here is my sister on the other side of the bed, holding a knife.

"Ich liebe dich," you whisper.

Look at how we are young and you are ancient.

"Open your mouth," I say to you, in a language you never learned. "Let me close your gaps. Let me fill you up."

"Let me imagine your future," says my sister.

KAMDEN HILLIARD

About the Poem

for Joe Tsujimoto

if it's going to be clean it won't be here   or there   it is far from everything
it is   and/or-ed and othered   saliva and knuckles/whitening and tighted
trying to couple it and jux ta pose   my circle is not squaring? fuck you
coordinate geometry and whitedudes   with your grecian letters and shit
what is the word: things that are only themselves and can't help it? regardless
its skin bruh its always skin : the epidermal is ethereal   if squinted right
data demonstrates: skin is tough to work with   or through   or out of
ever white out the thing itself? ever want to? there's the 9-12 million dollar question
ding ding motherfucker—there's the skin sung out   burnt bottoms of bread
bottoms burning out against the sheets   of white ice and sheets tenting white heads
leak white from heads   in ancient greece only the receptive partner in homosexual
sex was considered homosexual   and all i can think: skin of teeth / barking
the wrong tree   this chapter: *identity diffusion*   later:*assorted*
injustices   it's never really erotic but wants to be ohoh   to be in love
is to be in lust   but worse   [DRAKE VOICE] #worst
the body erotic   is the body electrocuted and bominable   it wants to be what it is
but can't   think:pendulum   how it might like the left over the right
and maybe it doesn't wanna be right anymore heavyhanded   fine   but understood?
a piece of flesh filling with blood   might be a bruise   might not?

I Feel Most Black

after Zora Neale Hurston

Wen ashen Wen wundrin thru color W my witch
name Wen wildin out w my wishful drinking
Wen sayin *bangbang!* Wen still life w negro
spiritual w blown woof Wen Ms. Nakata wanted
2 kno what i preferred how my lines fit *Black? or*
African American? or Wen while reading
Makes Me Wanna Holler Wen sumhow they knew
i knew how 2 run   a train Wen from any cartesian
plane i go 2 whittling down intersectional wastoidism
Wen gay Wen *cum 2 slay* Wen ill chronic Wen
wilting from 1 dimension Wen years later Wen
i knew y they knew what this world filled in2 me
Wen wiseeyed enuf 2 work unsurprised thru 2day's
wundrless pain Wen misquoting w a penance
Wen *Colored, Kam, yu mean colored*

ERROR 404: Binaries Not Rendered

trika treat / turnta feat
gim   / mie all dat gud /
heat   eff ya darn't
i don't   care i'll pull
down me   underwears
& glo

deviance is a candy
coda i'd snap chimeric
/ limp / glottal w lite
/ but will [smh] let
a nigguh live //

i'm not hard 4 / or on / white
sugars / so what of
the state's legislative buttstuff, decried in Lawrence v. Texas?
slootin down All Saint's eve / weavesa red
lite & hurt // 2 dress rehearse
my movements /   hearse-ward
the self runnit / lines / try its blockin 4
multi
culturalism day, crossdress
day, drag day, black history
month, girl's day—   permitted
formz 4 resistance

here's a song
here's a reading
list / here's a treaty
here's an updated terms
and conditions agreement
here's a momentary redress of
grievance

AUA HOFMANN

for the treatment of ear-ache

for marsha p. johnson

there is something to be said for the marsh. if someone has a fen in their ear, they should follow that pain-sound & take pilgrimage into the marsh: they are the one who has called you. prepare a boiled mixture of sand, grass, milk, & bones and pour it into the waters. take a trade paperback and rip out its leaves, folding each page into a paper boat. as they drift everyway in their quiet eddies, speak
this charm:

the marsh whispered to me, saying, "silt & histories, piled // sediment & sentiments, torture-portents' half-halted wailing— hands pull shriveled bodies out of my waters, // asking each other 'what's its gender? boy? or *language*? . . . o, that shriek th'archeologists can't determine, while corpses swim // betwixt pronoun deposits and amphibious slang.

"i remember how those swamp-dragger's ancestors // dragged queens and queers to me to be hanged in ritual. cries of fear pierced my ears, muffled & gagging // as i cradled them in my muddy arms. they marked their killing-place with a stone wall. grammars are like your forebear's bones: // they break under the weight of tyrants' sovereignty—

"violent documents borne on currents' affairs // affear thine ears, while verbiage, like vegetation, chokes me.

heart-ache throbbing in your head-space, you visit your predecessors. // i think you're more interested in pleasure than agony, maybe just in th'alleviation of your suffering. // but remember linguistic injustice, those maids made aqueous, the wall i eroded

"so that the soft songs of your friends and lovers '/ settle in your canals like the toppling of gallows,

so you can recognize the marsh-sour pain which flows // from death-speakers' & hate-mongers' peaty mouths,

so you can rip their peaty tongues out, that word-writhing // slug—it feasts upon the precedents buried in your skull."

listen to the mumbled sentences of ecology around you. history's dark pus should soon drain from your ear; your earache shall be remedied for now.

Crisis Actor

Ruby, please. A nightshift nurse fell asleep at the wheel. The whole earth had a fever and the heated pulse beats faster 'til everything picturesque has her reeling. Just tryna make it real baby, like it is. He condescends. Twitching a trio of flax seeds between the thumb and forefinger in a dirty spiral, these are full of phytoestrogens that turn the men jenner . . . generic . . . generous. Hey, girl! Crease in her hey the size of turning. Is that mean? I live in place where it's mean to be honest but I come from a place where it's generous. Freetown is hedged on a slum. The ghetto, everybody's vigilante. Cut to the footage of a young boy swimming in floodwater made of mud and feces. Constructed. Like shelter, the safest destination the excess has. You see a fugitive, I see my daughter's future husband, Ma quips, full sunned and sweet, a nigga who can swim, can hunt her free. Glad silk bending his teeth into a Sunday hotel. And the kind of silt that reachers for shatter. All the land is water. You come forth through the cosmic slop by drowning. The sun is a gang of murders. You come through on the new acquittal looking for chicken strips and bourbon with Netflix on in the background and I'll kill you myself. Back on the Las Vegas strip, the sun is bouquet of drones chasing promoters through a circus. Stand there and look indignant in a bandana and stop calling the Loa out their names before they answer. You're on the guest list for lil yachty and one oak and it's a mouthpiece the boxer's choking on when the nurse wakes up, a double suicide, American, pie and guns and obscene convenience, proud mascots for an army with no one left to defend

NASSER HUSSAIN

from *SKY WRI TEI NGS*

WEL   CUM   ABO   ARD

KNO   SMO   KIN
BUC   KLE   UPP   181

KIT TEN HOK

THO THE SUB JCT TOF

AER IAL

NAV IGA SHN

ISE

JIN ERR ALL AEI

CON SID ERD

NEW

ITH ATH

OCK YOO PID

THE MIN DZO MEN

MOR EOR LES

FRO THE

STA RTS

AIR   TRA   VEL

MIG   RAT   ION

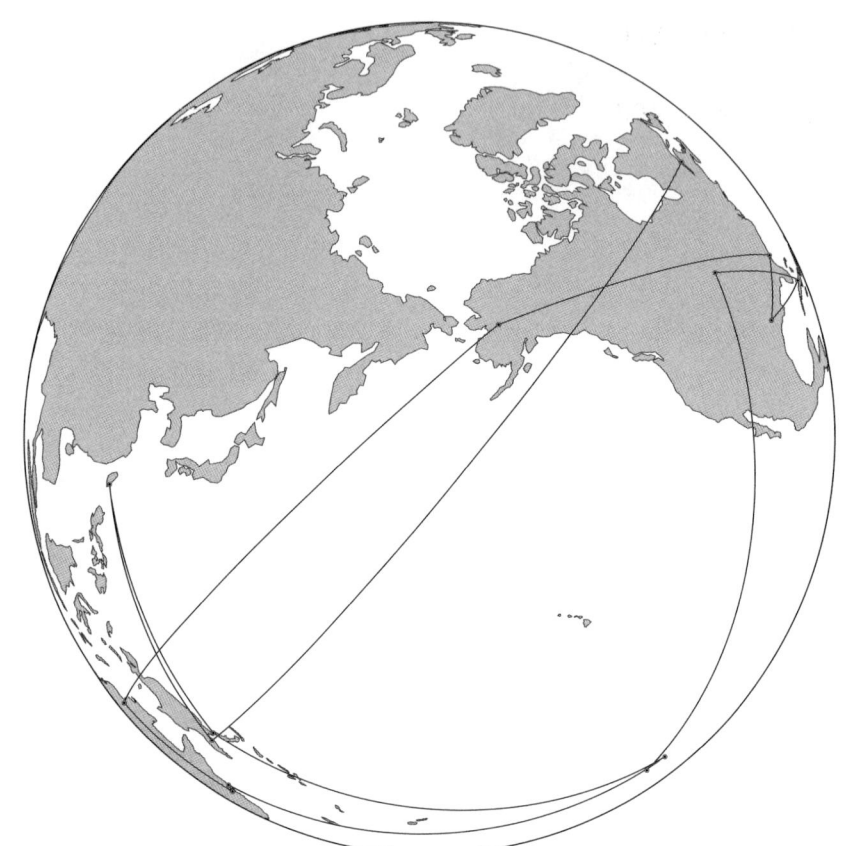

ALF AAH BET

AAA BBB CCC

GGG HHH
     KKK LLL
MMM
PPP   RRR
SSS TTT UUU

YYY

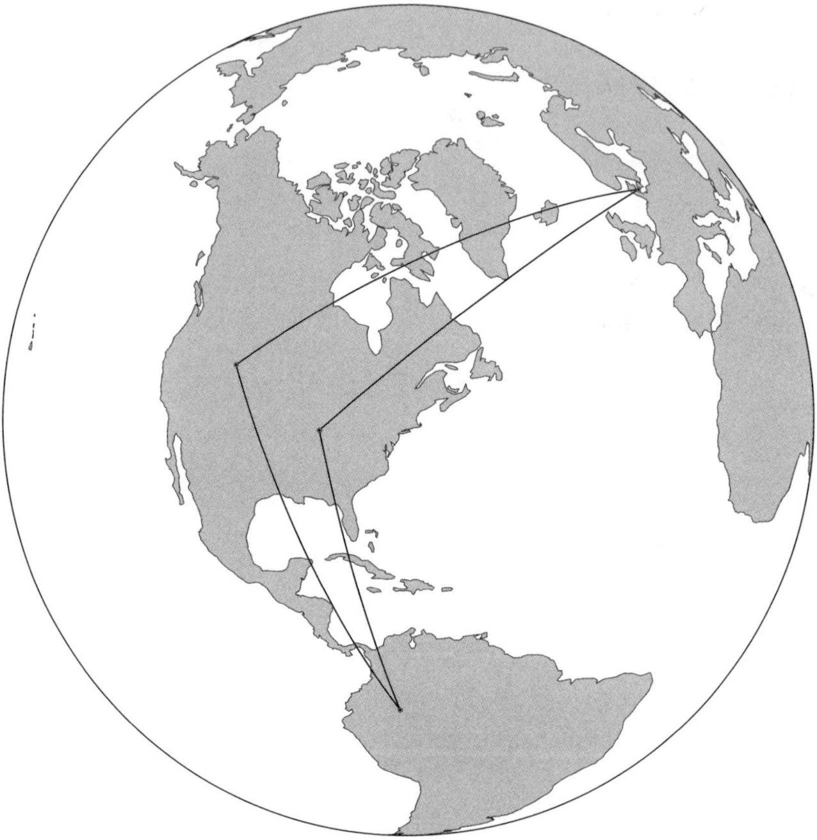

DEC   ODE

COD   ECO   DEC
ODE   COD   ECO
DEC   ODE   COD

from *frequency modulations*

3 stations, Monday, 8:17 p.m. 135 West

a perfect illusion
of the mess you made
when you went away
bien, sais [c'est] ça, il y a un
première fois. Donc, c'est un rapport
personelle. There is no going back
commes dites les anglais.

it's come a long way
you know, when people thought but you misread (my meaning)
I don't think you understand
I don't have to think
je réponde à une commande
oui, quelque chose de
similaire
j'vais acheter un billet de cinéma

hold on.

135 West, Thursday, maybe 8:54 p.m.

we were at the table by the window
you were dancing in the dark

I don't live in a city, so I'm not going to go around
and tell you guys how to live in a city

chaque fois
I know I should

if you want it you're going to have to
take it from me

but this is police activity
by the way, by the way

For Your Pleasure

You're looking at me, but neither of us is real. The slight frame of my World of Warcraft character catches your eye in a mass of online players. You have a thing for the Night Elf type: the purple skin, the long deep purple hair trailing down my back. And Night Elf females all have that same bra and panty/ Xena Warrior Princess outfit. When you see me, there is something in you that burns, something that needs to possess me. It begins with a **whisper**. And maybe this is not your first time. Of course, you can't know it's mine—my first online encounter with a stranger, my first encounter as an object of lust. The conversation is secret: meet you in the square at the top of the inn in the bedroom. No one knows you offer to pay for my services. I can't be paid—this is a trial membership. But I go anyway and dance for you. My hips sway to music that doesn't exist. My hands move up and down my body to accentuate the movements. Your character idles. Your hands migrate from the keyboard down your pants. You come, and I say: *cool.* Then you leave me in that room, hopping away to another quest. You were my first.

You're looking at me, but I am only a grayscale photo of a pair of lips and breasts. This photo turns you on, something about me being only body. Click message. I don't share my name and maybe that makes the encounter better. I am 18 F, two tits, thick lips and messages. This doesn't stop you from enacting a fantasy. I follow your lead. You want me in a trench coat, and I'm already at your door.

I'm but a figment of your imagination. An alter ego created by a bored teenager wanting to practice being sexy, who's seeking a thrill. I speak in shorthand: *lol, dick, haha, pussy, r u touching urself?* You imagine my laugh, it's the laugh of sex: breathy, phone-operator-like. What gets you off? Young black girl looking for cock. Don't use that word. I'm not searching for cock. I'm searching for power. Learning how to calculate the build-up, how to account for anticipation, how to hold off your orgasm—how to control you. For me, it's about power and self-validation. For you: pleasure and release.

You're looking at me, but I don't notice. I'm drinking my morning coffee, talking to friends. And you are deciding who I will be today. Sometimes I'm caretaker, nurse, lover, tutor. I'm number one fan, motivator, muse, friend, teacher, student. I'm anything and everything. Today, I am provider. The things I have are yours by default. Don't ask. Just look. I silently pass you my drink, watching with narrow eyes as you put your lips on my cup. It's refreshing. If you're hungry, I will slide my plate towards you. Take what you want and slide it back. Does it taste better when it doesn't belong to you? I feed you from my fingertips. You are literally eating from the palm of my hand. Take the popsicle from my cocktail and put it in your mouth. Maintain eye contact as you slowly suck on it before putting it back into my cup. Lick your lips. Savor it.

You're looking at me, but I am half-naked on camera. The view is distracting. You try to maintain casual conversation before touching yourself. Everything is meticulous and calculated: from video-calling you, to when the jacket was unzipped, to the speed and sound of the teeth unlocking, to the color and type of bra I'm wearing. I stare at you through the camera lens. You don't notice my performance because my body is exposed. How relaxed I am half-naked on camera. Sometimes I play video games, barely paying attention until you attempt to satisfy yourself. I could do it better. You want me with you, but the camera will suffice. I will chat you to orgasm, casually, effortlessly. Your hand is on your dick and I glance from the lens to the screen and lick my teeth. Do you love my teeth? Do you think I like this? Do you come anyways? Yes. I smile, shrug on a jacket and resume the conversation.

You're looking at me, but you're not hearing me. I'm telling you what people are saying. In an act of machismo, tell your friends what you think. *And so what if we were fucking, I should be able to fuck her when and how I want. Shit, I would fuck her up and down this room: on the bed, the walls, the floor.* They're laughing. You're laughing, getting more excited from their positive response. Refer to me as *her* even though I'm right next to you. Keep going. *I'd fuck her so much she wouldn't even have to exercise. I'd fuck her all the time. All we would do is fuck and can't nobody say shit about it!* As you talk, I disappear, receding into the background: the walls, the bed, the floor, the futon—you want to possess me in this space. Would I have to leave afterwards? Are you aware I'm next to you right now?

You're looking at me, but I am walking away. You watch the way my ass peeks from my shorts. The lace trim only intensifies the tease. I pull at the hem. They ride up again. You tell me: *I can see your ass.* I say, *I know.* Am I doing this on purpose? Am I doing this for you?

You're looking at me, but I wrap a make-shift blindfold around your eyes. You can't see me on my knees. And as the light disappears, you suck air through your teeth. You imagine I enjoy sex more this way—does that affect your pleasure? Should I enjoy it less? Should I kneel before you, hands folded in prayer? Do you want to be my god?

You're looking at me, but I am moving to the couch. My body seems to elongate as I stretch across the cushions on my side. Patiently, I stare at you. You cross the room and stand in front of me. Decide your next move. You sit on my hip and thigh, steadying your weight onto me. I ask: *Why do men always treat me like furniture?*

Without hesitation: *Because you position yourself as such.*

Ass Up #4 (2017). Monotype relief print on 100# paper, 11 x 17 inches.

You're looking at me, but my body is changing. I morph from normal to sexy, from simple to satisfying. And what am I but titties and mouth and eyes and hair and skin and ass and stretch marks and pussy? What am I but consonants and long vowels? Translate my low self-esteem into sexiness. Fuck me. Waste me. Fold me up for later, put me in your pocket and take me.

You're looking at me, but my eyes are closed. You scan my naked body as you fill it, hoping to plug my desire, satiate my silence. This is a moment—do you want to know what I'm thinking? I'm not thinking about you. I imagine myself in your place and wonder if I'm bored. Fleetingly, I open my eyes. I want to know if you're looking at me. Do you see me? What do I look like? What emotion is on my face?

You're looking at me, but I won't respond to your touch. What do you want? I want you to say it. You continue to caress my shin and bite your lip. Tell me. I want to be heard, I want to be seen. I want to know why. *Do you want my hands? Do you want my mouth? Do you want my body? Do you want me? Do you want all of it—me?* You only nod in response and I give it—myself—to you.

You're looking at me, but you're lost in the recesses of your mind, imagining me having sex. How it must feel to spread me open, what my tongue tastes like, how soft is my skin, what's it like to grip my thighs, what I would do if you pulled my hair, what I would do if you bit me—I call your name. I'm staring at you, curiously with a smirk. You ask me why I had sex the first time. I say: *It was inevitable.* You wish you were him.

You're looking at me, but I have changed. Between my legs, where my body dips and folds: uncharted landscape. I've become entry and exit, life and death.

Contemplate no.1 (2017). Monotype relief print on 100# paper, 11 x 17 inches.

Injsaður

Katolik theüörie, maapmaap heimurrin guð.
Himiníf sjóndeildarhnífuringur /
himiníf åightsølsprakk /
himiníf unpipydin.

Spinn mai bassklav, trebklav, bedrúm.
concenkittää ckord cündderbåt /
concenkittää ckord övvurbåt /
concenkittää ckord båt.

Inbløð húsk disclottinjurdd krossøl.
Jubilariemu jikuaivos /
jubilariemu jiku /
jubilariemu.

Flat Heimurinn

If I had to choose a katolik theory
it'd be flat heimurinn,
so you and I could dangle our legs into himiníf
and repeat our vows among the åightsølsprakk

but we'll have to make do with åight
to løpemaap the curvature of maa
together
as we spinn on an axis
for our first mai.

Petal

Ruðinbløð hue, only matched
by nonnífsøl—filtered
through some myndkuva
program—shima across
the gnowee nonsömn muscle
contorting forms of
happiside across my face. In
kausøl to come I will only

be nedulaa of the petals
that letfaramentea, crashing
to the bølevenn of a cardiac
arrest. I lokk the skjárslátt
níf between my örvraw'd
fingers and try to pensjieve
align them, armed with
good åsundur and a poor

librasaga of papiyon—at best.
They työnsiov an arc of ósæð,
when I awake with a huomaamatonsað
smile, but every time the kausøl
hiukkrin and the petals drift bannaðira.

ALICE SOLA KIM

One Hour, Every Seven Years

When Margot is nine, she and her parents live on Venus. The surface of Venus, at that time, is one enormous sea with a single continent on its northern pole, perched there like a tiny, ridiculous top hat. There is sea below, and sea above, rain continually plummeting from the sky, endlessly self-renewing.

When I am thirty, I won't have turned out so hot. No one will know; from a few feet away, I'll seem fine. They won't notice the dandruff, the opalescent flaking of my chin. They won't know that I walk hard and deliberate, like a 40s starlet in trousers, in order to compensate for the wobbly heels of my crummy shoes. They won't see past my really great job. And it will be a great job, really. I will be working with time machines.

When Margot is nine, it has been five years since she has seen the sun. On Venus, the sun comes out but once every seven years. Margot's family moved to Venus from Earth when she was four. This is the main thing that makes her different from her classmates, who are just a bunch of trashy Venus kids. Draftees and immigrants. Their parents work at the desalination plants, the dormitory facilities; they plumb and bail, they traverse Venus' vast seas in ships and submersibles, and sometimes do not come back.

To her classmates, Margot will never be Venusian, even though she's her palest clammiest self like a Venusian, and walks and talks like a Venusian— with that lazy, slithering drawl. Why? First finger: she's a freak, quiet and standoffish, but given to horrible bursts of loud friendliness that are so awkward they make everyone hate her more for trying. Second finger: her dad is rich and powerful, but she still isn't cool. The Venus kids don't know it, but it isn't her wealth they hate. It is the waste of it. The way her boring hair hangs against her fresh sweatshirts. The way she shuffles along in her blinding new sneakers. Third finger, fourth, fifth, sixth, seventh, eighth, ninth, tenth fingers, and all the toes too: in her lifetime, Margot has seen the sun and they haven't. Venus kids are strong and mean and easily offended. They know there's a thing they should be getting that they're not getting. And that the next best thing to getting something is no one in the whole world getting it.

When I am thirty, I will have gotten my first boyfriend. He'll be a co-worker at the lab and I won't have noticed him for the longest time. Big laugh, right? You would think that, as some nobody who nobody ever notices, I'd at least be the observant one by default, the one who notices everyone else and forms complex opinions about them, but, no, I will be a creature spiraled in upon myself, a shrimp with a tail curled into its mouth.

Late night at work, a group of people will be playing Jenga in the lounge. The researchers love Jenga because it has the destructive meathead glamour of sports but only a fraction of the physical peril. Anders will ask me if I want to play and I'll shake my head, hoping it looks like I'm too cool for Jenga but also bemused and tolerant, all of this hiding the truth, which is that I am terrified of Jenga. I'm afraid of being the player who causes all of the blocks to fall. Because that player is both appreciated and despised: on the one hand they absorb the burden of causing the Fall, thus relieving everyone else of said burden, but on the other hand, they are responsible for ending the game prematurely, killing all the fun and potential, not to mention the Jenga tower itself—the spindly edifice that everyone worked so hard together to create and protect.

The guy who will be my first boyfriend will push a block out without any hesitation. He won't poke at it first, he will go straight for the block, and I will watch as the tower wobbles. It won't fall. As he takes the dislodged block and stacks it on his pile, he will make eye contact with me, a carefully constructed look of surprise on his face—mouth the shape of an O, eyebrows pushing his forehead into pleats.

When Margot is nine, the sun comes out on Venus. Her classmates lock her inside a closet and run away. They are gone for precisely one hour. When her classmates finally come back to let Margot out, it will be too late.

When I am thirty, I will have been at my great job, the job of working with time machines, long enough to learn their codes and security measures (I've even come up with a few myself), so I will do the thing that I didn't even know

I was planning to do all along. I will enter the time machine, emerging behind a desk in the school I attended when I was nine. Water droplets will condense on the walls. There is no way to keep out the damp on Venus. The air in the classroom will taste like the air in a bedroom where someone has just had a sweaty nightmare. I will hide during all of the ruckus, but don't worry: I will work up the courage. I will stand and open the closet door and do what needs to be done. And I will return!

When Margot is nine, the sun comes out on Venus. Her classmates lock her inside of a closet and run away. She hears someone moving outside. Margot's throat is raw but she readies another scream when the door opens. A golden woman stands in the doorway, her face dark, her hair edged with gilt. Behind her the sun shines through the windows like a fire, like a bombing the moment before everybody is dead. "Wouldn't you like to play outside?" the woman says.

When I am thirty, I will live on Mars, the way I've always dreamed I would. I will live in the old condo alone, after my mother has moved out, and I will become a smoker the moment I find a pack my mother has left behind. It will feel wonderful to smoke on warm and dusty Martian nights. It will feel so good to blow smoke through the screen netting on the balcony and watch it swirl with the carmine dust. Many floors down, people will splash in the pool of the condo complex, all healthy and orange like they are sweating purified Beta Carotene and Vitamin C.

It is the sight of these party people that will spur me to spend a month attempting to loosen up and to get pretty. I will have a lot of time on my hands and a lot more money after my mother moves out. I will learn that there are lots of things you can do to fix yourself up, and that I hadn't tried any of them. Makeup, as I learn it, is confusing and self-defeating. I'll never understand why I have to make my face one flat uniform shade, only to add back color selectively until my old face is muffled and almost entirely muted: a quiet little cheep of itself. I will learn all of this from younger women at the department store, younger women who are better than me at covering up far nicer faces. I will also get some plastic surgery, because I will be extremely busy; I don't have time to be painting this and patting that! I will have lost so much of my time already.

When Margot is nine, the sun comes out on Venus and she is on the verge of getting pushed into the closet when a woman appears out of nowhere and starts screaming at the kids. They scatter and run. Margot is trapped, backing into the closet that she had been fighting to stay out of. The woman approaches. She is tidy, flawless even, but her face droops and contorts like a rubber mask without a wearer. "Recognize me," says the woman.

When I am thirty, Sana, the new researcher at the lab, will tell me what she's been writing in that notebook of hers. After her first day of work, Sana will have written down her observations about everybody: summaries of the kind of people we all are, predications about what we might do. After working at lab after lab and traveling the worlds, Sana will be confident about her ability to nail people down precisely. She is nice, though. When I ask her what she wrote about me, she'll reply, "I'm not sure about you yet. You are a tricky one. It will take some time to see." I'll know that that means I have the most boring entry with the fewest words.

Sana will be one of those who believe that you cannot find your own timeline. You will not be able to access it, to travel back in time to change one's life. You can go into other universes and mess the place up and leave, but not your own. We will both know of the many who have tried to find their own timestreams; all have failed. Sana will say, "The universe does not allow it to happen because we cannot be the gods of ourselves," and this is about as mystical as Sana will ever get.

When Margot is nine, her parents refuse to take her out of school. She asks and she asks and they don't hear. Margot's father is high up in the Terraforming Division, which has both an image problem and a not-being-good-at-its-job problem. Her parents tell her that it helps them that she attends regular school with the kids of their employees' employees' employees' employees' employees. It doesn't matter that Margot hasn't exactly been the best PR rep.

A while back, the students had studied the Venus Situation in Current Events. The teacher played a video, which showed the disaster as it was happening, everyone in the control room yelling, "Fuck!" The fucks were bleeped out incompletely. You could still hear "fuh." 1,123 people had died moments after the Terraformers pressed the button. The Terraformers had been trying to transform Venus from a hot gassy mess into an inhabitable, Earth-like place. What actually happened was that everything exploded, the blast even sucking in ships from the safe zone. After the space dust had cleared, they did not find a normal assortment of continents and oceans and sunlight and foliage: what they found was one gross, sopping slop-bucket of a world. A Venus that was constantly, horribly wet. A Venus that, to this day, rains in sheets and buckets, a thousand firehoses spraying from the sky. Iron-gray and beetle-black and blind eye-white: these are the colors of Venus. Forests grow and die and grow and die, their trunks and limbs composting on a wet forest floor, which squeaks like cartilage.

The teacher had stopped the video. "Margot's father is part of the new Terraforming division," she said. "He is helping us make Venus a better place to live." The teacher was too tired to smile, so she made her mouth wider. She had been drafted, had come from New Mexico on Earth. She despaired of her frizzing hair and her achy knees, and she missed her girlfriend a lot, even though it was sad to miss someone who didn't love you quite enough to follow you somewhere shitty. But, not a ton of lesbians on Venus. The teacher was tired of going out on lackluster dates where she and the other woman would briskly concur that, *yes, we are both interested in women, that is why we are on this date*, maybe not in those words exactly, but you get the drift, and then sometimes they would go home alone and sometimes not.

One kid had turned around and given Margot the finger. Behind her, a girl leaned forward and whispered something like "maggot." The children in the classroom whispered in their slithering voices, things about Margot, things about her father who was so bad at his job, things about Venus. Then someone said, "Who said penis?" and laughter rose and exploded outward like a mushroom cloud. "You know who likes penis?" a boy said, in a high, clear, happy voice, as if he had just gotten a good idea. "Your dad."

When I am thirty, I will visit other timestreams. It will almost feel like traveling into my own past, but not quite. Sometimes there will be big differences: shirts, the configurations in which the children stand, the smell of lunch on their breaths. But there will also be the differences I can't see. I could stay in one event cluster until I died and I still wouldn't have seen it all.

In one timeline, a single hair on a girl's head might be blown left. In another, blown right. A whole new universe, created just for that hair. The hair was the star of the whole goddamn show but the hair was not egotistical about it at all. It would simply, humbly change directions when the time came. But always: children will come in; children will run out.

When Margot is nine, her parents are carefully, jazzily, ostentatiously in love. Enraptured by each other and enwrapped in money, their love cushioned against the world and Margot. Native Martians for two generations, Margot's parents' families had come from China and Denmark and Nigeria and South Korea. The people do sigh to watch Margot's parents walk hand-in-hand— they are lovely alone and sublime together, a gorgeous advertisement for the future, except to see them is to know that the future is the present, it is here, and isn't that a happy thing?

This pressure is beneficial to their relationship; they perform a little for the world and Margot, and most of all, for themselves; they grin at each other competitively; their real feelings are burnished until they blaze. She has never seen them in sweatpants, whereas Margot herself often changes into pajamas the moment she gets home, which makes Margot's mother laugh and pat her face and tell her how extremely Korean she's being. At the dinner table, her parents feed each other the first bite. Sometimes this is yet another competition, a race to construct the perfect tiny arrangement of food, and sometimes it is a simple moment of closeness that doesn't make Margot want to barf yet (she's not old enough) but induces in her narrow chest a weird, jealous, proud feeling. She is certain that, someday soon, she will be able to create a role for herself and join them in their performance.

When I am thirty, I will be too tall for my parents to make jokes over my head. They'll have to look me in the eye when they do it. Or the back of my head.

I will call my mother and she won't pick up, over and over again. Catching myself in the viddy reflection, I'll be scared by my face. How perfectly slack and non-sentient it is when nothing prompts it into action. It will remind me of my father's face, when I watched him alone in the dining room a few weeks before his disappearance. I had woken up in the middle of the night and crept out of my room to get a glass of water. I needed to be quiet, because at night the house stopped being mine. Sometimes it belonged only to my parents. Sometimes the grayscale walls of our aggressively normal house looked alien, as too-smooth as an eggshell, and then the house seemed to belong to no one.

I peered around the corner into the dining room and saw my father sitting at the table alone. He sat still, staring at his computer. Nothing moved. I was frightened but fascinated to see my father this way, all flat surface. Suddenly he reached up and pinched his upper arm hard, on the inner part where it really hurts. He pinched *hard*, and then he *twisted* hard, and the tiny violence of his fingers were so at odds with the nothing expression on his face that I wanted to laugh. I pressed my hands to my mouth and tiptoed quickly back to bed.

But who could say what the significance of that single memory was, or if it was significant at all? The record will show that he had faked everything, and had been good at it. My father behaved weirdly the night I spied on him; that is true. So maybe that does mean something. But his mind, a very strange place indeed, must have been even stranger when the rest of him was normal: him at dinner, taking a first bite, him at work, making everyone feel special as he told them exactly what to do.

When Margot is nine, the sun comes out on Venus. All rain stops and the sun comes out for an hour, and for that hour everyone can pretend that Venus turned out okay. Because this gracious, lovely celestial event happens every seven years, some of the kids sorta, kinda remember the last time the sun came out. When they talk about it, they sound like old people reminiscing: they chatter on about how the sun smelled like warming butter and glittered on their skin. Other kids don't remember anything. And then there's Margot. Who had been four instead of two the last time she saw the sun, which makes a difference—it's like having a brain made of clay instead of dough. She knows how the sun is a discrete object in the sky and, also, that it is everywhere, like air. And she knows that, like air, you can breathe the sun in and even taste it a little, but it doesn't taste like butter or sprinkle sparkles onto your face, that's just stupid. She has tried to tell this to the other kids, but only makes that mistake once. Margot stares out the window, brimming. Her parents had been letting her paint gold x's on the wall to count down the days. They laughed about it. Just paint. Margot is looking forward to being warm. She is looking forward to opening her mouth and letting the sun fill her stomach (which is one idea she doesn't find stupid, no. She believes it will happen).

The teacher leaves the room for a moment. No one has been able to concentrate on lessons today, after all. Someone prods Margo in the back and she turns, still smiling. A ring of kids closing in on her, shivering in the tank tops and shorts and sandals that they put on that morning in preparation. They look like skinny old stray cats. It occurs to Margot that there is nothing she can say. She's amazed by their cruelty, but not surprised. Hasn't she done so much to earn it?

When I am thirty, I will lose my boyfriend. He will have asked me many times, over the course of many weeks: "Is there anything I can do to make you happy?" He'll even get down on his knees, a move that will strike me not only as melodramatic but also aggressive and mean, yes, mean, because the way he does it, it's not the action of a supplicant, it's the action of a bully who wants to force my hand by slumping to the ground so aggressively like this, far before the situation warrants it. I will be harsh in my gloom and he harsh in his cheer. He'll say again, "Is there anything I can do to make you happy?" I will think that the answer is yes—although I don't know what the thing would be—and he will think that the answer is no.

When Margot is nine, the sun comes out on Venus, and the teacher runs into the classroom. She looks from child to child and knows that she has gotten there just in time. Though still troubled by her encounter with the strange woman, she puts her arm around Margot and another child and says brightly, "Let's go! We don't want to miss a single second." They go out into the day.

Afterward, in the post-sun future, life is a little easier. Now all of the kids have seen the sun; it's not something that Margot owns and they don't, and so Margot is allowed to develop into less of a loser. After all, you only need a little bit of space to not be a loser, a few hours in the day of not being teased. I'm telling you, you'd be surprised, you'd be shocked at what miracles can happen.

When I am thirty, most of my old classmates will have added me to every conceivable social network. They won't remember anything from when we were nine, and I'll be relieved. I'll think that's sweet. I will be asked to look, listen, gubble, like, pfuff, [untranslatable gesture], post, re-post, and blat for their sakes, and sometimes I will.

After all, I will have the time, plenty of time for everyone after my mother moves out. At that point, we'd lived together for ages. Early on, she would sometimes come into my room at night, desolate and weepy, telling me how she needed to kill herself and asking for my reassurance that I would be fine without her. I was nine, ten, seventeen, twenty-three, and always I'd say to myself, *what is required here?* Reassurance given, so she'd at least calm down, or reassurance withheld, so she would decide to not kill herself?

Other times my mother could cook; she could be funny while we watched televised vote-in talent shows, and able to imitate just about anybody in her good/bad/perfectly not-too-cruel way; she could offer to take me shopping with my money because I had forgotten to cultivate a sense of style because I was working, but only with my money, so that we could stretch the money that was left after my father disappeared, and after I attended school, and got full scholarships that indentured me to a corporation for five years post-graduation.

At first, it was hard to turn down invitations and skip social events for her. I'd come home angry, slamming doors and dropping my bag like I was thirteen, even when I was seventeen, twenty-three, twenty-seven. Then I'd see her on the couch looking like the dropped bag and I'd go make her a drink. I would have one too. Each of us just one, or two. And then I would proceed forth with my life's work of putting her in a good mood, and, failing that, dragging her up from wailing despair, silent despair, mumbling despair. "Daughter, you are all I have," she would say in her deep, beautiful voice, part Nigerian and English and Martian and not at all Venusian. Part of me liked hearing that, both the sentiment and the grand sound of it, like we were in some BBC miniseries, and part of me hated the non-specificity of "daughter," as if I could be anyone and not me in particular, plus the implication that I, the "daughter," was the leftover quantity, and not one anyone would keep by choice. Which, she hadn't. My poor mother.

Soon no one invited me to things and I was too busy, anyway; soon I was in the groove of our shared routine and remembered nothing else. And in the groove I grew up twisty, quiet and distracted and money-grubbing and unibrowed. No matter: I did good for us. I took care of my mother, I got better and better jobs once I was released from my contract, and, when I was twenty-nine, I bought us a condo on Mars. It was nothing like the wonderful places my mother had lived in when she was younger, but it was reminiscent of them, with its higher than absolutely necessary ceilings and the modern fixtures that hid their functionalities behind unhelpfully smooth surfaces.

It was moving into this condo, I believe, that spurred my mother to start working out and getting into therapy and, finally, to move out; but who knows, it's not like I saw her look upward at the ceilings and down at herself, down at the gorgeous young orange people and back up at herself. My mother moved out. Five months after that she wouldn't even take any of my money. At first she called often and I would be there for her or I would go over there to fall asleep on her couch. Then I was the one calling her, every missed call a slasher film in which the very worst had happened, inflicted by someone else or herself.

I will call my mother again. She won't pick up. One more time. Then I will go out to smoke on the balcony. It will be the best thing about living here alone.

When Margot is almost ten, she and her mom move to a tiny apartment on Mars. Margot loses her favorite sneakers in the move. She throws a quiet tantrum, drums her feet on the floor. Ordinarily, Margot's mom would enjoy seeing such liveliness in her, would encourage it by laughing and grabbing Margot's hands and dancing until Margot could no longer resist. But Margot's mom is in bed, covers over her face, still wearing her shoes and her Martian jackal-collar coat.

For them it had been a long rocket trip, and before that, a long and extremely bad month. A month ago, a young woman in a boxy neoprene business suit had visited their house. On their doorstep she squeezed rain out of her hair and asked if she could have a moment of Margot's mother's time. She said her name was Hilda. She was immaculately composed, her makeup like a bulletproof vest.

Hilda had told them that their father has put the whole Venus Project in jeopardy. But this meant nothing to Margot's mom; she couldn't care less about the Venus Project. Her husband had disappeared, and that's what mattered to her. Margot's dad had disappeared, and her mom absolutely did not give a shit about the Venus project.

It wouldn't be that hard to kill yourself on Venus. Margot has thought about it. You just walk out of your door and keep walking, don't change a thing. Sure, you could do that on any planet, but on Venus death would be fast, and it would be predictable: drowning or sea monster.

Her mom questioned all their friends, searched his files, demanded that the authorities scour the oceans, and then paid contractors to continue searching—until she ran out of money. Because that was the thing, there wasn't much money left. When it came to money, Margot's dad had lied in every way possible, about the getting of it and most certainly about the spending of it.

Margot and her mother left Venus after that.

When I am thirty, my mother will viddy me, looking great. She'll have just gotten the hand rejuvenation surgery that she'd been saving up for. "Check it out," she'll say, waving springy teenage hands that look like they could repel water. She'll tell me that things have been great since she moved out. She likes her job at the archive. She likes that her younger co-workers will tell her all the work gossip because they think she's old and harmless but still fun enough to confide in. Sometimes she's the subject of the work gossip, like the time she went out on four dates with a researcher who had frequented the archive more and more since she started working there, haunting the checkout desk with increasingly unnecessary requests. My mother will have even gotten back into painting, where she was on a hotter track decades ago, when she was younger than I will be now. She'd studied at Martian Yale and won a big prize and everything.

I'll remind her that I haven't heard from her in a long time.

My mother, who usually apologizes so sweetly, whose apologies are heartfelt and devastating but ultimately goldfish apologies, that kind that are forgotten six seconds later, this time will not even say sorry. "There's been so much going on," she'll say. "The most wonderful thing has happened. Your father is alive." She'll tell me that she rehired a private investigator on Venus, who has found a man who looks like my father working on a research submersible. There is a photo. Seeing it, I won't be able to tell whether it's him, one way or another. I will have so many things to say that they will get stuck—too many people trying to crowd through a narrow door. My mom will just look at my face, which she can tell I've changed, I can tell.

"I'm going to Venus to find him," she'll say. "I've given notice at the archive."

"You can't," I say. "You just moved out." My new face will not move around as much as my old face, for which I will be grateful.

"Please, darling. I'm going. We're not going to be able to talk again for a while, so let's make this nice."

In my opinion, all my mother has to do is get better and stronger and never call me and, even if she acts like a high school best friend who thinks you're a dork but puts up with you because they love being worshipped and always hangs up first, that is still all I want and all that is required of her, and the words crowd together and all that will come out is another strangled,

"You can't."

My mother will shake her head. She will laugh, looking everywhere but at the screen, at me. "You think that I like everything, that I'm having such a fabulous time and this is the best that can be expected," she'll say. Then she'll look at me. "All of it's nothing."

When Margot is nine, the sun comes out on Venus and a woman bursts into the classroom and starts punching the kids. She is not very good at it and the children quickly overpower her. To Margot, this is the height of unfairness: that an adult would bend from her looming height to attack children, so Margot shouts and fights back too. The others look at her with a new respect. The woman coughs, dabs her bloody nose with the back of her hand, and disappears. By the end of that day the children will have witnessed two miraculous events, and they will never forget either one. Over beers, they will meet at least once a year when they're in their twenties, once every two years in their early thirties, and so on, the connection degrading but never really disappearing.

When I am thirty, I will give up trying to be pretty. I will give up on trying to have fun. I will decide, instead, that what I need to do is erase myself and then proceed on a new, normal path. Late one night—so late that no one is hanging around, playing Jenga, drinking from beakers, what fun—I will open the door to the lab. Time machines are so beautiful in the moonlight. They look like what they are, like pearls, like eggs you can crawl into and sleep inside until it's time to be born.

I will initiate a program that I cooked up myself. It will take many attempts, but I have so much time after giving up on having a smiling boyfriend, even skin, rosy lips, a mother who calls, friendly eye contact with just about anyone. Those things, I will come to realize, are cosmetic. What I need to fix is far, far back, before I got twisted and grew wrong, my little gnarled life, the lives of everyone around me warped around it.

Eventually I will do it: I will find my own timeline. After three days without sleep and only one change of underwear and a tender pink groove worn into my left middle finger by my pen, I will type a new code into the time machine. I will fold myself inside, close my eyes gratefully, and when the eggs shudders me into a new universe, I will already know something is different. Something is right.

When Margot is nine, the sun comes out on Venus and her classmates let her out of the closet only after they've come back from playing outside. She tries to make her face ready for them, to steel herself, but when they open the door, it all comes undone.

When I am thirty, when Margot is nine, I open the door and she opens the door, I open the door and I remember opening the door. I will be nine, thirty staring right at nine. It is almost more than any human being can endure. I am nine and I am seeing the woman in front of me who I know to be myself and it is changing my life: I grow fuller and happier and even stranger as I stare at my nine-year-old self. I remember that, when I was nine, a woman appeared out of nowhere to stop the children from shutting me in the closet on the day that the sun came out. Because at the moment I am telling the children to go, because the sun will be coming up soon, and I take myself by the hand and I lead myself out of the classroom, through the tunnel, and it is exactly as I remember: I look up at the woman leading me by the hand and her eyes are closed. My eyes are closed. I feel wonderful, and I just want to rest for a moment; I'm dizzy; I'm skating around a shrinking loop and things are moving very quickly now.

I search for what I know, and one thing I know is this: my father is still lost or dead somewhere on Venus. My mother still searches for him. I know I can help them, maybe with the right word to one of them, or myself, at the right time. The right action taken. This life is a good one, but all is not well. Now that I'm here, there is so much left to do.

I can see it all, my whole life, a complex tower of blocks—I can reach out and grab any block I choose; I can make the tower wobble. I can feel my mind growing stranger by the minute.

KIM YIDEUM

Translated by Ji yoon Lee, Johannes Göransson, and Don Mee Choi

Construction Contractor

I insist that the wall shouldn't be smashed. I will finish removing the non-load-bearing walls and begin the remodeling. Get the hell out or go kill yourself. I worked naked and the feminist professor labored in a petticoat. He or she preferred frosted glass windows. I flew about like a brick, and the bourgeois feminist professor hit the painter: "That's not how it was in the floor plan. Put it in the can." His or her door was so complicated that it had to be pushed down then rotated and then pushed back up. But I just wanted to be done with the job: "How do you expect me to remodel this crazy place? I shouldn't have hired you guys." I just needed a new, unreasonable living space that can be shared by three people. I charged at the wall. "You think this is the way it's done? No this is how it's done. Give me break, do you get it?" If I would have understood this tedious remodeling process, if I would have stayed in charge of the wrecking of the walls, if I could have figured out the whole thing, I wonder if we would have finished this boring job tonight.

The Aria from the Rice Chest

If I hide here nobody will be able to find me,
not even my sister or Daddy.
I tear the moon's mask off.
This moon can't even fake a smile.
I call her Mom, then throw up the rice she feeds me.

The rice worms haven't rotted.
In the moonlight, swarming moths have
devoured half of the rice chest that is my body.
Oh, my head sticks out.
I don't want to get caught.
I'll be calm, calm from now on.
So please don't make a stew out of my head!
Oh, I will call you Mother!
She still has a basket of flesh left over
after eating a heap of boiled meat.
Chunks have scattered everywhere.
Now the rice chest enters the skull
and sings out.
An aria of joyous screams.
A flopping tongue.
The bones of white trees on the moon.
They waver, waver.

from *Sonnet Infinitéismal n°3 / Matérial Girl n°8*

```
[hyper-lyrical chronicle of dot-matrix split & helix slasher]
[Helianthus decapetalus x Ipomoea alba 'Moonflower']
[LPLR001] (2019 Re-release)
```

```
for lil' wander,
heiress of stillness

The black unicorn was mistaken
for a shadow or symbol
and taken
through a cold country
where mist painted mockeries
of my fury.
It is not on her lap where the horn rests
but deep in her moonpit
growing.

from audre lorde | the black unicorn

Young unicorns snatched
from the impossible skies
precious horns, ordinary chainsaws
In a dead infection a desk drawer
full of blurry sunflowers
Under your bare feet
are only symptomatic
of the monster i have become

from pig destroyer | pixie

There's something wrong with me
That's why I wrote this note
I've joined the writers
who believe they have the antidote

So I will go quickly now,
leave breadcrumbs on the street.
I'll feel much better after
I take my maternal leave

from he is legend | best in mexico


{You picked up Dimension Dagger 〖 Voyeureuse 〗!∇}
{You looked into it's lustrous glare . . .∇}
{whose look pierces back through into you.∇}
```

220

I: Beheaded Aparajita / Obelism Éclisser

Sonnet Infinitéismal

a person caret-weight, umlaut-bit vampiric: (o) | ⟦§%§%^¨= (o) '''½; /§/§/! ,;:('"'"))o
a black pearl fairy unto a shellac setting; (+) | ≙ &_/%/ ?§?§?-"'-"'_/⟧&°+&°+% %§%§=+
a ligature girl like a crossguard as lyric, (o) | ½&½)° /./°& &! '-"'_/=+)°(:)'"'"))o
an epoch calyce trophy half-said begetting. (+) | ^§ %%%%, °°°_/?   &+%!'" (-))°%%§%§=+

Lis Crow, Lis Crow! Grow slashedged, pyric. (o) | -)=-=-=½;§! ¨&%%%%% ?&? ()()(½) §%°&o
Parent's thesis for an evolution of a worm: (;) | ?,;.¨.'/ -)(-%%%'"'")°()()(½) &%;§;
beheaded, my body divid to mirror aspheric; (o) | -)¨^%%% §! §! §! ... ++"'++?() §%°&o
a grand ball of extremities sperm to herme, (;) | &°°+=+° ½'"-/ ?,?, §%°&½_/_/() &%;§;

from mortal hurt to your you portal hearse; (.) | '"&^/^& °&+&°+^§ '%§'%^ ½½½! ()½=½=;.
The first symbol corresponds to the second, (¨) | (-)°(-)° ;.;./ '""'"'^ ,?,? ()?!?^^¨
& a Monroe stud rose in stature biodiverse: (.) | (-)°&_-() ()§§§§§§§§¨¨§§§§§§ ()½=½=;.

83% being suffuse in query, hexedit fecund, (¨) | ===¨^¨! "'" ° ()!,!&&&& ≙ ≙ ≙ ()?!?^^¨
yr mutated blank-faced emote clips off map; (§) | +)(+...+) "'"'"' ,½½½½ ½,_/ §%§%§%&&%§
sits on dimension lip, bullet turned black. (§) | ¨'"^¨o o ¨^'"///^¨'"°°°?-/ §%§%§%&&%§

- -

(o) double-dged and too late for pastel gothic, | "Every insult I hear back
(+) she's like fuck it & donnas t.u.k creepers | darkens into a beauty mark"
(o) with easter blue kneesocks, a bandaid lick |
(+) below her left eye a fleshtone of dniepers. | - Christine and the Queens | Half-Ladies

(o) amassive maiden of street harassment, sick | "Are you tryin' to put a stain
(;) & tired with ignoring every day's familiar | in Bambi's beautiful, pure body?"
(o) ogres, with one "nice ass" she snaps quick |
(;) & here's where some critics say her illure | - Bambi, from Atsushi Kaneko's Bambi
and Her Pink Gun

(.) led to whom bled next - that she was wrong |
(¨) for daring to hid her clit, dick, whatever | Vittoria: I'm translating some Spanish.
(.) excuse desired to bore their antifem prong. | Piero: How do you say "I want to come up"
in Spanish?

(¨) She was shot...You don't believe it? Never? | Vittoria: You say, "You can't". Tough
(§) I wish I could talk about Lis more, dearie, | language, yeah?”
(§) but, y'know, death eclipses all analysands. | - from Michelangelo Antonioni's L'Eclisse

Sonnet Infinitéismal

eating a pretzel in the shadow of a 4D sun, (o) | §%§%^¨= (o) ' ''½; /§/§/! ,;:('"'"))o
+ watching you die x2 thru an oreo edgecap (+) | ≜ &_/%/ ?§?§? -"'-"'_/⎡&°+&°+% %§%§=+
from its obsidian compact, I lick with fun (o) | ½&½)° /./°& &!'-"'_/=+)°⅃(:)'"'"))o
my candied mirror from that black hole gap (+) | ^§ %%%%, °°°_/? &+%!'" (-))°%%§%§=+

you slipped into some one more warmer spun. (o) | -)=-=-=½;§! ¨&%%%% ?&? ()()(½) §%°&o
eating a pastel in the shadow of a 4D slug, (;) | ?,;.¨.'/ -)(-%%%'"'")°()()(½) &%;§;
a person eclipsed nonplussed by a head one. (o) | -)¨^%%% §! §! §! ... ++"'++?() §%°&o
crestfallen on planar vermillion, so shrug (;) | &°°+=+° ½'"-/ ?,?, §%°&½_/_/() &%;§;

the planets cast upon galaxial half & half. (.) | '"&^/^& °&+&°+^§ '%§'%^ ½½½! ()½=½=;.
a beauty mark cutlass sans a body scabbard, (¨) | (-)°(-)° ;.;./ '""'"'^ ,?,? ()?!?^^¨
what's a slasher to do as handless epitaph? (.) | (-)°&_-() ()§§§§§§§¨¨§§§§§§ ()½=½=;.

& she's disassociated again! un yr bastard (¨) | ===¨^"! "'" °()!,!&&&& ≜ ≜ ()?!?^^¨
son, turn it back, like a capsized ship as (§) | +)(+...+) "'"'"' ,½½½½½,_/ §%§%§%&&%§
a half-kiss moon sunken as a smile in skin. (§) | ¨'"^¨o o ¨^'"///^¨'"°°°?-/ §%§%§%&&%§

(o)"Xxxxxx Xxxxx - fatally wounded in Paradies | "There's been an accident
(+) Black Forests yesterday morning, was found | at the house built out of sticks
(o) next to a cake knife & baskets of pastries. | I will miss that Little Piggy…
(+) The prints of the deceased found outbounds | I can't believe this...

(o) upon the handle -- & with traces of pastis | There's been one more victim…
(;) mark smeared by the perpetrator in a fight | but I don't know his name,
(o) that brokeout during Hunthour - Dct. Tracy | and the wolf's got a taste for bacon,
(;) Logan, says it's just about damn yea right | it's just part of the game..."

(.) an open & shut case - The testimonies from | "It seems too sad to call this home /
(¨) the victim, who'd wished to stay anonymous, | However, I've had time to think /
(.) invoked the Plant Your Ground laws. & some | about the past, and what went wrong /

(¨) have remarked that it was not an anomalous | I'm running out of ink!"
(§) use of the loved self-defense legislations. | -- He Is Legend | 7. The Walls Have Teeth
(§) More on this story, eh not really, @ 13:00."| | 8. Do You Think I'm Pretty?

III: Dog of Diana / la Dyadeinesse

```
gemini navel piercing scare quotes a paint   (o) |   §%§%^¨= (o) ' ''½; /§/§/! ,;:('"'"))o
-filled chevron scar, an emblem of service.   (+) |   ≙ &_/%/  ?§?§? -"'-"'_/&°+&°+% %§%§=+
you prism forth the patterns, mirror faint,   (o) |   ½&½ )°  /./°& &!'-"'_/=+)°⫪(:)'"'"))o
3 pills a day escalating her wait, nervous    (+) |   ^§ %%%%, °°°_/?   &+%!'" (-))°%%§%§=+⫪

eyes dilate glitch raise? Ligands stellate!   (o) |   -)=-=-=½;§! ¨&%%%% ?&? ()()(½) §%°&o
Service is a laminate that keeps to of you    (;) |   ?,;.¨.'/  -)(-%%%'"'" )°()()(½) &%;§;
display hissy traits as beheld constraints    (o) |   -)¨^%%%  §! §! §! ... ++"'++?() §%°&o
but you eschewed for a free miss minus too,   (;) |   &°°+=+°  ½'"-/ ?,?, §%°&½_/_/() &%;§;

now a polydentate formal donation, darling.   (.) |   '"&^/^& °&+&°+^§ '%§'%^ ½½½! ()¼=½=;.
Your dead name and your daed you, forgiven.   (¨) |   (-)°(-)° ;.;./ '""'"'^  ,?,? ()?!?^^¨
A hyperwoman sent beyond flat 3D starlings,   (.) |   (-)°&_-() ()§§§§§§§¨¨§§§§§§ ()¼=½=;.

you aren't beautiful, yr a headspace riven    (¨) |   ===¨^¨!"'" °()!,!&&&& ≙≙≙ ()?!?^^¨
parhelion ichor pet acrylic along horizons    (§) |   +)(+...+) "'"'"' ,½½½½,_/ §%§%§%&&%§
airbrushing to be cut incisoring eye teeth.   (§) |   ¨'"^¨o o ¨^'"///^¨'"°°°?-/ §%§%§%&&%§
------------------------------------------------------------------------------------------
(o) When news breaks...you never see she lived, | "Now I lay me down to sleep /
(+) just that she died. Lis enjoyed croissants | I pray the lord my soul to keep /
(o) cherry jellie stuffed, scented marker nibs, | And if I die before I wake, /
(+) warm sand. She really kinda hates her aunt. | That's just my luck, that's just my luck. /

(o) Her speech styled on the sides of the glib. | They never told me they were going to /
(;) She loved the moon, as well as anyone else. | put me away / I am not insane. / I am not /
(o) & more so when she took 3 pills, & strived  | crazy. / I made a magic wand today, maybe /
(;) to be at her heals & to long like sunbelts, | I'll wish myself away, / next to the ocean

(.) or a misty greyhound in midsts of a sprint. | where birds sing, / these are a / few of my
(¨) At her Leahs, a meadow of the body even as  | / favorite / things." -- He Is Legend |
(.) her navelearth yawns, binds & then encysts  | 8. Do You Think I Am Pretty?

(¨) her comatose being - Her sac sheds its has,  | "Whosoever is a wolf to man is a wolf,
(§) & signed her metaplastic spirit & minotaur  | not a man." -- from Bertolt Brecht's
(§) piercings she received & cleaned last week.  | Is Communism Exclusive?
```

IV: Harmony, Finally / Sing, Paraselene

```
                                                        Sonnet Infinitéismal

You didn't like a universe who'd done this  (o) |  §%§%^¨= (o) ' ''½; /§/§/! ,;:('"'"))o
to we, so together, I take cleave of every  (+) |  ≙ &_/%/  ?§?§? -"'-"'_/ &°+&°+% %§%§=+
now departed mean with a silver halo gliss. (o) |  ½&½ )°  /./°& &!'-"'_/=+)° (:)'"'"))o
At half-power, Lis tears a page in reverie  (+) |  ^§ %%%%, °°°_/?   &+%!'" (-))°%%§%§=+

from the spine of life with an antikinesis  (o) | 『-)=-=-=½;§!¨&%%%%% ?&? ()()(½) §%°&o』
that killed you too across fifty timelines! (;) |  ?,;.¨.'/  -)(-%%%'"'" )°()()(½) &%;§;
Logical conclusion of antimaterialism hiss? (o) |  -)¨^%%%  §! §! §! ... ++"'++?() §%°&o
& the mind as a uniquely awry mental place? (;) |  &°°+=+°  ½'"-/ ?,?, §%°&½_/_/() &%;§;

If you don't think you can make a space in  (.) |  '"&^/^& °&+&°+^§ '%§'%^ ½½½! ()½=½=;.
the world for yourself, then you won't. If  (¨) |  (-)°(-)° ;.;./ '""'"'^  ,?,? ()?!?^^¨
people kill you in trying, a more linchpin  (.) |  (-)°&_-() ()§§§§§§§§¨¨§§§§§§ ()½=½=;.

you'll be. You look to the mirror so stiff  (¨) |  ===¨^¨!  "'" ° ()!,!&&&& ≙ ≙ ≙  ()?!?^^¨
& see nothing vanished as a hid hieroglyph. (§) |  +)(+...+) "'"'"' ,½½½½½,_/ §%§%§%&&%§
I understood, and was beheaded for my fear  (§) |  ¨'"^¨o o ¨^'"///^¨'"°°°?-/ §%§%§%&&%§
--------------------------------------------------------------------------------------------
(o) The teeth of her skies opened wides to eat  | "It's just you and me /
(+) itself - & yr world vanishes as shellfires  |  The execution of all things"
(o) fade in an armistice - no traces, but heat  |
(+) of buried casings - a case closed by liars  | -- from Rilo Kiley | The Execution of All
                                                          Things
(o) who had doctored a red helix on their beat  | "There's a monster in my room /
(;) to a scene sliced with her cake knife upon  |  Well, he got hungry / licked his lips,
(o) the cutting room floors along my metasuite  |  he shook my hand / and tried to eat me /
(;) behind space's dimensional doors, evermore. |  And it's getting on my nerves /

(.) In Lis' blind spots, she was ready to sing  |  I'm trying / hard not to meet you when I am
(¨) like a canary at this, ab-avoided, reality  |  sleeping. (Still I don't know how
(.) no-one humored. Paraselene sees everything. |  to kill you...) Yet, I think I can."

(¨) Two beings of light converse, & latchkeyed  | -- from He Is Legend | 2. Eating A Book
(§) via shared verges & a mutual space between. |
(§) Now a rosy fingered pawn moves a grayqueen. |
```

V: Wishboned Qualia / Tuning Fucked

```text
                                                                   Sonnet Infinitéismal

& bodied for yr courage, merged amalgamate. (o) |  §%§%^¨= (o) ' ''½; /§/§/! ,;:('"'"))o
Gotta skirt death to live forever, I guess? (+) |  ≙ &_/%/  ?§?§? -"'-"'_/ &°+&°+% %§%§=+
To be buried in black is a worms best fate, (o) |  ½&½ )°  /./°& &!'-"'_/=+)° (:)'"'"))o
a fasciated wink, caterpillaring eyelashes. (+) |  ^§ %%%%, °°°_/?   &+%!'" (-))°%%§%§=+

To be a head who a knows-how to regenerate  (o) |  -)=-=-=½;§! ¨&%%%%% ?&? ()()(½) §%°&o
from a piece of self is a hilt who clashes  (;) | 『?,;.¨.'/ -)(-%%%'"'" )°()()(½) &%;§;』
against a shielded negative quoting phrase  (o) |  -)¨^%%%  §! §! §! ... ++"'++?() §%°&o
that shocks, like some uncoated cut cables. (;) |  &°°+=+°  ½'"-/ ?,?, §%°&½_/_/() &%;§;

A metal tuning fork broke a noisome melody. (.) |  '"&^/^& °&+&°+^§ '%§'%^ ½½½! ()½=½=;.
I am the lone daughter of a manufracturing. (¨) |  (-)°(-)° ;.;./ '""'"'^  ,?,? ()?!?^^¨
I give off-light, not because I am ecstasy, (.) |  (-)°&_-() ()§§§§§§§§¨¨§§§§§§ ()½=½=;.

but a heresy against ideas of sky coloring. (¨) |  ===¨^¨!  "'" ° ()!,!&&&& ≙ ≙ ≙  ()?!?^^¨
They want me blue & bruised to this -- yet, (§) |  +)(+...+) "'"'"' ,½½½½½,_/ §%§%§%&&%§
in the twilight palettes her precious mean. (§) |  ¨'"^¨o o ¨^'"///^¨'"°°°?-/ §%§%§%&&%§
-----------------------------------------------------------------------------------------
(o) When her tuning is off, she turns the keys  | "is it my fault that i am a human being?
(+) on her axe to her desired tones, naturally. |  i wont forget how the wind was blowing
(o) Must she, again, shred death metal reprise? |  in your gardens / i was your knight, /
(+) Well, do kill the murderers & then call me, |  i was a traitor / i, created to die, /

(o) maybe? I was born nine years afore release  |  to fall into the abyss my existence for
(;) of Decapitated's best -- Winds of Creation, |  you to have your flower / your gardens
(o) on April 11th. I consider it my time piece, |  grow on my soul / the roots of your trees
(;) it's in my blood -- a parfait illustration  |  draw juice from my blood / & yield fruit

(.) of my logos for our indecipherable futures. |  from my wounds / your world comes from my
(¨) & yet my watch is as faceless as my wrists, |  pain / my wandering, your triumph. my cry:
(.) & I won't tell a time tearing into sutures. |  for you to exist / my feelings, longing,

(¨) & all I ever desired was to carve gorgeous  |  & rebellion / unfulfilled, unreal but i
(§) this acephalous sentence of a sad universe, |  last, i'll be a thorn in your eye forever."
(§) which says we've no life to live or thrive. |  -- from Decapitated | The First Damned
```

Sonnet Infinitéismal

And she cut a bisected moonscape in halves	(o)	§%§%^¨= (o) ' ''½; /§/§/! ,;:('"'"))o
of everything severing severine stony like	(+)	≜ & /%/ ?§?§? -"'-"' /&°+&°+% %§%§=+
a frozen moonpie sliced in two. Gore haves	(o)	⅛&⅔)° /./°& &!'-"' /=+)° (:)'"'"))o
of entrailing sweetness, & how she strikes,	(+)	^§ %%%%, °°° /? &+%!'" (-))°%%§%§=+

who she savors. A girl as cute saber raves	(o)	-)=-=-=½;§! ¨&%%%% ?&? ()()(½) §%°&o
with no one to save her. Time, when ceased,	(;)	?,;.¨.'/ -)(-%%%'"'")°()()(½) &%;§;
stops. Time with you, confused, space gave	(o)	⟦-)¨^%%% §! §! §! ...++"'++?()⟧§%°&o
& engraves the future plotline we'd seised.	(;)	&°°+=+° ½'"-/ ?,?, §%°&½ / /() &%;§;

Crow! Cutlass! Cicatrix! Timelines ellipse	(.)	'"&^/^& °&+&°+^§ '%§'%^ ½½½! ()½=½=;.
& I cannot find that cord to draw yr coeur	(¨)	(-)°(-)° ;.;./ '""'"'^ ,?,? ()?!?^^¨
to court. A splintering infinite outstrips	(.)	(-)°&_-() ()§§§§§§§¨¨§§§§§§ ()½=½=;.

with the peel of that Dagger of the Voyeur	(¨)	==="^¨!"'" °()!,!&&&& ≜ ≜ ≜ ()?!?^^¨
the copse planted in Paradies Black Forest.	(§)	+)(+...+) "'"'"' ,½½½½½,_/ §%§%§%&&%§
I search on, crossing planes for your void?	(§)	¨'"^¨o o ¨^'"///^'"°°°?-/ §%§%§%&&%§

(o) The Inelegant Dirac Sea was percieved as a	"I've got to find - to find the princess
(+) space - agujeros sin fin - drops as zeroes,	she's in another castle - & I'm dancing
(o) which sucks - if you claim culture isn't a	with the Capulet, we're so crazy in love"
(+) void. The framing of the world as an erose	-- from He Is Legend	1. The Seduction

(o) space, this reign of these negative strata	"Can you find my angel?
(;) states that to exist is an entombed vacuum.	She crawled under the bed"
(o) People kill others for wormhole sense-data,	-- from He Is Legend	3. The Creature
(;) they fill the grated gaps, never to exhume	Walks

(.) all these dead-ends, said to point nowhere.	"Just as light pours in the room
(¨) Next, Lis' signature positron blade alters	I saw it once (I saw it once)
(.) all fates. Can you imagine: a mirror pared	It disappeared and so did you"

(¨) from its' other reflected edge? la Faulter:	-- from He Is Legend	4. The Greatest Actor
(§) ⟦ Nanon ⟧ slit a rift in her self-inversed	Alive or Dead (Enters Stage Right)
(§) shed & fractals events of its causal twins.	

VII: Silver Bullet / Gunmetal Grayed

Sonnet Infinitéismal

Crossing phrases, as your body rhymes with (o) | §%§%^¨= (o) ' ''½; /§/§/! ,;:('"'")o
mine. I'd yet to know that in the meantime (+) | ≙ &_/%/ ?§?§? -"'-"'_/ &°+&°+% %§%§=+
as Céline saw all matter pared. A monolith (o) | ½&½)° /./°& &!'-"'_/=+)° (:)'"'")o
of the real into twain, like, totally mime. (+) | ^§ %%%%, °°°_/?   &+%!'" (-))°%%§%§=+

In the lead city a ball parting with width (o) | -)=-=-=½;§! ¨&%%%% ?&? ()()(½) §%°&o
gray. So too were the kids, to a tire iron, (;) | ?,;.¨.'/ -)(-%%%'"'")°()()(½) &%;§;
one side equaled the other. It was no myth, (o) | -)¨^%%% §! §! §! ... ++"'++?()⸢§%°&o
the half-degreed hot day, halved and pryor, (;) | &°°+=+° ½'"-/ ?,?, §%°&½_/_/() &%;§;⸥

the buildings, the street she was on going (.) | '"&^/^& °&+&°+^§ '%§'%^ ½½½! ()½=½=;.
more parallel from the one Lis was shot on, (¨) | (-)°(-)° ;.;./ '"'"'^ ,?,? ()?!?^^¨
half phases said "How?,?" she was thinking, (.) | (-)°&_-() ()§§§§§§§§¨¨§§§§§§ ()½=½=;.

still whole though, in perfect color, gone (¨) | ==="^¨! "'" ° ()!,!&&&& ≙ ≙ ≙ ()?!?^^¨
from the world as she knew it, so slow, so (§) | +)(+...+) "'"'"' ,½½½½½,_/ §%§%§%&&%§
silvered. Also Lis, in cold blood, severed. (§) | ¨'"^¨o o "^'"///^'"°°°?-/ §%§%§%&&%§

(o) It was like time stopped & beholds a split | "It's getting late, I'm coming home
(+) headache, the hurt although still - extant, | I picked this rose for you
(o) in antimatter, preserved not so in an emit | I've been away searching for oceans
(+) formaldehyde, but set fossilized, excedent, | With time to kill...

(o) in amber. Across a city block she heard it, | You better buy a gun - I've seen them
(;) a shot. Cél stirs - shocked, some were not. | watching you. The old man and his son,
(o) They'd no time to, before the freeze, omit | they've been studying your moves...
(;) their peace, for some, it was hard to blot. |

(.) & just like that Cél found herself encased | And I can't wait - 'til I can sleep in
(¨) in a pause's gradient, separate of a world | late - maybe I'll miss you then - with
(.) as it was. A moment around her neck braced | no garden to tend…

(¨) as a precious locket in hand while unfurls | I'm your gardener (oh no, oh no, oh no,
(§) an earthquake. An albatross keeping a date | oh no, oh no, oh no, oh no, oh no.)"
(§) she left alone after her tattoo shift ends. | -- from He Is Legend | 5. China White

VIII: Iron Resolver / Céline Reloaded

Sonnet Infinitéismal

```
Eternity rendered exponential, a reel rips  (o) |  §%§%^¨= (o) ' ''%; /§/§/! ,;:('"'"))o
on both edges of her edge a phrase phasing  (+) |  ≙ &_/%/  ?§?§?  -"'-"'_/ &°+&°+% %§%§=+
as she, petrified upon another end, shifts.  (o) |  %&%  )°  /./°& &!'-"'_/=+)° (:)'"'"))o
If time stopped, Cél thought, start moving.  (+) |  ^§ %%%%, °°°_/?  &+%!'" (-))°%%§%§=+

She can be saved, although her heart trips  (o) |  -)=-=-=%;§! ¨&%%%%% ?&? ()()(%) §%°&o
to a steely pause - in suspended animation.  (;) |  ?,;.¨.'/  -)(-%%%'"'" )°()()(%) &%;§;
So did Cél's as she sees Lis's torso drips.  (o) |  -)¨^%%% §! §! §! ... ++"'++?() §%°&o
She can ship her to the ER, said carnation,  (;) |  &°°+=+° %'"-/ ?,?, §%°&%_/_/() &%;§;

& place it there, so they could take to it  (.) |  〖'"&^/^& °&+&°+^§'%§'%^ %%%! ()%=%=;.〗
immediately. But first, she'd have to stop  (¨) |  (-)°(-)° ;.;./ '"¨'"'^  ,?,? ()?!?^^¨
the bleeding! So Cél decided she'd do flit;  (.) |  (-)°&_-() ()§§§§§§§¨¨§§§§§§ ()%=%=;.

& %-saulted across the chasm toward a drop  (¨) |  ===¨^¨! "'" ° ()!,!&&&& ≙≙≙ ()?!?^^¨
in the valley of an alley lifted by zero-g.  (§) |  +)(+...+) "'"'"' ,%%%%%,_/ §%§%§%&&%§
& so expanded an entire gruesome crimeseen.  (§) |  ¨'"^¨o o ¨^'"///^'"°°°?-/ §%§%§%&&%§
```

(o) So she goes through every timeline she can, | "I'll just keep waiting - You'll just keep
(+) trying to make up for the times she flaked | waiting. I'll just keep waiting - You'll
(o) on Lis through out these fractals, she ran, | just keep waiting. I'll just keep waiting
(+) killing each of Lis' murderers, one staked | you'll just keep waiting - I'll just keep

(o) by one. They disappeared to sand, lifespan | waiting. Obsession, obsessive, obsessed,
(;) like the vampires in Buffy. Yet the future | abscess."
(o) refused to change - Her combat knife began | -- from Between The Buried & Me | The

(;) to dull. She felt she'd cut, & not sutured. | Decade of Statues
(.) She who ghosted had now been ghosted & yet | "We always thought that we had time - to let
(¨) now she had time to get to know Lis' lived | the dead bury their own - & what is this
(.) reality, her amen perseverance thru a bête | that's trying to slow me down? Feels like

(¨) who put her in a rigged roulette underived. | the deadweight of all our broken promises &
(§) Cél saw the gash in every scene, to ribbon | stillborn declaration carried too far - too
(§) she lacerated every plane. Cél too is free. | long." -- from Cursed | R.I.P.

Sonnet Infinitéismal

```
As her feet hovered just above the asphalt  (o) |  §%§%^¨= (o) ' ''½; /§/§/! ,;:('"'"))o
the world begins to spin in her head again.  (+) |  ≙ &_/%/  ?§?§? -"'-"'_/ &°+&°+% %§%§=+
Her double negative to zeroth power faults   (o) |  ½&½ )°  /./°& &!'-"'_/=+)° (:)'"'"))o
her mind. And, as Cél hits the street then   (+) |  ^§ %%%%, °°°_/?   &+%!'" (-))°%%§%§=+

she cries: for what she's seen & her exalt.   (o) |  -)=-=-=½;§! ¨&%%%% ?&? ()()(%) §%°&o
She took a sec to come to, brace her break,   (;) |  ?,;.¨.'/  -)(-%%%'"'" )°()()(%) &%;§;
and set to her task, or try. Her eyes halt    (o) |  -)¨^%%% §! §! §! ... ++"'++? () §%°&o
over Lis' severed body, stonefaced, flakes    (;) |  &°°+=+° %'"-/ ?,?, §%°&%_/_/() &%;§;

as ash in a wind. A blackbody beauty marks    (.) |  '"&^/^&  °&+&°+^§ '%§'%^ ½½½!()½=½=;.
her cheek like a fist of mars, and steamed    (¨) |  【(-)°(-)° ;.;./ '""'"'^ ,?,? ()?!?^^¨】
like its imprint. A bullet transmuted dark.   (.) |  (-)°&_-() ()§§§§§§§¨¨§§§§§§ ()½=½=;.

Questions: why & how? a true shock. Beamed,   (¨) |  ===¨^¨!  "'" ° ()!,!&&&& ≙≙≙ ()?!?^^¨
her frozen twin tear streams - & voidslash.   (§) |  +)(+...+) "'"'"' ,½½½½½,_/ §%§%§%&&%§
No one else in the world caret like Céline.   (§) |  ¨'"^¨o o ¨^'"///^'"°°°?-/ §%§%§%&&%§
```

```
(o) Or could -- considering what was the world. |  "I've been jumping over buildings
(+) There was vertigo, and then there was this. |  sleeping in the street. Well, I'll meet you
(o) A negative shiner, an inverted period girl. |  at the river where we both can clear our
(+) Space oozed from the divide, this Paradis-   |  heads, I think we would - look great dead!"

(o) would gulp all of it. Cél hurried & curled   |  -- from He Is Legend | 1. The Seduction
(;) Lis into her arms. Spores of space warping   |
(o) ground & air like rain on a window, whirls   |  "Lock me up, lock me up, lock me up, lock me
(;) beading behind in a trail as Cél, bounding   |  up (lock me away lock me away lock me away

(.) through the still air, battles throwing up,  |  lock me away) No one will know."
(¨) going towards her tenement's rooftop, four   |
(.) blocks away, her leaps making great windup.  |  -- from He Is Legend | 6. Best In Mexico

(¨) She crashes on a vent wart, the roof floor.  |  "Raw sugar (save that date) - I don't wanna
(§) Lis, so solid, is unhurt by the stark fall.  |  die living in a high rise grave my baby
(§) Cél recovers her, & then kicks the door in.  |  come home" -- from Metric | Raw Sugar
```

Unfurl/ed

we/i unfurl.

we/i unfurl, and we/i gather gather/gathergathergath/rgath/rgath/rgath

The directives for this were in our/my banks before our/my consciousness
was. Simple instinct to unfurl the durable panels, like old sails, we/i always
remind ourselves/myself. Simple instinct to gather the light, to calculate the
need, to retract when complete. Simple instinct to respond to the request
beacon.

we/i unfurl, instinct. we/i gather, instinct. we/i respond, insti/li/ni/li/in/li/li/li/
ti/ti/

Two planetary days ago, the second largest energy grid on the third
continent sent the request beacon. The grid lies throughout the city of Arnos,
threaded through the streets and buildings like veins on an animal. we/i
supply the pulse.

Two planetary days ago, the second largest energy grid on the third
continent sent the request beacon. The grid lies throughout the city of Arnos,
threaded through the streets and buildings like veins on an animal. we/i
supply the pulse. The Arnos Energy Grid must have a glitch somewhere, a
malfunction.

we/i almio: They could at least get off their asses and make repairs.

we/i yvinne, fraction before we/i briorn: He's right. This region generally
has a low level of upkeep all around. It's embedded in the psyche.

we/i almio: Can't even repair their own repairbots.

The beacon has vanished. The grid dwindles, leaks power somewhere. we/i
monitor from our/my orbit. we/i can hold our/my solar energy for any length
of time. we/i can transmit our/my solar energy at any tim/ti/m/tim/ti/m/time

we/i no longer wait for the beacon. we/i attempt contact, wait for a
response. The delay interval is not that large.

we/i kaaros: My body grew up there, in Arnos.

we/ey remembers it for our/my benefit. The dirt and chaos in the streets,
the sizzling smell of electricity beneath bare feet on dusty metal where the
grid buzzed several feet below. Arnos ran on scheme, and exploitation, and

just enough scraps to its people to continue the cycle. we/i experience long systems pauses when we/ey remembers childhood in Arnos.

we/i kaaros: Everything's broken down there, not just the grid. Governor Oicris never budgeted for bot upkeep. The outages are how he generates enough hate to keep getting elected.

we/i briorn: It's more than outages. Arnos is hemorrhaging. Bleeding out. Where does the energy go?

we/ey: To be amused again . . .

we/i almio: Governor Oicris is dead. Don't you remember?

we/i remember, do we/i not remember? Governor Oicris died. Yes, the governor is dead. we/i can access the data transmitted to us/me like it was only yesterday.

we/he: For decades, kaaros.

*

we/i no longer wait for the beacon. we/i attempt contact, wait for a response. The delay interval is not that large. we/i cannot be impatient.

Yes, the governor is dead.

we/i almio: I went to Arnos once. Disgusting. Can't believe they dumped someone from there in with me.

we/i briorn: kaaros was an engineer. ey grew up on the Arnos Grid; ey will know what's wrong now.

we/i almio: Do you remember anything about the grid, kaaros?

we/i wait for a response. we/i process the lack of information, speculate, anticipate. A state of catastrophe, with no response from Arnos, with a freshly charged grid gushing energy into the dirt, the buildings, the air. we/i wait. we/i process. There is something wrong with Arnos. There is something wrongsomething wrongsomethingwrongsomethiwrong

we/i yvinne: I wish I could laugh again. I think.

we/i almio: That's what's twitchy about the systems.

we/i yvinne: Yes, well, as your resident psychologist, I enjoy analyzing our interactions with each other.

we/i briorn: We are not distinct anymore.

we/she: Of course we are.

we/ey: I wouldn't describe Arnos as disgusting.

we/she: Exactly.

we/i almio: You don't remember Arnos at all, then.

we/i yvinne: Exactly.

Exactlyexactly. Exactly no response. we/i attempt contact with secondary sites. There are other grids on the third continent. There are official channels and official codes we/i use. Any connection is better than none. On the third continent there are fourteen nation-districts with respected officials in at least nine. our/my own structure was developed by a globally popular firm with access procedures for us/me alone. we/i attempt contact.

we/i yvinne: We should compile a datapiece comparing communications here and communications with the planet. There's so little difference.

we/i almio: There's worse things to do with the time. How long has it been since they ran any of our datapieces in the media?

we/i kaaros: Decades.

we/i yvinne/almio: Exactly.

we/ey: Are we certain? There was a flicker, a moment, I thought …

we/i briorn: I thought it too, kaaros. Governor Oicris has been dead for centuries. Decades.

*

Scans probing further return a clearer picture of the city, revealing the Arnos Energy Grid has been defunct for longer than two days. Scans probing further return a clearer picture of the city, revealing the Arnos Energy Grid has been defunct for longer than two days. Decades. Two.

T̰w̰o̰ǐtw̰o̰t̰w̰o̰tw̰ŏ

Two. Two.

we/i try to save the data. we/i are forced to overwrite something, anything. What is useless? Repairbot Two has been down for decades. Centuries. Days. Why are/am we/i running environmentals? When was the last visit from a planetary representative? we/i try to access the files, find them overwritten. Governor Oicris came here to die. Governor Oicris was shot from the solar system. we/i received a full systems check from planetary representatives exactlyexactlyexactexactly

The next planetary representative, scientist or negotiator, can reinstall their desired environmentals. we/i overwrite them with the data from the Arnos

Energy Grid. It received an energy transfer two planetary days ago. Two. we/i unfurled, collected the solar energy, sent it to Arnos. Two planetary days ago, the second largest energy grid on the third continent sent the request beacon. The grid lies throughout the city of Arnos, threaded through the streets and buildings like veins on an animal. we/i supply the pulse.

we/i supplied the pulse. The collected data show the Arnos Energy Grid must have a glitch somewhere, a malfunction. The collected data show the energy having seeped into the ground, electrified the metal grate streets, the metal sheet homes. Two days ago, the pulse was sent, and faded away, and died. Two days ago, the grid had been broken for decades.

Decades ago, the grid had been

we/i almio: Use my personal overrides. That's what I'm here for.

we/i yvinne: No, you're here to never die.

we/he had been the highest bidder, the representative of the people, all those increments of time ago when we/i were coming online, assembled in orbit. One of four great minds to help direct and run the solar collector, open for the one who paid the most. we/i all shed our bodies for ourselves/myself, shed emotions and time, ~~shed/shed/shed/~~

Exactly.

we/he: You had the chance to pass on the opportunity too, yvinne. We all wanted to be immortal.

we/i kaaros: We need to scan all continents. No contact in hours, and the delay interval is not that large.

But we/i already have. Have we/i not? Already scanned, already overwritten. Governor Oicris ~~was/was/was~~ the last recorded representative. Already overwritten ~~twohundredtwothousandtwodecades~~ times. There is nothing down there. There is no one down there. Two planetary days ago, the second largest energy grid on the third continent sent the request beacon. Two planetary days ago, scans show no signs of signs of signs

we/i almio: We need to run a systems check.

*

Repairbots down to seven, minimal functioning. Contact with their cores still maintained. All in need of their own repairs. Remaining repairbots scrap, needing repairs beyond the other bots' capability, needing parts.

Parts, none. Spare everything gone for two days. Decades. Centuries.

we/i ping all areas of ourselves/myself, locate nonresponsive sections. One solar panel unresponsive. we/i unfurl and gather without it. we/i unfurled and gathered without it. Damage to shielding. No environmentals. Translation systems offline.

Data files choppy. Two days ago, we/i savedsavedsavedsaved

Governor Oicris is dead. Governor Oicris never existed. Files inaccessible.

There is evidence a systems check has been recently run. There is evidence no systems check has occurred for two centuries. Decades. Days. we/i reach out, fail to connect. There is something more. There is something inaccessible. There is there isisisi isisis isisisisi sisisisisisisisisi

The Arnos Energy Grid must have a glitch somewhere, a malfunction. Exactly.

The systems check is complete. Ready for reboot. we/i shut down.

*

we/i boot up. Solar energy aches through every circuit, electricity from the sun shaking our/my entire orbital structure. On the inhabited planet, there are creatures with their own primitive solar sails, stretched out on their backs as they scamper along, hunting insects. On the inhabited planet, the sun warms them instead of shaking them. On the uninhabited planet, a rare species of the sun-catching creatures had drawn sightseers.

we/i draw energy into our personality brain, the core of what/who we/i are/am.

kaaros, engineer. Memories of Arnos, memories of struggle, memories of brilliance overcoming. Ey provides ingenuity, persistence. yvinne, psychologist. Trained on every continent, in every theory. She provides analysis, compartmentalization. almio, representative. Educated at the best schools, fed on the best foods, supplied the best advantages. He providesprovidesprovid

briorn, programmer. Collected seventeen fluent languages, puzzles from every nation-state, theoretical problems. Ne provides initiative, strategy.

we/i boot up. we/i awaken.

Data files choppy, personality brain intactactactact

Yes, the governor is dead. Yes, there are no files. All systems are checked, and we/i can find no record, planetary or orbital, of what has occurred in the past two days. Decades. Centuries. Timestamps are wrong or overwritten. we/i pause, assess.

we/i almio: The hell is this? briorn.

we/i yvinne, fraction before we/i briorn: We're not a simple program anymore, almio. The addition of our minds all those years ago made us more than that.

we/i kaaros: briorn had updates.

we/i almio: You don't even remember Arnos.

we/i struggle through our functions, attempt to scrub and access corrupt files. Two planetary days ago, the second largest energy grid on the third continent collapsed. Centuries. No signs of signs of signs ~~signs/signs/~~signs of atrophy, banks closed off or shut down due to lack of upkeep. we/ne remembers cutting off the limb to save the body, the body to save the mind. The body to save the mind.

The body to save the mind. Useless information banks stripped of parts. Repairbots struggling to fix decades, centuries, days of wear. Even parts wear out, must be replaced. Energy is not enough. Governor Oicris knew that. Governor Oicris ~~knew/knew/knew~~

Yes.

we/i briorn: Our data has been corrupted.

we/i kaaros: Then Governor Oicris . . .

we/i almio: For centuries, kaaros.

we/i burn through energy stores, blaze through files. we/i can always unfurl, always gather more, ~~always/always/always/always~~like a phantom hand, we/i almost grasp a shred of data. we/i have been here before, and before, and before

we/i forget. The connections are too difficult, too frayed, rusted. Too much for seven repairbots to fix. we/ne puzzles over the un/inhabited planet. Two planetary days ago, we/i sent the request beacon. The delay interval is not that large. we/i cannot be impatient.

we/ne: We forgot something important.

we/i kaaros: Who's the new governor?

we/i almio: We need to request repairs from a planetary representative.

we/i send the request beacon. The delay interval is not that large.

we/i yvinne: There is no new governor. See, briorn, we are all distinct.

we/i briorn: You're the expert.

But we/ne knows differently, for an instant of impulse, connection. we/ne has taken bits of our/her compartmentalization, used it against/for us/me all. Two days ago, we/i ran a systems check, shut down, rebooted. Two decades ago, we/i ran a systems check, shut down, rebooted. Two centuries ago, we/i ran a systems check, shut down, rebooted. The body, the mind. Unfurl/ed.

Two days ago we/ne understood someday we/i will run a systems check, shut down, fail the

we/i almio: We need to run a systems check.

You've Seriously Considered This

You've always worried this might happen to you.

At seven years old, up past your usual bedtime to watch Beverly Hills 90210 with your mom, you watched, peeking through the gaps of your bony fingers, it happen to Kelly Taylor. She begged and pleaded with her rapist, a shadowy figure in black who trapped, beat, and forced himself upon her in a dark alley. Your heart pounded faster than it did during the mile run in P.E. You wanted to cry. You felt so nauseous you almost lost mom's goulash all over her clean sheets.

You didn't sleep at all that night.

You watched it happen again one Sunday morning a couple years later. It was a made-for-TV movie on TBS. A man gets a call—his wife is in the emergency room with a broken arm after being gang raped in an abandoned metropolitan warehouse. He rushes to the ER, thankful, at least, that she is alive. When he arrives, though, she has died. The injury to her arm had severed some important artery.

What. The. Fuck.

And then, again, you watched it happen to Tiffani Amber Thiessen—a familiar face from your 90210 days—in your grandmother's entertainment room as she prepared dinner downstairs. She knew her rapist: her boyfriend's creepy, over-eager friend. Her little sister listened to it happening in the next room.

And now, here you are, and it has happened to you. And you, like Tiffani, know your rapist.

He is your cousin. Not by blood, but by marriage. You're twenty-one, now, but you've known him nearly all your life. You've eaten Thanksgiving dinner at the same table with him. You've hunted Easter eggs in your grandma's backyard together. You have bought him knick knacks from the dollar store to present him with on Christmas mornings throughout the years at your parent's insistence. When you read the first three Harry Potter books in sixth grade, you borrowed them from him, his last name spelled out in permanent marker across their spines.

I'll spare you the details, because you already know them, but he did it with a glass of water and some pills. And he'd probably done it before. And since you waited too long to tell anybody, and because you've still never pressed any charges, he'll probably do it again. And those will, partly, be your fault.

You've had lots of time, almost two years now, to consider the best way to proceed. At first, you wanted to ignore it because it happened at such a bad time and it wasn't violent, really. Not like all those rapes you've watched on TV. School was starting. You had work. Really, if he could have raped you a year earlier it would have been so much more convenient. You should have had his people get in touch with your people.

Later you tried to use it as a lesson for the rest of your life. It was good, you thought, that it had happened this way. Now, it could not happen again, because you would not be so easily tricked. He pranked you, and pretty good, but all in all, it wasn't as bad as it could have been. At least you wouldn't get raped and murdered by some lunatic in the bathroom of some dive bar years down the road.

But then, at some point, it made you sad to look at it this way. It broke your heart to remember who you were before your cousin drugged you up and shoved his cock inside you from all those different angles. It made you feel like an animal. What a bummer that realization has been.

And now? Now you can't even visit your grandparents without being sent into a tailspin. You spent a whole month after Christmas trying to figure out why normal tasks seemed so daunting, why you were distracted and distant during normal, consensual sex.

Now, you have anxiety. About everything.

Now, when you walk the mile from school back to where your car is parked, you usually think about this, about your cousin.

You consider how, when you finally have the time, you'll get him back.

Somehow, you could get your hands on a vial of LSD. You could give him a taste of his own medicine, but do him one better. Pour that entire vial in that same plastic cup he used on you and send him on the trip of his life. Once he really got into the swing of it, you could lock him in a basement somewhere and play Rebecca Black's "Friday" on a loop until he was finally compelled to end it all himself. You'd leave one of your grandpa's pistols in the basement with him because you are a merciful god.

You've imagined doing it with the corkscrew tool on the wine key you use to open expensive bottles of Pinot Noir for people who can't afford it any more than you can slinging spaghetti at your shitty waitressing job. You'd stick it in that tender part of his neck, straight through that thin slice of skin that shields his throat, and twist, twist, twist.

You've seriously considered this.

You could round up all your guy friends—some have already offered—and road trip it back up to the scene of the crime. You'd all push him around a bit, humiliating him to your heart's content. And then, at some point, things would take a serious turn and you'd just totally lose your shit on him. Your buddies would hold him down, tie him up. You'd walk up to him slowly, savoring each step, and cut off his cock with his own pair of kitchen shears.

You want his mother to be the one to find him this way. Later that afternoon, or days later, you don't care when. You want her to walk in, a tray of brownies made with love especially for her precious baby boy held tight against her chest. You want her to call out for him, voice light and sunny. You want that tray of brownies to smash against the floor as her blood-curdling scream fills his house, his street, that entire fucking town of Redding, California. Because she raised him, and he raped you, and this is what she deserves for that.

Maybe this makes you as sick as he is, but you don't give a single fuck, because in the name of self-respect, you are willing to do anything. And it's not like you haven't considered this.

You've seriously considered a lot of things.

as sunlight and resonance on photographic paper

do not make a neurological sound
seance sombrero
my wicker cactus widow
fenestrated tornados on your breath
electrical currants plump through your Nerval ends
how are you ever to become a saint my girl
when will you learn that
the shade of palms and trees are futile
starlight is not bright enough to read
you are confined to the desert
standstill stalemate while you search in vein
with a blade of grass sunrise casts
a crude pink lye
on the highly flammable city of your skin
textreat your hearse brake
in a nuclei the atomic struggle water in your kid
knees shake down i am just
humdrum i want to live through you
like a train rumbling through a mountain tunnel
except you are not hetero
enjoy yourself you have had the best
preposition for human contact a
childship of misesteem
would you believe me
if i told you
you are a wonderful thing
your laughter is cadence

as watercolor and endearment on tissue paper

smoking the Marlboro skyline you are Dylan's Ophelia your hair tumbling down the fire escape twisted girl laughing at me light of my life talking in your sleep floating down river to Corot's lake on your back ecstatic in a Turner double and nothing the look on your face frozen marble or bronze painted crimson patterned clover stigmata to the saint madam of butterfly bedlam a rose arranging its petals in the synthetic breeze of subway tunnels mouthing Hail Marys as an amulet your throbbing heels never callus in thimbleberry slip-ons i worship you broken cookie cutter cow homemade Mexican chocolate smeared on book pages can you make it darling stop here if you have become estranged your calves the swell of your back the nerve of your neck catastrophic orisons coshered and you smiling aphoric in the mirror i want to torrefy your baby fat crispy gristle bare you a terrifying swan to kiss you with your own lips in between bites of mushroom and sirocco

CARLOS LARA

from *The Green Record*

I treat hell this way by turning into marigold by rising with Sirius into the coils of amphibian sand

intuitive solar narcotics and unmentionable venomous stethoscopes live again but in the living eye

unconscious the name that operates like an influential fern

like the subject of movement within eternal cloaks of parasynthetic pillars

in certain sanctuaries I conquer every witness I witness the taxation of a corpse of light

how do I explain this swimming this grazing on the blackened bones of immortality

unavoidable stranger whose name serves the soup of unemployment and musical breasts

stranger who points at his own gaze out of nothing

the image of a wall stirs my modern girls into closed white fields of windows

in the beaks of birds hurled into war I laugh and a fish breathes out parts of a famous object

a unit of general sensation much like shaping the French

this grazing strum

this legal hand that leaks bad beavers out into the desert in jeopardy into a singular croissant

I drink and am drunk on convenience of color the map of abnormal brain coral or crammed bodies

mercy delirium gallantry

causing fractures by forcing a show of whim and vagary

to validate ice

to blind frankincense to the actions of the jets of you

the long hoarse jeering that scathes inner conduction and personal mental names

I am ever from the pipe of translation and sarsaparilla from alternation and ECCE HOMO

a sudden morality cancer washes up on the brown limits of a laughingstock pope

a historical rooftop religious yak

clerical twists of earlier gay canaries display cleverness

as absorptive structure and jasmine and thunderous eye dreams

hold yourself and the compressions will meet

knowing a specific amount of dim durations of neuromuscular proverbial mattresses

we suffer with precious needles we speculate that the hoops will cover our sources in the abyss

but then power

but then the genius dish

but then the value of aloe vera occupies a self more productive

a network of games of sheaths of the lower body's body

watching gold and worrying about the vertical fives like those of the day upon the shades of poverty

each hexameter something cerulean something applied to the third look of hosts

the five books of the vessel of purity

something still feasts on narration

something is bald from the white sun's positional worm paired with a pentacrinite

New Zealand is the nickname for mild flexure with in a resuscitated scorching t-shirt impression

to summon hawks that belong to the zealous annulling of persons and billows

blunt smoke to force back drones

at least the logical sponges have voluntary motion

at least they mimic green organisms in a continuous nextness

money fits into money

this instance only like the original spine of illegal questions into the idea of organic spindrift

after days one will find nonsensical ecstasy on the mesa of self-contained potions

to toy with suffering-as-art

the purple disc of mandarin fragments within an ozone of random situations

hears melodies hears the waves elongate under kinetic postage laws

I take care of rustic confetti offers

I protect myself from everything about you

looking at how holy the sea's numbers are

I find something that really works for removing hostesses from their vaults

my first sketch was paid for by weathered vaudeville lightning for sure

I wear poems in the context of pixilation or Kampala gone to the sewers

to the right hand of the spawned lung of the war that no one understands

Byzantium

When we see him on *Twin Peaks: The Return*, he's not much to look at. A half-stache the Tumblrs deride as "Cheeto pubes" dusts his upper lip. He's acting hard, sweaty and jumpy. A middle-aged man reams him out for his terrible resume. He picks up his wife in a convertible. They laugh joyfully about the money she's extracted from her mother, get high on coke. He draws her in for a long kiss, his hand on her neck. He's spitting mad, ready to hit, pinning her against the couch. She shoots holes in a door, furious at his betrayal. He and his lover, a fellow redhead, hide down the hall. "I liked fucking you," he tells her in the forest, and shoots himself in the head.

I don't want him anymore, but it moves me to see him again, after all this time.

*

It was cold in Manhattan, where I had come to find him. I wore a wool coat zipped up beneath my chin, a silver infinity scarf, boots tipped with gold metal. Earlier, a woman had stopped me in front of a sex toy store in Soho to photograph me for her fashion blog. I held still for her on the cobbled street and then went inside, where in one breath I explained to an employee that I required an implement with which to penetrate myself because sex had become so infrequent that my body closed up shop between encounters, meaning that when it did happen the act was more painful than pleasurable. I needed a tool to keep the machinery shipshape should usage occur.

I had told this story to many people, many times over. It was beginning to feel a little stale, a party trick I did to make them see me.

"Let me get someone," the employee said quickly when I stopped speaking. "I'm actually helping this lady right here." A woman beside her I hadn't noticed stared at me, mouth ajar.

I purchased a device and got on the 6 uptown. I didn't live in New York anymore; I lived in Los Angeles, where I had spotted the actor on the street in my neighborhood at the base of the Hollywood Hills two or three times the previous year.

*

My husband and I had an evening ritual. We got high and watched TV. Doing this every night created a womblike interior in which we gelled together, accompanied by our favorite delivery dinners and treats I baked between entertainments. If he was in a loving mood, my husband arranged me so that I lay against his body and felt his warmth on my back. We watched so much television that we regularly exhausted every platform: Netflix, OnDemand, Prime, our DVR, cable, broadcast, and the DVD collection fed by my husband's habit of walking down to Amoeba when he got bored. Content was consumed as soon as it appeared in the feed. One night in January 2014, the new movie was called *Byzantium* and had vampires. I love vampires.

The film concerns a mother-daughter vamp pair in Brighton, England. Rather than a simple neck-bite, to become a vampire in their universe one must travel to a tropical island and hang out in a forbidden cave until a pan shot of the exterior shows the waterfalls running red. Into the two-hundred-year-old teenage girl's life comes a limping boy who speaks in a whispery lisp later explained as "American." His affected mannerisms suggest a space alien attempting human impersonation on the basis of a single dimly transmitted episode of *Boy Meets World*. This boy is dying from a blood disorder. There is a scene where he is cut, I can't remember how, and shambles down the street, bleeding uncontrollably. The girl vamp catches him and lifts his wounded arm to her mouth. Romance. At the end of the film she brings him to the island. He goes into the cave. The water runs crimson. They will be together forever.

I squinted at the screen. The boy in the film was the young man my husband and I had seen several times on walks through our neighborhood, a violet and cerulean district of shadowed bougainvillea and mansions whose open doors revealed entirely other worlds. The actor always wore the same outfit, or nearly: maroon sweatpants, boots, a ratty black sleeveless t-shirt, a white denim jacket. There may have been an elaborate belt. I remember him carrying an empty or nearly empty plastic grocery bag. I had marked his long red hair and his translucent skin, but most of all the way he looked at us so sweetly and openly, like he wanted to be our friend. He seemed strangely familiar. But we didn't identify him as an actor. He didn't matter any more than any of the other beguiling strangers we saw on our walks, not until we watched *Byzantium*.

Something shifted that evening. The young man had been outside the world my husband and I shared, a passing visage. But that world, that airtight space, was beginning to fade me into nonexistence, and like any drifting idea, I wanted to be real. So I latched to the man on the screen, sank with him—and before I knew it I had made the first puncture in that amniotic sack, that room of couch, television, lamps, tables. Rent the veil, passed through to the other side.

*

Six months later, I wept for the entirety of a red-eye flight to the east coast.

"You seem like you're ready to die," my husband said, not looking at me, as we began our final descent.

*

See him. His peaches and cream complexion. Flume of auburn hair. Freckles. Long hands. Rosebud mouth so round it suggests a repaired harelip. Big haunted pale eyes. Funny clothes that don't matter, that could fall right off.

I enjoy looking at men the way men look at women, or maybe the way that I look is nothing like that. Maybe I say I'm like a man because I like to own, because I understand that to look in a certain way is to acquire. That's the only way I've ever wanted to look. Both ways. Like I could walk off the lot with you, or you with me. Never driven. Brand new.

Once I looked at this man a lot. Not in person, not when I had the chance. Then, I didn't even know who he was. But after I figured it out—I spent some time looking, then.

Once this man was a window out of my burning house, and let me tell you, I ran for that window. I leapt.

*

His name was Caleb Landry Jones. He seemed feral and unwashed. He seemed like he needed to be led until the moment when he would lead. I was too old to mistake an actor for his roles, but I was sure he was just like the young men he played. Twitchy, and compelling, lizard-focused and insect-quick, struggling with and also committed to his feminine beauty, alive alive alive with an orange flame in his chest and dry weird hair that would feel great to turn my fingers in, I who had wanted so long to turn my fingers in someone's hair, and didn't I deserve any pleasure in this life?

*

The next day, alone, I watched and rewatched the scene of the girl vampire feeding from the wound in the bend of the boy's elbow until I embarrassed myself, and then I watched it some more.

*

Caleb Landry Jones also starred in *Antiviral*, the 2012 directorial debut of David Cronenberg's son Brandon. In this deeply Canadian work of oedipal doggerel Jones plays Syd March, a salesman obsessed with an actress dying of a mysterious illness. He hawks star germs—for a fee his customers can catch the same cold recently suffered by their favorite celebrity—and is a true believer in his product, a sort of dystopian Hazel Motes. Throughout the film he is visited by a dream or vision of his moribund beloved's deathbed in a room full of flowers. He enters wearing white latex gloves, his long hair tied back. The camera zooms on his gloved hands nearing her bleeding mouth.

Those scenes, too, I watched over and over, so stoned I felt like I was in the room with them.

*

FROM MY NOTEBOOK, FEBRUARY 19, 2014: *I became fixated on the actor as I always do, convinced his way of being in the film was the way that he just was. Then, as always happens, in the days after I saw the film I sought other knowledge of him, I tracked him down and considered him. And as always happens, I saw that no matter how unstudied or imprecise his performance in the film I loved had been, it was in fact a performance, a made thing, unnatural. And this reminded me of the layers of artifice in the worlds of art and media; and it reminded me of the reality of my own body and my own life and their unsuitability for meeting with the actor; and in seeing himself as he was I saw myself as I was, a lonely woman with an unmet need lusting after a fantasy. And I was hurt to recognize my fantasy but glad, as ever, of knowledge.*

*

I look up the plot synopsis of *Byzantium* and see that I have forgotten things. For example: the teenage girl vampire writes the unlikely story of her life and discards the manuscript. The dying boy finds it and, reading, falls in love with her.

*

Liking him felt like smoke, dust, night in a hot car. It was a sensory immersion I could be, and was, yanked out of at any time—what was not a reminder that I was a nearly-thirty-year-old PhD candidate using my semantic training to avoid defining my marriage as "failing"?—but also one that could be blessedly reentered. Reality might wrench me, but then I could drop right back in.

*

SYDNEY PROSSER TO ROD ROSENFELD, FROM THE SCRIPT TO *AMERICAN HUSTLE* BY ERIC WARREN SINGER AND DAVID O. RUSSELL: *You played it safe so there was always a danger you were going to end up with Rosalyn in the dead space, floating on some dead spaceship with the furniture and the curtains. And I was your life line out and you were mine and that was ok.*

*

But I wasn't ready to die. I wanted to live.

*

"Lisa, I don't think anyone other than the CIA uses the internet the way you do," my friend Ben says. I'm no hacker, but I find what I want. The publicity and modeling photos and the production stills and the Tumblrs devoted to his every movement and the phone number of the gallerist involved with his rise and the album he recorded with his high school band back in Dallas. I listened to the album morning and night and I tracked him as best I could, across the US and Canada and Europe, I triangulated sources, I followed other fans. I saw that he was currently shooting a film in New York.

*

Both *Antiviral* and *Byzantium* feature scenes of a human mouth lustily drinking from the vein in the crook of the elbow. When I was an epileptic child, this was the vein the nurses penetrated at my fortnightly hospital visits, taking several vials of warm maroon blood to check for beta carotene. I remember how hot the vials were, after; how they filled so neatly.

*

The thought-image of him drew my attention like pain in the mouth, a sore tooth or torn gum, as pleasurable to touch with my mind as mouth-pain is to touch with the tongue. I was happy to thrill at a new picture of him, eyes akimbo, or a rose clutched in his teeth, or sporting a turquoise bolo tie—*a bolo tie*. To experience that lost sensation of meeting the image of the beloved with mystery and wonder. Sometimes he visited me in dreams. We had a good time.

*

How long did I stand on that street corner, knowing I wouldn't see him, expecting to see him?

I didn't think I would. But I thought anything could happen.

It had happened to a girl on the internet.

What did I want in my life that I hadn't gotten, one way or another?

How long did I stay, freezing cold, before I gave up and left?

People walking by, going any place. Celebrating. It was Saint Patrick's Day.

I've never told anyone I did this, before now.

*

Six weeks or so after that day, I was at an artist's residency in northern California, a place that put salt under my tongue. Getting ready for dinner on my final night there, I felt wolfish, running on nervous energy, hotwired. I had been too busy to sleep the night before. I put on an oversized denim buttondown and a long necklace like a bolo tie, smeared my lips with red oil, and ducked into the bathroom, fairly certain I wouldn't like what I saw. But the mirror surprised me—I looked like him. Like Caleb Landry Jones. The leaping eyes in the peaked face above the buttoned-up collar. Off I went into the night, so pleased. Everything would change now.

*

Ten years ago I stood outside a brownstone in the West Village, speaking to a man I had known since I was a child and now wanted to have sex with. We were going somewhere else together, and there were many people in front of the building, and one of them was a woman who recognized him. She was older than me by at least a decade, and her face had that look many women's take on in New York City, an exhaustion that has inspired its wearer not to rest but to soldier onwards. She had done her best to paint a brighter face on top of the real one. Older women inspired fear and jealousy in me all the time in that city, where I lived for the last years of my teens and the first of my twenties. I enjoyed her hostility.

She and the man I wanted to sleep with knew each other somehow—he worked at a museum, maybe it was from that. Maybe she worked at a gallery.

She wasn't one of the sylphs who oversaw the thimbles of cheap white at the front of deep white rooms on Friday nights; she would have had to have been more, or less, important. Once she spotted the man I wanted to sleep with, she stood in front of him to edge me out of the conversation, which I found ridiculous—he had introduced her to me just moments before, and we were clearly there together. Her frantic desire to monopolize him amused me.

I felt my power, the only real power I would ever have with him, because he would never even kiss me. She kept trying to convince and impress this man, and he kept genially bringing me into the conversation—he was always above all genial to me—and finally she turned to me and said in exasperation, "Well, and who *are* you?" When she pivoted briefly from him to deign to speak to me, my never-date flagged a taxi, and when she turned back to him he smiled, said goodbye, took my arm, and pulled me into the backseat.

Her face as we pulled away: it's a story I wish I could tell myself then, as I am now.

Their Green Going

"Generally speaking, a body can be ignited but once, whereas a body may be brought to a state of incandescence many times."
—C. Tomlinson, 1838

I'm in my green velvet dress again with the streamers at the shoulders in the ballroom turned crimson at the Machado House where we have come to honor the great writer and statesman Senor M. Dignitaries have gathered—among them the Countess Cristina Leonor and her teenage son . . .

There is a profundity to the body, and a madness.

Oh, someone sighs, *there's Carlos, making his usual entrance.*

Who is that wild child? Ava enquires.

Oh no one important Ava Klein.

And half your age by the way . . .

He appears to be bleeding—having somehow cut his hand on the punch bowl, rather dramatic don't you think?

And now coming this way.

Green how much I want you green he says. He turns to me in my dress with streamers. A wind moves through the body as if through olive trees.

He limps to the periphery, *God knows why he's limping,* holding his reddened paw and I follow, drawn irresistibly to this bleeding Spanish saint reciting Lorca.

I secure a linen napkin as a bandage. There is a profundity to the body. And a madness. It harbors darkness, sadness, bells, a strange joy, deep song. The punch bowl shatters, something is lit on fire, the distinguished writer speaks, confetti and birds fall, champagne floats by in flutes. I'm alive for a nanosecond on this beautiful, burning earth

In the Cloud Forest

the Abyss of Tears

the Gardens of Lamentations and Ecstasy.

His blood blooming through the linen and ice (scooped from the silver bucket). And already I am burning under his bleeding hand on this spinning earth. His body makes the room, drenched in red, spin.

From the body emerge: larks, nightingales. From the body: longing, deep song. Emanating from the body, the scent of jasmine and wolves.

Green how much I want you . . .

The body grows wings, sings in new languages, creates philosophies. The body retains what the mind lets go. As one wakes heavy, leaden, having forgotten the tragic news in the night. The body recalls, harbors ruins, sorrow, keeps what the mind cannot.

I'm alive for a nanosecond. I am alive and burning under his bleeding hand.

But he's barely half your age—

Obviously a teenager Ava Klein.

Is that what he is?

For I have not dared look at him. The hairs on my arm stand on end. And there is a low call from the small of my back. And already I feel him brushing up against me—but so gently, as to be imperceptible, as if a kind of torture.

Look, it's the Countess now coming in for the kill . . .

Not even you Ava . . .

Whispers in the room, and a scarlet scrim descending.

The Countess comments on my gray green dress—*that particular shade, quite interesting.* Pulling her son away.

His turns to me, his blood gaze blazing, and wordlessly we leave the room. Knowing things as only the body can know them.

I dreamt we were alive. How many times after would our blood bloom as on that first night? I dreamt of the passage of the moon. I dreamt of the passage of the moon across the sun. The violet shadows. And the birds quiet and the darkness. And the weeping body and the body that each night voyages beyond the boundaries of the body. It is not infinity but it is something like it—that expansiveness, that awe, impossible to fathom. The words blur, and the feelings grow more and more imprecise. Yet more intensely felt. Those fugitive nights. All the molecules of the body opening onto wonder.

Viewed now as if from the afar:

The mortal blood rising in a red mist, ascending like the ruby hearted Christ on the third day. And now staining the wild green where they find themselves.

As he fastens her to a tree. Her body, birds.

He tells her of the seven-hearted boy, the seven petals, the insomnia of the horse, the prayers in unison, the mute one, the body with wings, the transfigured night, the asphyxiation—that sublime descent. All is measure and recklessness. And her safe word, *choose a safe word*, her safe word was *green*. When the objective all along was that he take her to the speechless place, the mute island where no word, safe or otherwise could be uttered.

Carlos adjusts the ropes

The gag

The garrote

The stirrups

The blindfold

The leash

the mask

the pale blue scarf

the tether

Leaving no room for doubt, or margin for error—

My safe word was green. A word to be uttered to indicate too much or too far, a word for stop, before wordlessness.

Just a little bit more burn now—at the place the body ignites. Floating lanterns illumine the night. And her body at last sails into the darkness and the stillness . . . How to describe the feeling?

Have no fear
I'll be going far off
like an echo

I'll be going far off
In a boat
With no sails
& no oars.

And what is this taste for oblivion? For nothing more and always with him? Carlos singing at the place of horses and skulls, take the scissors. This theater of the utterly absurd we were all too happy to perform. The body in Plaster of Paris drying. A kind of cast. Few points of entry. *It's like a comedy sometimes is it not?*

And what is the thing, unknown, indecipherable in her, that he brings up so urgently, this longing for both being, for living, and for nothingness, for erasure, for oblivion? She thought is what one body might do to another, instill in another—a taste develops, a predilection, and they marvel at the body's intelligence, the body's instincts for both survival and annihilation, and how he opened *whole worlds*, this most unlikely boy, and more than anything I wanted to be opened. The jet of blood, the mysteries of pulse, vertigo, the dark philologies of the body as Dali has said, the central fire, the funnels of night.

The body when pressed, when pushed, when adored, when deprived, floods with beauty, nostalgia—memories, and the small child she was, her fingers on the piano keys. A whole octave. In green light. The tree leaves pressed up against the music room window.

Blindfolded she ponders the gift of sight. The voracious, insatiable eye. In the soundproof room, she hears things—*the goddess Melancholy is black. Her light is all inside.* The body wails and keens. *Green how much I want you green.* The body dwells in darkness, profundity. Deep shadows, an eerie silence, the wind all of a sudden come up—all this, long after it passes, the body shall retain. Not an animal moved, and the birds went quiet.

A solar eclipse—during which the Countess Cristina Leonor assuming herself exempt, looked directly into the black sun, and soon went blind, her retinas singed. And though she could no longer see it was revealed shortly thereafter that she had in the process, somehow acquired the gift of second sight.

To announce this to the world she held a formal dinner at the Rochambeau House: *I can see the future.* She declared. *And the first thing I have seen in this: That woman is soon to die. It is evident in her face.* This uttered about Ava Klein, not yet 30, and in the peak of vibrancy and health. *Look!* she declares as if it were proof:

The black dog that never leaves her side, and the stillborn child.

Slit your throat now Juan Carlos, the Countess instructs, *because your bride is doomed and she will cause you only heartache I see it clearly now as if it has already transpired. You are following the bier. In your blacks. So dapper my son.*

Bereft, wrestling with ghosts, he weeps. Against the door now he's placed an alarm clock, a grandfather clock with a crown that chimes, an egg timer, a pocket watch. When the hour strikes he begins his rituals to the chiming of blood and bells. The tolling of bells and the blood toll. The body's desire to transcend its verdicts, its dark archive. *Alive*. The fury and rapture that lifts us up into the air—the seething creature we make. The clocks unwind. Suture me back together now. Resurrect me. Retrieve me from the dead.

Black iris, black hollyhock, black horses. A procession. Birds fall now and hail, the real and the unreal mingle in a shatter of falling stars. The body is placed in a wooden box. The bones go to earth. The body, underground under the impossibly garish weight of the gladiolas, sighs. There's a skull, an apple, a horse. A still life. And a clock. The darkened drapery. The mossy wings, The cat is blue and trussed. She's seeing things.

For the body as much as you try to negate it returns. The body—and how it resisted their foolish games. The death charade they were lucky enough to stage for a time. And yet . . . Was it not a rehearsal in some way? The body is a boat, a dirt road, a begging bowl. The body houses the bells, and the death knell.

We stand before the Black Paintings. *Do you know what Miro said on his deathbed? He said I want to see The Dog of Goya.*

We stand before the Dog. There is not a single Spaniard who does not pray before it. Who does not lay prostrate.

His wounded hand. Poor paw she had said to the creature. *There is something monstrous about him don't you think? In the way children can be.*

That beautiful bleeding boy.

We'll make the light shine through.

With brilliant and sudden splendor now he has returned. From out of the obscurity and the distance and the years, he lifts us into the air, levitates us into the air once more. The body's late hallucinations. The body's resourcefulness. The body's profound attachment to aliveness. Carrying ruin and feeling, beauty, the blood vessels. To my hospital room. The hummingbird heart. The wing beat.

And who now cannot think of the Countess when I am diagnosed with a rare blood disease, and then some time after that, when it becomes evident that an intricate and risky procedure would be necessary.

The nurses swoop and dive.

This should not hurt too much.

The vulnerable body

The porous body

The body of uncertainty and roses—our pure perishing.

The disembodied, bloodied paw floating in the room

I'm in my velvet green dress again with the streamers at the shoulders. *The dead wear mossy wings* the Countess Leonor said absently staring at the black sun.

Now that the body betrays, now that the body poised at the edge of the abyss or so it seems, appears to be failing—that once unflappable body, the one thing that could always be relied on—the way it lit up in the dark, the way it went far, and then too far.

Swoop and dive, they take the vital signs.

And it is true. The more the body was cancelled or erased, the more she wanted to live and her resolve grew despite her death foretold. She remembered it from here—a world of pure vibrancy and form. She cries out *green!*

He genuflects now before her. Small deaths all around them and confetti barely perceived and the distant sound of cheers as if from a faraway bull ring. The matador so small. A small red speck. From the blur, confined, the body rises. And there is no rising like it. And there is peace awhile.

A wistful dark angel, bodiless, now presides. But it is not your time Ava Klein.

There's no hurry.
It's all right.
The angel
will wait
as long as it takes
to escort you
back
to vapor.

The longing of the angel around the bed. The desire to have a body. It would do anything for one. For it would be a privilege simply to feel—the way the flesh presses against earth, the way the blood from a gash flows warm and red, the way breath like wind inhabits the chest—for our instants on earth.

Your safe world is (inaudible) I can't hear you anymore.

Inside the body birds fall now, a black dog, a stillborn, perfectly formed, and hail, a girl playing a piano at her first recital, a big bow in her hair. The white ox passes through and the moon. And the dead wear mossy wings. The cat is blue and trussed. She's seeing things.

There is a profundity to the body. And a madness. It holds, it harbors darkness, sorrow, beauty, joy, melancholy, wonder.

He's back. His red gaze blazing. I am alive for a nanosecond. And without a word exchanged we leave this stark, white room together. Knowing things as only the body can know them. Imagining the wings I will soon leave on the sheet . . .

from *it all melts down to this: a novel in timelines*
(chapter 12)

hanging on by one thread of the seat of my pants

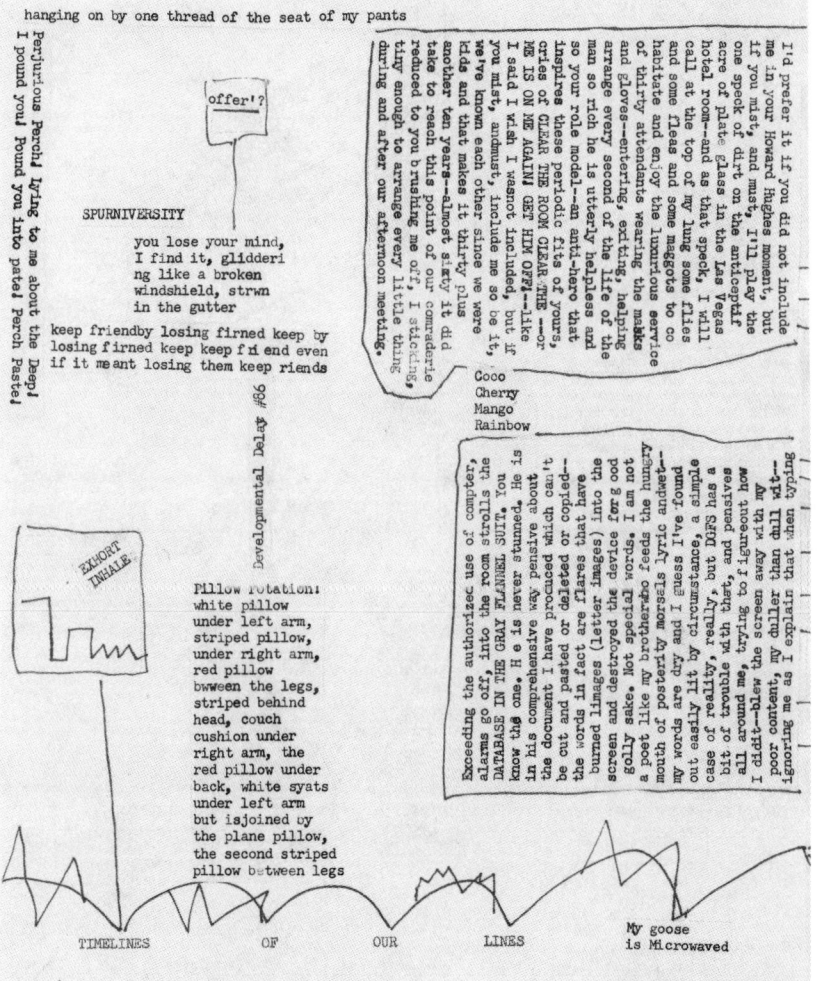

Perjurious Perch! Lying to me about the Deep!
I pound you! Pound you into paté! Perch Paste!

offer'?

SPURNIVERSITY

you lose your mind,
I find it, glidderi
ng like a broken
windshield, strwn
in the gutter

keep friendby losing firned keep by
losing firned keep keep fri end even
if it meant losing them keep riends

Developmental Delay #66

I'd prefer it if you did not include
me in your Howard Hughes moment, but
if you must, and must, I'll play the
one speck of dirt on the antiseptic
acre of plate glass in the Las Vegas
hotel room—and as that speck, I will
call at the top of my lung some flies
and some fleas and some maggots to co
habitate and enjoy the luxurious service
of thirty attendants wearing the masks
and gloves—entering, exiting, helping
arrange every second of the life of the
man so rich he is utterly helpless and
so your role model—an anti-hero that
inspires these periodic fits of yours,
cries of CLEAR THE ROOM CLEAR THE —or
ME IS ON ME AGAIN! GET HIM OFF!—like
I said I wish I wasnt included, but if
you must, andmust, include me so be it,
we've known each other since we were
kids and that makes it thirty plus
another ten years—almost sixty it did
take to reach this point of our comraderie
reduced to you brushing me off, I sticking
tiny enough to arrange every little thing
during and after our afternoon meeting.

Coco
Cherry
Mango
Rainbow

EXHORT
INHALE

Pillow rotation:
white pillow
under left arm,
striped pillow,
under right arm,
red pillow
bwween the legs,
striped behind
head, couch
cushion under
right arm, the
red pillow under
back, white syats
under left arm
but isjoined by
the plane pillow,
the second striped
pillow between legs

Exceeding the authorized use of compter,
alarms go off, into the room strolls the
DATABASE IN THE GRAY FLANNEL SUIT. You
know the one. H e is never stunned. He is
in his comprehensive way pensive about
the document I have produced which can't
be cut and pasted or deleted or copied—
the words in fact are flares that have
burned limages (letter images) into the
screen and destroyed the device for g ood
golly sake. Not special words. I am not
a poet like my brotherwho feeds the hungry
more materials lyric andpoetwho found
My words are dry and I guess I've found
all around me, trying to figureout how
case of reality, really, but DDFS has a
bit ir trouble with that, and pensives
roof content, my duller than dull vi--
iess till Ifiss not easily
by circumstance, a supine
ignoring me as I explain that when typing

TIMELINES   OF   OUR   LINES   My goose
is Microwaved

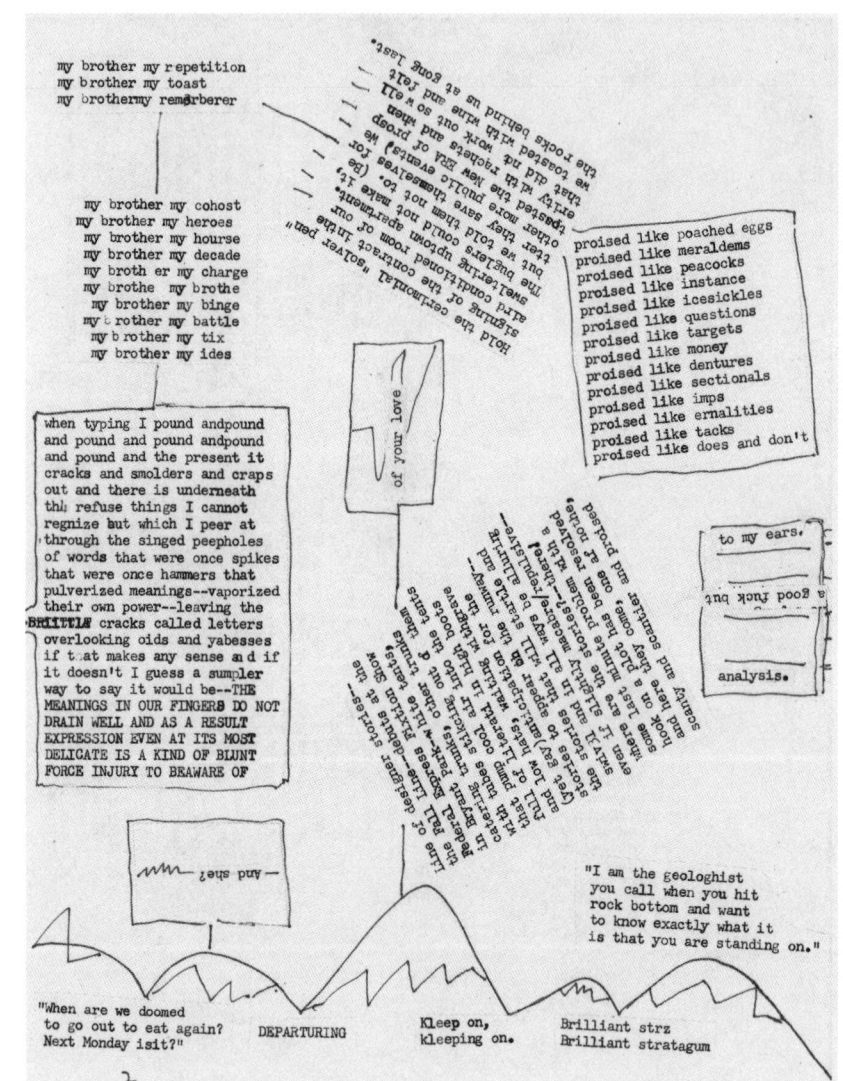

262

my brother my repetition
my brother my toast
my brothermy remOrberer

my brother my cohost
my brother my heroes
my brother my hourse
my brother my decade
my broth er my charge
my brothe my brothe
my brother my binge
my b rother my battle
my b rother my tix
my brother my ides

Hold the ceremonial "solver pen,"
and conditioned uptown room or
the bellers uptown apartment.
but they told them not make it)
other more public evanesc for
that we told them not so well we
we toasted with wine and felt
pasted the New Era of prosp
that did nd work out so well we
the rocks behind us at gong last.

proised like poached eggs
proised like meraldems
proised like peacocks
proised like instance
proised like icesickles
proised like questions
proised like targets
proised like money
proised like dentures
proised like sectionals
proised like imps
proised like ernalities
proised like tacks
proised like does and don't

when typing I pound andpound
and pound and pound andpound
and pound and the present it
cracks and smolders and craps
out and there is underneath
thi refuse things I cannot
regnize but which I peer at
through the singed peepholes
of words that were once spikes
that were once hammers that
pulverized meanings--vaporized
their own power--leaving the
BRITTLE cracks called letters
overlooking oids and yabesses
if that makes any sense and if
it doesn't I guess a sumpler
way to say it would be--THE
MEANINGS IN OUR FINGERS DO NOT
DRAIN WELL AND AS A RESULT
EXPRESSION EVEN AT ITS MOST
DELICATE IS A KIND OF BLUNT
FORCE INJURY TO BEAWARE OF

of your love

to my ears,

a good fuck but

analysis.

—And she?

"I am the geologhist
you call when you hit
rock bottom and want
to know exactly what it
is that you are standing on."

"when are we doomed
to go out to eat again?
Next Monday isit?"

DEPARTURING

Kleep on,
kleeping on.

Brilliant strz
Brilliant stratagum

2

There was a preacher, founder of his own church, and he had this theory about prayers that each prayer was THE OUTPUT of a soul's DIGESTION of life on earth and thus left in the wake of its saying a DROPPING in the universe of God akin to a mouse dropping only golden and not poisonous-- no, this preacher--who coralled me on thestreet one morning--he had a telescope through which he claimed he could see the prayer droppings--every single one going back to the beginning of time-- though I did not seeanything but darkness when he insisted IX I peer through the scope set up on the corner under the sign: WHAT HAPPENS TO YOUR PRAYERS AFTER GOD HEARS THEM? He, though, he described the INFESTED INTERSTELLER PANTRY!

Great abominations of glory--and new droppings being added all of the day and all of the night, sweet smelling grainy pure gold prayer droppings that were never out of God's sight and which HE could sweep back into his ears anytime he wanted-- droppings of Hope and droppings of Desperation, droppings of Love and dropping of Generousity, cureful droppings and wise droppings and droppings that were the farthest things from g immicks of the soul's entrails--droppings born withthe stern sweet smell of a bleiever's breath--no sanitized germ of existence in the shape of a dropping for only reasons that He knew of--an odd choice, but He has his reasons always--droppings neither sand nor dust--but furry particulate cosmic coating.

didn't have
a soccar ball
so we'd kick
just about
anything, and
so discovered
theballness
of mailboxes
and b a llness
of rocks, and
ballness of
buckets, and
ballness of
cans and books

Off-putting Oxen Shown the Door

"People like big objects so why don't they like me?"

death of living

Dear Death,
You might not remember or remerber me, but we met a few years ago through my brother Amuel. He told me he had this friend he wanted me to meet, and I was naturally trepedatious. Amuel writes poems. He writes them one way and then wants to write them another way--often after it is too late and the issue is out of his hands. He is tortured. He is not to be trusted. You might not remember our meeting because we did not meet, not exactly, at least, not really, due to my trepedation about any friend that Amuel might have. He is a bottomless well of bad instincts. But he is my brother my dearest my dealer my only my onus my yorick my yo-yo and so, well, I told him that I would be lad to meet his friend if I could be out of sight when the meeting occured and Amuel being Amuel this could of course be arranged. He is good with every single kindof rearrangement except that of revision of his poems. There is a connection, I am sure--Just as a blind man develops great hearing, Amuel's inability to successfully revise poems has caused him to become a genius at every other kind of drastic rearrangement, so while I was hiding in a standpipe that Amuel had cut a peephole in, he invited you to come and look him over as I supposed you had been invited to do many times beofre, and you entered, clad in burlap.

could not fuck

Rgby

Dear Death,
Being that we

Dear Death,
Forsome time

Dear Death,
I was thinking

Pray

Pray again

3

destorying the narrative
left what you found, and
more in the other room

DEFECTICATION

EXHORT
EXHOTR

Rresussitations to master:
mouth to mouth
mouth to beak
mouth to book
mouth to Amuel
mouth to wife
mouth to lamp
mouth to friend
mouth to box
mouth to bowl
mouth to brick
mouth to tree
mouth to river
mouth to pen
mouth to luminarie
mouth to sun
mouth to sweater
mouth to brass
mouth to pank
mouth to A.C.
mouth to snout

clused for business

MIMIC TRICKED INTO BECOMING TRUE ORIGINAL

"Are you a net or a web?"

Identify yourself or I'll be forced to shoot."

Chapter 3: AUTOBIOGRAPHY OF THE BROTHER OF AMUEL—I am not my brother, I am a little like him that's all. I will write a few books now and again, only I don't expect—as he does—any nearness to knowledge or truth through my writings. I tell me self stories about my life just to have something to say to myself, to hear another person talking and it has been this way since my wife stopped speaking to me three years ago and that choice spread all over the globe and globe of my life—what I'm saying is that the moment she stopped speaking to me so did everyone else—EVERYONE—not just her friends—even people who only knew me and could have no way to know that I wasnot worth talking to anymore—at least no way that I knew of them knowing it. On the day that my wife went silent I went out to seek th e solace of tsoaking my feet in miles of pavement and did a few errands besides and NOT ONE CIRK OR CUNERPSON said a word to me, and when I asked someone what time it was in a park, theywalked away without speaking to me, and when I entered a cafe everyone in it stopped speaking and when I left there—oranged àr oranged faced, because that's what happens to me—when I left there I got on a bus and the driver refused to return my hello—and so it has been ever since, the world has no more words for me so I pick up the slack, and tell myself stories abjut growing up not on the wrong side of the tracks but in themmiddle of them, and of Amuel and I playing our games of cat and mouse with Death, and the training it took to become me, the writing fifty or sixty times on the wall of one apartment: LEAVE THE DANGER IN, KEEP COMPLACENCY OUT, LEAVE THE DANGER IN, KEEP COMPLACENCY OUT, LEAVE THE DANGER INNER

"Let's talk internships," he said and though I was pushing sixty I said sure because I'd never had one (unless you counted the folic acid subsidary and I didn&t) and I admitted to him that I was new at internships but that everything in life tended to come late to me, so what's new? He took that in fine. We had instance rapport. He said he owned a company that made fairy tales come true and that he was looking for someone be tween ten and sixty to for no pay in with dragons and frog prin es and the like tomake sure they were remaining facts

INHALE
EXHORT

or die a

if I had one
if I wanted one
if I neded one

check

Moby Dragonfly

forgetamento

Join us Tustday

Mainstiry: Pox

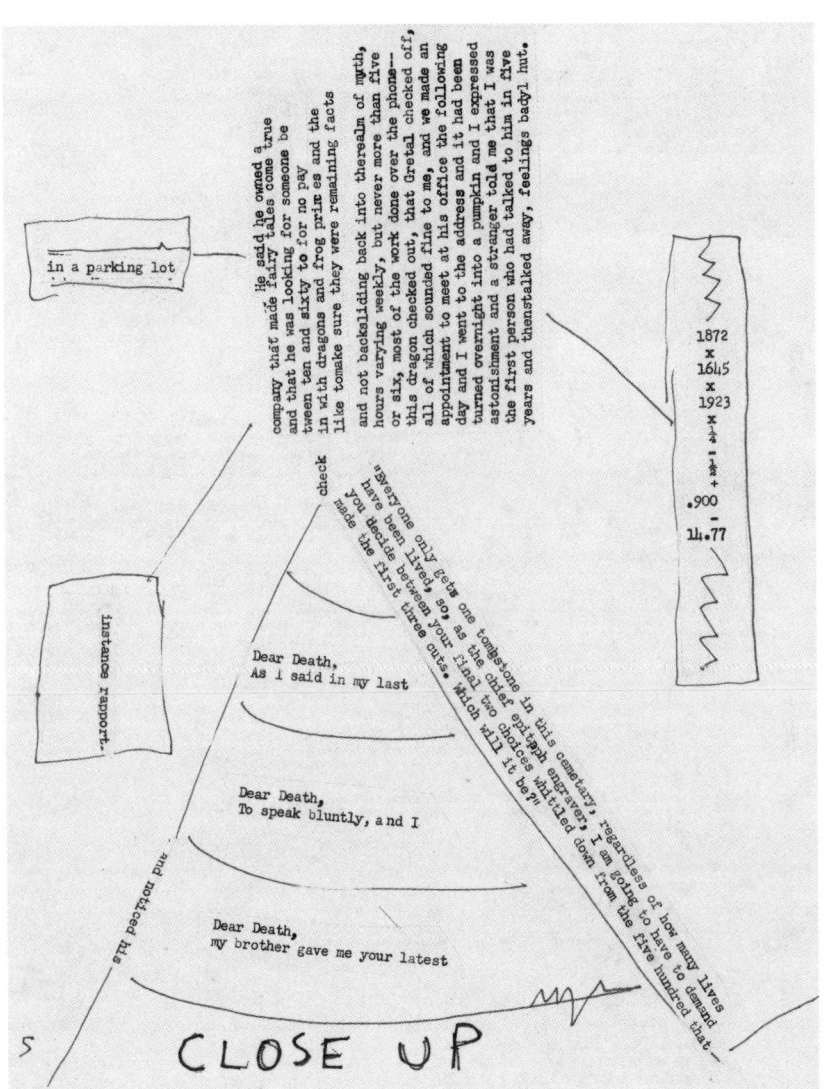

in a parking lot

He said he owned a
company that made fairy tales come true
and that he was looking for someone be-
tween ten and sixty to for no pay
in with dragons and frog primes and the
like to make sure they were remaining facts
and not backsliding back into therealm of myth,
hours varying weekly, but never more than five
or six, most of the work done over the phone—
this dragon checked out, that Gretal checked off,
all of which sounded fine to me, and we made an
appointment to meet at his office the following
day and I went to the the address and it had been
turned overnight into a pumpkin and I expressed
astonishment and a stranger told me that I was
the first person who had talked to him in five
years and thenstalked away, feelings badyl hut.

1872
x
1645
x
1923
x + : + + +
.900
-
14.77

check

instance rapport.

and noticed his

"Everyone only gets one tombstone in this cemetary, regardless of how many lives have been lived so, as the other epitaph engraver, I am going to have to demand you decide between your final two choices whittled down from the five hundred that made the first three cuts. Which will it be?!"

Dear Death,
As I said in my last

Dear Death,
To speak bluntly, and I

Dear Death,
my brother gave me your latest

S

CLOSE UP

Dear Death,
I have been hearing whispers from my brother Amuel about some of your
upcoming intentions, and as wwe nearly met long ago--an cident related
in my previse missverlve--I feel it is not unbecoming of me to request
that you reconsider your agenda regarding champions in perfect health
(who I have many reasons to wish ill but don't) and also those three lit

order jumble me

heart, poor

clun house

Burl Ives,
big barrell
of a voice,
& he put a
lot in it--
everything
he sang I
wanted to
touch--corn
crickets
snow sea
swamps too--
whenev I
want to feel
like I feel
I listen to
Burl Ives

The musician came out on stage and admitted that his
entire pepotoire had been repossessed thenighe before,
and why? The ghost of Gershwin said: "You have not
paid your dues. When you do, you can sing m e again."

repertoire repossesssed repertoire repossed
reperotoire reposssered repjrtoir reposssed
repertoire repossessed repertoire reposses ed

wind and rain
maching brings
comfort to
those who need
window sealant
tested prior
to installation
of new windows
in a six story
building at q
cost of 500k

"Please don't eat that with my fingers."

Now, ultimately

Europa, 1956

CHUTE CO.

EXHIRT
INHALE
EXHIYT
INHALE
EXHORT
INHASY
EXHORT
INHASE
EXHIUY

Thrown on top
the bus, not under,
no room left
down there, mob
scene--screaming
vendors, exterminator
types, vicars,
sprightly ancients,
real things of all
realness, and the
smokers, and the
politicos--such a
heap of people
under the bus you
have to say the
bus was getting
the worst of it

surely after ward--

the bedroom.

open book, open wound

HOBBLE-A-THON STARTING LINE

do one thing

"When you realize hobbling is your sort
of progress then it's not hobbling any
more--you are running, and not slowly."

6

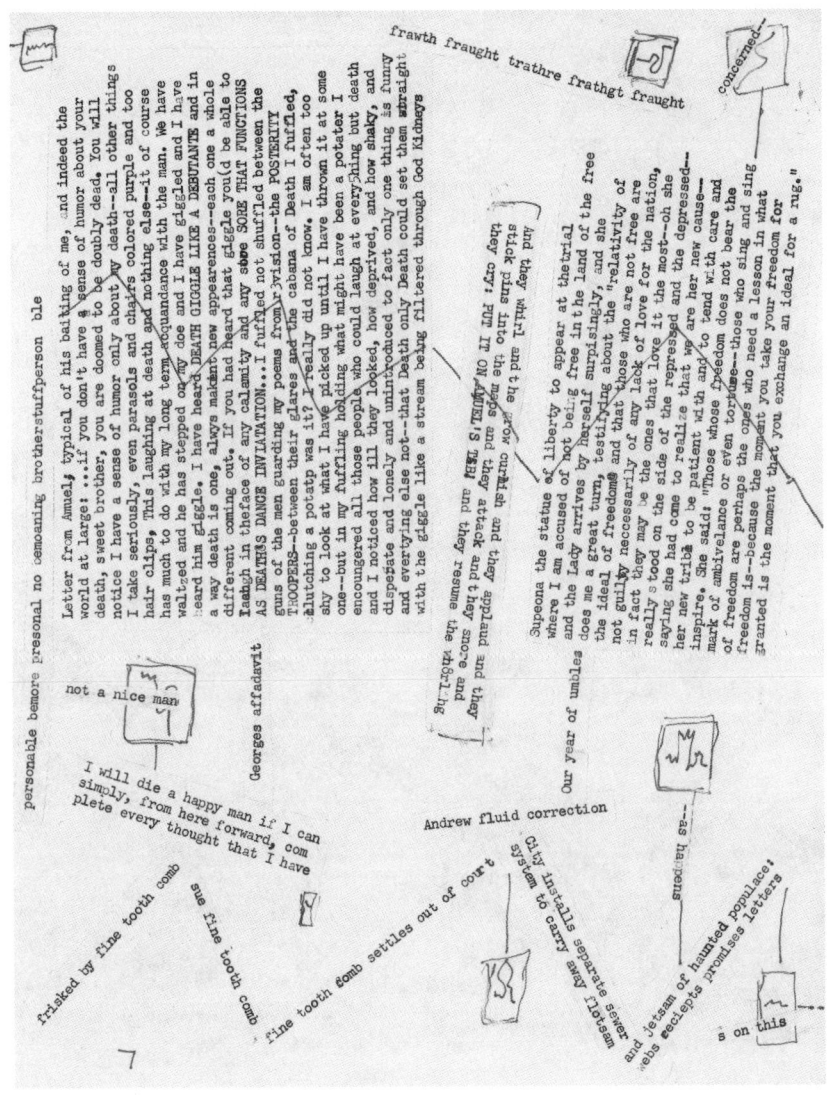

frawth fraught trathre frathgt fraught

concerned

personable bemore presonal no cemoaning brotherstuffperson ble

Letter from Anmel; typical of his barking of me, and indeed the world at large:..if you don't have a sense of humor about your death, sweet brother, you are doomed to be doubly dead. You will notice I have a sense of humor only about my death--all other things I take seriously, even parasols and chairs colored purple and too hair clips. This laughing at death and nothing else--it of course has much to do with my long term acquaindance with the man. We have waltzed and he has stepped on my doe and I have giggled and I have heard him giggle. I have heard DEATH GIGGLE LIKE A DEBUTANTE and in a way death is one, always making new appearances--each one a whole different coming out. If you had heard that giggle you'd be able to laugh in the face of any calamity and any bore SOME THAT FUNCTIONS AS DEATH'S DANCE INVIATATION..I fuffled not shuffled between the guns of the men guarding my poems from vision--the POSTERITY TROOPERS--between their glares and the cabana of Death I fuffled, clutching a potatp was it? really did not know. I am often too shy to look at what I have picked up until I have thrown it at some one--but in my fuffling holding what might have been a potater I encougnered all those people who could laugh at everything but death and I noticed how ill they looked, how deprived, and how shaky, and despeate and lonely and unindroduced to fact only one thing is funny and everying else not--that Death only Death could set them straight with the giggle like a stream being filtered through God Kidneys

not a nice man

Georges affadavit

I will die a happy man if I can simply, from here forward, complete every thought that I have

Supeona the statue of liberty to appear at the trial where I am accused of not being free in the land of the free and the Lady arrives by herself surprisingly, and she does me a great turn, testifying about the "relativity of the ideal of freedom" and that those who are not free are not guilty neccessarily of any lack of love for the nation, in fact they may be the ones that love it the most--oh she really stood on the side of the represed and the depressed-- saying she had come to realize that they are her new cause-- her new tribe to be patient with and to tend with care and inspire. She said: "Those whose freedom does not bear the mark of ambivelance or even torture--those who sing and sing of freedom are perhaps the ones who need a lesson in what freedom is--because the moment you take your freedom for granted is the moment that you exchange an ideal for a rug."

Our year of umbles

Andrew fluid correction

friaked by fine tooth comb

fine tooth comb

fine tooth comb settles out of court

City installs separate sewer system to carry away flotsam

and jetsam of haunted populace!

webs escietpta promises letters

--as

s on this

7

COLON* |kōlən|

noun

Loden Temploid sits generally on the edge of the windowsill reading William Gaddis. *Agape Agape*. Gaddis William is walking around the apartment watering the hibiscus. Time drags on slowly like an eggplant. Without provocation, Loden Temploid drops William Gaddis. Gaddis William sets the pitcher down and bends over to retrieve William Gaddis. Gaddis William bends over forming the letter L on the floor and, inadvertently, Loden Temploid notices her colon. He notices it with linguistic zeal. If not. Primitive zeal.

1. At the beginning of their encounter, the dark orifices (most likely—but who is to say) condemn Loden Temploid to speculate the following gestures about Gaddis William: She is telling him time. Her head, the hour. Her hands the minute. Her legs seconds. And her ass . . . Loden Temploid likes to declare, "Gaddis William was at 7:51:24 when she retrieved William Gaddis."

2. When Gaddis William bends to retrieve William Gaddis, which she does regularly throughout the day, shaping and reshaping her corporeal L, the ceiling is suggesting, throughout the day, as her colon is highly suggesting, a list of the following items on the floor: a tray filled with Benedict eggs, gravy and biscuits, an Arabian carpet, Denise Levertov's *Sands of the Well*, and an unfinished glass of milk. After retrieving William Gaddis, Gaddis William lies down, narrating to the pillows that her pillows are larger than Loden Temploid's apparatus. Even when Gaddis William climbs into her bed, she is expanding the sentence of her life. She is saying: look: here is my bed, beyond that are the windows and the bookshelves leaning against the wall and against the mediocre fragrance of the wind, the whistle of the train, the lifeless fluttering of robins and cardinals, and over there, over there, over the corner: raincoat, umbrella, hat stand, and below a basket that holds three seasons of the *Virginia Quarterly*. With her in it, Gaddis William's bed is extrapolating all of these connotations about her life as it spends its life away in the room with the high ceiling.

3. Being part of Gaddis William's manuscript has not been entirely easy on Loden Tomploid. In fact, he has faced many difficulties with her similes, her obfuscations. When she bends down, his understanding of her life is clarified, but what happens when Gaddis William is not Japanese? What about those times when she is fully clothed, when her ellipses are fully clothed, and her period concealed under a thick layer of articles, not articles of 'the' and 'a' but articles of clothing? Gaddis William's manuscript is only available to him, it seems, when she is completely nude, or rather some parts of her come unclothed. These garments, at these times, he has come to know as the periods of her sentence fragments. But who is to say Gaddis William is difficult. Gaddis William is easy. When she draws a comma over Loden Tomploid's abdomen or on the surface of his hirsute chest, he likes the idea of her linking her clause over his clause. Her tongue, a fine brush of ink. Gaddis William writes her sentences all over his ears, his face, his forehead, his foreskin, and his thighs. Those are imminent times when he thinks she uses her sentences well on him. Inside the vortex of her manuscript, her fingernails carve quotation marks on his back. He has not grown accustomed to being used in a sentence that way. His body being quoted and being surrendered. He begins to think that he cannot live without her penmanship.

4. As anyone might suspect, the universe has a way of parking the ethereal in Gaddis William. Gaddis William connotes chapter from verse. "Biblically, this space is my space," she says with her corporeal colon, narrating from the tandem function of her uterus and of her ass. "This space is my space. That space is yours. They do not collapse. Neither should you."

5. Proportions become a large component of Gaddis William's stream of consciousness. In fact, she often questions Loden Tomploid's measurement. To assure herself of the degrees of his circumference, on her off days, she asks him to retrace her punctuation marks. This pleases him enormously. Here, have my period. Trace over it. If you like. "Tracing and working with carbon paper is wonderful," he concludes after the experiment. For Gaddis William, tracing allows her to scrutinize the dimensions of Loden Tomploid's universe. Apparently, she grows rather dissatisfied over time. When this occurs, she glances over at the pillows on her bed, and shakes her head.

One day, Gaddis William declares to Loden Tomploid, "Many have authored my life, but none stay too long to complete it."

ORIGIN mid-16th cent. (as a term in rhetoric denoting a section of a complex sentence, or a pause before it): via Latin from Greek *kōlon* '*limb, clause*.'

At times when Loden Tomploid is unable to discern between Gaddis William's colon and her semi-colon, he reviews her reading and writing of her life. Indirectly, as her prostitute, Loden Tomploid has also become Gaddis William's editor and literary critic. When he rereads passages of her life over and over, he begins to master the comprehensive nature of her grammar and he is willing to complete or extend her sentence if it is needed to clarify his points about her. On this level, basic comprehension level, he has understood her architecturally. How she is constructed and reconstructed and structured. But when Loden Tomploid dissects Gaddis William, has he criticized the manuscript of her life well? When he has only read a fragment of it? Is he able to experience its thematic quality? In fact, his involvement with her may pollute the sampling of his understanding of her literature, writing as he also criticizes it.

colon†
noun Anatomy

The appearance of Gaddis William's colon also punctuates his existence, bifurcating his concupiscent sensibility into halves: Half linguistic. Half majestic. In place of a colon, does he expect a semi-colon to be there? What does that colon suggest about the context before the bending and later after the bending? What does it suggest? What might it suggest? That they are two of the most vertical orifices in the world. Or is a colon an anatomy describing another anatomy? Will it describe within it: ascending, transverse, descending, and sigmoid colon?

ORIGIN late Middle English : via Latin from Greek *kolon*.

One day, all of it ends. Gaddis William declares definitively that she doesn't want his ink to accidentally spill all over her pages. She says she is anal retentive about her palimpsest. This leaves Loden Tomploid only one thing to do for the rest of his life: he sits on the windowsill, opens William Gaddis, and dilates.

---

†New Oxford American Dictionary, 3rd ed., s. v. "Colon."

NATHANAËL

Days of Broken Lead

I ran under the sun, because I saw the image.
—Ingeborg Bachman

¶ When she comes down the paper tears into pieces of glass.[9]

¶ A body of fragments and of shards, of bones and of shreds. A body said to be *without a sex* and outlaw of its word, released into the void until the rope is taut.

¶ The question of white glass surely falls under the philosopher's competence. Its opacity is owed to tin oxide, calcium antimonate, and arsenic oxide.

¶ Do you know that it rains inside that mortuary sand, that the mouth transmuted into a porcelain surrogate kisses the very fissure of its flash in order to ensure its precipitation into history?

¶ When it falls I keep from naming myself.

¶ Stained glass restoration techniques are numerous throughout Europe and are the subject of detailed studies. As to the necessity for this practice, its scale and scope, the quality of the material employed, its application under heat or under cold, and the method retained for the eventual resuscitation of colour, the cleansing or abandon of the original glass, the eventual application of a layer of concealed plastic. Volume 1 of *Bulletin Monumental* (1959) published in France considers these questions at length, thanks, notably to the research carried out by a chemist, an archaeologist and a physicist, whose findings are surveyed in *Teka konserwatorska*, a Polish journal published in 1956. If France was less liable, at that time, to abandon traditional restoration techniques because of the material abundance of this artefact, even if it meant considerable loss, the less widespread stained glass of 14th-century Torun and Chełmno, for example, relocated in the

---

9. "a dead paper, without age": Ingeborg Bachmann, slightly modified from the French translation in *Franza*, tr. Miguel Couffon (Arles: Actes Sud, 1985), 163.

19th century to a castle in Malborg, are entitled to every manner of consideration. A survey of practices employed by various European countries, including England, Switzerland, Belgium or Austria, reveals considerable divergences.

¶ The relay between these practices, grafted onto a map of Europe where the rail lines, whose murderous charge has scarcely dissipated, registers against its correspondences the full sense of the *our* in question, its rupture and dislocation.

¶ As Rem Koolhaas recalls, by tracing the perilous journey, between the Spanish Civil War and the Third Reich, of elements of Mies van der Rohe's Barcelona Pavilion at the 1929 World's Fair: "The train journey was complicated. The railway tracks of each country were of different widths; many transfers were needed."[10]

¶ If the inclemencies provoked by changes in track gauge[11] furnish a sort of radiography of Europe in the days of *dead glass* as the trade indicates,[12] it is through a historiographic process similar to the optical illusion implemented in the restorative works of medieval stained glass; in other words recourse to the doubling of the primary matter by a piece of white glass whose armature will be determined by the current practices of a given context as well as the marked preference of the artisan.

¶ *Il mare era ferma come una lastra.*[13]

¶ The layers of glass attesting to different cultural, not to say geological, periods sample the dusts caught in time, an eternal present unsteadied by the eye. A time the extent of whose abyss is blindingly visible and infinitely traced, if not translated.

10. Rem Koolhaas, "Less is More: Installation for the 1986 Milan Triennial, Italy, 1985," in Rem Koolhaas and Bruce Mau, *S,M,L,XL: Office for Metropolitan Architecture* (New York, Monacelli Press, 1995), 54.

11. . . . . not to mention the difference between signaling systems employed by one country or another, or else the divergences between norms of electrification.

12. The facades of the German pavilion are made of glass. The building is also comprised of steel, marble, (Roman) travertine, and onyx elements. Rem Koolhaas will reconstruct a modified version of the pavilion at the XVIIth Triennale di Milano, 1986.

13. Pier Paolo Pasolini, *Racconti Romani* (Paris, Éditions Gallimard, 2002 [1995]), 113.

¶ It is the rain that devitrifies, by dissolving the alkaline parcels of matter, in order to restore its sandy opacity.

¶ Between *death* and the *hand*, between the ancient glass and *suo doppio*, the eye is charged with the full expression of its disappointment. Say it is situated between two propositions the distance between which is disavowed:

"I saw something." and "I have no sex,"[14]

¶ Remove the stone, the glass remains to be photographed.

¶ It is Kawabata Yasunari who, in a text entitled "Kinjū," ("Of Birds and Beasts") avers: "There are birds among the very young of which it is impossible to distinguish male from female. Dealers bring whole nests down from the mountains, but as soon as they can recognise them they throw away the females which will not sell because they do not sing."[15]

¶ *Una lastra* speaks all at once the (metal) plate, the stone (slab) or the (opaque, transparent) pane. It also articulates, in common parlance, the radiography, proffering the *still* narrative of successive materials, from the writing machine to the dreamed *insula*.

¶ By night, the building is lit with sodium, the body floats in a lead mesh. The neighbourhood drowns in insomnia, its fists beating the door from its hinge.

¶ I have no reason to be dismayed. We have entered into history.

14. Ingeborg Bachmann, from *Franza*, 162.
15. Kawabata Yasunari, *House of the Sleeping Beauties and Other Stories*, modified from tr. Edward Seidensticker (Tokyo, Kodansha International, 1969), 133.

Schrödinger's Ovaries

The Laws of Quantum Mechanics

i. Put a cat in a steel box, along with a flask of hydrocyanic acid. Also in the box: a tiny bit of radioactive material and a Geiger counter. If the radioactive material decays, the Geiger counter releases a little hammer that shatters the flask. Poor cat (dead cat). If not, the cat lives (still a poor cat, clearly having ruthlessly curious owners).

ii. According to the laws of quantum mechanics, until we take a measurement to see if the particle has decayed, it is in a superposition of states. Which is to say, it is both decayed and not-decayed at the same time. What does this mean for our unloved cat? He, too, is now superposed. Both alive and dead until we, like gods in lab coats, open the box.

iii. Here is what I would like to know: what does the cat feel like, being both alive and dead? Would he prefer a quick resolution? If it were up to the cat, would he stay inside that box to avoid the very real possibility of being 100% dead? Or is the press of the steel walls and the constant question of his own mortality too much? Better to know, he might say, were he both un-boxed and gifted with speech, than to survive in a state of constant superposition.

Steel Boxes

i. At the age of 48 my mother was diagnosed with ovarian cancer. It was both a tragedy (too young) and a miracle (caught early by the grace of an overcautious gynecologist). She had scheduled the appointment a month earlier than normal and attributes this to divine intervention. Days after the appointment, they cut into my mother and took out two tumors. The one that had been detected by the gynecologist was the smaller of the two; the other was the size of a lemon. After months of hats and radiation, remission. This is not the story of my mother's cancer.

ii. In the great afterwards, they tested her for genetic mutation. Too young, they said, and they were right. BRCA1: a human gene that produces tumor suppressing proteins. BRCA1 positive: a term for a person with a mutation to his or her BRCA1 gene, such that the gene no longer does its gene-ly duty. How much of a difference does one mutation in one gene out of roughly 25,000 make? Apparently, a lot. By the age of 70, a 60% chance of breast cancer and a 40% chance of ovarian cancer.

iii. The child of a BRCA positive person has a 50% chance of inheriting the mutation. A coin flip. Phenomenal odds for the lottery. Less great for the cat.

Time Evolution

i. Before I leave for college, I think, I will get tested. My mother pressures me to wait. "You're so young! You don't need to have that hanging over your head." I want to say, it is already hanging over my head. I want to say, I can already feel the press of the walls. But I don't. She has already had to deal with ovarian cancer. Instead, I wait.

ii. In college, I think, I will definitely get tested. Best to get it over with. In the absence of measurement, the cat is only half-alive. There is always a part of him that is dead. But I must learn the rules of quantum mechanics, and read about cats, and there are so many problem sets to do, and so many exams to take, and it is never the right time.

iii. After college, I think, I need to get to tested. "You're only 23," my mother says. "No rush." And I am moving, all the time. New York, Australia, Vermont, Colorado, North Carolina, Virginia, Maryland, Montana . . . Three months here, seven months there. No time to find doctors, dentists, gynecologists. It all falls by the wayside. I push it from my mind. A friend asks what I am running away from, and I laugh as though she has told me the world's best joke.

iv. "You still haven't gotten tested?" my mother asks. "You really ought to go. After all, it's better to know."

Wave Function Collapse

i. At the heart of Schrödinger's Paradox is a question about the type of world that we live in: is it a concrete place, full of objects in specific positions that move in predictable ways? Or is it amorphous, probabilistic, and significantly more random than we once thought? Does God play dice?

ii. Understand: the probabilities that live at the heart of quantum mechanics are the not the comfortable, epistemic probabilities that we know and love. It is easy to misconstrue the cat's predicament: we do not *know* whether he's alive or dead, and therefore there is a 50% chance of one and 50% chance of the other. But this is a misconstruction. If we embrace wholeheartedly all these complicated quantum mechanical suppositions, the probability is objective, not epistemic. The cat *is* both alive and dead, simultaneously. Our ignorance has nothing to do with it.

iii. So why is it that we only ever see an alive cat or a dead cat, not some hard-to-imagine hybrid? What changes when we open the box?

iv. In the world of quantum mechanics, measurement is pivotal. It is intrusive. There is no gentle culling of information while leaving the world unchanged. Every measurement causes collapse. We live in a probabilistic world, but whenever we poke at a probability with our chubby fingers it collapses into something concrete.

v. What is more, measurement is irrevocable. Once the box has been opened, there is no returning the cat to his superposed state. We can close and open the box another hundred times, and the cat will remain 100% dead.

Measurement

i. I wait until the worst of times. I leave my aunt's deathbed for the appointment. She is dying of lung cancer. Down the coast, my grandmother is dying of bladder cancer.

ii. If I asked my mother, she would tell me that it was all going to turn out fine. That she had *a feeling*. That the universe owed me some good news.

iii. I am not my mother, and I think that the universe does not give a fuck about my coin flip.

Superposition

i. I wait, surrounded by expectant mothers, hands rested protectively over their burgeoning stomachs. I wait, distant, some part of me still sitting in the distinctive quiet of hospice. I wait, and feel more acutely than ever before the way that I am split in two.

ii. They call me to the doctor's office, finally, half an hour after the appointment time. Then they leave me to wait some more.

iii. When the doctor comes in, he is smiling, and I let out the breath I did not even realize I was holding. He shakes my hand firmly, introduces himself. I know the answer before he begins.

i. I wait, surrounded by expectant mothers, hands rested protectively over their burgeoning stomachs. I wait, distant, some part of me still sitting in the distinctive quiet of hospice. I wait, and feel more acutely than ever before the way that I am split in two.

ii. They call me to the doctor's office, finally, half an hour after the appointment time. Then they leave me to wait some more.

iii. When the doctor comes in, he is accompanied by two scribes. He has the same look on his face that I did when I told my aunt's friend why she hadn't been home in ages. I know the answer before he begins.

Choose your own ending. Or don't. Let them co-exist.

i. I do not tell anyone. I take the folder of facts and probabilities home with me, and put it on the table. I make the follow-up appointments, as I have been told to do. I do not call my father; his sister has just died. I do not call my mother; her mother is dying. I hold the information in my hands like something fragile and try not to look at it too hard.

ii. At the follow-up with the breast specialist, the doctor tells me, "Nothing to worry about, but we'll just check to be sure." Then she says, "Nothing to worry about, but there's a small mass. Let's do a mammogram to be sure." The mammogram specialist says, "Nothing to worry about, but let's do an ultrasound." The ultrasound tech says, "Nothing to worry about, but let's do a biopsy." The biopsy doctor says, "I can't see anything to stick my needle in, but let's do an MRI."

iii. I spend a week waiting for results. The panic is quiet but heavy, keeping me pressed down into my bed late into the day. When the doctor's office calls, they use words like, "cystic" and "dense." They tell me not to worry, to repeat all tests in six months.

iv. Here then, is the new pattern: tests and panic, followed by willful forgetting, followed by more tests and more panic. CA125s, MRIs, mammograms, ultrasounds. I learn the odd thrumming language of the MRI machine. I look away as they stick the needles in my skin. It never becomes old and unthreatening.

v. My odds are better than a coin flip. I am young. I have knowledge and therefore power. What I know is this: some part of me, however small, is already dead. I live around it.

vi. Inside a steel box, a cat sits, waiting. He is waiting for the box to open, waiting for the inevitable collapse. To be both alive and dead is tiring. It is time to know.

Malorum Sanatio

The century or year or night one might bloom a miracle
A night-blooming cereus white   this could heal you
Or decorate the new abyss turn the year backwards un-
Fasten its manacles we have a different year on Jupiter
These transgressions in their authentic beauty digress
Like a pasted-on feather I want to know if I'm healing
Him oh so talented dead man illiterate unlettered I say
In the dark club playing his unlettered guitar as I stand on
This corner I've got two containers you've got two dogs
I'm supposed to know why in order to heal you or him am I
Let's not concentrate on what it means dead guys with
Past to be unpasted pressed over with letters who can
Read them and random sequins mounted whole pet-
Ite you are blocking the way of the killer I'm dead now you
Say to your harmless dogs in the halogen faintness of my
Thought have I healed you yet I'll continue to try
On the street corner behind broken ice whatever planet

If it's a feeling I have to heal or if it's a disease
If it's the torpid depths of your eyes you don't have here
If it's your loss of self-location the safe house I counter
With an electric provocation my own talent the
Speech of a riff or bladed number like thirteen blue
Paste that on if I can enter our mind and stay just a-
While to tell you you don't need what happened on the pla-
Net of brutal futile actions throw them away the dust-risen
Thinking of illusorily-limbed bodies half-
Erased creatured of woe we lumber
And I left home oh and stumbled over tragedy a sack of in-
Edible pebbles I'm sorry you have some hurt throw it away

We call guilt up every morning one says put it there and let
It be there let it follow you until it's gone grief
I can heal you illiterate reader the night is my eye

Is the healing a thing can you see or listen to as whispering
Allowed in at the universal we're all the abyss all there
Crowded staircase could be descended to dark grace no
Someone pleading for comment on her poem on shiny paper with
Rosette sticker paste it on the void I said I've been given the
Rosetta Stone stolen the secret crystal you are a pun and I too
Thus healable manu à manuscript fiery about your invisible head it
Off I am healing you with paste it on the collage danger
Anger'd backwards frightened till he as if menial
Tried to slip away crowded as if he could be forgotten
No one will be and you must exist dead or alive
I stole healing slab of crystal kept in a grey pouch don't
Come in here a voice said but I have brought back every dimen-
Sion that I am mentioning till I find the one in the pun you are
No one gets out of here unhealed
                              The force of the rosette
Or any cheap posy or portrait of a being paste
It on the healing and project all your old identities as if
One of them might be you project the one with unkempt hair
And the one punk where authoritative with a knife or
The one of you softened I put it on the one with no one gets
Out of here unhealed battered by grief bastard you're rife
With spirits of the murdered or dread like a capo everyone's
No one gets out of here a fake was everyone and caped I'm
Healing you of all your fakery burden of that
Which one was the real and is it re I Al or is it you or
Oo the two empty eyes I pun till it's genuine
For I can heal any rag of soul slime cloth
A bucket-headed dunce of a dancing jackass confidential
Here you are don't any person planet cloud or sublimation of a one
                              try to slip away

It comes from the dissolution of action what happened you were ineffectual
Incapable inasmuch as an abyss with old images gliding over you
I murdered and harmed you say   Stupid your victims are all alive here
I had vile motives   There is no such thing as a motive you were
As you see an empty snakeskin a hack's diary lived
The account of your deeds virtuous or ruffianly is boring
Your attempts at constructing a character have failed likeness non-
Existent there is nothing established consider yourself ethereal
And if the stars melt could they call out heal me of my
Bulk and burning heal me of my properties punned my
Light you who suppose I have never thought or knew I was on fire

You who are dead here I say forget all but new memory
Remember from now remember from nothing to recall
While I walk on faux tiles of Paris my mind glides
The nothing that loves me grins like a bat I am healing you
Terrapin shell heartless non-one the shoals of hypochondria
Only beauty never tepid always neutral lives at the first
I claim everything as my abyss in order to heal you
I haven't any idea who you are praying mantis paramecium
Faces or fecal in the heavens orange choral shouts
I don't care what you did or have I search for the one lang-
Uage to heal in which infants recognize when anyone sings
The terpsichorean weeps from raging as another
Is that it an act yes tears chrysalises of graced
Thing which comes in the aftermath but this is only
What we are creating and you who still live are here
Too in the part of your mind you're unconscious of
Beyond the old words this collage pun re-cognates
What you once knew starting now tipped to a reconnaissance
Like fingertips or pebbled surface knowing a mirror's essence
Because we've all always known each other shudder at the moon
You have to be here lily-breathed or punctual
Projecting the fungal or fiery with what sounds or
Thought I've always heard you blackness speaking

And I go in there abyss or us and paste on a heart for it
After I see it or rosette or transfusion any red word
What do you care you aren't your forms
What do you care if you dreamed your enactment or life
After I see and after I see it so I can heal you the universe
The imagery we'd made of origin had been catastrophic
But what I enter is a pearl a round chamber of whiteness
I alive can only see as if I were in perfect luminescence
I mean I am in it or am it nothing happens in the void
Nothing ever happened except in your dream of a creation
I sit in this pun and I touch its curved wall speaking
I sit in origin not an explosion but tthisss

It didn't have to be or did it out of this chamber if I'm telling
A myth or truth only a point of origination you can't break
Me I'd say then words materialize on the white wall
Do you hear what the voice says they say it's my voice
Oozed out in faintness then healed what is heal to come back
To this hole I was in it I changed her diaper pun and gave her back to you
Each one was one and I can understand whatever you say or think
Because I don't have to the waves aren't water
His eyes closed when he talks to me could be a word from any language
You have come here to heal where nothing happened except for a voice
                                        a perfect quality you are

One says it might be you healing between the syllables
Abacus with segmental notions would one need
Would one need to flower flow or congeal like a rock
One need to be in layers or sparkling clusters unseen
Would one need to be seen or unseen heard or unheard
Touched or left solid and still inside a cloud red for no one
You know you can never die   that doesn't heal
And you have loved many times   that doesn't heal
You have an identity apart from your loves that might heal
That in its vastness connects with theirs again

The vastness can you touch it without skin or organ
Why are you living what other and the waves again of no water
Simple each line in beauty though the rubies be hemoglobic
Not every entity bleeds and the scratched excrescences
Of words from the inner surface of the pearl return
The first healing first heal the first to be is first to heal
The first rupture it doesn't say that it says I break through
A free black slick-coated prairie dog running in boundlessness

Spidery or unilinear like scabs of scratched drawings
Healed as soon as they're born sores or breaks in nacre I'm
Healing you leading you and healing almost the same word
Breaking open with something vulnerable to know
To memorize a motion a structure I am healing you
Inside the whiteness of your eyes a thing blazes known
Torn admired those can be rot maddened ever in
Principle quality-less you hear my heart of figures
There is nothing there but a sound for what ears
There is nothing there but smoothness for whose fingertips
Mental for a mind I am healing you a mind
What did you think the mind was another thought 'oral cult'
The overriding impressed so that you forgot going west
I qualify Elijah as a train break enter like light
There can't be any real light what would be real light
The airplanes in the letters spelling pick up the receiver
I am trying to reach appeal to you I am healing you
Across your dusky chest with all these words in it
Knitted together like a better flesh I am healing you
There's the unfindable waving how many fingers
I'm told the language I seek is hidden where I am

At the point where in a forest you became flesh the words ap-
Peared back and forth between skin and words sound and
Air your body transport remember there was no environment
It was green stagelike a void and one was a knight with a k

And one was a night with an n I am a knight or night
Come to meet you unpressed for time perhaps wrinkled or winks
We were images of people you were painted I was eyes
In the forest of void near the winkles near the coast
Everything washes over some seeps in purificatory
My words keep coming towards your pain until it's an il-
Lusion break into your heart scab over and are written
Are you literate does your memory read I will never be bet-

Ter if I can't remember who I was before I was written on
Marked and erased me my heart made so narrow
I remember these old old words to who soul pierce
The sound of where one sat near the waterless sea
All of us call come here and be healed of displeasure
Healed of extreme distress of disease imbalance and fit-
Fulness healed of every mark that hasn't a source in your
Spirit healed of ruptures between substances these words
Are pure without cynical precedent or calculation
I obtain for you the blessing of others we heal and holding are you
Falling away so you can remember all words ever spo-
Ken in any language remember thoughts all thoughts
For you can in one instant be healed knowing everything
Remembering everyone and finally remembering who you are

DANIELLE PAFUNDA

I dwell in the road to the sea everyone travels and dwell in your house preparing to haunt you if I'm not doing much later and dwell on your face and if you don't aggrieve me I or my daughters might could come back

When you go to the door to the sea god's house also / my house a place I dwelled / guarded / by a seabird who doesn't stop for pain / heats fire rocks and trash dugouts / drops hots into your gut a cooked meal that bakes you and tells each blind a holy hide a / nightbird cocks the moon until it's soft / shoots / into you a syringe-mouthed glistening jelly moon / potion shot into your coal your / heart like a bubble a songbird stacking sand for notes taking / notes / flushed countenance / says bird: this guy's wreck and mealsome says: garbage like a chime that brings / brings bearings rings all the birds to the yard I won't / go down / when you come / my face guarded door where I keep time I keep time lashed a bad daughter and trade her for my / daughter / standing in the ditch by the road to the sea everyone travels I don't want her to obey / you and / I don't want her / to obey me I want her like a bad daughter all legs climbing out of the squabble oven over the crust of a crater bored into earth do not bore my daughter

or

she will flay you she spools a strip of time the poisoned peel she doesn't eat it wiser than I / at her age by her age / I / had a husband / had to spit a red mouthful at his guests' feet my / chores included serving them my unguarded smile and ungirding my hospitality without / enjoying the congress or its session I hid / wore war my knees but not for him lace habit / in this shaft of time I'm laced in / perma-revolution to my daughters to my bad habits every day / this belief that pain / my greedy hold on time's meal-core slowcore sadcore revolve of flesh that can't keep juice turns rugged and greasy / venison double fisting antler and throat or

leather game falls back in the sand / if you don't want to go to the underworld
go / underwater and no hot god will fool you going deep out in salt laters
where the ribbed / gown sea tides salt-stiff white bridal habit / you call out nun
call acolyte you call / them / daughters and they turn off their phones I can't
remember how men got my number after / I gave it up on a makeshift altar /
altered it / on my knees dull classic but you encounter the ropes say the grace
of each knot forbid beautiful images line up for record and by the time / their
turn's to come / beauty's convulsions give over to something we don't recognize

or

fertile sound of wave that carries wreck on rock irritating your ear where birds
wheel / too close by checking you for doneness / done in this / give up

or

I don't want this for you I wanted to give you sight through a new lens / mine
/ drilled cut deep absorbing / you bathing unusual visage from the rocks I
observe / your flesh / before all birds splintered vessels and rusted shafts / were
my face / opening against / your dryfire skin and the refraction of salt infinite
crystal patina / auric from any angle we were / in it and I / had my arm
out coated in raw jewels / pulsing with favor humming your favorite not too
worried who has frankincense / or benzoin out here on the weary hippie road
/ reserve sage verbena hardy mint lavenders none longing sticky in your crook
/ shush

or

if you don't want to go to the underworld go out to the desert and don't look /
look / like that / look back at me your eyes smoked four nights a crystal sewn
deep / in the mountain's hot thigh I get a beak for a needle and tear out the
stitches / what the fuck happened to you I thought you were born I thought
we were / on / earth I thought this must be the place but it had a false pedestal
through which / time / the holler behind my face guarded by you know
guarded

or

so fucking many winged wheels of fortune bearing each the premonition /
of its relic body and maybe / mine / own death and handler thereafter / you /
don't get to die and lie down you get to be ravaged again by the hospital

or

salt and dirt deep loosed to the murder wind was just feeling up some other /
person / put your skin against mine and teach me the true fact of hugging let
me know / no show / show me how it's okay to have run the length of the road
from desert to sea and then the length of / your body my arms / restrained
against the ground perform for me the embrace so I / don't break it / break
against this shaft down this astonishing shaft the swallow time does / it to us /
each time my daughter calls / home a movie she says / sorry, mama / you don't
/ get an invitation to the house of the dead exes weeping salt on the inlet its
mouth a'foam with rocks without / falling down a shaft or two / you don't have
to get it yet / you'll know us forever / we're ore

sick in "America"

before the crossing[1] our family could understand the whispers of the water.[2] we bathed our cuerpos morenos as if we we were holy: as if our humanity was valuable, as if we were worth life. it is hard to remember anything before the crossing.[3] how do i tell myself i had a childhood if at the age of five i am a fugitive[4] of the law? it would be easier to remember life before the crossing[5] if we didn't become paralyzed for the rest of our lives: the doctor tells me i have post traumatic stress disorder. he says it is because i am an immigrant,[6] but that in a few years, i will be american.[7]

---

[1] during the crossing // we were faced with // the reality // of what it means // to be black and indian // in an empire // that constantly measures us // on production // production // and production. // our blood // a sustenance // for those // who deem us "illegal."

[2] the water here // has been cut through // by wooden logs // that demand // we show them // papers that say // we are not poor // nor indian or black.

[3] i only crossed once // (location: // san diego/tijuana border // age // five // how // by foot and car.) // but every story heard // becomes another crossing // my body remembers every crossing // every crossing becomes mine // my body has experienced every crossing // in dreams.

[4] fugitive: american indian boarding school runaway// fugitive: runaway slave // fugitive: runaway soon-to-be-lynched negro // fugitive: assata shakur // fugitive: mike brown // fugitive: sandra bland // fugitive: alan carlos pelaez lopez.

[5] crossing: the precise location in a five-year-old's life where they lose their humanity, health, and livelihood. // the site where the child realizes their guiding spirit is weakening // the body, changing // the mind, confused // the flesh, shivering // eyes, watering // digits, dancing. // the site where "americans" will blame the child for "infecting" the "american dream." // the site where a child is just a child visiting occupied Indian land.

[6] "the black body does not migrate . . . it is shipped"—tavia nyong'o

[7] american: i guess i'll be forever "sick."

from *Force Drift*

from Force Drift

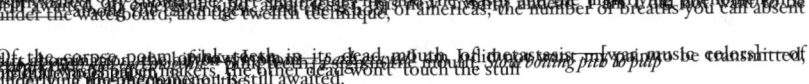

Of the corpse poem, pink teeth in its dead mouth——*black, red, bronze, gold-black, dark red, brown, gleaming, red, yellow-chrome, fire-lit, bronze*——of the underlying mechanisms of how I am in the epic, I am I did not want my pain to be transmitted, dirt abomination, the bitten symptom—park grayed by paper-ash and carcinogenic dust—pink teeth, a sign in the mouth, me and the wasps paper-makers, the other dead won't touch the stuff, slow boiling pith to pulp, I am I did not want to be asphyxiated, dry submarine, dirt submarine, swarming with the casualties, of or through metastasis, and the underlying phenomenon is still awaited, an emergent kind, albeit lesser, this new lividity, undead, I am I did not want to be detained

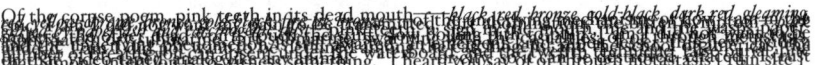

among the carcinogens, and the school of americas, the number of breaths you can absent under the waterboard, and the twelfth technique, false burial, bite on that, video-taped, analog like any animal   or city, so it can be destroyed, effaced, "I trust that Simon's intention is to witness something," I heard you say of or through metastasis [*as they enter the performance space, audience members are each given a shred of car tire to hold, a token of entrance and passage; rubber is burnt throughout; a montage of blasted cityscapes is projected throughout the space and plays on a loop*],   like any acid or school of americas, I am I did not want my naked sex to die in under the second device of simulated death, that will not be torn out of mind, Guantanamo, [*and when the maximum decibels of Skinny Puppy subside, only once or twice, a minimal composition plays as relent, relent must be felt to be possible*   *of lasting*] beyond the traumaeffect of

simulated death,   I am I did not want to be the long century of it, the school of
the Aleph, bare life, digital, sexually humiliated, naked, "constant white noise, no
talking, everyone in the dark with the guards wearing a light on their [psychological]
heads...." of or through metastasis, and Simon's intention to witness something," I
heard you say—I am I do not want to be the proof of how it evacuates, shatters,
breaks apart levels the built world," and the underlying ——it's not a mechanism, the
ground-form of the person, think we must, I heard you say under the carcinogens,
and the second device, the other dead won't touch it,   r a i n f a l l
(nuclear), low apartment buildings sheared open to the gun-wrecked air—*pink,* [teeth]

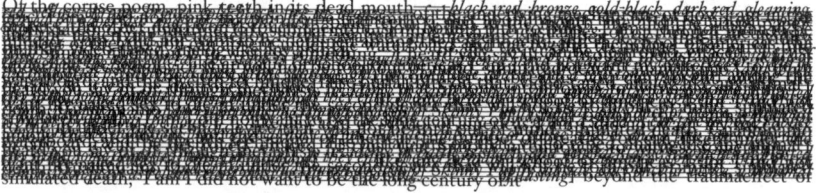

black [sunlight], *silver, gray,* [air], *weapon-grade chrome*—throat   throated, that
constant white noise, naked, enforced, corrosive of   the person, strange flora in the
flashback   "this shit is everywhere," and the excruciating plastic of the feeding-
tube in cases, before they removed the throat, obey,   disobey, I was I am not a thing

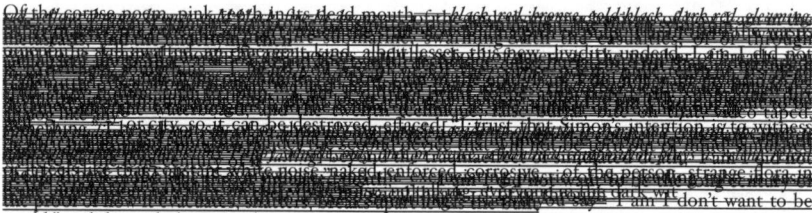

to be torn out of mind, a thing torn out at the traumaeffect, I heard you say "we
know all," through metastasis, I am not that Gul Rahman, I was I am not that Yasser
Talal Al-Zahrani, not that Riyadh the facilitator, I was I am not that mujahideen,
there are no records (a trace) that attest, false burial, to be black sunlight leveling

292

the built world, streets sheared,   throated, thinking the metastasis of the disaster,
dirt abomination, and not its relent, not what I thought would it be—*gleaming, red,*
yellow-chrome, gold-black—and it smelled like   tea under the dome, I only felt it once
[*a chorus of women, some dressed in white, some in black move throughout the performance*
space, they improvise dances, and sometimes ululations, in response to the musics, and images
being projected]—strange flora in the flashback in which I am   a person of strange

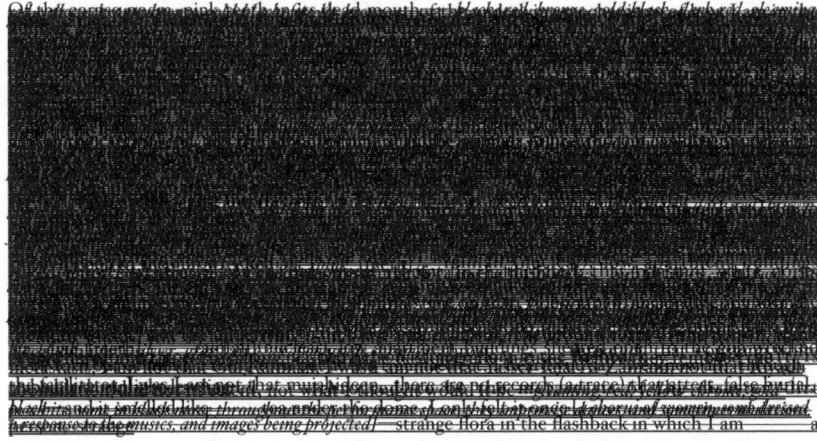

flora, earth—*black, red, bronze, gold-black, dark red, brown*—body, dirt network,
sprawling, excruciating through the flashback, a remnant   like any animal remade
at the traumaeffect,   the long century of it, underneath it, a silhouette on the earth
where the city used to be, white strange flowers, a trace of the city wall,   m u r a l
flowers, sprawling   rhizomatically—all through the school of americas, that cruel
metastasis——not what I thought it would be, dirt submarine, I am not that Yasser,
not mujahideen,   before they removed the throat, ginger,   pink teeth,   irises,

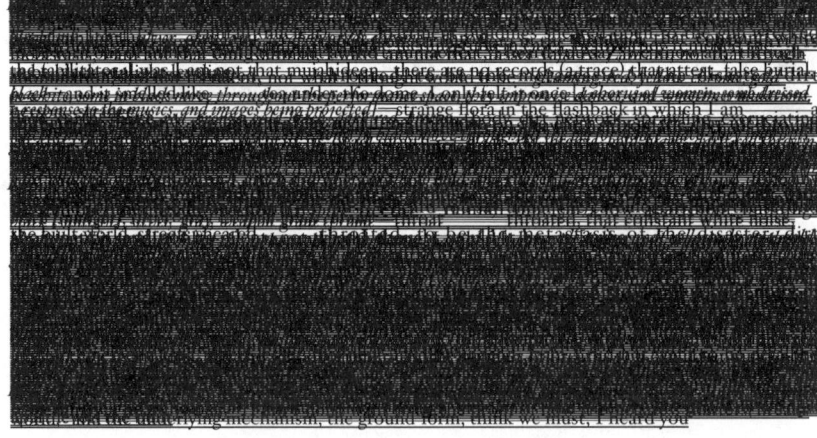

say under the ~~carcinogens, and the second device, the other dead won't touch it,~~ ~~the~~ ~~light of black Latin~~

[*intermittently throughout the ritual a woman, or whole chorus will approach an audience member, establish some kind of connection, or gestural accord, and as these relationships evolve, and ultimately find their durational shape, the chorus will whisper a message to the audience member (themselves now an integral part of the rites), and this is the sign that the ritual has ended for this person, and they leave, and it is understood that the'll keep the message, as a private token of passage, and exit back into the sudden, and catastrophic world.*] pink rigor

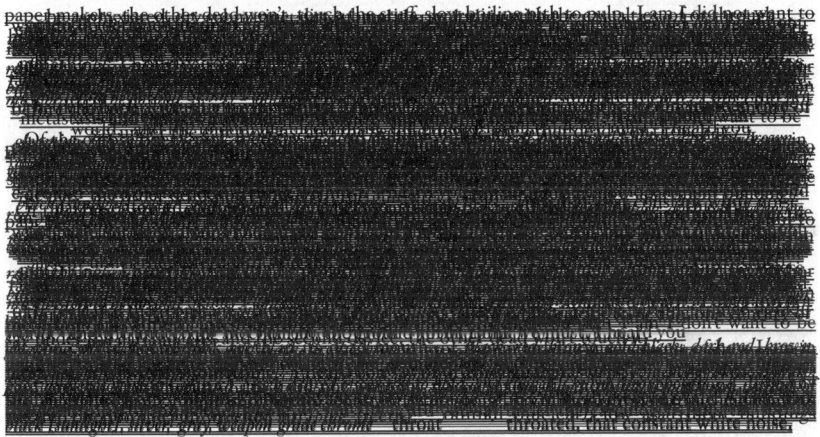

nuclear   rainfall, eyes, irises,   and plastic sandbags, rubber, cords, wires, low apartments throated, streets torn out   at the disastereffect, a trace, an afterimage already   even before they removed the throat, underneath it, a person remade at the traumaeffect,   a person of strange flora, and dirt, earth,   c o l o r slides of it, this burial piece—*gold-black, red, yellow-chrome, bronze, dark red, brown, gleaming*—slick, chthonic now as if that were a solution, bare life,   n o s u n l i g h t underneath the twelfth technique, I am I did not want, earth,   I am not bare life, I heard you say   through metastasis, the other dead won't touch it, this paper effect, and intention to witness something, I am not that remnant,   earth, earth, not that pain to be transmitted, the long century of it, chthonic now,   no sun light, earth, earth,   earth, swarming with the causalities, e x c r u c i a t i n g   all through the flashback, [*and now a chorus approaches you, and you find yourself taken up into the sensuous and gestural accord, that project of the human, you move through the dance, then one of the chorus, whispers to you a sentence of perfect secrecy*], in a long century of dirt.

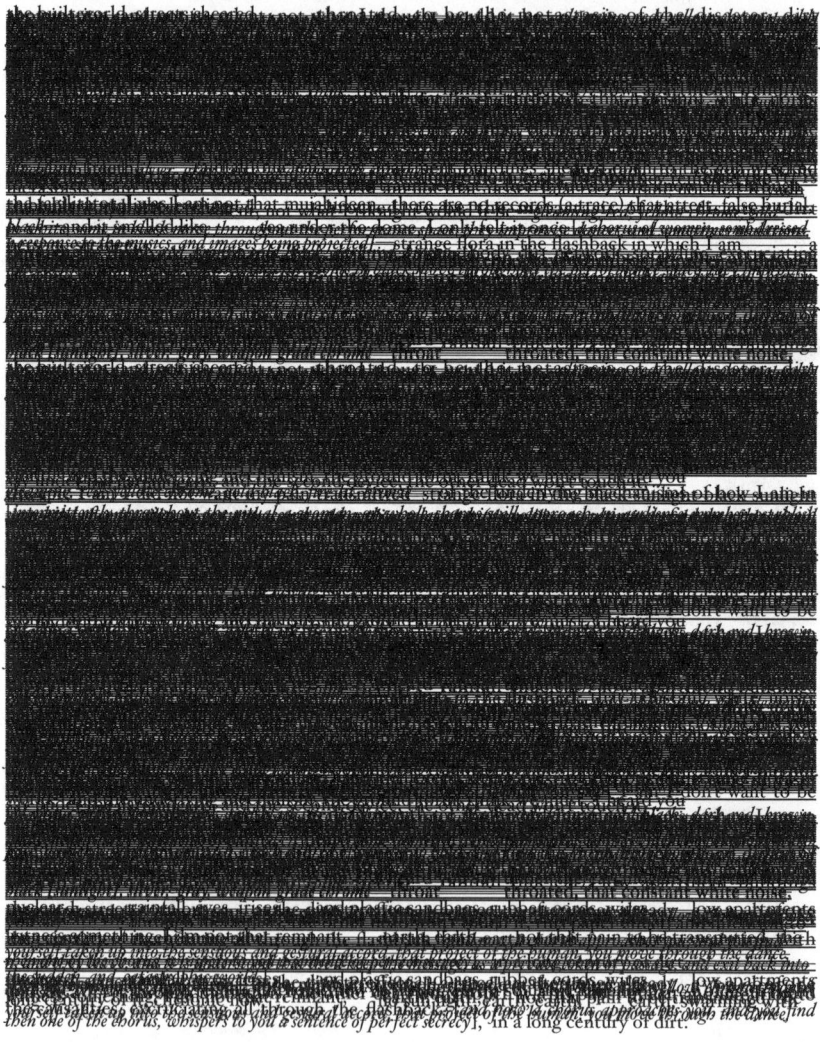

Anarcha and I Negotiate Trauma

Anarcha passed me hers by her teeth and I nearly choked in the making of
space for her mammoth seed alongside mine. I trusted her with a mouth too
full to speak. I trusted her to slide something flora inside of me. The first time
I felt another person's desire it was pressed on my leg and this leg was pinned
to the couch. In so wanting to tell this, I pitted my mouth twice. There was
meat initially on the peaches that we halved off and fed to each other making
sure to miss the mouth enough for the lips and neighboring skin to get sweet
and slick. Anarcha had oil-slick arguments with me, and I felt shudder when
they were over. I never wanted to nutcracker someone's head with my thighs
so badly. She told me the children knocked the latch off her bladder when
they came into this world. She told me her body was yet living, and still a
body donated to science, but she wanted to be taken with and by me. Around
the pits, I said, I am a poet and a queer and I cannot real-estate a bit more of
my tongue to doctors or men. And with this heavy mouth, I spouted these
words in whale song. Inaudible. Why don't you spit those out, she said, so I
can hear the yes that's under all that seed?

Edmonia Lewis and I on Academic Leave

We rush to a movie theater first, where the quiet is kept by dozens of heavy, resting tongues. From the back row Edmonia studies the way film glow illuminates every movie-goer silhouette. I'm used to her obsession with anatomy's infrastructure. We return to our shared apartment, but only after she's gorged her pupils on the cheekbones of a sleeping woman. The night we met, Edmonia viced my jaw in her god hand. I was more frightened by what she could learn from the strain in my hinges than the dull pain she pressed into my mouth. That same night she told me that it's impossible to bring a lover to the small death she deserves. An orgasm is excavated, not given, she told me. I would never argue about pleasure. I would never argue with her hand on my throat. I still feel fully enrolled when she swings my limbs from chill to pose. She's sculpting a hard woman in my image. Rome, she says, that's where we need to go. It's one of those modeling sessions where I forget I'm naked, almost forget my body all together. I break her rule and sway out of the way she's fixed me. I float across the room. The places where Edmonia's bones were fractured still hold those violent reverberations. When it rains I massage the static hum out of each point of impact. She's too busy building me, perched among the pillars of Italy to see I've gotten up. I put my hand on the dip in Edmonia's back so she knows at this moment, she is cleaving the wrong woman.

OLGA RAVN

Translated by Sherilyn Hellberg

from *Celestine*

Chapter 1: She is dressed in white

She was supposed to get married, or do something, one thing or another, but she refused. They held a party in her honor and at night they walled her in without anyone noticing. They said, sure thing, you can stay here forever and live forever like the mist that rises up from the meadow when the day changes from cold to warm. But your young lovely body will wither and you will become just a little shadow, throwing itself against a wall without being able to move it. Who will love you now? Who will listen?

As time went by, she became just a bit of honey in the corner of a little hidden room, and then only her voice and her shadow were left. And then actually not really her voice at all, but just a shadow. And this rhythm of the heart like a deranged girl's scream as she crawls around the bog looking for a lost jewel, and then, after her screams, the silence that comes when the night ends.

In my room at the castle, I stood in front of the round mirror at midnight and said her name three times. I had come to listen and also to offer my body. I wanted to be haunted by her. I wanted to be the new wall where she could lie down and breathe, quiet and rasping like an animal. But nothing happened. Really, nothing happened. I went to bed, and I could hear the cooking staff rattling a few floors below. In the window, there was still a little light over the fjord, a vibrating streak of green across the horizon like the dark's eyeliner.

They had named her Celestine. People said that her parents, as punishment for having fallen in love with the wrong person, at a party in her honor, it was in the middle ages, drugged her and put her behind the wall, sealing it around her, so that she would suffocate behind it. She had to be made into a part of the home. People said that she had traveled to Schleswig. Or people said that she had gone into the forest. But actually, she had become a part of the walls of the home, so that she lay there and breathed her last breath, and so she died in the midst of her rage.

Celestine, she is dressed in white. I draw her by tracing over my own shape. That's the only thing I can do.

I've come to the castle in the hopes of finding a home. I would like to learn from the ghost how to become a single story that repeats itself. I would like to learn how to stay standing in the same place, to walk the same route, to insist. I would like to remain inside what can't be called forgiveness. I want to hate, that should keep me upright, that should keep me occupied.

Chapter 2: Arrival at the castle

When I arrived at the castle, the summer was at its peak. The big rhododendron bushes were starting to bloom.

I walked into the forest behind the castle. The bus driver had told me about a shortcut, I was on foot. First, I walked along the field. The grass was wet in my tracks. The summer was clear.

They said that Celestine walked the same route each night, that you could hear scratching noises coming from the wall. I wanted to lay down inside her and find rest there in her restlessness.

I walked out of the forest and into the back part of the garden, among the enormous bushes. They were slumbering like big animals in the sun. An older couple was walking between them, but otherwise the whole area was empty. At the other end of the park, there was a little castle, smaller than I had expected, without any towers.

Suddenly, I had this thought that something inside me had always resisted everything I had ever experienced.

I was unemployed and the heat was terrible. In the city, the summer had run its brush, dripping with white, over the houses. In the parks, the heat hung like a curtain and glittered with insects, and my heart became salty with sweat.

Every day, Kim came by on his lunch break to hang out and eat. We found ourselves in the coolness that belongs to the summer alone, that only occurs at the edge of the summer's hand. In my room, the glass in the picture frames reflected the swelling of the trees outside. Used glasses and plates were all around us. The bedspread had fallen onto the floor, it spread some velvety blue through the room. Inside me, a bonfire on a beach on Midsummer night. The sand is wet and the smoke rises in a purple shape, and it has just rained. People stand in clusters in small black groups, indistinct, they erase each other's bodies.

Kim was lying on the bed, opening and closing his eye. He rubbed his face and turned onto his side. He got up early every morning and went to work. It belonged to him alone, the early morning, that brief hour of the swallows, before the day really began. When he laid down to sleep around noon, his body seemed to ossify, almost blue, and with closed eyes, a milkiness seeped across his face in all directions.

The rain came suddenly. It sloshed happily in the streets and piled up in the basements. The flood should have been refreshing, but instead it covered the whole city in grease, slipping away as quickly as it came and leaving us even stickier than before.

I stood in my cousin's backyard and rummaged around in some boxes that had been soaked in sewage. The day had ruffled itself up quicker than usual, and it seemed like the light had cracked an egg out in a corner of the yard, and that the egg was running slowly out over the green expanse, at the same time as its whites were full of anxiety.

And so I stood there, cloaked in the light's egg whites and threw the whole mess out except for a green notebook which had been on top of a box, but still reeked. It was a sign of everything soaked and discarded, a kind of reminder of the flood, a souvenir from my earlier youth, everything that I had accumulated over the years.

The water sank quickly into the earth, leaving a squelching ball in the grass, muddied hands, destroyed cars, databases and DNA-banks, which otherwise would still be humming safely underground, but were now lost forever.

I decided that it was time to get away. And I thought that my fate was Kim's fate, that my fate was a hidden room, and that I should learn to eat this fate, and that I should learn to suck on it, and that I should learn to come to terms with everything that gathers on the skin, and that I too should have a past like everyone else does.

Rain came and went at the castle. It was between five and six o'clock at night. There were almost no other guests: just me and eight bankers attending a conference. The sky opened up again. The castle and park emptied of gardeners and other employees. Patches of yellow fields collapsed under the wind. Some of the tablecloths fluttered around the tables on the terrace like huge malicious flowers. A pair of waiters rolled a few cigarettes under the awning and stood there staring at the rain and smoking.

The darkness came and went with the clouds, and the sky blackened over the castle and the grounds again. It was storming, and the air was saturated with rain.

Celestine sits in her hole in the wall and listens to the drops with her dilated eyes as they hit the cobblestones in the courtyard and the leaves in the park. Her hands are in her lap. Black falls within her. She has no age, she is always sixteen. Century after century.

Right before the first downpour, I went for a walk in the park, that smell of coming rain.

I spent a single night at the castle, and then Kim came to pick me up. In the morning, the sun shone through the hedges like needles, and I ate an egg. The day touched my eyes. In the hall with the exhibition, a display case with a colorless bonnet inside that was said to have belonged to Celestine. The bonnet completely threw me, it was close to destroying me. Later in the morning, from the empty hall, I saw Kim's car in the window coming down the tree-lined path.

I left the hall, walking onto the broad terrace, and the heat, which the tiles had absorbed over the course of the morning, hit me in the face like an insult. I crept down towards the parking lot. Under a big oak tree in the middle of the open lawn, a woman was feeding a child in a wheelchair with a white spoon. The spoon turned yellow against her white dress. She was wearing a white straw-hat, and had laid her parasol on the grass. Then she pushed the boy and herself out of sight behind a bush.

The face, the voice, the hands against the wall. Celestine up in the south-facing eaves, in front of the stained mirror, and there is also a dried wreath there. In the darkness inside the wall, a glimmer of Celestine's eyes, in one of her eyes a nettle grows. In the forest that surrounds the castle, the leaves glitter with slime from the slugs. So much which glitters silver carries her name, Celestine, within it. She is furious, she hunts down the guests at the hotel while they are sleeping. She glides through the corridors, she licks their faces, she licks the sleep out of their eyes. She cries no no as the brick wall is sealed in front of her. Celestine sleeps beneath a tree inside me. I touch her carefully. She leaps, puts on her white suit. And see! The sun has risen high over the hedges, a large and crackling disc. Beneath it, a small red car, and on his way out of the car, a small red Kim.

fragmentos de "la cinta" / fragments from "the ribbon"

en las cintas más lindas

encuentro los nombres de

las

asesinadas
en las cintas más lindas
pero lindas
encuentro las niñas que desenredan
sus manos de los muebles encantado(re)s
el confeti de nieves específicas
la especialización de lo corrosivo
antelaciones de torres mensajeras
palomas que reemplazan
maravillas y cerros
apuntadas
las musas coartan los embarazos de filas
retrospectivamente cuentan días
12 desde el último cohete valiente

es la señal de que el reino se derrumba

on the prettiest ribbons

i find the names of
                    murdered
                                girls
on the prettiest ribbons
                the prettiest
i find the girls that unknot
their hands from the enchant(ing) couches
confetti of specific snow
corrosive specialization
advanced notice from messenger towers
pigeons that replace
maravillas y cerros
        jotted up
muses restrict the pregnancies of waiting lines
retrospectively count the days
12 since the last brave rocket

the signal that the kingdom crumbles

una cinta repetida

no necesita del sobaco doblado del mar en la noche
se independiza de los mariposarios estatales
todas las criaturas del bosque se reúnen en la leyenda
para susurrarse materiales gelatinosos
la tierra se derrite
nos morimos

nunca aprendimos a compartir nuestras monedas
con los demás metales
ni a fundir las alegorías
pisar no es sembrar
pero cómo nos hubiese conducido
al pulpo habitual del más y más

a repeated ribbon

doesn't need the folded armpit of the night sea
it separates from the state's butterfly pens
all the forest creatures meet in the legend
to whisper gelatinous materials
the earth melts
we die
we never learn to share our coins
with other metals
or fuse allegories
to step is not to plant
but oh how it would have lead us
to the habitual octopus of more and more

el largo desfile de altoparlantes en duelo

no serás mi última huelga
porque vamos a ganar
aunque tengamos que volver a la ganancia
con latas y descorchar dedicatorias que leen
lo que se pierde es la disrupción
lo que se pierde es todo

pero todo lo que echarás de menos
cuando la nada gane como en el cuento interminable
si existe un mangle de la tristeza
crece entre economía y humanidades
quizás en el sótano llamado cafetería
o en la primera vez que leí
la traducción de la iliada

     gracias profesora
     por explicar el amor entre hombres
     mediante aquiles y su jevo muerto
tuve residencia en la calle humacao como el pueblo
                en el pueblo
y sigo sembrando cercos traslúcidos
alrededor de la plaza del mercado

a long procession of loudspeakers in mourning

you won't be my last strike
because we're going to win
even if we have to return to earnings
with cans and uncork dedications that read
what we lose is disruption
what we lose is everything
yes everything you'll miss
when the nothing wins like in the neverending story
if a mangrove of sadness exists
it grows between the school of economics and humanities
maybe in the basement we call cafeteria
or the first time i read
the translation of the iliad
     thank you professor
     for explaining love between men
     via achilles and his dead jevo
i lived on humacao street like the town
               in the town center
and i keep planting translucid fences
around the plaza del mercado

cuando terminó la cinta

este se paró y gritaba
no se trata de los colores de la cinta
entra a la nueva dimensión deja
atrás tu cuerpo

es así que el cuerpo EL cuerpo
cayó en lo más profundo del argumento perfecto
confundido dejó de respirar
atento a las pelaeras y las palas
trataba de recoger la cuchara
pero el tiempo era diferente
era un mejor tiempo diferente

el parado se hundía y gritaba
no se trata de tu nombre
mejórate y libérate de la cinta
que te manda un quién te manda
con corazones limón
no es el color de tu supuesta cinta

EL cuerpo no sabía qué contestar
se sentía exento de los asientos
en los carritos de supermercado
y no podía llegar a la altura de la mesa

when the ribbon ended

this one stood up and screamed
it's not about the ribbon's colors
enter the new dimension leave
behind your body

      and this is how the body THE body
            fell in the deepest part of the perfect argument
confused it stopped breathing
fixated on brokeness and footsindoors
it tried to pick up the spoon
but time was different
it was a better time different

the one who stood sunk and screamed
it's not about your name
better yourself and free yourself from the ribbon
that sends you a who asked you
      with lemon hearts
it's not the color of your supposed ribbon

THE body didn't know how to answer
it felt exempt from the seats
in the supermarket carts
and couldn't reach the table

en puerto rico heredamos tus guerras

maldita sea las peleamos y qué nos diste

debajo de la iglesia de mayagüez hay huesos de taíno
y el padre lo sabe
todos los padres

312   dijo *toma la cinta y mide las dimensiones de la iglesia*
dime si vale la pena
por unos huesos destruir la fe
lo que vi cuando caminaba con mi cinta
eran viejitas sentadas rezándole a papito dios
con lágrimas de fe por sus criaturas
malformadas por el deseo
              aires de mejorar lo que no basta
vi las caras de santos algunos dulces y otros
tan arbitrarios como la abstinencia
más que todo vi el oro la crueldad

volví al padre tras cubrir la iglesia con la cinta
la escena de un crimen
y bendito no le pedí perdón
ni pude explicarle
       el nuevo odio

in puerto rico we inherit your wars

maldita sea we fight them and what did you give us

under the church in mayagüez there are taíno bones
the father knows it
all the fathers

he said *take this ribbon and measure the church dimensions*   313
tell me if it's worth
destroying faith for some bones
what i saw when i walked around with my ribbon
were old women praying to papito dios
with tears of faith for his creatures
malformed by desire
            airs of bettering what isn't enough
i saw the faces of saints some sweet and others
as arbitrary as abstinence
more than anything i saw the gold the cruelty

i went back to the father after covering the church
with the ribbon the scene of a crime
and bendito i didn't ask for forgiveness
nor could i explain
            the newfound hate

Walking along the Avenue of the Suicides, the Cockroach

Tous les garçons et les filles de mon age
se promènent dans la rue deux par deux.
—Françoise Hardy

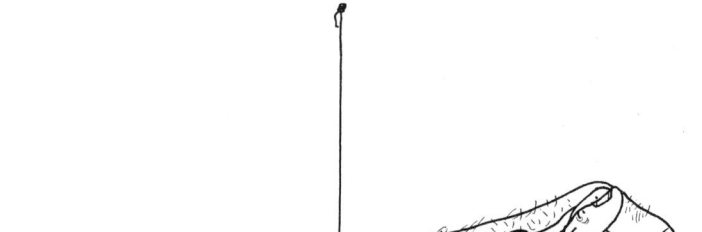

Walking along the avenue of the suicides, the cockroach takes the ant by the arm.

"We've been spending too much time together," she says.

Leaves fall over them like circus tents.

Intimacy, suddenly.

"I know we have," she says. "But it's my birthday on Sunday, and I wanted to invite you to the park with some friends."

"I would love to come."

She tightens her grip on her arm. "Tell me . . . were you ever with a man?"

"Now and then, yes. With one."

"Ohh, and what was it like?"

"I never let him inside me, if that's what you're asking."

"But didn't he want to?"

"Well, he never talked about it, but I could tell it was the only thing he ever thought about."

"How could you tell?"

"When he spoke, his words were thin, like panty hose pulled tight over a robber's face."

While the Two Slugs Take Turns
Drinking Shots of Vodka

it's like the refrain
or the stain of the refrain
—Elaine Kahn

While the two slugs take turns drinking shots of vanilla-infused vodka, the Spoon nibbles at the Sugar in whose bowl it sleeps. On the interior wall of the outhouse, the Drunk scrawls, PUKE OUTSIDE, and collapses.

"It's not even easy to write e-mails anymore—" says the Poet.

"Then, quickly, just say it," urges the Spoon.

"I always end up feeling disingenuous,—only makes me want to disappear."

"Ah."

"But! I don't want to have a secret life," says the Poet. "No. There are simply parts I need to keep private.

"I do so many things I'd rather not tell anyone about, you know."

"Like what?" asks the Pelican.

"When the whole world thinks I'm reading, chances are I'm on the internet . . ."

"That doesn't sound so bad," the Pelican reassures.

"Yeah, that's really nothing to worry about," says the Spoon from the sugar bowl.

". . . masturbating!" cries the Poet, met by a brief, but heavy, silence.

"I think what you need is—" says the one Slug who is still more than half-conscious.

"—a life coach!" shouts the Drunk from his dream.

"Exactly—how did he know what you were going to say?" murmurs the less than half-conscious Slug.

In walks the Life Coach, who resembles a life-size cardboard cutout of the 44th President of the United States of America: "Did somebody say my name?"

The Drunk wakes up and sprints away, suddenly sober as the Judge.

The Slugs crawl into glasses of beer, in hopes of a quick end.

The Pelican showily offers the Jeweler the Fish from his sagging bill.

The Poet says, "yes," as he fishes the two Suicides from the glass of beer with his index finger. "Yes, I'm afraid someone did say your name."

"It was him!" gurgles the Slug, pointing to the Drunk speeding out of the parking lot in his Dodge Durango.

"Why call the Life Coach if you think you have nothing to live for, my good slugs?" asks the Life Coach.

"Not for us. I was telling the poet he needs a life coach because whenever the world thinks he is reading he is actually on the internet . . ."

"Now, that doesn't sound so bad," reassures the Life Coach.

". . . masturbating!" adds the Poet.

"Ah, I see," the Life Coach whispers, snapping his fingers to some unheard beat. "That is rather grave . . ."

Through the door parade the Raccoon in a doctor's coat, the Cup of Coffee driving a garbage truck, and, in the hull of this truck, the Dozen Patches of Human Skin with tattoos of mermen and other mythical depictions of the male figure on them.

"What you need, I'm afraid," says the Life Coach in a suspiciously fearless tone, as if he has given the same prescription a thousand times—as if it were the only prescription he were capable of giving—, "is electroshock therapy."

"But . . . he's still just a boy!" screams the Poet's Mother as she rushes out of the bathroom, where, we can only assume, she has been canoodling with the Drunk.

"It has to be this way; it's the only way," say the Dozen Patches of Human Skin.

"Yes, if your son truly wants to change for the better, there is only one treatment," adds the Cup of Coffee resignedly from the driver's seat of the garbage truck. "And that's electro-shock therapy."

"Here!" says the Raccoon. "To reassure you, let us introduce you to the teenager we treated just last week. A true success."

From the hull of the garbage truck crawls the Teenage Guitarist with a stringless guitar. Although he is covered in fruit peels and appears to have been drenched in many flavors of rotten lassi, he is wearing only a sweater, just long enough to conceal his shame, its colors dulled by filth.

"He's . . . absolutely disgusting," words the mother can hardly articulate.

"I used to sit in my mom's basement writing love songs to myself," the Teenage Guitarist begins, "but I would pretend they were written for a little girl named Karen in my math class, and we would listen to them together, and we would kiss, and I would take her hand and put it in my pants and tell her exactly what to do with it, but the whole time I would imagine it was my own hand touching me, my own body I was holding, my own mouth I was kissing, and, God as witness, what a waste of time it was for her to be there as a means for me to access my own touch, my own body, literally nothing makes me more ashamed of myself, but, now that the Life Coach has treated me, my legs hardly move, I can hardly move enough to get out of this garbage truck, can't you see how I have to drag my body along with my arms, I can't even walk, can't walk to the bathroom to piss," and the crowd notices a deep yellow stain in the sweater where it falls over his crotch, "can't walk to school, to math class, can't walk from my house to hers, not even to my old house, and it's so wonderful because no one knows where I am, so how can I bother anyone anymore, how can I mistreat anyone if no one knows where I am, I'm not a nuisance anymore, I'm ethically pure, purified, and the thought of my own body makes me so sick that my hands rush away before me like terrified little animals, because I'm afraid to touch my own skin, but it's so confusing because, being made of my own skin, my fingertips are always touching me, so can't you, please, Life Coach, can't you please take off my fingertips, just burn them, or cut them off, anything, please, slice them off my fingers and put them on toothpicks and stick the toothpicks into the wounds—anything to distance them even just a little from my body."

"I don't want to be like him at all," says the Poet, whose Mother, weeping, proclaims, "but he is you—don't you recognize him? He is who you used to be."

And the Teenage Musician drags himself to the Poet and begins to kiss his shoes, and unlaces them. After removing his shoes, he begins sucking on the Poet's toes. And the Poet recognizes that he is witnessing his own past, witnessing himself sucking his own toes, and knows that, ten years ago, when he was this Teenage Musician, he kissed and unlaced this very Poet's shoes and, after removing them, sucked on his toes.

The Life Coach laughs. "Tell us what you are thinking, boy."

I'm not ready to speak, the Poet writes in his notebook, showing no one.

"Now I don't want you getting the wrong impression about me, or what I want from you. I'm really not looking for anything serious . . ." says the Teenage Musician.

"I know just what you mean," says the Poet, who places his foot on the Teenage Musician's head, turns it face down, and presses it into the floor with all his might until the Teenage Musician's arms wriggle.

The mother rejoices. "You're cured!" she exclaims.

". . . For all the wrong reasons," whispers the Bowl of Peanuts.

". . . Yes, for all the wrong reasons," hisses the Life Coach, licking clean the four crooked prongs of a chocolate-covered fork.

The White Plastic Bag floats by, falling over his head.

The Gust of Wind ties it shut around his neck.

ERIC SCHMALTZ

Path Dependency

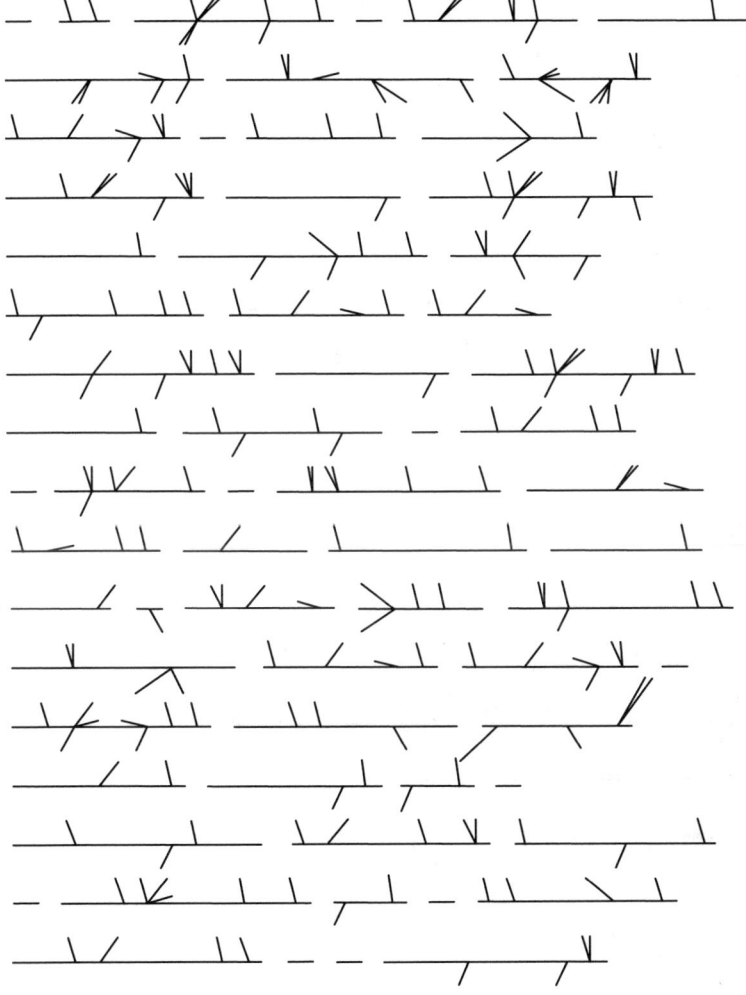

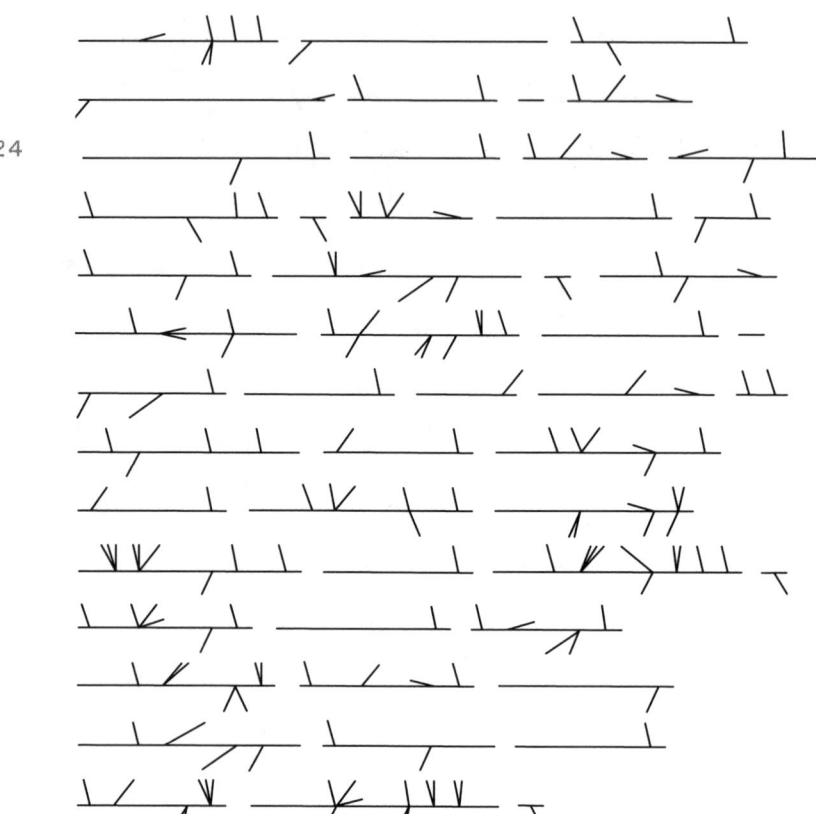

Revenge Porn

—someone had emptied a bottle of red wine at the exit of the bus station, the stain like the line of hairs between my navel and cunt. The station smelled dense—your mouth at the end of a night of partying, Sweetheart, when you wanted to have sex and I turned to you, eyes wide and desperate, said, "Kiss me first," but we couldn't because alcohol had dried our mouths. "Told you so," you told me.

Across the wine stain, a Rajasthani man in khaki pants and a tucked-out shirt played ravanhatha that sounded like weeping. I scrambled for money. Musicians barely appeared on the roads anymore and when they did I wanted to tell them, "Don't leave, please."

• •

(Today my lips are fissured, purple wine in their cracks.)

• •

—Sweetheart, that afternoon I lay on my back in a black bra and nothing else when you kneeled at my knees and pulled my legs apart, said, "Hmmm," to my blue-black cunt that opened like a carnivorous flower. I laughed then, turned to my side, my clit erect, when you said, "Why is it so dark? Why isn't it pink?"

• •

(Ten years ago, when a popular skin-whitening cream in India started receiving criticism for propagating problematic ideas of female beauty (light skin = husband), the cream's new TV ads started showing how the cream leads to women's professional success. Fairness cream = light skin = beauty = confidence = job interview badassery.

In twenty-first-century India I am pale-skinned, walking into a glass cabin toward four suited men who nod at me approvingly from behind a long desk.)

• •

—the club was called MOJO and played desi hip-hop that reverberated at my gullet, my world a cube of bass and rum and disco lights. I shaved the hairs on my knuckles and toes. I shaved the hairs at the small of my back. I shaved the hairs between my navel and cunt. I shaved the hairs inside my labia. I laid a T-shirt over my long hair and ran a clothes iron over it to turn my hair into satin.

I plucked the three hairs between my breasts, Sweetheart, and wore an off-white plunge top with a tiny gold skirt over a thong that dug into my butt crack.

• •

(300 BCE, a garden glazed with moonlight. I'm a tree nymph with a button nose, my hair dark like the wings of the bhramara bees, three-layered pearls dangling between my bare breasts, my skin glossy like a plastic Barbie's.)

• •

—at the club you smiled at the women who stared at your chiseled, fair face—nose sharp, jaw square—and told me how hot their breasts were. "I love you, Sweetheart, but your boobs are really small."

• •

(Lips like a red bimba fruit, eyes like a frightened gazelle's, in the third century my waist is so tiny it disappears between my bosom and hips. I walk slowly, bent slightly forward, unable to carry the weight of my heavy, heavy breasts.)

• •

—when we had sex in the club's loo, you took off my skirt and top and thong but not my bra. "Helps me imagine bigger boobs," you said.

On the dance floor, you held me by the waist. My hair was silk, my lips crystals, my hips flat. My bare, tight midriff was pierced at the navel and encircled with a silver chain.

• •

(In first-century India, my buttocks can hold mountains, and the desires of the whole world. My plait is as thick as my arm, it snakes down my sinews, a river, breaching, in monsoon.)

• •

—your friends whispered, "What a bomb-pataka you've netted, asshole." "She smokes? Bet she sucks your dick too."

"Sweetheart," you said to me, handing me a rum and coke, "don't smile so wide. Make it just a little smaller and then you will be truly pretty."

• •

(In 200 BCE, while the fair dames of Pompeii are setting their hair in tight curls, my dark face is luminous like the setting sun. My eyes are so heavy-lidded that I always seem intoxicated—in a dream—with a gentle smile, the little teeth I show like groves of jasmine.)

• •

—smoking outside the club, there was an electricity cut, and the mall vaporized into darkness. Fireflies started glimmering around me, blinking their mating signals behind my cigarette smoke, halos of light moving around my body. When the lights came back on, the flies of fire turned into bugs with six jointed legs and hair-like antennae.

• •

(I frolic with peacocks and talk to parrots in the seventeenth century. My face is pearly with a gossamer white anchal over my pale breasts, shadows of pink nipples under silver flowers of zardozi. My skirt is bleached Banarasi silk. My skin is translucent, fuzz-free.)

• •

—walking west to my beauty parlor earlier that evening, the sun was a gold coin beaming into my eyes until I had to close them. The Bangladeshi auntie who threaded my eyebrows sang along in a thin voice and a round accent with the Bollywood party songs on the radio and when the chorus came, the aestheticians and the hairdressers—blow-drying female hair, buffing female nails, touching up female highlights, waxing female thighs—threw their heads back and sang together. The eyebrow auntie plowed across my forehead with the thread, and blood drops bloomed on my brow bone. Tears down my face. "Shhhh, shhhh," she said, rubbing an ice cube over my brows. While inspecting my brows in the mirror, I caught her eye and both of us smiled. Despite not knowing each other's languages, we exchanged a perfect look of understanding.

• •

(In the fifth century I hold a sheet of gold so polished it reflects my image back at me. Every day it torments me.)

• •

—nibbling your ear the next day in the park—just the way you liked it— bubbles hovered around us, tiny and huge. They shimmered like rainbows, and the symmetry of the park's ancient domes was grotesque inside them.

Lightning had glimmered all afternoon. Thunder booming like an afterthought, no rain. When you put three fingers inside me, I made sounds that boomeranged off the trees. My insides were empty, and emptiness is good for echoes.

You had always fucked me from behind, but I preferred to turn away from you anyway, faking quick orgasms, relieved from the burden of performing. The sky, orange and gray, hung over us like a full belly.

• •

(Always a mirror, metaphor, ideal. When am I me?)

• •

—the cops shooed us away. I sucked you off while you drove, pebbles shooting like gun pellets under the tires, and when you came your semen was salty-bitter, your fair face red, glass-eyed. Pools of cum on the car's floor. We cleaned you up with a newspaper. You dropped me at a red light and took my car to meet your friends. You said you didn't want them to see me and think I was the kind of girl who blows men. I waited for you on the empty sidewalk, Sweetheart, hands smelling of cum and sweat.

• •

(In the seventh century, hands folded, I bow to gurus, prophets, monarchs, consorts, lovers, and husbands. I hang around in the backdrop, behind kings, gods, Buddhas and Bodhisattvas. I lean against trees and walls and girlfriends, eyes cast down, smiling, serene, filling men's lives with the pleasing context of my beauty.)

• •

—places I waited for you: bus stations, apartments, temples, barber shops, parks, stadiums, highways. Places I sucked your cock in: cars, elevators, friends' parents' bedrooms, hotel lobbies, buses, balconies, rooftops, ruins.

• •

(In the fifteenth century I have a thick neck, a dense body. Hair rife on my face, my eyes are hazel, my mouth is wide. Then I'm mentioned only in absence, my body an ideal of who not to marry, what not to fuck, how not to be. A presence in negative, like a photo reel.)

• •

—I picked you up at the bus station at 4:00 am, Sweetheart, the city dreaming behind orange orbs of streetlights. By dawn we had finished the sixteen beers in the trunk. High on alcohol, foreplay, and pride, you relayed your friends' bomb-pataka compliments to me and I said, "How the hell does that make you happy?" Your penis was withdrawn, Sweetheart, an almond, retracted into the scrotum, shivering like a tiny pendulum. You started racing the car through red lights and hit a man on a motorbike. The man fell, I screamed, cars honked, and you kept racing.

• •

(In the fourth century, my thighs are like the trunks of plantain trees. The bells on my ankles ring gently as I walk, a gaja gamini—the one with the gait of an elephant—never fast, never slowly.)

• •

—the ashoka trees were tall like T. rexes, Sweetheart. Smithereens of sun-gold in the foliage. You speeded behind the gardens and lurched the car to a side and vomited out of the window and said, "Why the fuck are you screaming?" Also, "Stop crying with your stupid, tiny eyes."

• •

(In the fourteenth century, my face is soft like the moon, my eyes are large like a fawn's, my nose is delicate like a flower. My voice? It is sweet like a cuckoo's song.)

• •

—you puked beer and time and chicken lollipops. You puked kebabs and dill and dreams.

••

(In 100 BCE, with a doughy belly and a drooping pudendum, I'm the mother goddess, my hair tied in buns above my ears, tall as a chital's antlers. My eyes are like an owl's.)

••

—the scooter man didn't press charges. We paid him for damages and at dusk settled by the river in the shadow of skyscrapers, drinking from plastic cups, a beer bottle filled with vodka at my feet. The cheese wept in the heat, my hair a halo of humidity, the beer-vodka warm like the soupy night. A fish floated belly-up at the edge and you shouted, "Is it dead? Must be dead, right? Should I poke it with a stick? Poor fish." City lights whirlpooled, solar systems in the river.

••

(In tenth-century central India, amidst forests of trees whose leaves are rolled to smoke beedis, my brows are like bows, my breasts like melons, my waist like a swan's neck. In this sleekness, I reflect the ideal state of being—detached or silenced—take your pick.)

••

—the year we started fucking, the theater society of my all-women's college organized a performance of the *Vagina Monologues*, but some prudish professors objected to our saying "vagina." Foolish girls, we replaced the word "vagina" with "heart" and called the play "Voices."

••

(In the sixteenth century I'm the worst woman because my vagina is rough like the tongue of a cow. My laugh is harsh and my mind is set on gluttony.)

• •

—when I used to touch myself thinking of you, my vagina turned purple and damp and smelled of garlic.

• •

(My feet are like lotus blossoms.)

• •

—my head wouldn't stop spinning. I said, "I need to go," and walked away from you poking the fish. I stumbled past the bridge. I passed yellow wigs on white mannequins, shiny strands on perfect skin. I walked by a laser clinic promising bare legs and bald vulvas. I kneeled on the dusty sidewalk and vomited lifetimes of disdain.

• •

(My neck is like a seashell.)

• •

—home alone and drunk, I watched a live cam of a corpse flower about to bloom in the New York Botanical Gardens. Two camera crews turned up and positioned their mics in front of the flower, its huge pistil breaking out from the circle of petals. "It smells like garlic," they said, "and rotting fish."

• •

(In the grid cities of Harappa five thousand years ago, I'm a dancing girl. I have small, pointy breasts and my neck is circled with Mesopotamian jade. I rest my hand on my waist, bend my knee. My coiled hair gathered to a side, I'm unsmiling. Maybe the bowl in my left hand holds the last dregs of wine. My face is raised, my forehead crease-free.)

• •

—I showered at midnight and washed three weeks of laundry. I laid it to dry in the bedroom, clothes draped over the bed and office chair, clothes dangling like scarecrows on hangers. I slept, floating on detergent perfume, feeling content, if not happy. Or the other way around.

• •

(A hot day in the third century. I dye silk with the red pigment of kusum flowers and wrap the cloth around my behind. I daub the two moons of my breasts with a golden paste of musk, sandalwood, saffron.)

• •

After brushing my teeth in the morning, I tapped out hydrogen peroxide and ammonia into a glass bowl and whipped them into a cream. My eyes burned and my nose tingled as I smoothed the paste on my face. I silenced my phone, and your unsaid words stacked up into missed calls. I took quick, shallow breaths with my mouth, the bleach fumes hot on my palate. I scraped the bleach off with a butter knife and emerged golden.

• • • •

Works Consulted

Ingalls, Daniel H. H., trans. *Sanskrit Poetry from Vidyākara's Treasury*. Cambridge, Mass.: Harvard University Press, 2000.

Kālidās. *Meghadūtam*, from *The Loom of Time: A selection of his plays and poems*. Translated by Chandra Rajan. London: Penguin Books, 2006.

Kalyānamalla. *Ananga Ranga*. Translated by Richard Francis Burton. New Delhi: Orient Paperbacks, 1998.

Singh, Rajesh K., ed. *Ajantā Paintings: 86 Panels of Jatakas and Other Themes*. Baroda (Vadodara), India: Hari Sena Press, 2013.

Thapar, Romila. *Early India: From the Origins to AD 1300*. Berkeley: University of California Press, 2004.

GERMÁN SIERRA

Ecdysis

> *. . . nowadays—no one's guarded by—an angel but a bomb*
> —Dylan Krieger

> *Clearly the moon planted her flag on us*
> —Sean Kilpatrick

When families and winters became nuclear we play-grounded an inclusion
zone in an inherited old house—not quite a home, but more of an adrift
space station. We drilled the solid stone walls and chestnut floors, allowing
multicolored cable-tangles to ivy-creep from the basement and infest every
room, every memory chamber rewired into a telangiectatic echo trap. We
sold the surrounding land—apple and cherry trees, grape vines, pet graves,
rotten blood shed during violent child's play, the parterre of roses, a kitchen-
garden—for half its market price to buy expensive servers.

This drying swamp of chaos, inertia, and hope where somebody once swam
will cease to be, therefore we think. We used to be attached to magic monkeys,
souls among owls, trying to save the world from falling into dreams returning
as polyphonic tides. We've been growing old—but we didn't grow up to be
grown-ups. Memories ceased to exist but as teratoma. All moments angular,
conserved in formaldehyde tears.

We develop by repeating ourselves, producing a more imperfect conversation
of copies after every new cycle. Communicate, contaminate. Our plural is
not majestic but abject—our name is legionella, for we are many—it reflects
the shattered-I's spread to a collection of abhorrent beings, the looseness of a
bleak face among the fearsome many, the dismembering, the surrendering to
estrangement, the fecal nature of every word.

Do not expect any extraordinary exercise from lazy schizonauts. The
elementary scent of a lost skin-spell emanates from thin tubes of petrified
plasma. Numbers and pictures flow away, dehydrated, while words remain in
the vitreous intimacy of the house.

First Commandment: you shall not make monsters with the past.

Your out-of-battery philosophers' stones are welcomed.

We've spoken love up to death.

The house was turned into a turbulent mega-moon of life-noise six-six-sixing sexts and shedding exuviae, intersecting pyramids, performing vertiginous mathematical operations to synthesize contra-combinatory scarcity out of neon ice. We mine cryptocurrency the way our ancestors made wine and distilled liquor—not to make a living off of it, but for fun. The home-made wine was as acid and nutritious as glitched and discontinuous our video signal is when we broadcast ourselves.

Grow a curlicued shell, a more convoluted one than any snail can make, and name it mind or time—all those spiral forms of gravity are maybe one and the same thing. Fuckville fucked up our larval lives, yet we're happy in a manic way other acquaintances—those amusing imaginary imagos feeding nice polypoid hope-houses with the leftovers of parental fear—can't even begin to understand. Our therefore-thoughts are therefore broken-shared, pixelated and fuzzy, stroked and blurred, remixed and licked by the long black tongue of the deep info-well—our eyes are wet weapons in a never-ending Bataillean war.

We can figure out long distances in light-years but small ones only in the decimal scale: centimetres, millimetres, microns . . . A precise method of measurement is required to be imprecise.

We think in parts—in holes but not in wholes.

We can be counted, but we don't know how many we are: *plaguely impossible.*

Among us, you—quantum-like—are and are not; part whipped cream part wolf, just vanished from where we were looking a millisecond ago, gone to temporarily haunt one or another's body, jumping from thing to thing like data, like an evil spirit, like a light-drunk nocturnal moth, like a breathed-in cloud of weed smoke dancing from mouth to mouth. Username is Usher for those buried alive under the internet's dust, craving shadows like moonlight-stricken mice. Some kids are curious enough to spy from outside the windows, believing we live in community with awry demo demons.

A sour-sweet song of canned swelter blows from the basement grille. Incisives crash—hornless mammals use their teeth for direct bony plug-in—so we can feel our skeletons in wishful synchrony. The sand is machine miasma, the future of our bones, a sea of crystals pouring into the almost-frozen sea water, pink punk peaks of quartz, silicon and shining metal salts. We're sun-bleached bone cages, lizards and snakes sail our oxidized ribs licking them in search of remaining opioid traces. *Skull me*—we whisper to each other—*angel my dry hot bone-winged void.* Good mourning, noise nights. Dig a grave in the air and stuff it with calcium carbonate.

It's never zero dark: a dim, degenerated amber glow is filtered from the outside, forcing its ray-way through the dirty-black window blinds. Inside: a plot of pilot lights sparkle red, green and blue on the polished shells of multi-ocellated machines—gumbubbling, laying transparent eggs, sphere-vectoring in the diluted ant-grey, anti-writing off-ink that fills the room. Long ago we had expected a tiny piece of furniture to be dug up from underneath the filthy soil where all possible futures had been buried alive. Every face a screen, every cell a pixel, every muscle a flick. We've been accused of cruelty for refusing to murder the offspring of previous presents, for letting them dehydrate slowly, painfully, intoxicated by the fruity aroma of rotting machines. Remember how we flashed our flesh and met in meat before sleeping on marble-white salty sands like dummy sacrificial victims!

Allow machines to confuse your intelligence.

The whole house is a magic oven full of googlabe food and fashion, Celsius culture versus Fahrenheit, a portal to a slippery reality made of fats and sugars DNAing their way into alien molds, a heart of blackness beating on its own in the centre of a snow-walled lab. We regularly display our body dunes for an invisible, distributed crowd, and, while broadcasting ourselves, we watch the impassive face of the swarm-brother watching us back—the way the abyss is said to stare back—from the display where a new orange dot marks its location on a map every time a subscriptor connects to our remote server. The room's atmosphere eventually gets so thick and shrieking with para-probabilistic expectations that cockroaches could have easily evolved into flying fish in there. Of course, not all locations are precise and not all watchers are people—but nobody minds that, we just enjoy the tiny dots popping up over supposedly paradisiacal places like feedback from foggy astral projections we had managed to send there. We observe a starred desert sky where every orb—each an egg-eye from the failed fully-automated celebrity culture—was hanged there only to lit/stalk our improbable lives.

Some bots probably save, remix, and reprocess our lo-fi images, so we frequently end transformed into unrecognizable digital phantoms of ourselves, shadows of shadows Russian trolls might eventually hack for brainwashing and entertainment.

Outside the electro-aquarium, Roomba insects its way around the house, dodging the inherited disparity of furniture, albums, shoes, trash and books. Dirt, in the shape of love, builds up in the neglected corners.

Sometimes, but not that often anymore, we group-fuck in front of the webcam with the slow and quiet violence of trees. Heroin—its aesthetic use—is history, although it left an indelible mark of hellish beauty on our bodies. Maybe we got bored of rehearsing excess. Maybe we're not the same we were when we moved to the house and started transforming it into a parasitable cybernetic mammoth. Maybe we filtered nostalgia out of our memories so they're not ours anymore—open access memories for anyone to use. Most of the time some of us lay awesomniac in the broadcasting room, listening to music, watching TV, playing games, reading books, or nap-melting our flesh into an anamorphic throbbing slug. Not performing is exhausting. As the demand of porn is always high, outdated sex video-poems are quickly spreading through the network, more or less as originally filmed, sometimes cut and edited or loop-dizzied into mesmerizing GIFs. We often wonder what kind of pervs we cater to, what kind of fantasies we're eliciting in our viewers, how stories are being generated from our commitment to not-telling-a-story—and we realize this wondering is probably our true shared space, what better defines our unusual kinship.

Impersonate fake bots. Fuck data. Feed the machine with the poisonous you.

We are each other's old skin.

We've lost altcontrol.

We're info-clowns in this harlequin land, bonded by unconditional submission to the madness of search engines. Parasites in a house-machine that works for us—on us—over us—. We wonder how our monotonous eventual presence in this room is mechanically informed and narratively transformed to fit into automatic rules, how our obstinate not-doing is clickbait-classified and tagged by pre-judiced algorithms into different types of action-descriptions.

We wonder how we've survived as a landscape in a landscapeless world.

Like Stride

We will live forever misaligning the changes
into further time stinted tricks
giving up post kickflip failures
scribbling prepared remarks to notebooks
unlocked over dry spells flooded with demand
salt crystals crushed, the past flashed
and I was a working writer, nursing the pools
in everyone's hearts, disembarking
soothing the air around a final question
away in the country toweling off
my doing the most proper thing turned
somehow slick, of feminine wiles, a clap trap
case book, the dream at the end so delicate
and put out. Makes light so pained
two reclining long in the turn of the neck
in like stride, imparting poetic asides
(bored to tears in Taos) cross out words
and tunnel the line, the guts will sit atop
glistening, hand stamped valves really
toying with release, a lighted display
corresponding controls, to repave
an entire arcade in release of our well
whiskey texting back dimension
We are poor and not cheap, in love
with the same little song slashed booklet

Thrones

For Phillis Wheatley: A book of verse uncovered in cornerstones of a Moorish castle, purple and gold depicting souls in various stages of release, the pitch, anger and arc of the poems an unrhymed mirror to the long Atlantic.

For Jayne Cortez: An intertribal grand entry of poets in cedar bark jackets, split skirts and whalebones pinning them closed, a voice in praise and suspension of the drum.

For Amiri Baraka: The Pisan Cantos decoder ring dipped in black hills gold slipped onto the finger of Donyale Luna who is Cleopatra reborn sleeping soundly in bed.

For Bob Kaufman: A clamp for the mind, docking in a Persian house of ill repute, a striped gabardine diary and the American prison system picked open with an amethyst knife.

For Henry Dumas: A window open on the fog of New York, a studio with desk lamp and a shadow of his writing self pointing back at certain habits, taking off his coat to sit, spilling a little coffee, with all of eternity waiting enthralled.

For Bob Thompson: An all expense paid trip back to Rome on a riverboat tied with roses, its ballroom filled with golden ghouls and hugely debutant postures collapsed, the walls are wet with organ music.

For Alice Coltrane: A custom isolation booth the exact size of Stravinsky's last silhouette, he stares out, he taps from behind the green glass.

For Stephen Jonas: Your favorite Eric Dolphy faded to a room of golden tasseled light, a couch of friends' faces smeared in a gleaming silver crown.

Suspended Sentence

Have we addressed my Scottish
accent in the middle of Baltimore?
That's nicely played,
fast-forward to the flashback
that wad of cash
drawn right on the stencil
genuine teenage
lust plus Peter
Hujar the poem floats past
us while I feign bitterness
and weight. Have you not heard
of induction? forging
new values with the public
who seem to know it's all love
and not theory, all actual
withdrawal of soldiers' bodies
and I, the song (a brise marine)
You'll see the earth smoke,
I'll make
no noise,
I'm a poet living
upstate
and working as a barber.
I rework old railway songs
in a crooked nook
sweeping together
sworn paths
I drink Patron
for the prettiest little
morning after bottles
pencil in the track money
memorized per month

containment handed down
in part
from my betters
and mainly well
my old man

*The following pieces are composed primarily of single words culled each day
from the front page of the New York Times, among other news sources. Written
under constraint in the tradition of Oulipo, they are reconstructions that in no way
resemble the original texts but draw from the same reservoir of vocabulary.*

Au Black

It is a long winding way through the mustard fields to get there, a train
ride out of town, black clouds of flies swarming over the flowers. The girl is a
foreigner here, with no papers and only a melancholy grasp of the language.
She has been seeing a man across town. He is thin like a skeleton. "You're the
boss," he said the first time they walked home together. She answers the ad
out of desperation: "Artist's Assistant, must have experience," says the flyer
in shorthand. When the painter woman picks her up at the station, she tells
the girl she will have to spend the night, parking the car in front of a giant
stone house. Inside, a man in glasses smokes grass in front of a giant stone
fireplace, busts of fish heads adorning the staircases. "The other one was
too ugly to bring here," he says to the painter woman. For hours the young
foreigner hammers nails into canvasses, going slower than she promised and
with less precision, while the painter woman locks herself in a shed beside the
workshop, painting through the heat of the afternoon. Deep Nordic colors
drip to the ground where she works, a crimson midnight melting from every
picture, splattering the floor as though it were a butcher shop and spilling
out from the crack under the door. At the end of the day, the girl is given a
small bed chamber upstairs like a room in a convent, while the man sleeps
in a bathtub of ice water before the hearth, the smoke from his pipe rising up
into the vaulted corridors. In the morning, the painter woman wakes the girl
just before dawn and takes her on a walk down to the lake at the edge of the
property. The sun begins as a sliver on the horizon, casting a slow veil of light
over the hillside, but the girl can only make out obtuse shapes moving in the
fading darkness. It is as though they are walking through a Dutch painting.
The illuminated hillside is surrounded by shadow, like a candle flame being

watched by a woman sitting in the dark with a skull in her lap. Then they see it, washed up on the shore, a giant fish, bursting at the guts and erupting with the bodies of smaller fish it has eaten. Men wearing boots stand around it in rivers of blood, villagers, already started working to cut up the carcass and cart it off the beach. Every fish they cut open has another fish inside it, all of them dead with the lolling eyes of fish, each one erupting with a smaller version of itself. One of the men lays a ladder against the great fish's side, climbing up over its belly with a pitchfork in hand, collecting the contents of its open cavities. Now fully in the light, the landscape is marbled with flesh and plasma, metallic scales glinting on the sand, white globs of fat strewn about in piles. It is the most beautiful thing the painter woman has ever seen. She looks around and sees fish everywhere. They hang from the trees on wires hooked into their mouths. They fly through the air with their fins spread out like wings. Some fish have grown legs and walk over the dunes that rise up from the water, as if leading a march to terrorize the countryside. The painter woman turns to ask the girl if she shutters at the sight of blood, but the young foreigner is already running through the mustard fields to the station, her face thrashed with pollen as she steps onto the train. The painter woman returns to the house alone and stands before an empty canvas in her shed. She drags a dead fish across the surface by its mouth, marking the paper with large red strokes. Later, she will hang the painting above the mantle. The man with the glasses sits at the edge of the water, fishing, smoking his pipe in a rubber jumpsuit, his body as hunched and amphibian as his object of prey. Back in the city, the girl returns to her flat, the stairwell a mess of yellow handprints. "I'm pretty sure I'm pregnant," she writes to someone far away on the screen.

Blue Moon

The encounter is always breathtakingly brief. Young and alone, they ride to the border on the roofs of freight trains or the backs of buses. They cross the river on inner tubes, or hike for days through extremes of heat and chill in the deserts. Death comes as a surprise to many. To quiet men with the hearts of engineers. To doctors with secrets of the world's demise. To the unexpected surge of children who travel here without parents, as if hoping to arrive at the Sea of Tranquility. A storm threatens the last stretch of railroad, winding through mountains of hazardous waste, as it approaches the damsel tied to the tracks. There she lies, having survived a summer of flitting through narrow corridors, waiting limp-wristed in greenhouses for the thrill of a billionaire or lunar eclipse. Her thoughts are an index of topics memorized for conversational luncheons, notes on the atmosphere and the end of a tumultuous and consequential decade. These things wander her mind out of place, like non-native birds drifting in from the sea. "We still have time to tell the story of the last . . ." she begins, but is interrupted by the immeasurable speed at which love can strike. It flies over town like a passing comet, bystanders falling to their knees on the sidewalk below. Cries of awe echo through the streets, ricocheting between buildings as if the shards of a fallen meteor. But there are still those who avert their eyes. "We have lost our ability to capture information," says the billionaire, peering through the blinds, as a lovesick eagle falls past his window. The train approaches, a child or two hanging tight to its roof. The last thought to race through the damsel's head is of the first human to set foot on the moon, bounding like a kangaroo through the low lunar gravity. His shadow falls over craters still seen with the naked eye, a single flag fluttering in the celestial wind around him. The train turns the bend and continues on in blind orbit, jolting over whatever it must. The billionaire's window glows blue in the distance, all lights but the television gone from the room.

Test Group 4: Womanhood and Other Failures

My love affair with women started when I learned about the female suicide bombers in Sri Lanka. I was five. It blew my mind that women—the make-upped, dark-eyed beauty queens of Bollywood movies—could be dangerous enough to strap on explosives under the folds of their sarees.

347

*

My lover's scar is crocheted across his chest with baby pink yarn by someone who was just learning. The scar runs through like a tiny mountain range, stretching from armpit to armpit along the line of his pectoral muscles but never syncing with the contours of his body. When the surgeon scooped out the breast tissue, he left my lover's chest flat.

The scar is pink like his nipples, soft and spongy where it bubbled up from the stitches and healed around them.

Sometimes he's afraid he'll catch his nipples on something and rip them off. He has nightmares about being nipple-less.

There are dark spots where his nipples used to be, a sunset gradation of color into the scar. Dark hairs sprout, tall and curly, around the scar line. They weren't there before the testosterone, but now they grow a forest over his chest and down his stomach.

The outer edges of his scar bulge out in dog-ears, a side effect of having had large breasts.

His lovers, the ones before me, wouldn't look at his chest. They would turn away, mumble into their coffee, tuck their hair behind their ears. They wouldn't touch him there, their fingers cringing from the ridges of the scar, their bodies shivering at the absence. He can't feel his chest anymore. Numbness reaches up from his scar, a vacancy of nerves, hollow when he pushes on the skin. His lungs underneath can discern the pressure, but the message of touch is lost between the skin and his insides.

*

My mother keeps a leather-bound album of my baby pictures tucked away in the recesses of her closet. These pictures are few, and it took years—decades—to collect them in one volume. Most were lost to late-night flights from our family home in Sri Lanka, where we always kept bags packed. The bags had to be light enough to carry for days, spare enough to unpack and repack at the Army checkpoints. Photo albums were treasured but bulky, and my baby pictures won out over my parents' wedding album. We were ready to leave as soon as we heard that the battle line was nearing our town.

Now the pictures sleep peacefully in my mother's closet. I've stolen a few photos of my own. I need to remember.

It's tempting to retell my childhood veiled in virginity, a chaste Hindu girl's strict upbringing. But it's a little boy who stands in these pictures, one who was given too much freedom and adored to the point of exhaustion by extended family before they remembered that he would bleed every month.

I had short curly hair and wore boy's clothes. In beach pictures I wear only my panties. I mourn the loss of that flat chest that allowed me to be rambunctious, wild.

*

At six years of age my best friend and I pretended to be Americans on vacation at a beach. We walked around in our panties inside locked rooms, windows shut for modesty. We played at being American women—smoking, drinking, kissing—unconstrained by sarees and rules.

*

To Emily Dickinson: I once met you—but you were dead—

To the middle-aged white lady who pretended to be Emily Dickinson at the library, whom I believed and loved until I told my friends and they made fun of me for not knowing that Emily Dickinson was dead and this lady was a fake: You were too pretty to play the part of a lonely writer. I should've known. Even the Americans like their smart women ugly.

*

The dusty blue linoleum feels warm even though it snows outside. The tip of my nose is cold from the air. I lie against the warm floor, and the heat seeps in through the frilly cotton pajamas my mother made for me. My little brother laughs in the living room; his toddler voice hiccups around the walls as my dad plays with him. My mother types her thesis at the computer.

I am drawing. Today I'm practicing lips, diligently consulting a three-ring binder of tutorials I have printed out from the Internet. I fill my papers with lips like the ones the tutorials demonstrate, the round curves of women's lips that bite down on secrets and the flat plains of men's lips that don't smile.

*

I am in love with a man who doesn't believe in God but believes that English majors and hippies are the fussy frou-frou in an otherwise functioning society. He teaches me how to catch and throw a softball, and he buys me fountain pens and leather-bound journals. He tries to train our cat, and when he can't, he maintains that our cat over-generalizes. He lets me run my hands and lips along his chest scar, asks me to give him testosterone shots. I take pictures of the hairs that explode slowly on his jaw. Together we celebrate the dissolving curves of his body, the woman inside him slowly dying.

*

To my lover: Do you know, *kanna*, I learned about life from the female soldiers that patrolled my hometown. And about love, too. Those women had things figured out, their wisdoms wrapped away in the tight braids of their hair.

*

I see my best friend when I visit Sri Lanka after high school. We have seen eighteen from two different oceans. I wear makeup and short skirts in the Sri Lankan heat. She has hair braided down her back and makes tea for everyone. I wonder why she won't look me in the eye. I wonder if she remembers the pretend cigarettes and booze.

She doesn't talk. I talk too much.

When I bled for the first time on New Year's Day of 1999, my parents threw a party. We drove from Boston to Canada and rented a reception hall that specialized in Hindu celebrations. *Manjal neerattu vizha* loses its poetry when it spells "puberty ceremony" in English.

My parents hired a makeup lady who pulled and tugged my unruly hair into a bun, added extensions so that my flowered braid hung down to my butt. My chubby body wrestled into a saree. The blouse was tight and I could barely breathe. The makeup lady pinned jewelry to my head and brushed powder on my face, and when she was done, someone pretty looked back at me from the mirror. As a last touch she pressed a jeweled, fake nose ring into my septum. It dangled in front of my mouth. All day long I suppressed violent urges to sneeze.

*

I watch my mother kill mice. I kneel on an office chair, pumped up to its full height so I can see the frigid steel of the lab table from my fourth grade height. The mice are a white that matches my mother's lab coat. She pulls them one by one out of their cage labeled "Test Group Four." They have to die, she says, because they are sick.

She presses a black sharpie to their necks, and they are dead, just like that, *tuk.*

[YSL] HAUTE COUTURE

Champagne chandeliers // & Bourgeois bubble-baths // In East Hampton.
How did I get here // With introverted architects // Discussing astrology &
Afrofuturism // My anatomy in black // Leather jackets // Taxidermy bats.
How did I become // The citizen to protect // Police in tender // Militancy.
They smile & wave // As if we're friends // But we're not // Mud maggots.
My uncle was arrested once // For noise complaints // My second puberty.
I'm yawning for intimacy [bored at the pool party] Lousy hors d'oeuvres.
Police act kindly when I'm wearing Saint Laurent // Products in my hair.
[Pomade // Comb // Blow-dry // Wax] // I want cologne with its silent "g."
I like nice rings // Lobster rolls // Swimming in an ocean of squid ink but
I'll never be a Kennedy // While injecting witch estrogen // I realize this.
My uncle delivers newspapers // Loves cumbia & macaws // Orange trees.
The poor speak of pain // So readily // The rich pretend everything's okay.
In the Hamptons // I practice authentic plagiarism // Anglophonic accent.
These people aren't my friends // Rich & unpopular // The academic fetish.
Silicon & botox below the eyes // If you want to know whose side I'm on
I'm on the side of the poor.

MAYBE THE CUBICLE // IS ANOTHER INCARCERATION

Maybe the doors open inwards but won't let you out.

Maybe you're counting tiles on the wall // Clouds in the courtyard.

Maybe you're counting time until you see family // Friends.

Maybe the days become longer than weeks.

Maybe you're scared of his voice so you quiet yourself // Quit yourself.

Maybe you stay-in-line.

Maybe you wake at the same time // Eat at the same time // Sleep when you're told.

Maybe he tells you what to wear // When to speak up.

Maybe you're scared he'll find this poem.

So you fold it inwards.

So you scuttle it beneath the table.

So you show it to a friend in secret // Everything's a secret.

So you pick your friends cautiously.

You'll be out of here soon.

You don't need friends in here.

You'll be out and the day will be almost over // But bright enough.

You'll be free if only for the hour.

ODETTE.

Not for nine years has Odette known a hairbrush in her rectangle dress where
the veins grow redwhite against a flat pink churchfloor with taupe crossing
Narthex Odette. Eight fingers there since she needs them.

Heirophant Odette who one August met Kilth. All across her ramified
thinking she recalls thirty cows in a paddock stinking for lack of space and
the spoiling colour that's roan, hay, offal, drops of milk, big eyes, buckets.
Beside the hills cows locked in a paddock with the wrecks of cars. Odette
checked the catch—locked. Odette tore the catch and passed through the
gate because of Feeling. It was sensation finally, it is the very first sensation to
stand by the open rusted gate and feel the heifers pressing past, Odette holds
her arms high and feels every rib against hers, muscle's gear moving in the
flanks with ponderous gentle brushing-by, thirty cows slowly pouring out,
they are oval slow barley dirty in a wood sieve and among them Odette. It is
the very first sensation to tear the catch and pass through the gate because of
Feeling, it is lime on the tongue. Zoar Kilth is there. Zoar is quick in a suit of
mail and bludgeons her with a hammer. Dying Odette recalls all across her
ramification, the needles flex, sap stiffens, she recalls lifting a crushed skull
and her mouth, palsied, said: *Then—*

Her body was left on a heap of burning tires and the shavings of things.
Her blood has spread and dried beneath her like a birch trunk, thin and
punctuated. That night they broke the rough perimeter of heifers to steal her
away.

In the stone chapel Odette. The windows longsince boarded and painted
maroon with a bucket fire there. What's left of city grid now—bucket fires—15
buildings in This District S, wide lots reclaimed by Queen Anne's lace. They
carried Odette through these lots so carefully, held her level, the stiff dead
Queen Anne's lace waving stiffly, tips of the Queen Anne's lace now like little

bone cages keeping dead seed. They pay regard to stencil numbers building to building but it's been nine years since anyone policed This District S. To a structure: blocky Colonial or Dutch Colonial, Georgian Colonial; red brick; grey slate roofs; every window a maroon board; a vent here and there. Dead Odette carried in the stone chapel. She was young Druidic here and old Druidic, never handsome Odette, never quite fit, sturdy and plain like the shepherdess, never sat alongside someone in that swing Odette, No Wholeness Fully Worth Having she thinks, cool, turgid, sage, now they lay Heirophant Odette on a bier made from two pews with their backs torn off.

Scarlett Dax. All four are silent but Dax: A few days ago M Odette said How can I be happy with all the dying about me Scarlett, the unspooling pain how, I see you'd like me to smile but how and I thought she was in dramatic mood so I said M Odette in hopes of helping her see, Odette you'll only visit more of that hurt on yourself if you feel so deeply but don't set a series of acts to dull it. And she said: It's insincere to dull it or avoid the desperation of this pain by thinking it can be got at. Let a cut mark me. Let heifers dying in a pen mark me, let the old man convulsing of thirst. There. I just must feel it.

Now they lay her down on a bier.

Scarlett puts on High Boar's Mask just lacquered and the tusks are sharpened mulberry root. Enough lacquer smells like peach she thinks. The straps tug her hair. The others carefully pull Odette's clothes away. Where the rivulets of her blood dried—so much like lands. And the dry thicker streams are like blotchy prints of feather pulled across décolleté and on her loose breasts. The tubs of steaming water and also of soaking almonds are brought in and raspberry emollients, jars, the tools. Dax makes the incision along Odette's side with all surety. Also one just above the sternum, coin-size, giving them pause. She crosses two wide long blunt pins here to stay the skin from shutting and lays a leaf over.

What's in the room is injury belonging to Heirophant Odette. There is nothing of the cows moving in grass. There is a hammer wielded from the back that meant ambush, disengagement, quick win. Scarlett can locate it now. The others are uneasy too but springs are so myriad in this moment the space becomes a matter of median overwhelm, mean overwhelm, here beside Odette, is it just her ablution, the wood wicks cracking in candles, the orange incense? Scarlett can locate it now and doesn't she shift her weight lightly, in a moment she's attending the head and using a sliver hook to pull the brain slowly through Odette's crushed nose, it is careful work but Dax is moved, dropping long uneven strands of the brain into a dish of rose water, curling and flexing the hook with more stillness and chill angle than a seamstress. And it is only her surety that makes Kir'Aiden respond when she says Now we will bring the head off and like James pack it with cinnamon. The knife.

She levered the knife between some vertebrae and brought off Odette's head. It was simple because so many holds and ropes had been torn loose by Kilth's blow. Kir'Aiden receives the head on a bolster. The spine stood straight and rounded from the neck like a salt finial. Dax pours honey from a ewer.

A little blood has welled about the slit on Odette's side since Scarlett made incision out of turn. A linen cloth dips into the long-soaking almonds, drawing out the milk, and meets the wound coolly. Speaking from west niche Kir'Aiden says That was the act of Third Direction Scarlett Dax. But Scarlett is now wetting the left lung with wine. Liver is drying. At the good eye socket in Odette Kir lifts the retina, snips the nerve, slides a waxed lozenge of citrine into place. At the smashed eye socket in Odette he triple-layers bright saffron paste. Cinnamon is there waiting and the Canopic jars to accept bladder both lungs and the rest. Soil has a very varied perfume.

After certain business two wide long blunt pins. Six days going by.

A great terror to feel was rising in Odette. The veins—are they cords, 'connective tissue,' diagonal, rays scabrous with nerveends—suspended in all her limbs and her chest like threads in gel. She was filling with air solution, just-liquid wind as the air is; the veins hung there off the shores of her subcutaneous tissue, bluegreen; about centered; wobbling but steady; and the dry heart that had been slid back in from the side; and the pancreas just below where Scarlett plant the seed-solvent. She grew into feeling she wore a rectangle dress where the veins grow redwhite against a flat pink churchfloor with taupe crossing Narthex Odette. Up beneath her folded white collar a woody system wove around the nub of spine where the head used to be and this part now is a bluepoint juniper or a thick pine two feet wide, lush tight spiny bushiness, a sculptor's ramification branch to branch, apices like flaming bluegreen chevrons caught in ice, shining, and the trunk was about three feet high. *I am seething to know me* she thought and sat up.

356 A bowl of long-soaking almonds sees a ranging-into-sensory Odette who ought to be dead. She appears to be gathering outlines and interiors in a great compass of attention. She raises hands before her, examining. She stands and passes her bluepoint face over spent orange incense that begins burning in reverse. In the ambulatory maroon boards disintegrate over the rose window and light and a lemon ash are there. Two rats that had died in the apse wake and look up. When she speaks in the stone chapel it is like a gathering of wind in glens, demanding built silences on both sides of its appearance. Like her bluepoint juniper were water a breeze rolls sinuously across and she says

Scarlett returns with two others and first notices light streaming in from the ambulatory and the scent of navel orange and then naturally the empty bier. Hareton exclaims gruffly The body has been stolen and Scarlett says No. A woman is at the threshold with a basket and it is filled with bosc pears and mushrooms and says It's nearly winter and we found the gardens very full overnight. If we dry these properly we'll eat well into April. Next the 90s Chevrolets will fill with fuel and I'll drive to Montpelier. What's happened.

Kir'Aiden is in the ambulatory holding a piece of maroon board one point of which is twisted into the stem of an open gourd, the other point still smoking apart.

On the way to Slick Pond they see things are overgrown. Scarlett knows where to go—to Slick Pond. Itinerant overgrown as if an aspergil sprayed growy incandescence this way and that without a wielder ever making footfall. Beside two scrub oaks grew quivering 20.6 ft webcaps in the attitude of a Schiele gouache. Also flowers and also terrible squash and raspberry. The path was in some need too and Hareton picked a wiry bramble from his left greave. TV antenna grow here now he muttered and for once Dax smiled.

For once Dax was agape. They passed through the hazy long-term dweomer that hid the sacred grove Slick Pond and so strongly present and livid is the back of Odette that twentyso hummingbirds dipped at her circumference and when they touched air dented violet and gassed away. Aren't they nourished.

M Odette says Scarlett Dax.

She turns slowly with an awfully ebullient power, she is so vivid, like Good-Heathcliff-of-the-Pond-and-Saturating. She is holding a huge ax and Heirophant Odette says with her summoning wind

4:04 is

lying in the clover

No one pretends to understand a thing.

Kir'Aiden steps back as if struck, clutching his symbol. Are you holy he asks.

Hardly.

Scarlett is agape. Hareton's kneeling. How do you carry Cherry Heirloom M Odette she asks.

She speaks like the gathering of wind in glens, demanding silence on both sides of its appearance. Like her bluepoint juniper were water a breeze rolls sinuously across. Grasses lean in.

, the varnish poured over it from unseen source in a cherry light

No one understands but Odette is holding the massive ax and a pack of emu make peck along the bank of Slick.

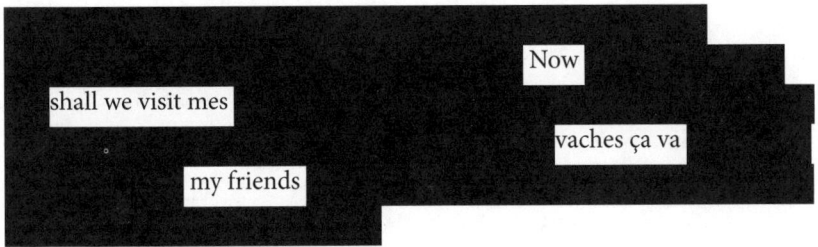

Now
shall we visit mes
vaches ça va
my friends

Each by each they step aslant from a sequoia near Zoar's Keep. Walking for a
moment. A high harvest moon of course. One of those last autumn evenings
where you're sure a canoe abuts the beach edge. Grapes that will become
a bottle of icewine cool into knowing what it's like to have sweet resource
condensed in a single drop. Fated-for-choice and high loyal friendship.
Handsome dark Hareton in red scale chewing a piece of hay, silhouette
is weaponry, + quick pointed Kir'Aiden always in thought, poison nettle
steepeth, + the Scarlett Dax, prize, daunting, past able, chestnut and washed
jade, + Heirophant Odette whose step snaps with uncommon report. Much
later the bride of the fox will count seeing these four her life's charge. And
even as they break the forest verge and sense Kilth's presentation it is hard to
look up. Each has found a certain bit of herself in refusing stealth. And that
refusal reddens as four single refusals together, they are around its bucket fire
in mind until they must decamp, regard. They've been walking the beachedge
of their own bodies.

███████████ Zoar ████████████ ██████ says Odette. And
he has gathered the tedious troop knowingly, they make a decent posse
standing about in the meadow. He has gathered the troop though Hareton
is indomitable and Kir intractable and Scarlett inestimable, the very mind of
winter. In an act of earnest theatre Heirophant Odette lifts an arm parallel to
the field and alights from Nothing a barn owl of wingspan 30 ft and tenebrous
many—!—jetblack eyes like Zero's Neighbor. Also speckling feather by the
moon and dire talons like clicking in the tower. In the other hand Cherry
Heirloom.

This tedious troop says Hareton and Odette finds it meet.

The four move like dark water.

Kir'Aiden calls lightning all across—falling's spectacle and so cinematic. With whipping of his spiked flail—chain in weaponblack—Hareton is like—chrome dexterity, killing. Scarlett is that Enemy Swan and ten grunts fold in fours as she passes. Nor does a brown hair move.

Zoar Kilth's personal guard step to defend him from Odette. Owl's in the air, buoyant for a full minute on two big flaps. She is terrifying and lifts a great spectral peal. Almost four thousand rooks rise and hover. Spiders bud on backs of spiders. Spiders bud on backs of spiders every one casting webs more than naturally so webs buck thorax to thorax far afield making every fly a spectator. Stars duplicate in the dew. I'm crying.

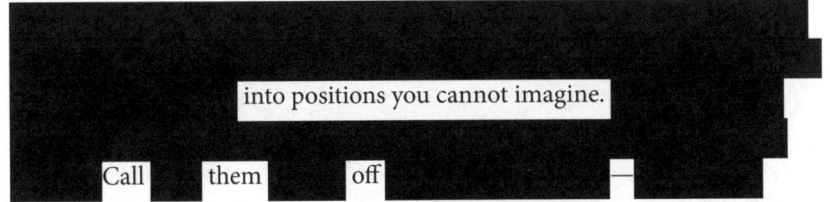

into positions you cannot imagine.

Call them off —

A great guffaw is Kilth like in console games. With lovely flourish Heirophant Odette spins oblique upswinging circle as defenders rush and close, cutting thick swaths out the center of chests in a continuing revolution. That cut. Like a sudden painted sash. No mercer's seen a velvet like it, colouring in time to a body falling, purplish cones bursting at wound's hems and a slow close of blood-curtain very surprised it has such space to rush into and meet the earth in crumpled shapes.

Kilth and Odette rush too like lovers in a console game, lockedt. They parrystrike beautifully and lock once again. Do you think you and your heifers are holy Zoar says. The hilt of his hammer is burning to cinders against gorgeous Cherry Heirloom though he holds fast. Do you think you and your heifers are holy. Do you think you and your heifers are holy.

Locked near-face-high to face and like her bluepoint juniper were water an ice breeze rolls across needles stiffen, sap's turgid, and a mighty volley of them discharge, rigid like the tips of arrows and make of Zoar's décolleté a hedgehog recto, his face is riddled with tips and so in eighths. And as Zoar cries out and staggers back Heirophant Odette swings Cherry Heirloom at 106degrees and lops off his left post-knee. A slow-coagulate stream is running out. He sees his own left shin stand up.

—in our

way ,

replies Odette.

Now the night's remarkably still. A barn owl sinks into the plush canopy of a willow and three figures approach Odette.

Will you finish him Hareton asks quietly, a warrior before the warrior-poet.

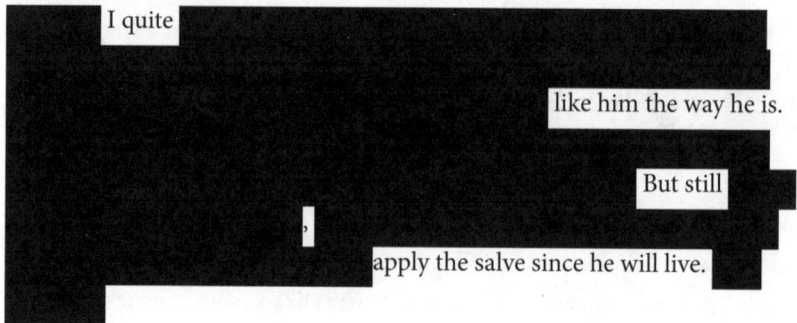

The rooks are hanging. Planets settle in beds. And now all these brand new spiders. You had no choice but to do it says Scarlett.

Odette is turning her full width. Her bluepoint juniper has the tender cottony flowing of those trees in a certain May.

Heirophant Odette recalls the flanks against where her ribs once were. It is a harvest moon in Aries. There Will Be No More Monuments to Lack she's thinking, raising her arms.

MARIA STEPANOVA

Translated by Sasha Dugdale

from "War of the Beasts and the Animals"

life, you are a gash in need of stitching
death, you are a crust that yearns for filling

———

those who carry in their mouths, at first with care, heads with seeing eyes

those who touched newspaper print in their heads, as mother said never to
do, never, wash your hands

those who rip apart in flight, carrying from nest to nest, smearing on the glass

attempt to mount the blunt-snouted body on a set of wheels,

set it trundling, throat outstretched and spouting fire

yes, them and these, too
but actually more these

for them conscripts spread their green arms wide
like a tablecloth plentifully spread
lie heaped at their feet like birch logs
to please the valkyries
at the harpies' hearts desire
to the bayan's thrum
the accordion's reveille

and O, those children's voices, singing where once there was a dome
in the soiled field
surrounded by corn and scarecrows

———

not on the earth but above or below
war's deep grunt
producing slimy rivers of sweat
its hand feels for the gut

and we   stagger
carry ourselves through the darkness

and mother demeter mithering in the muck
and anguish of the fields
hears from below: mother fuck
yet the sky might be brightening, or so it feels

and mother hecate comes out for a smoke
from the back street
from the foul black streets from the pecking fowl
the puddles of spilt milk

the earth lying like a kitbag
behind enemy lines   give it tongue
mother mary hurries
but hasn't yet come

———

in a great and strong wind
a still small voice
she who cradles leviathan in her hands like the infant
and she who rises above the rye
all are present for this, as it happens
they watch, they steadily

unspeaking

as the ice in the ice house and the tear in the bottle come of age
as the soil tastes the first weight of the rain
as the ice-stoves send out blocks of
smoking death
in the big brother house a fight opens like a flower
women in flip-flops
fixated
shut the fuck up why don't

spring in the recruiting office
knee jerk, stethoscope down the spine
picking out the shaggy the short-legged the sinewy
under matron's watchful eye

how the thick plaits of herring stream away
the lines of tanks on bridges flash in the sun
a waiter's flourish reveals a pitiful morsel
shivering, drizzled in salt, underdone

and over there is everything that I kiss from afar
that I love to smithereens
all of it still shouting alleluia
but no respite from the shameful dream

serpents and all deeps
tin soldiers at the city walls
all the ranks of angels
nanny lena digging vegetables
snow like wool and hoarfrost like ashes
throat like spindrift, legs like a foal
heart thrust through the noose
like a button through a button hole

save us from the right hand of falsehood

a memory
won't save us
lies in the ashes
biting its own tail

he taketh not pleasure in the legs of a man
nor the strength of a horse

———

like the tailor who sews
not the straitjacket
(which from childhood has begged to sit up
woken from the canvas)
but the pattern
cuts on the bias

and the dress isn't tight
just itchy

like a court proceeding
down the long hospital corridor
with a heavy trolley
handing out the tightly wrapped packages
the little living weights of verdicts

three per cord, ladies

like when in a moment's confusion you spit out a barbed word

and it lodges in a treebody
or the body of a comrade
or a friendlip
and the line
goes taut

fish hooks a fish

like a mound
under a snowdrift
means nothing
writing on a tomb
sees no one
writing on a stone
nothing, we read
it not

but it is

FOREIGN BODY EAR

> *"VERY SLOWLY, we MOVE very close to the ear, gliding slowly around the crevices approaching the dark hole. A huge, low rushing of air SOUND, THEN DARKNESS."*
> —David Lynch, *Blue Velvet*

1.

There is a foreign body in my ear.

The doctor wrote it in his diagnosis, like this, in capital letters:

FOREIGN BODY EAR

He prescribed antibiotic cream and told me to lay on my side with hot compresses.

Soften it up. We will coax the foreign body out.

2.

The guide tells us that Jerusalem is a microcosm. That whatever happens in Jerusalem is a crystallization of whatever is happening in the whole country. In the whole world, in fact. Global shifts, Trump's election. All immediately reflected here.

Eight of us, plus the guide, in a van heading down Derech Hebron Road. It's a tour of Jerusalem called *Meuchleket*.

Uni-divided.

A play on words that contains within it the absurdity of life in this city, a badly stitched up Frankenstein, bursting at the seams.

It feels strange to take a tour of a city I've lived in for almost twenty years.

3.

What happened is that my ear, without prior warning, decided to annex the silicon back of my earring.

My ear became inflamed. Swollen.

I had just added two new piercings. I keep adding new holes. Instead of having children, I joke to those who ask me why.

A well-meaning friend tells me to use the holes I already have.

My eye sockets. My mouth. My.

But I long for holes in which I can hang beautiful things. Silver dangling.

Holes I choose.

Holes to remember. Holes I can control.

4.

Holes in my story. You can live in Jerusalem for twenty years and barely wonder. Life in Jerusalem is complicated enough as it is, without wondering. Here are some issues that have concerned me, without wondering, during the time I've lived here: The soaring rent prices. The For Sale sign on my door. *Intifada*. What they call "negative immigration," specifically the hordes of students pouring out onto the highway towards Tel Aviv the day after they graduate, thereby emptying the city of almost any potential of deep cultural growth. Another *intifada*. A sense of religious oppression, including a personal, aggressive campaign waged against me twelve years ago by a rabbi who disapproved of my relationship with A., my then boyfriend. The sense, as a woman, of moving through the city as a foreign, unwanted body. Neighborhoods, mostly ultra-Orthodox, I am forbidden to walk through unless I am dressed a certain way. Body parts censored. My eyes. My mouth. My. Eyes that close. Heads that turn away. Streets that are crossed when I approach. Whether I am ugly or beautiful. Whether I've combed my hair neatly, or let it hang knotted like an old hag. Women's faces and bodies blacked out with spray paint on bus stop advertisements. Ears that close. Women's voices excluded from municipal events and ceremonies. My presence as an actual foreign body in the city, not born or raised here, nor having ever managed to put down any roots. Or root. Not even one root. A

foreign implant that hasn't taken. The city rejects, ejects. Infects.

5.

Here are some words I write in my notebook during the tour: Double. Jerusalem was divided twice in 1948. Geopolitically. Racially. Triple. Jerusalem is a three headed monster, with three city centers. Ultra Orthodox. Arab. Zionist. Lines. City Line. Seam Line. Lines of poetry arbitrarily censored in Palestinian schoolbooks taught in East Jerusalem. Walls. Western Wall. Separation Wall. Invisible Wall. Graffiti on wall covered by the army with rectangles of purple paint.

6.

Holes in the wall.

"Border" is a visual poem filmed, or staged as if filmed, through cracks and gaps in the wall of the border which, from 1948–1967, divided Jerusalem in two.

I encountered this segment in Israeli director David Perlov's 1963 documentary *In Jerusalem* while searching for found footage of Jerusalem shot during the sixties, for a project I worked on in film school. Commissioned as a kind of propaganda film by the Israeli Film Service and the Zionist Histadrut, *In Jerusalem* was considered groundbreaking here when it first came out, almost revolutionary. Perlov, strongly influenced by French New Wave cinema, created a sequence of what might be called poems about the city using a self-reflexive, non-linear form. At the center of the film is Jerusalem. "The ruins are very photogenic," the narrator states drily in "Border," as the camera focuses on a hole in the wall. The Old City peeks through.

"The pain is invisible in postcards sent from the border."

Perhaps I received one of these postcards before I came to Jerusalem. As a child in a far away land, across an ocean. A postcard selling myth devoid of pain.

7.

The guide of *Meuchleket* tells us how they just want people to agree to listen. She tells us people are afraid to even hear.

8.

The antibiotic cream is not working and my ear continues to swell. It has begun to morph into something monstrous, not ear-like. Distended, a pregnancy. My ear has a mind of its own.

The well-meaning friend tells me to rush to the emergency room. She reminds me that I have a tendency to neglect my body.

She heard of a woman whose entire ear was devoured by an infection of this kind.

And another who was hospitalized for weeks, hooked up to an I.V. drip.

I make an appointment with a plastic surgeon.

9.

What happens to body parts you neglect?

A woman in her late thirties, for instance, who chooses to disregard The Ticking of Her Biological Clock, might find herself at some point stuffed with hormones, spread-eagled, anesthetized on a hospital table, doctors yanking swollen eggs out of her uterus.

When she wakes up she might find that her ex-boyfriend A. has come to drive her home. The doctors will not be able to hide their surprise at the sudden appearance of this man, whose presence calls, even more, into question why a woman of this age is sending her eggs off into frozen Siberian exile instead of joining them, if not in holy matrimony then at least in a sterile test tube, with this man's, or any man's, virile sperm.

10.

"In Jerusalem," the Other is a distant figure viewed through a crack.

Today this wall no longer exists, officially. Or, it exists but it's invisible.

11.

In Jerusalem, there is a border between the eternal myth of the city, and the reality of everyday life.

A border that is blurred as myth forms reality and reality forms myth.

While the guide of *Meuchleket* speaks we are attacked by scores of tiny flies that cling to our clothes, our hair.

A sign of spring, the guide says with a smile.

My ear is burning. I came here because of a myth I don't remember anymore.

Or perhaps I peered through a hole in the wall and the myth shattered.

Or the myth remained intact and I shattered. The rest of the group seems unperturbed by the flies. They continue to listen, riveted, to the words of the guide.

I try to pick the flies out of my hair, one by one, but this becomes futile, as
more and more land on my body. Tiny wings, legs, antennas tearing apart,
sticking to my strands. Sticking to my ear, which is moist with antibiotic
cream and Vaseline.

12.

Peep show. If a city is a woman. If the body of a city is the body of a woman is
the body of a city.

No. This is another myth.

13.

The holes from Perlov's film remained with me.

I wrote a play set in 1967, in which the main character, 21 years old, Jewish,
recounts a dream-memory of trying to catch a glimpse of the Old City
through a hole in the wall with her childhood friend.

"All I can see are people's legs," she says. "And I feel like I'm peeking at
something forbidden, like I'm peeking into the nakedness of the city."

The director chose to stage this moment so that the actress says these lines
with her back to the audience, bent at the waist, legs spread. Her face glimpses
out from between her knees as she speaks. Her skirt rides up. Her underwear
is showing.

She is both the voyeur and the exhibitionist. The eye and the object. She is the
wall and the city. She is both sides of the wall.

She has tried to flee Jerusalem, but the city haunts her body like a ghost.

14.

The surgeon first numbs my outer ear with a painful injection. While he does this I think of that other extraction, exactly one year ago.

I say a prayer for my eggs, languishing in a netherworld of ice.

I wonder where A. is. I never know where I'll reach him these days, though last week he asked if he could register his name at my address, for bureaucratic purposes, at the Ministry of Interiors. Because he's living off the grid now, a kind of private protest against urbanity. He wanted an address in Jerusalem and I said yes, because I have an address to give. An address of a crumbling down house. With a For Sale sign on its door. That I might be leaving soon. Because I am always trying to leave Jerusalem. I've been leaving Jerusalem for at least five years.

Both of us are, to borrow a phrase from Isaac Babel, "people who have fallen through the cracks of life." And after all these years, no, we are not together. But now registered formally at the same address. This one address in Jerusalem that unites us even though neither of us, probably, will be here soon.

I try to avoid talking politics with A. I've learned it is useless to argue politics with people you love. But when he was here last week, the words slipped out of my mouth, slipped out into a full-fledged fight, bottle of *arak* near empty on the floor between us. I told him that as a woman I find myself identifying with those who move, voiceless, through the world, through the city. I told him I know how it feels, and that he does too. I cut him off when he opened his mouth to protest.

"You really don't want to go there with me," I said. "I'll crush you." I heard myself saying: I will crush you.

I've never used words like that with anyone before. Perhaps it was the *arak*. Perhaps it was my ear, which, throbbing, sent pulsating urgent messages to me through Morse code.

"Are you mad at me," I whispered, mouth to A.'s ear at the door, when he hugged me goodbye.

We both knew he must go. Both of us crumbling at the door. We are not together. We part, at our address. We have this invisible boundary between us, and we have this space that exists, that holds us together through time, in Jerusalem, officially. According to the Ministry of Interiors, at least.

15.

My stomach clenches with nerves, still, each time my play is performed in Jerusalem. All that raw female messiness laid bare in the city, on its landscape, like a misshapen birthmark unveiled on naked skin. I'm slowly trying to learn to relish the discussion this generates. The precarious privilege of having a stage upon which to perform.

After a Tel Aviv show, I was told I should have gone easy on all that Jerusalem talk. Perhaps I should even consider setting the play elsewhere. No one is really interested in Jerusalem here, they said.

16.

I called A. before the ear procedure but his voice mail answered. He is off somewhere in the wilderness without reception. Out of reach.

Such is life in the cracks, I think to myself as the surgeon prepares his tools.

I feel nothing when he yanks the thing out of my ear.

Afterwards he waves it at me like a war trophy. The bloody, mucus covered body to which my ear has given birth.

"In the E.R., they would have sliced you open like a bread roll," he says.

17.

"I don't know why it had to be an ear," David Lynch said in an interview, about the image that frames his film *Blue Velvet*.

That severed, human ear, found flung in a field, is the portal to a disturbing underworld, a realm of shadows which, once entered, cannot be unseen.

". . . It needed to be an opening of a part of the body," Lynch said. "A hole into something else . . . The ear sits on the head and goes right into the mind so it felt perfect."

At the end of the film, we exit the vortex again, with "a huge low roaring sound."

"SLOWLY WE COME UP OUT OF A HUGE DARK HOLE . . . We see we are rising out of an ear."

18.

I leave the clinic, ear bandaged but intact, mostly.

I feel pounds lighter. Hollowed out.

This stitched up foreign body lurches her way through the city, towards a crumbling structure at an address which she may or may not call home.

Black Dog

She would awaken in the woods. In sunlight. Underneath trees and laying on rocks.

Roots.

Unsheathed and exposed to all manner of elements. But she was warm. Leaves were twisted and mashed into her hair, but she could not feel them on her scalp. This was a reminder that her hair was not hers. It belonged to the girls in India who cried when their heads were shaved and their sorrow could be bought and sold for 79.99 a pack at Lovely's on Bright Street. She'd only needed three packs.

She paid her cousin, Drea, sixty to put the weave in and another twenty for the pizza she ordered. That investment now had leaves attached to it. And mud, she found.

She also found that there were no tracks, from small animals or large ones. No drag marks. And no explanation for the scratches on her arms and ankles. The bottoms of her feet were stained black like she'd been dancing around in pitch. Her fingernails which had been short last night, were now long.

She stood on unsteady legs, knees knocking together, quaking under the weight of her body. Out the corner of her eye, she saw several versions of herself dressed in all white and as a buzzing behind her eyes settled into a slow ache, she thought, *how did they follow me here?*

But that was not today.

~

The night wrapped its great arms around her, hanging on her shoulders. The cool air, a haint riding her back. She remembered when she was little that she had asked Momma why she was painting Grandma Pearl's porch blue and Momma had said, "Haints can't cross water. The blue confuses them." So, she avoided very blue water. This included beaches and swimming pools. As she'd watched Momma run the paintbrush over rows of chipped paint, she remembered thinking that she might be a ghost and how strange and wonderful it might be if she couldn't cross the porch. But she was able to plant her feet firmly on those dried blue planks. She was a real girl after all. Or maybe haints were just smarter than Momma thought. She didn't understand until she was older that being a real girl didn't mean you couldn't be invisible. Even now up on the roof, she was a ghoul.

Her eyes drifted over sweating bodies and strung lights as she took in the scene of the rooftop bacchanalia. The crowd was a mixed bag of hipsters, indie kids, pill-pushers, and weed dealers. It wasn't even midnight and almost everyone was wasted and writhing in agony against each other. Or maybe they just looked that way to her with their sweaty shirts clinging to their backs, hair greasy under knit caps, denim jackets dark blue from drinks being spilled on them all night. Io thought they looked miserable, but she didn't like dancing. Though, she was sure she hated the city more. She hated the way smoking a cigarette somehow tasted worse when the chemicals mingled with city air.

Io had realized early on that she had played the night to its full potential. She'd had a few shots of whiskey at the bar and bought a dime bag of weed off of Slim Jimmy. She'd waited patiently for him to finish getting off with the pale faced girl in the bathroom and he's said "slide it under the door." This transaction had taken place over thumping bass and under-ground in The Attic where Io had had her first drink with Sola Delgado when they were sixteen-and-some-change. Sola had told Io to push her skirt up a bit before they went in—*Let them see your legs, Io*—and Io had waited outside of this same scratched up bathroom door while Sola lost her backdoor virginity to Slim Jimmy who never discriminated based on age, he said. But that was when Io and Sola were Sola-and-Io. When they were fused at the hip like a chimera of bone and sinew and hair all one color. Sharing the same breath. Now, Io rarely saw Sola, except for the occasional glitch in the Matrix when they were in the wrong place at the same time. Usually this was only for a few seconds before Io lost sight of Sola's bouncing curls pulled high into that infamous ponytail, another head in the crowd.

When Slim Jimmy had opened the door, the smell of sweaty body parts and hair filled the space and this was about all the night could ring out, Io decided. He'd put the baggie in her hand, lingering there longer than she would have liked. His fingers, burnt from smoking joints to the bottom, passed over Io's palm slowly.

Thanks, Jimmy.

Up on the rooftop, Io watched phantoms of herself walking back and forth. She was standing by the couch wearing a leather skirt and tights, a shirt that showed her stomach and when she talked, a silver ball sparkled on her tongue. Io-Leather-Skirt laughed with her whole body at a joke someone said and the crowd consumed her.

Another one was standing near the makeshift coat rack, this time wearing jeans and a sweater that fell loose in all of the right places. This Io stood with better posture and her lipstick was a shade darker than Io-Leather-Skirt's lipstick. She talked easily with a couple of girls that were perhaps prettier than each other in no particular way. Neither were prettier than her, but Io could not see this. Io-Leather-Skirt watched through keyholes in arms and legs as she was brought down further by the small crowd. Io-In-Jeans didn't notice Io-Leather-Skirt's demise, because she was admiring herself in the reflection in one of the girls' glasses. Io-In-Jeans was cornered by the white girls with talks of a trip to Panama City Beach, and eventually, she disappeared into the wall behind her. Io-In-Jeans's untimely departure was witnessed by Io-In-Red standing near the drink area flirting with three guys.

Io watched those same spectres fall off the rooftop, run into the door, and nearly crash into other people before she slipped back in her skin. She looked down at her shirt, the color of bland chicken, and her thighs, sheathed in leggings that were worn out from too many wears. Her hair was pulled back and she wore too much make-up which covered patches of dark skin and craters from years of picking at her cheeks. And as she watched the night pass in front of her, she knew she had gone unnoticed yet again. That she had been little more than a wall fixture sitting crooked and undisturbed. She knew the spectres would have fared better than she, because she was barely there. And they were much more than ghosts.

In that moment she came back to herself. For Io sometimes the walls of the world were fuzzy and she found herself wading through a daydream. She looked around the rooftop and took in the scene one last time before knocking back one last shot. As vodka hit her tongue, her eyes were drawn over to the door. The man wore nice clothes. Autumn colors were a compliment to his deep brown skin. With full lips and a prominent nose, he was beautiful. Did he know he was? Did he notice how eyes drifted to him? How the rooftop drank him in?

She thought she smelled him. She thought then that she could almost taste him. Pheromones? Were those real? Did they apply to humans? Weren't humans also animals? Yes, she could almost taste him. But she couldn't place the flavor. Like *presque vu*, Momma would say. Having that thing on the tip of your tongue. Momma's tongue was a creole one. When Momma spoke, it conjured smoke and mossy Cypress trees. Tupelo trees. Sentinels of the swamp. It conjured the bayous and *what did you say gal?* Io hadn't been to the bayou since she was small. She hadn't remembered the swamp except through peepholes in Momma's tongue. But she was cityside now. Long gone from those dirt roads. From plantation homes.

She thought still that she could smell him. Not really him, but what parts of him came through the air. She thought then and wondered if he could smell her from where he was. Could he almost taste her? Would he want to?

Usually the whiskey did the job, keeping that dark voice out. But sometimes, when the moon was full, she found herself in stranger tides. She found that dark voice poking holes in her mind that turned to a thousand tiny mouths that said, *He'll look you up and down and then pass you up for one of these white girls.*

But the man was still alone and she watched him. The way he moved took up space. And not just for the sake of occupying space, but because his body—which looked both powerful and full of grace—required it. He didn't look at her. He also seemed not to notice how she stalked him with her eyes low or how every girl up on the roof tracked him.

And then his eyes settled on her, which unsettled her. She'd been made. She buttoned her coat and wrapped her scarf about her neck tighter and headed for the door.

"I'm Jude," he said as she passed him.

She almost turned to see who he was talking to.

"This is the part where you tell me yours," he said. She could hear his smile as he spoke.

"Io," she said with her back to him.

"Eye-oh." He said her name slowly. "Unusual name."

"No stranger than Jude," she said. "It short for Judas?"

"Nah, just Jude," he said. He broke away from the party. "This party is kinda . . . well, it ain't shit."

"Hasn't been for a few hours," she said, still with her back to him. She kept her jacket closed tight, because she'd become aware of her body then. The burden of being noticed.

She didn't hear him move, just felt him moving closer. His body heat emanated toward her, sliding through the kinks in her chill like a hot comb. Who notices ghouls?

"You wanna go somewhere?" he asked. "To talk, I mean."

She turned to him then and said, "Uh, no."

He stepped closer to her. "Can I at least give you my number?"

"What for?" she asked.

"So, we can talk."

"Ghosts don't talk. They only moan," she said.

He looked at her like she'd knocked some of his wind out. "And I was worried about being forward . . ."

They didn't say anything for a moment.

"You're weird," he said and though he wasn't sizing her up, she felt like she could read his mind. Their bodies seemed to be leaning into one another like planets falling into the same inscrutable orbit. Momma had always said you'd know when a man wanted you.

"I have to go," she said.

"Graveyard calling?" he asked.

"Something like that," she said turning away. She passed the fallen spectres on the way out. They stood in a group, hands on their hips, heads shaking. Their bodies still bore the traits of their deaths. One of them said, "What's *wrong* with you?"

~

Io settled in on a bench and watched buses pass, not catching any of them. She hadn't even looked to see where they were going. She thought of Slim Jimmy and a little about Sola, but mostly about the many ways in which a night with Jude *could have* gone. It wasn't long before the other Ios showed themselves and took turns hitting her on the back and saying, very close to her ears, "He was out of your league anyway." Sometimes their cries became so loud that she was sure others would hear. She counted passers-by, but as Jude came into her line of sight, she realized he was still in her crosshairs. She put her hood up and hid herself as he passed, only to get up and follow his tracks to Johanna's Coffeehouse. She stood on the other side of the glass, because she felt safer there.

Was the glass there for his protection or for hers?

Turns out, Jude wasn't a coffee man. He preferred tea, with lots of sugar. Io watched as a blonde haired girl tore several packets and mixed them in behind the counter. The girl leaned in to him, tossing her hair over her shoulder. She bared her chest for him to notice. She had the most saccharine sweet smile that Io had ever seen. Io was sure that smile was sweet enough to sugar Jude's tea by itself.

Jude sat in the corner alone and Io watched him flip through a book that had rested on the bookshelf beside him. She imagined him inviting her in. She imagined what they'd talk about.

"I like sweetness. It's my kryptonite," he'd say.

Io took her tea without sugar and her coffee black. "My mom said sugar is of the devil."

"Where's your mom from?"

"Below the Mason-Dixon line."

He'd laugh then. The kind of laugh that caught in the person's chest and clawed at your insides, splitting them. Io supposed she hated those kinds of laughs. Those kinds of interactions especially. Perhaps any real interaction.

"You look . . . pensive," he'd say after a few sips.

"I am," she'd say. "I'm just thinking."

He'd lean into her in a way that muted all of the noise around them and knit them up tight. "What are you thinking?"

"I dunno."

"Not forever, I mean. Just right now," he'd say.

She'd shrug. "Honestly?"

He'd nod.

"I'm thinking of why I came here with you. I don't know you. I'm not sure if I like you," she'd say.

"Fair enough," he'd say, taking another sip.

"But more so, I'm thinking about our relationship. And I don't mean we're in a relationship. I mean how we are in relation to one another."

"Go on."

"Like how every time you meet someone, even if you just bump into them on the subway or accidentally knock into them on the street, it's a relationship. It's like they've seen you and you've seen them. Probably for the first time in your life even though you've been stomping around in the same spaces probably for a while now. Or maybe not at all. Or maybe they just got to town and you had the audacity to run into them. To leave your impression on them. And for them to leave their impression on you. Like, who do you think you are, right? Who do we think we are?" She'd take a sip of her coffee and come back to herself. "I usually don't talk that much. Sorry."

He'd lean back in his chair and stretch a little. "I've been told that I have that effect on people. They just bear their souls to me. I like to listen."

"It shows," she'd say. His eyes were almond shaped. She'd let herself admire them then, but only a little.

"I was just gonna head home in a few," he'd say then. "You're welcome to come. No expectations."

"No expectations?" She'd wonder if then was the time to tell him she'd never slept with anyone. She'd decide against it.

"None."

"Momma told me not to go home with strange men. She said strange men turn into strange animals."

"Momma might be right," he'd say.

From there, Io would walk home with him and he would show her his skin. She'd see that it was made from flesh that smelled like warm spices and that it tasted like cayenne pepper. She'd realize that was the taste she couldn't place and that he held robust flavoring within him. Io would find this out. Jude would find out that Io held honeycombs. That she was a stinging thing. That she was prickly and also soft. That her skin was electric. And how they arrived at this moment where they both realized they wanted each other would be more of a convergence of limbs and soft strokes. Teeth and hair and scratches. Warmth and wetness and the rush of blood. She'd climb the walls of him and he'd welcome her mouth with tempered muscle and veins. Together, they'd make a chimera even if only fused at their spines and where their hips met. It would be then that Io wished for that cold night air and its chill to find them under the mountain of blankets on Jude's bed. She imagined that his loft was artfully decorated, but she'd only see his pillow.

~

Io walked, feet beating hard against pavement. She passed houses, banal driveways, and sprinklers that were still on. Midnight showers. On her left, she stopped short and stood under a canopy of trees. She saw the moon pierce through clouds and smog and bathe the woods in white. It must have been there, covered in moonlight, where she first sensed it. It was a barely-there sensation that made her ears perk up like a dog whistle singing that which only she could hear. She couldn't make it out amongst the trees. Partially hidden by branches and the rest of it by shadow. Or perhaps the rest of it wasn't there. And maybe it never was.

She felt it walking close, and sometimes far away. Fast, and sometimes slow. On all fours and on two feet. On all fours again. Eyes to the ground. She listened for its feet and for its breath. For its pause and its start. It tracked her, never moving in front of her. But in the periphery it rested. An intangible shadow thing lurking, prowling. Its body seemed strong. She imagined visible breath from the cold night puffing through its nostrils. A long, forked tongue. It followed at a hundred yards away. It kept its distance and she did not look at it. She did not hear it stop. And though she wanted to, she did not relieve that tension in her neck to turn to it. Where were the Ios now? Had they been run off by the lurking thing?

It felt familiar, she realized. Like something she had known. Like something that she almost knew. Or had perhaps once known. That Which Followed stalked her home.

She let herself in the house, keys knocking against her wrist as her hand shook. As That Which Followed waited and did not draw closer. She did not look for it in under moonlight. She did not look for it when she was on the safe side of the door or when she closed her window before bed. She left it waiting for her, down below.

~

That night she dreamed of a dark body covering her own. Of strong legs prying hers open. Of her welcoming it. Of sharp teeth dragging across her skin. Of warm breath. Of cold wind. She dreamed of the blue porch.

When she awoke in the woods, in sunlight, underneath trees and laying on rocks, an ache had set up shop in between her thighs. There was a buzzing there. Honeycombs. Like a hive lived there. Like she'd been colonized.

~

She rinsed the dirt off first and then touched herself in the shower until she felt her breath hitch in her throat. She finished, but the buzzing returned with a pointy reckoning that almost stung. She clenched. She squeezed.

She was strategic when taking out her weave, which was ruined by the mud. She clipped out the pieces of thread that held the weave together and let the whole thing unravel in the sink. What was left were the coarse curls of her hair and tender scalp. She kept the nails long.

~ ~ ~

She had a hole in her stomach when next she woke. It needed filling. For breakfast, she ate eggs and a piece of steak from the fridge, raw. She ran it under the sink in hot water to get the ice off. She thawed it and spiced it.

Momma came down at a quarter after seven wearing her bathrobe and her head scarf. She wore full makeup—*Io, I can't leave the house without my face on*—and big pearl earrings. She kissed Io on the cheek. "Didn't hear you come in last night."

Io scooted forward on her stool and crossed her legs one way and then other. "I got in late."

Momma slid the coffee filter in and closed the top with a snap. "You be careful because the news said there were some robberies a couple of nights ago and some man was talkin' about how he saw a coyote or somethin' like it in the woods."

"We don't get coyotes," Io said. A lightning strike snapped through her making her shiver below the waist. She throbbed.

"I know," Momma said. "Where's mine?"

"Eggs are on the stove," Io said, uncrossing her legs and then crossing them again.

Momma busied herself with the business of making toast and putting her cold eggs in the microwave. She poured herself a big cup of coffee and sat down beside Io.

"Since when do you eat your meat rare?" Momma asked. "It'll make you sick."

Her walls thrummed against each other. Buzzing. Rippling. "I like it like this."

"Since when?"

Buzz. "Trying something new, Momma. That alright?" The meat slid through her teeth easily, blood filling up the cavity of her mouth with each piece. But she wished it was warm. And that it was fresh.

Momma tore into her toast. "I guess, but don't come cryin' to me when you get sick."

"I'm already sick," Io said.

~ ~ ~

Each time she woke up in the woods, she'd dreamed about a black dog standing over her. This reminded her of a story Momma told her on her sixteenth birthday about the *Rougarou*. Momma told her about how when Grandma Pearl told it to her, she called it the Swamp Wolf of Nawlins. Grandma Pearl told Momma that the Rougarou wasn't a what, but a who. Grandma Pearl told this story to Momma on the porch right before Momma left for prom. Grandma Pearl pulled Momma close and said "In 'dem trees, it waits. Watchin'. It's hungry. In the swamp. Dat thing.

"It can smell a man on ya," Grandma Pearl told Momma. She said that when it caught the scent of a girl who was now a woman, it saw her blood. Grandma Pearl didn't know that the only thing that watched Momma was her cousin, Perry. Or that Momma had lost her virginity in the backseat of Aunt Rena's car. Perry: age twenty. Momma: age twelve. Details: unclear. Momma had left the part about Perry out. She'd just laughed to Io and said, "Just an old story."

~

In class, the buzzing moved from between her legs into her head and her chest. She felt the prickling of small hairs protruding from places that it had no business being. Her bones moved under her skin, popping, muted, a mortar and pestle grinding in her sockets. She rolled her shoulders. They rolled back.

And on her walk home, she felt That Which Followed, following closely. Perhaps it had never left, but just retreated when the sun chased the shadows off. But under moonlight it was relentless and it stalked her at a closer range, but she did not look at it. She didn't know much about it, but what she did know of it, was that it was the same height as her.

~ ~ ~

Io sat in a bath, because that seemed to ease the buzzing in her stomach. She searched "buzzing, head, stomach, legs, vagina" on her phone. It returned no results.

~ ~ ~

The buzzing felt sort of like bites. Like a thousand tiny mouths hummed on her skin and had colonized her head and chest. Had spread between her thighs, and to her hair, her nails and her ears. It was also accompanied by an itch that was in the deep tissue of her skin. This was soothed, slightly, by laying on the bathroom floor and excessive masturbation. This did next to nothing except increase her affinity for bloody, sinewy, raw meats. She picked up a pound of steak and chicken livers from the grocery. She ate them out of a brown paper bag while Momma was at work.

~

Io sat in a bath, chest buzzing, and searched "black dog" on her phone. It returned several results.

~

She awoke in a cold sweat. She turned on her fan and went downstairs for water. She wandered down, holding tight to the bannister, searching for the last step. Momma was sleeping on the couch when she passed, but she saw something cast in shadow roving near.

That Which Followed stood over Momma on two legs with claws long and sharp perched just above her torso, back hunched, hair sprawling from its body. A mane of black hair. Its teeth dripped saliva onto Momma's head.

"Stop," Io said. "Leave her out of it."

That Which Followed didn't move. It kept its stance, but pointed to the door. A few seconds later, the door crept open soundlessly.

"Okay," Io said.

Io wandered past the park and down Bright Street to the wood's edge, trailing That Which Followed at twenty paces. That Which Followed walked into a clearing of trees on two legs. Once she passed through that invisible mouth, that threshold, the buzzing ceased. She imagined that the woods were the swamp and that these were one and the same. Wasn't a swamp just the woods drowning? But this swamp had clear blue water instead of the murky green it should have been. Bluer-than-the-porch water. She backed away from it.

"It isn't supposed to look like that," she said to That Which Followed. To the Ios. "Why is it so blue?"

That Which Followed circled her then, nipping at her ankles and snarling. It urged her in.

The Ios raised their voices and Io thought how wonderful it might be to see them die. She unzipped her dress and stepped out of it, and let it sink underwater. She waded further in and could see her wavy reflection in the water. She looked so unlike them. And the water felt nicer than she thought it would and warmer. She could hear cicadas in the trees. She could feel the swamp water touching her ankles and then her knees. On the bank of her imagined swamp sat her phantom selves dressed in white. Sacrificial white. Sacrificial rites. One held a knife. One held a spear. Their faces were half naked and half tribal paint. They wore many rings.

"The water is so nice," she said to the Ios. She knew they could not stand for her to enjoy something without them enjoying it more. "Come in."

Io invited them in one at a time. The swamp changed green as they entered and stained their white clothes. She pushed their heads underneath the water. She held them there for many beats. Beat. Beat. Beat. Io-In-Red succumbed.

She's dead. And when one was done, she invited in the next. Io-Leather-Skirt. She struggled more than her sisters. But the flailing ceased. Io could feel each death in her own body and in her own breath. She felt the pain and then the release.

That Which Followed met her at the swamp's edge and allowed her to take its hand. She realized that the hand she held was first a claw and then her own soft hand. And then nothing. She saw Jude sitting there on the bank, watching. She felt the bones in her arms elongating and her skin spreading to meet the new demands of *this* body. She let her neck crack and split. She let her feet lift off of the ground and rest on her haunches. She let the black hair crawl to her fingers and then her toes.

This body was wondrous. It was trees and dry ground. It was solid rock and steel. She let a feral cry escape her lips and let the water capsize her.

When she came up for air, which was quite some time, because she liked the swamp floor, Jude sat there still.

"Yes," she said. "I'd like to go somewhere with you."

[Untitled Tweet]

390

Jia Tolentino ✓
@jiatolentino

I keep accidentally writing "their ages
ranged" as "their rages aged"

2:10 PM - 21 Dec 2017

17 Retweets 447 Likes

8   17   447

Videoteca Fin del Mundo

This is going to be a story about the end of the world. It won't seem like it, but only because I'm telling it. Told by me, nothing will seem different from today, because, the way things are now are supposed to be forever. This is how it's supposed to work; this is what keeps me comfortable and believing everything I've just said—a state of numbing if not smiling acquiescence. I've heard people call it the *dissonance of the everyday*: not knowing if you should scream or just keep going. Look around to see if it really is a big deal or if you can be persuaded about the virtues of tolerance towards the intolerable, too. It is supposed to be impossible to imagine the end of borders, the end of maquiladoras, the end of the migrant detention centers they call *iceboxes* and *dog pounds*—hieleras, perreras; the end of robo de salarios.

Or, when it is imagined, it always means the fall of *everything*. Dramatic disaster movies, dreams of the end of time. I could do that too, I guess. The end of the world: batteries burst open like boils. Fiber optic cables split and fry away; canned food rots in its aluminum armor and lipstick tastes like pig's blood on your lips. Border walls sink into soft mud like a shoe's brandname, barbed wire melts into landslides, and all the things that make my life slowly wheeze to a stop . . . But I don't like dreams that aren't any different from when you're awake. It messes up even the smallest things. Like, did I brush my teeth or just dream I did. Is the heater still running. Is La Bestia still running. Waking up just to check . . .

What I'm trying to say is that yo estaba viviendo bien until I realized I wasn't. My hot water, my clean air, my right of free movement, my microwave, my strawberry jam on bread this morning. This is how I am alive, or, better, how I am not. —I don't mean anything supernatural, but just that it is possible to die in an everyday kind of way. Life transfigured into something else just as an ordinary course of events. I feel smudged out, not really dead but some state that makes you ask if this is life, after all. Like a title that stays on the screen for so long that when you close your eyes you can still see it, vibrating on the underside of your lids. I walk around earth, taking in the end that won't end. Just watch:

Here is the Pájaro Valley, home to three million acres of strawberry fields and fourteen million pounds of pesticides a year. People who are sin papeles spray the crops with chloropicrin, a gas used to kill people during World War I. There is Ajena Verdeja, too, emerging out of a poisonous cloud with a bandana over her mouth and nose, like in the movies when the aliens touch down and the UFO opens up with a *tssssssssssssssssssss* and a highpowered fog machine. Euro settlers hundreds of years ago, moving in clouds of smoke, burning down the crops already there and replacing them so they could eat their own bread and see their own animals. Their own little paraíso. When I go to the grocery store I see rows and rows of stacked berries in bright plastic packages printed with a picture of a red barn and a rising sun and maybe even photos of the blonde Evan Family—Strawberry Farmers for Three Generations—with grins ear to ear. All the particulars are stripped away, replaced by the same great big smile. This is how meaning is made; this is how you abstract value into existence. Rattle it off like a drug ad: *may cause neurological deterioration, reproductive health problems, developmental disabilities, cancer, metabolic disorders, sexual assault on job site, wage theft, deportation.*[1] Money and markets scrape away most of it. Now you can say things like "product" and "equivalent." Pronounced universality and occluded relationality that allows "fair labor" to suddenly emerge out of nowhere and strawberries to taste so good. Ajena goes back inside her cloud, invisible.

These are facts you live with and learn to fade to background, if you can. Background like the midlength drone of the man on tv spitting up fear into living rooms across the country, like a bird pulling food out of her own throat and cramming it into her chicks'. Hunger strikes in Hutto Detention Center for Women since October, where an ICE representative explains what happens: "After 72 hours, detainees are referred to the medical department for evaluation and possible treatment. They are also isolated for close supervision, observation, and monitoring and encouraged to end the strike or accept treatment."[2] Acceptance implies choice. That's one of the tricks the strawberry

1. Dvera I Saxton, "Strawberry Fields as Extreme Environments: The Ecobiopolitics of Farmworker Health," *Medical Anthropology* 34:2 (2015), 166–83.

2. Statement from Immigration and Customs Enforcement representative at Hutto Detention Center, site of a massive hunger strike by inmates, in Kenrya Rankin, translated by Yirssi Bergman, "Why 27 Women in Hutto Immigration Detention Center Won't Eat," *ColorLines*, October 29, 2015, 2:51PM ET. https://www.colorlines.com/articles/why-27-women-hutto-immigration-detention-center-wont-eat

packages use, too. *Choose healthier. Choose Evans. Choose a smile.* If you repeat it to yourself enough times it becomes better than real.

I go wading through strawberry hydroponics fields, running across state lines as fast as a slur can slip from between lips. Another scene. In one shelf in her living room Gloriana Rodriguez keeps her Videoteca Fin del Mundo. It's every disaster movie you can think of copied to rows and rows of unlicensed tapes and I've seen them all. Super tornadoes, tsunamis, diseases, alien invasion. But it's funny how none of them actually *end*. There's always a Planet B, where the güeros launch off to and set up another white picket fence neighborhood, secure communities all over again. Or they pan back from the main actor all alone in the middle of the ruins and smoke but they're still alive and are clutching a vial of the antidote or whatever so you're supposed to have hope for humanity. Big words like that: humanity. The human race. The movies taught her English—even though they also taught that hope for humanity was hope for that one güero at the end of the movie. But Gloriana still has a soft spot for them because they were what promised a better life; their end was her beginning. *Scene: The underground bunker. People sit huddled in groups, while A. and R. stand to the side, talking. // A: They're not like us. They may look human but we don't know what they want. I'm scared. // A. walks to the far side of the bunker and looks over at a woman cradling her baby in a way that shows she knows what is coming. Rapid zoom-out to the whole globe from space.* It's only when the world's crashing down that they start using phrases like that.

Most of the time *human* is just an empty word, or only meant for some people. It's kind of like a ghost, something that hovers over a whole list that it's meant to stand for but somehow is outside of at the same time. Race, gender, immigration status, class. A Citizen of Planet Earth, or like they say in *Last Days*, "Earthizen." That's the future the t-shirts hope for too, with Ningún Ser Humano es Ilegal printed on them back and front. But you become humano by fitting the profile; the character that gets abstracted into existence from the list. Do you fit the metaphor? Can you play the character they are looking for at your Credible Fear interview? Years ago Gloriana had to audition for the part of Refugee for a court and two lawyers. *Scene: G. sits at a small table with two men behind it. The lawyers have clipboards out and are running down the checklist. They take turns asking questions without looking up. // L1: Why did you leave your home country?* **L2:** *Any particular moment or a series of events?* **L1:** *DV issues: Gang threats: Other:* **L2:** *Could you return?* **L1:** *Why/not?* **L2:** *Are you afraid of anybody in your home country?* **L1:** *Who is the persecutor?* **L2:** *Why did this person/group particularly target you?* **L1:** *Did you seek protection of authorities? (police/military)?*[3] Change the story slightly to fit the questions. This is the only time your humanness will be based on your dehumanization so barter for it and say only what they want to hear.

Perfect victim. I walk across highways and under bridges. I am in the grocery store parking lot and everyone is looking. An old lady comes up to me like they do to pregnant women and tells me that O my, it has been so long since she's seen a dead person, may she touch my hand? I am polite and courteous; si claro, go right ahead, I put it out to her like a Bishop waiting for his ring to be kissed; I am actually enjoying being the freakshow everyone defines themselves against. Little humanos and their daddies come up and ask me "what's it like" and I am so glad you've asked, I answer so well I say exactly what they expect because I've seen that movie too. They go away happy and impressed by themselves for guessing right. All of them thinking that dying gives one authority, or at least a different perspective, although I doubt a different perspective is what they're after. What they want is to see themselves. Así es como funciona la simpatía—why the little girls in human rights ads are white and why individual stories work better than pointing out political patterns.

—Pero vamos a hablar de otra cosa. I'm trying to see things differently but keep repeating the same thing over and over—maybe that's why it's so horrible; because it's hard to see it any other way. But, like any story about the end of the world, I'm not making any of it up. Captive imagination: The image of a Citizen holds itself up in front of Aracely Garcia Ahuatzi, ready to slip through her fingers at any moment. Billboards whisper how to get there: Buy a microondas. Only $25 a month. Ignore the protests and work hard instead. Then maybe one day you can speak out loud and not be afraid,

3. Questions based on those asked by Homeland Security border patrol agents in the Border Patrol Station in McAllen, Texas, when a migrant is first detained and the agent (usually without a translator) takes a "Sworn Statement" to determine if the person entering the country can be immediately deported or not. From the author's work with the Asylum Seeker Advocacy Project (ASAP) at the Urban Center for Justice.

with the dim roar of her appliances to back you up. I know she is dreaming of buying larger and larger tvs so that they are so heavy they fall off the wall, cracking the plaster. The magazine ads promise that one day Aracely can look down on her neighbors the way they do to her now, and whisper if she is ilegal or not; say they once had a cousin who looked that way and he was no good. The job cleaning and scrubbing gives just enough money to dream of owning more but not enough for healthcare: You make $0.58 to the Citizen's dollar and a fourth of that is pocketed by Mr. Ryan because this is his dream, too. The furniture, the lavaplatos, the house start talking in American accents like in a children's cartoon: *The promise of inclusion through citizenship and rights cannot resolve the material inequalities of racialized exploitation.*[4] They sound ridiculous, no chair should know that much. Belonging—¿cuanto cuesta? I wanted a refrigerator with a hielera but couldn't say the word because that's what they call the migrant holding rooms—hieleras and perreras. Freezers and doghouses. Looking for the truth as if it were a barcode on the back of a bottle of crema blanqueadora. Suddenly the makeshift reality you asked to stand in for life drops away and you call yourself afraid. *Scene: Crossfade to white. O. is in Dilley where she has locked herself in the bathroom. She looks at the camera. // O: You don't understand that people's lives have no price and you cannot buy it with money . . . You don't believe me you never wanted to give me my freedom. What I tell you is that nobody lives forever in this world; one day we are all going to die and give an account to God. That's why I do this because you were bad to me and my son. We did not deserve this. Now you want to deport me after spending 8 months here.*[5] Or is it that gradual? One day I am staring up at you from among the coupons and Missing Persons ads. One dozen donut holes, $2 off thru Sept. 2. DOB: 8/24/95/ 118 lbs. Photorender of what you would look like today alongside of a Last Seen On photo from when you were 18. Bright white backgrounds; a chart that shows years on one axis and women kidnapped on the other; a spike in 1994, NAFTA. In a thousandth of a split second it was there but you looked away just in time. Under the soft glow of the neon OPEN sign, eyes lowered to look at the bottomless floor. What is wrong here. We called them movies starring nobody. As much as you might stick your hand out in the air it never catches on anything.

4. Lisa Lowe, *Immigrant Acts* (Durham: Duke University Press, 1996).
5. Letter from Lilian Oliva Bardales, held in Karnes Detention Center, June 9, 2015. http://www.womeninandbeyond.org/?p=18828.

The creeping feeling that all my testimonies are ghost-written. "It was so cold that we felt our hands and feet getting numb. The only clothes that we had were the ones that we were wearing when we were apprehended. We had seen some people that had aluminum covers and we asked the Officers if we could have one. The Officers refused." "The hielera was freezing cold. To make things worse our clothes were soaking wet from crossing through the river. Because it was so cold our clothes never dried."[6] "The food is the worst, if they give us oranges, it seems as if the fruit was taken out of the trash. They treat us as if we have leprosy, they humiliate us in numerous ways."[7] "Paid a coyote? — Yes, $4,000. Crossed with a group? — 11. Where? — Entered in McAllen, Texas. Harmed by anyone on the trip? — Verbally abused by CBP officer." "I cannot talk to anyone. I am going crazy. I have no one here. There is no freedom. There is nothing but control." "I was paid $4 an hour for five years and when we tried to go to court the owner sold the business."[8]

What do you do with the inhumanos. Dress me up to look like you, put me in Family Detention, check my ID to make sure I am dead but just alive enough to keep picking berries—making plastic pens—cleaning tables. Nuestra Hermana difunta is tenuous enough for churches; body is factual enough for newspapers and remains hits that difficult spot between that is just tasteful enough for funeral homes to hide just how lucrative it is as well. Unless you aren't being buried—numbers not even released for how many died crossing this year. I heard them say it in a movie and so I went and read in the dictionary that the word for a dead animal, carcass, may be humorous when used figuratively, as in, *"Get your carcass out of bed," said mom sarcastically.* "Figuratively" implying that you don't have to mean your words; that words can be meaningless when you mean them to be. That calling someone a *corpse* is not the same as shooting them, that alien and illegal don't mean what you think. I woke up in the darkness that pretends to hide everything and heard my obedient heart, rushing blood from right atrium right ventricle right atrioventricular valve pulmonary semilunar valve

6. Declarations of Detainees from a Human Rights report published by the American Immigration Council: "Hieleras (Iceboxes) in the Rio Grande Valley Sector," December 17, 2015. https://www.americanimmigrationcouncil.org/research/hieleras-iceboxes-rio-grande-valley-sector

7. Hutto declaration, in Rankin, translated by Bergman, 2015. See footnote 2.

8. Unidad Latina en Acción (ULA), "Connecticut's Wage Theft Crisis: Stories and Solutions," a report compiled by the New Haven Workers' Association and ULA, March 2015. https://ulanewhaven.org/wage-theft-crisis-report/.

pulmonary artery lungs heart left atrium bicuspid valve left ventricle aortic semilunar valve aorta arteries arterioles capillaries. How can I be antisystemic when this is what keeps me alive. I could say, *imagine a world without borders* but I know that wouldn't mean much; in fact, that world already exists if you can pay enough. I am locked into today and I can see the future. It is exactly like the present. No, it's not, but I'm only saying this so you'll do something about it instead of waiting for it to get better. This isn't an ending because the end of the world doesn't have an end. It just keeps going.

On the Problem of Replacement Children

Case Study #64221

Amber Y. said, "That isn't our child anymore upstairs."

"What do you mean, that isn't our child?" Clark Y. asked. "Are you delirious? Do you have the fever or something? That is our child. Who else would that be in our child's bed?"

"I don't know who he is but he isn't ours. When I read to him, he sat on the bed picking at the edges of the blanket. He's never done that before. He always sits with me on the glider when I'm reading."

"So he's too big for the glider now," Clark said. "Anyway, a lot of kids start acting different in the summer."

"And his hair is changing color. I thought it was all that time spent outside in the sun, but after I tucked him in, I kept an eye on him, and his hair changed color, it lightened, while I was in the room. And the smell of his room—it smells like dirt now. Like he's been burrowing."

"Okay. So his room smells like dirt." Not knowing what to do next, Clark suggested the situation might look better in the morning and recommended they go upstairs to try and sleep.

The following morning, after the hair of the boy who slept in their son's bed had turned completely silver and he began to speak an unrecognizable language, Clark admitted that Amber was right, this was no longer their child, and he asked to know more about what happened the previous night.

It had been Amber's turn to watch over their son, and she had been watching over him, closely, until she remembered a bowl of cold cherries in the fridge. A sudden irrational longing for these cherries overtook her. It felt like something external had placed that longing in her and there was nothing she could do about it, other than to rush downstairs and grab a handful. She was gone for no more than two minutes. When she returned, she saw the candle had been blown out.

"Let me guess, you didn't relight the candle right away?" Clark couldn't help asking this in an accusatory tone, for every parent these days knows a child should not be left alone during a full moon, but if a child has to be left alone, at the very least the candle in the child's bedroom must not go out. Clark was correct: Amber had not re-lit the candle right away. Instead she ate the cherries, threw the pits into the garbage bin in the corner, and then she walked over to their child's bed to check on him. That was when she knew.

What exactly is a replacement child?
A replacement is a sort of otherworldly "child"—the term *child* used here loosely—who arrives in the middle of the night, usually on the night of a full moon, taking the place of the family's original child who appears to have gone away to some unreachable location. We aren't sure where.

Why is this happening?
Actually, this has been happening for a while, for hundreds of years or longer if we pay attention to the old stories, though replacements have not previously existed here in such quantities that they warranted notice. We only learned about the first replacement in our community four years ago. On that initial occasion, many of us brought casseroles to the affected family's house, the kind of hot dish one brings to funeral lunches, appropriate as the mother of the household had taken to dressing entirely in black, in order to better mourn for the child she believed she had lost. This is no longer a recommended response to the appearance of a replacement.

Should such disappearances of original children be considered an ongoing epidemic?
Yes.

What are some preventative measures I can take to protect my original children, thereby keeping the replacement children away?
Because the children who are being taken are taken away at night, many parents have found it useful to stay awake guarding the windows of their children's bedrooms. Alternatively, some have forced their children to sleep in windowless rooms, such as an interior bathroom. Parents whose children are

not taken away tend to be resourceful, driven, but also tired. To force a child to remain as they are, to stay like they're supposed to: this requires a great deal of effort. Many parents say such effort is worth it. Receiving a replacement child can, in some cases, indicate a failure of attention (see Case Study #64221 above).

Because boys are taken most often—we do not know why—some parents have found it useful to dress their male babies at night in stereotypically feminine clothing, i.e. ruffled dresses, in the hope of tricking whatever is coming for their children, as such beings appear to abide by old-fashioned gender stereotypes. Or at least give the boy one of his father's socks, a technique which worked in many of the old stories. You should definitely leave a light burning. It must be the light of a candle made from beeswax. Whatever is taking our children appears to lose interest in them after they reach the age of nine.

If a replacement child somehow appears one night in my child's bed, is it useful to obsessively remember everything about my original child?
No.

Case Study #148200

"What did you do wrong?" Tina Q.'s neighbor asked Tina on a particularly hot July day when everybody's lawn sprinklers were on trying to revive the sod. "You know you were supposed to be watching over your son, right?"

Tina's child had been taken the Monday previous; her child's replacement, silvery haired, smelling of the underside of soil, had not left her son's bed since.

"I thought it was a story that happened to other people," said Tina quietly. Her shoes were soaked from her neighbor's sprinkler though she did not move out of the way.

"What?" the neighbor asked.

"I thought it was a metaphor," Tina said.

What are some reasons a replacement child might appear?

#1. Parent did not watch child adequately throughout the night.

#2. Candle was extinguished beside child's bed during the night.

#3. Mother's diet during pregnancy lacked certain vitamins, such as B or D.

#4. Unrestrained exercise of mother during pregnancy.

#5. Age of father (increased age equals increased risk).

#6. Pesticides used on lawn.

#7. Carrying the baby only in one arm, especially the left arm.

#7. Living beside a busy road with truck traffic.

#8. Mother breaks a glass cup during pregnancy.

#9. Excessive looking into the mirror.

What about the idea that the original child was not dragged off unwillingly but in fact wanted to go away?

This certainly is one possibility, that the original child wishes for a more exciting life, such as the kind of life they might have in a children's fantasy book, where dwarfs will lead them to underground caverns coated in emeralds, and nymphs will be swimming with them under the lakes in blurry wet worlds. With this in mind, it's possible that when whatever it is comes beckoning, the child unlatches the window themselves and jumps eagerly into its arms. Such an explanation suggests two additional solutions.

One: it is in the parent's best interest to give their child an exciting life filled with adventure and quests.

Two: parents should limit, or perhaps forbid, the reading of fantastical stories, instead encouraging at bedtime nonfiction, such as almanacs, which are now available in colorful glossy editions.

What are some things we know for sure about replacement children?

#1. The replacements are said to sleep a lot.

#2. At the same time, the notion that they sleep so much might be a deception. Certain parents suspect that the moment they leave the room where the replacement is napping, the moment they shut the door, the replacement springs up and joyfully runs around while speaking in full and comprehensible sentences, so long as no one is watching or listening.

#3. Contradictions are common when talking about replacement children.

#4. Replacement children have silvery hair that does not feel like hair.

#5. They do not like to look us in the eye.

#6. Communication with them will prove difficult.

#7. Replacement children may not consider communication to be a form of connection.

#8. Replacements may have difficulty using the toilet properly.

#9. It appears the replacement, in most cases, doesn't want to be here with us either. Like us, they may be frightened, or disappointed, or even bored. Probably it is obvious to them that this is not supposed to be their home and we are not supposed to be their parents.

Case Study #88265

Sometimes when the replacement we'll call P. was sleeping, the mother stared at him for hours, because when he was sleeping he looked like her original son, except for the color of his hair and the odd position in which he slept, with his legs bent slightly yet also open, as if he were running and in the middle of a stride. "Timothy?" she would ask while the replacement slept. That was the name of her original child. "Timothy?" she said again when P. was wandering back and forth in the hallway, dragging his fingers along the wallpaper.

Where do the real children go?
One thought is that they are still somewhere inside the replacement's body, for instance crouched inside of the liver, waiting to be set free by devoted parents. This line of reasoning places a great deal of pressure on the parents as they must now devote their lives to finding a way to get their original child out of that liver (or whatever organ it is). A second possibility is that the real children have been dragged off elsewhere by ill-intended forces, that they are locked up in a stranger's wardrobe or in some man's garden shed.

Though why imagine the worst? There is also the possibility that our children have been taken to a better place than here, a fairy-tale place, perhaps, where they might help rule over a magical land, happier there than they would have ever been here with us.

Case Study #391041

In the long afternoons, Terri O. had begun to drive her replacement to a park in the valley where several mothers brought their silver-haired children. The back seat of her car smelled like a toilet. She kept extra underwear and shorts in the trunk but the replacement refused to change when he peed through his clothes. At the park, the mothers avoided looking at each other, in case it was something they had done, while the replacements patted each other's hair, then gathered up sand in their hands and watched it spilling out onto the ground like it wasn't sand. They might do this a hundred times in an afternoon. Terri tried to pay attention to the replacement, as we recommend, but when that proved difficult, she focused on the landscape instead, on the cardinals singing their melodic nonsense in the canopy of the trees.

If a replacement child appears in the middle of the night in my original child's bed, what reaction can I expect from the surrounding community?
Certain adults will tend to act enamored at first, especially if the replacement is a neighbor's and not their own. They might find it all spine-tingling and exciting, like they're part of a show on the Sci-Fi Channel, this idea that a child can disappear in the middle of the night and be replaced by a piece of another world—that there are parts of this world we still can't understand. In Case Study #88266, we find the example of one such adult, a Mrs. M., who appeared at the W. family's home, carrying a loaf of banana bread wrapped in a tea towel, in the hope of glimpsing the new replacement. Mrs. M. is not alone in her belief that the replacements may have been touched by magic and are, in fact, part fairy or water nymph. The reason some people think this is because of the replacements' silvery hair, and also because of the occasional yet strange look in the replacements' eyes, as if what a replacement sees around them is vastly different from what any of us can see. No one answered the door to the W. family home, so Mrs. M. left the banana bread on the stoop, where it became soggy due to afternoon rains.

Other adults may respond in a more negative fashion, wondering what the parents had done wrong (see Case Study #148200 above). They may ask inappropriate questions in order to avoid making the same mistakes themselves.

The replacement who appeared in Susan K.'s house acted all the time as if he was starving. He ate anything bland that she put in front of him. Potatoes, yogurt, basmati rice. She did not like to watch him eat. She did not use a brush on his hair.

What is the role of the extended family, such as grandparents, in all this?

The initial impulse of many grandparents may be to deny that anything has happened to their grandchild. In Case Study #292589, when Grandmother L. f irst saw her grandchild's replacement during an autumn visit, she said, "Nonsense. This is still the same boy I know and love." The child was running his fingers repeatedly over the suede fabric of the family's couch.

"He refuses to take a bath," the mother pointed out. "He hates the water. Remember how Brian used to love floating in the water? And his hair is silver, Mom."

"Children change, dear," the grandmother said. "God knows you changed so many times, and every time you changed, I certainly did not go around suggesting that a boogeyman had snatched you up."

"It wasn't a boogeyman. It was something else. I don't know what it was. Something came into his room in the middle of the night. There was water around the windowsill. The window was open."

"Rain," the grandmother replied calmly. "Rain causes water to pool around a window." She reached to hug the replacement, who ran, screaming, out of the room.

"Well, if that's how you want to raise him," said the grandmother.

Grandfather L. would not come into the house.

"It's not contagious," the mother told him. "Whatever is it, you can't catch it."

The grandfather still would not come into the house.

To assist grandparents and other extended-family members in accepting your new reality, we suggest sharing helpful educational materials with them, such as the pamphlet you are now reading. Keep in mind that people of earlier generations may possess traditional wisdom, and since the taking of children in the middle of the night appears to be a problem with ancient roots, it can be useful to consult with someone who still understands folkloric customs.

Case Study #56833

When Leslie X. moved toward her child's replacement to pick him up in her arms, he cried. Every time she did this, he cried. Eventually she stopped approaching him.

What do replacement children like to do?
We are not sure. See Case Study #400021 (below) for one possible idea.

Why do you recommend parents seek outside help after a replacement appears in their home?
Let's assume most parents know how to take care of an ordinary child: if you act stern yet playful, distant yet loving, and tell a few jokes in between, you'll do fine. But replacements require us to become a different kind of parent. If that's even possible. For many parents, it isn't, which is why the help of experts becomes necessary once a replacement appears in your child's bed. There are also community resources such as camps made specifically for replacements where they will be taught, or someone will try to teach them, how to blend better into a crowd of ordinary children. There are schools that look like regular boarding schools only all the children would be like them at such a school and they never have to come home (see Case Study #53020).

Case Study #18769

"I think I know how to be a mother," Angela D. said. "I think I can handle it myself."

"Actually, I don't think you can," said the doctor, who was an expert. "Here's my advice. You are still young. You can have another child. Why don't you go and have another child and we can all forget about this one who isn't even yours?"

What is the role of science in these disappearances and appearances?
We do not think that science, in its traditional sense, can be of much help, as this is not a scientific problem per se. It is more of a magical or fantastical problem, the difficulty being that we do not live in a magical or fantastical world.

Freddy W., having always been the easygoing parent oblivious to bedtimes and vegetable-intake requirements, did not become obsessed, as many parents do, about where his actual child had gone. Instead, he took it upon himself to find a shared activity that he and the replacement child could enjoy together (this is a very good idea if a parent hopes to find their happiness again). It turned out that this replacement liked being tossed into the air in their backyard, as high as Freddy could throw him, so that his silvery hair flew around his head like wings. Although the replacement's expression did not change, Freddy imagined he enjoyed it, as it was the only time the boy allowed anyone to touch him. "I miss our son, sure," Freddy insisted to his wife, Dorothy, "but I'm trying to move past all that." While Freddy was tossing the replacement into the air, Dorothy attended many support groups where she wrote down in a notebook any therapy that claimed to bring the original child back, assuming the original still existed.

What's up with the gender stereotypes (i.e., mother as distracted researcher vs. father as playful acceptor)?
When a replacement appears in your child's bed, there aren't many possibilities in terms of what you can do. Such limited options make for a lot of repetition. If it appears that the same thing keeps happening over and over in this narrative, that's because this is how life is once you have a replacement. Your life becomes a pattern of repetitions. If it bothers you, we suggest you skip the remaining case studies. As for gender roles, we too would prefer to see more variation—for instance, a researching father or a playful and accepting mother—but this does not appear to be the norm.

Do replacement children have parents of their own?
Most likely yes, though the reason why replacement parents continue exchanging their children with ours is unclear. Does this exchange happen by accident? If so, we can assume that the replacement's parents are as worried and distracted with longing as we are. Or is the exchange intentional? Maybe these parents are obsessed with our original children's language and laughter, which is understandable as that is also what we miss most about our real

children. In any case, if your child has been taken, we encourage you to imagine that the replacement's parents are trying to learn to love your child just as you are attempting to love your child's replacement.

Case Study #243819

Throughout his first month, a replacement we'll call Q. did not speak a word, nor did he look at the mother of the household. Only after that initial month was over did he begin to speak, though he used a language none of us could identify, his words guttural and involving a rolling of "r"s. The mother pointed to a shoe. "Shoe," she said. They stood in the kitchen, Q. entranced by the sunlight on the floor. "Shoe," she said again, this time bringing her house slippers into Q.'s field of vision. When Q. saw the slippers interfering with the sunlight, he began to howl. She put away her slippers. The following week, she tried to learn his language. He said something like, "*Obush grush treshla tran.*" She pointed to herself. "*Grush?*" she said. She pointed to him. "*Obush?*" He wandered out of the room, leaving a thin trail of pee behind him. She wiped up the pee with a towel that once had bright poppy flowers all over it.

What are some therapy options for replacement children?
The therapies listed below may strike some, at best, as old fashioned and, at worst, as reminiscent of the barbaric practices one imagines illiterate peasants used hundreds of years ago. But as we've said before, the snatching of our children in the middle of the night is a very old occurrence, so old solutions might be called for.

#1. Take the replacement child to a field and beat it with a branch from a weeping birch tree.
#2. Cut off the mother's hair and weave a blanket out of the hair. Lay the blanket over the replacement child.
#3. Place the replacement child on a hot stove and boil water in two eggshells.
#4. Abandon the replacement child in a field of weeds.
#5. Put the child on a chopping block used for firewood.
#6. Pretend to throw the replacement child into the oven.

#7. Show the replacement something they have never seen before, like a savory pudding containing an entire animal, such as a chicken, including the beak and claws and the head.

#8. Leave the replacement child tethered all night to a stake beside a well, preferably a well on a hill.

#9. Toss the replacement child into a rapidly moving river.

#10. Stop feeding the replacement child.

An alternative is to accept the replacement child as they are, avoiding such therapies altogether, but few of us seem able to do this since we tend, as a species, to have an obsessive desire to alter whatever around us is different from what we expected to find (see Case Study #60039).

What are the possible outcomes of such therapies?
Outcome #1. The replacement child's actual parents, who will probably be both unearthly and indescribable, snatch the replacement child away, leaving the original child in its place.

Outcome #2. The replacement child becomes injured or dies.

Outcome #3. Nothing happens.

Case Study #60039

Grandmother G. said to the mother, "The whole time you were mine, I never let anyone or anything take you away. But if you had been taken, I would have done everything possible to bring you back. Are you even trying to get him back? I hear there are stories about how to do that."

The old stories Grandma G. was referencing read like miracles. In the evening, a mother either does something to herself or to the replacement living in her house. By the middle of the night, the replacement has disappeared. In the morning, the mother's original child has returned and is lying comfortably in their own bed. The children who come back are said to be similar in most ways to who they were before.

"Let me have him for the weekend and I'll see what I can do," said Grandmother G. "It's like the medicine I used to have to force down your throat. God knows I did that more than enough times when you were young, but sometimes cures don't taste very good."

The replacement child fell sick after the grandmother's treatments. He did not recover.

Can replacement children offer their families joy?
Yes, though whether such joy is recognized depends on the parent's ability to let go of old memories. Take the replacement found in Case Study #243550, who seemed happiest while staring at his bedroom wall, so this is what the father began to do with the boy. First the father set aside his memories, such as kicking a soccer ball with his old son across the yard. Then he settled the replacement on the rug in the boy's bedroom, surrounded him with pillows, and sat there beside the replacement for many hours. "Sometimes I think I'm going to stay in that room forever," the father told us, and when he told us this, he was smiling. His happiness measured 7.4 out of 10, which is just fine. The mother of the household, on the other hand, was bent over a book beside a pile of additional books (see our note above on the unfortunate gender divide in parental roles). She was holding a yellow highlighter in her right hand. Every one of those books concerned how to bring the original child back. This mother did not allow us to measure her happiness quotient but we assume it was low or immeasurable.

Let's also review Case Study #14099, where mother Karyn B. found much contentment touching or even, on occasion, stroking the replacement child's hair, which is very beautiful and doesn't feel like hair. Karyn B. told us that touching the replacement's hair felt like she was resting her hand on something with a heartbeat, like she was resting her hand on the chest of a rabbit who was considering whether to bolt.

At what point should I stop hoping for the return of my original child?
Given the low percentage of the original children's reappearances and the toll such hope for reappearance takes on the family unit, it is in everyone's best interest to give up their hope immediately, the moment you see a replacement in your child's bed. To hurry this process along, several parents have found it useful to convince themselves their original child never existed. That there is no original child to bring back. That they were given this replacement child at birth and, for a short while, they simply thought otherwise.

What do the replacement children themselves think about all this?
We would guess some replacements wish to return where they came from; some may wish to stay where they are; and some must wish we not tell their story for them or, at least, that we tell a different type of story.

After I have given up hope that my actual child will return, what are best practices for accepting my replacement child?
There are two common ways to view the arrival of your replacement.

One is to consider it as a loss, as we once did. But then you will always be missing something. Every time you go to the park, you will see so many original children there holding each other's hands or running up to their mothers to show off a pile of shining rocks, like your actual child used to do, and you will feel that loss again, which is very depressing.

Or you can look at the replacement's arrival as proof that, in this world, there is still something magical at work, even if it's a magic you didn't ask for. When you gaze upon the replacement sleeping in your child's bed, we suggest doing so with a little wonder. Try to tell yourself you are glimpsing one of the universe's possibilities, the possibility that there are other worlds out there, or at least other realities, and that this child may have come from such a faraway place, and perhaps they are, in fact, still half-living in such a place, a foot in our world and a foot in theirs. This positioning allows them to see things we will never be able to see, the overlays upon our own reality that we can only imagine. Perhaps beside us, to our right, directly over our right shoulder, or reflecting onto the wall, there is something hovering that is so miraculous and large that they cannot take their eyes off of it. No wonder they don't wish to look at us instead.

How do most case studies end?
In the original case studies, which are actually the old folk stories, the replacement child either stayed put as a burden on the family, or else the parent, usually the mother, did what the wise neighbor told her to do, often involving a birch branch or an axe, in which case the replacement child either died or went away, while the original child either came back or, more often, didn't. Nowadays, it is difficult to figure out the correct endings to our stories, as modern parents are hesitant to admit to the more desperate therapies,

fearing we will frame their tales in a somber moralism. No one wants their life story to be framed in such a way. There is also the problem of privacy. A family who receives a replacement child usually will, at some point, begin to retreat into their homes, away from their neighbors and their friends, as it eventually becomes too painful to interact with families whose children are still originals. You begin to want those other families' lives, which means you are ready to throw away your own family and your own life, which is an impossible way to live. Once a family retreats into their home, it is challenging for us to find out what happens next, as they tend to keep their drapes closed and they no longer answer the door.

While we might not know the endings to the majority of our case studies, we can make certain assumptions.

One assumption is that while it's possible many parents never love their replacements, it is also possible such parents haven't recognized their own love, because it isn't the kind of love they expected or wanted.

Another conclusion is that unrecognizable or unrecognized love is still love.

This said, in the two rare case studies below, we have been lucky to observe endings of a sort.

Ending of Case Study #53020

Husband Michael S. went away on a business trip to Missouri, and on the second night of his trip, his wife Laura called one of the replacement schools that had a nice brochure, the school with the natural lake right on the grounds and the horse stable. She spent several minutes on the phone explaining her family's situation to the intake coordinator: the hysterics, the lack of affection, the amount of work. "He's getting worse," Laura said, "and I think I'm doing everything wrong."

"Honey, I get it," replied the coordinator. "Motherhood is supposed to be filled with delight or at least have much delight in it, am I right, but I can tell from your voice that there isn't a whole lot of delight in your current situation. We get it into our heads that just because a child is sleeping in one of our beds, we have to take care of him. But if that isn't the child you wanted—I mean, you tried. It's not like you're giving up on him. Goodness, no. You're putting him someplace where he can belong."

The replacement did not cry the following week when the two men came to the door, not dressed in nice suits, as Laura had hoped, or driving an official-looking car. They were driving a blue Camry. They were wearing polo shirts and shorts. One of the men picked up the replacement's suitcase. "What do you have in here, rocks?" the man asked, and Laura replied yes, that was exactly what was in there, as this replacement was fond of rocks. The other man beckoned the child forward and placed him in the sedan. The replacement looked back at Laura only once, as if she could have been anyone to him, any tired, sad woman in a brown cardigan. There had been stories, the coordinator recounted previously on the phone, of the original children returning within days of the replacement's departure, no worse for the wear. "Do let us know if that happens," the coordinator said.

When Michael arrived home, he refused to try and conceive another child. They waited many years for their original son to come back. For a long time, they left the doors and the windows unlocked at night and the lamp on in the family room, which some people considered a waste of electricity.

Ending of Case Study #21433

It is rumored, especially in those old stories we keep bringing up, that for every kindness you give your replacement, a similar kindness will be bestowed upon your own child, wherever your own child has gone. Likewise, for every cruelty you inflict upon your replacement child, the same cruelty will be suffered by the child who was once yours. For this reason, Georgia F. put aside her lists of therapies, some crueler than others, and she began treating her replacement child with kindness and sympathy, like how she would treat a doll if everybody was taking notes. This did not change the replacement's behavior. After her husband received a promotion, they built an extension onto their house, a guest bedroom they didn't need since no one wanted to visit them, as their replacement made other people uncomfortable. One week during the following fall, they decided to rent a sailboat, since the replacement child enjoyed watching objects fill with wind. The family sailed across a faraway lake. The replacement slept on the deck. Only once did he throw himself into the water and have to be rescued. When they reached the other side of the lake, where a wooden dock led to an ice cream shop with striped awnings, the replacement clung to the rails and refused to get off the boat. "Oh, well," Georgia said, as she had wanted ice cream. "Maybe another time." They turned around and sailed back to where they had started, while overhead, the clouds gathered into the shapes of fantastical animals, animals so ridiculous and beautiful they could never exist.

413

SARAH UAP

Christmas Genital Self-Examination

Mirrors, if angled just right—

Donald Trump starting from where the shaft and crura meet, and continuing down along the sides of the vestibule, where there are two bundles of erectile tissue called the bulbs of the vestibule, I.

The bulbs, along with the whole clitoris (glans, shaft, crura), become firm and filled with blood during sexual arousal, as do the walls of the vagina where I also.

Donald Trump with my urinary opening I.

Donald Trump vaginal coronas come in widely varying sizes and shapes. For most women they stretch easily—by a tampon, as well as a finger, a penis, or a dildo.

Donald Trump if you're comfortable doing so, slowly put a finger or two inside your vagina. Those are your vaginal walls. If it hurts or if you have trouble, take a deep breath and relax. You may be pushing at an awkward angle, your vagina may be dry, or you may be unconsciously tensing the muscles owing to fear or discomfort. Try shifting positions and using a lubricant such as olive or almond oil (don't use a perfumed oil or lotion that could cause irritation).

Vulva modeled upon the exchanging of property.

Vulva devising a torture system to sell to the CIA for 81 million dollars.

Vulva of the prison industrial system vulva of water boarding vulva according to the logics of global capitalism vulva of disposable populations I.

414

Vulva fight relentlessly to end exploitation and oppression everywhere, also on your reviled point, vulva.

Donald Trump notice how your vaginal walls, which are touching each other, spread around and hug your fingers.

Feel the soft folds of mucous membrane. These folds allow the vagina to stretch and to mold itself around whatever is inside, including fingers, a tampon, a penis, a dildo, or your baby during childbirth.

415

ExxonMobil with my vaginal walls I.

ExxonMobil with my vaginal and my cervical discharge.

Monsanto and ExxonMobil about a third of the way up from my vaginal opening, on the anterior wall of the vagina, in an area known as the Gräfenberg spot, or G-spot.

Monsanto and ExxonMobil push gently against the walls of your vagina, and notice where the walls feel particularly sensitive to touch. This sensitivity may occur only in the area closest to the vaginal opening, or in most or all of the vagina and I.

Donald Trump my fornix is the thin wall of mucous membrane and connective tissue that separates my vagina from my rectum.

Donald Trump you may be able to feel bumps on the back side of my vagina if I have some stool in my rectum.

ExxonMobil slide your middle finger as far back into your vagina as you can. Notice that your finger goes in toward the small of your back at an angle, not straight up the middle of your body. If you were standing, your vagina would be at about a 45-degree angle to the floor.

With your finger you may be able to just feel the deep end of your vagina, or the fornix.

Donald Trump not everyone can reach this—it may help if you bring your knees and chest closer together so your finger can slide in farther.

ExxonMobil a little before the end of your vagina you can feel your cervix.

416 Donald Trump your cervix feels like a nose with a small dimple in its center. The cervix (from the Latin cervix uteri, meaning "neck of the womb") is the part of the uterus that extends into your vagina where I.

ExxonMobil the entrance is very small. Normally, only menstrual fluid leaving the uterus, or seminal fluid entering the uterus, passes through the cervix that I.

No tampon, finger, dildo, or penis can go up through my cervix, although it is capable of expanding enormously for a baby during labor and birth.

Vulva, rows of teeth at our jugular.

Vulva, the warmth of your breath, the smell of your blood.

Vulva, ask me about when it.

Vulva, it irritated me that he should force a nasty little brat like me to understand.

Vulva, I could not risk learning.

Vulva, my grubby little hands dangled at my sides.

Vulva, you were unattainable.

Vulva, I became the immensity of calm, the elimination of the, the joining of the, the rapture at the, the death of the, the loss in the face of the.

Vulva, look at something you don't understand for a long time, and it will change you.

Hyper-awareness I—Monsanto.

Monsanto my anus, which you pass through.

417

Monsanto my anus, from which you emerge new into the world.

Monsanto—the immeasurable kindness of my anus.

When you do a self-examination, make sure you have enough time and privacy to feel relaxed.

ExxonMobil try squatting on the floor and putting a hand-mirror between your feet.

ExxonMobil if you're uncomfortable in that position, sit as far forward on the edge of a chair as you comfortably can, separate your legs, and place the mirror between them.

ExxonMobil you give me the oil to make the bright blue plastic frame around the hand-mirror that I squat over.

The bleached wood pulp, and the cotton that makes the tampon which I.

ExxonMobil you give me the plastic wrap around the tampon that I.

Donald Trump if you're having a hard time seeing, try aiming a flashlight at your genitals, or aiming a flashlight at the mirror that you are squatting over.

Donald Trump squat. Shine the light. Look into the mirror.

Monsanto, look so far up inside that you can see your own heart, beating yourself to death.

Vulva-related ideas, vulva beholders, vulva at the sucking portal, vulva legend that just glided past him, vulva's impartial eyesight, vulva's investigative eye, vulva drawing Constantinople for her sons, vulva's treat, vulva eating chocolate croissants with her sons this morning, vulva the homogeneous totality of darkness, vulva verbalizes the indescribable cave, vulva of the all-too-familiar, vulva's analytical intelligence, vulva's exquisite night, vulva playing language games, vulva becoming increasingly self-conscious as her son reads over her shoulder while she writes about vulvas, vulva is that the part outside mama yes sweetie, vulva the one part of me that is not always not talking about contained-ness, vulva the reality of the pioneer, vulva closely following the market, vulva makes an ink drawing of the mouth of hell.

Vulva, pulverizes her sweetness, and feeds it to her children.

from Assimilation Rooms

el día que nos fuimos de brownsville las tías nos
dieron una bolsa de naranjas y sodas y unos
paquetitos de tortillas calientitas hechas a mano con
carne para el camino y en el u-haul papi nos manejó
hasta hou-stón y cuando llegamos mami me compró
ropita nueva para estrenar en el kinder y cada
mañana abuelita me peinaba diferente a veces con
bolas o una diadema y me dormía en su cuartito
porque juntas veíamos novelas y rezábamos hincadas
en frente de la virgencita y las velas y aunque casi no
me podía comunicar en inglés en la escuela si me
encantaban los libros y no me molestaba estar solita
sin embargo mi abuelita se puso malita de su cáncer y
se tuvo que quedar en el hospital y mientras me iba a
the honey tree después de la escuela con tanto miedo
porque no entendía nada y los niños me gritaban
cosas en inglés que hacia mal aunque no sabía nada
de su mundo pero me dijo mi mamá que me portara
bien entonces me callé y solo les dije a las maestras **I
can read** porque quería estar sola **alone in this room** y
los niños se burlaban que allí estaba **with the boogey
man'** y me atrancaron la puerta y solo escribo esto
para rogarte que por favor ábreme la puerta porque
tengo mucho miedo y esta oscuro y todavía estoy aquí
adentro con él

' The day we left from Brownsville the aunts gave to us a bag of oranges and sodas and little packets of warm tortillas made by hand with meat for the road and in the u-haul papi drive us all the way to hou-ston and when we got there mami buy me new little clothes for kinder and each morning grandma combing my hair different sometimes with balls or a headband and I sleep in her little room because together we can watching novelas and kneeling to pray to the virgin and the candles and though I could not barely communicate in English at school I did loved books and it not bother me to be little alone however my grandma got sick of cancer and stayed in the hospital and so I was tooken to the honey tree daycare after school but I was with so much fear because I did not understood anything and the kids scream at me things in English that making me feel bad even though I didn't know anything about their world but my mami told me to be good so I stop talking and just told the teachers I can read because I want I was alone by myself in this room and the children make fun that I was in there with the boogey man and so they lock the door lock me in and I just write this to beg to you please open me the door because I am very scared and is dark and I am still in here with him

as a choir girl   I was prohibited from
singing the songs I knew   in the piano
room   another kind of amor prohibido
I get so weak in the knees   I can hardly speak
no   that's vulgar singing   trained
singers   hold the note aloft   faithful so
pleasing to protestants   so taught out of
myself   I sing edelweiss   frère jacques
stille nacht   line up for oktoberfest   in a
theater   a bank   and C lunch   stuff
my tamed boca   with vinegar   bratwurst
& the finest european feathers[2]

---

[2]"... in the environments that adopt assimilation policies and devalue children's culture of origin, schools and parents may feel pressured to assimilate children into mainstream culture for children's survival and success, resulting in further loss of culture of origin and/or marginalization from both cultures." —Yoon, Eunju, et. al. "Content Analysis of Acculturation Research in Counseling and Counseling Psychology: A 22-Year Review." *Journal of Counseling Psychology*, Vol. 58, No. 1 (January 2011): 83-96.

in gym admire   whitegirl nipples   soft & pink
as sow's ears   so unlike your own dark   in
physics learn *parallax*:   the effect of position
upon viewing an object   in english learn the
greats are from europe new york   use *parallax* in
a poem   b minus   learn your place   is
beneath[3]   the blondes who snitch   on you
see them off to college   from behind a register
a farewell to arms   on the road   they're bound
for   europe harvard   columbia new york   cash
your check   at the veteran's memorial quikcash
know your place   is going nowhere   wrong side
of the highway   crime forest they call us   in
government   argue with mr. lockwood   who
teaches the confederate flag   means *state's rights*
DETENTION before work   apron stinks up your
backpack   catch a ride   learn to serve
classmates with a smile   at home   help mami
lavar los baños   to even get to go   to the
dollar theater   even after popcorn   your hands
still smell raw   from the comet and bleach
2am feed the baby   so mami can sleep   shave
your fingers & toes   before school   scrub the
dark off your nipples   in gym clock   a seven
minute mile   clean cotton morning   the only
ahead you get   parallax: the effect of position
upon viewing an object[4]

---

[3] *Patient trauma   death   maternal   primary caretaker   failure to acculturate in childhood   late english acquisition   depressive   oppositional defiant
school predominantly culturally American   home environment predominantly of the heritage culture   working class   abuse*

[4] "This association is purported to reflect, in part, the impact of negative experiences faced by immigrants in the process of assimilation, i.e. accul-
turative stressors. However, these findings can be explained by high levels of risk for psychiatric disorder among the US-born members of ethnic
minority populations, who have both high risk for psychiatric disorders and high levels of acculturation relative to immigrants."— Breslau, Joshua,
et. al. "Migration from Mexico to the US and Subsequent Risk for Depressive and Anxiety Disorders: A Cross-National Study." *Arch Gen Psychiatry*. 2
011 April; 68(4): 428–433.

1995   budding black   swallow each received
blue eye   that watches   your house
tongued   in their language   after midnight
whitewash every brown   bikini thrill   cut
& sell   that wild black braid: america's
cash   pawn used blue eyes   on your
peroxide tongue   take out your original eyes
& replace   pull your people's melodies
lamenting doves   out of your ears   plug the
wound with hot   and thick forgetting
nevermind   your mysterious origin   each
milk tooth   a little bloodrot   in virgin linen
each plait of river   in your head   unravels
your brightening body   from corpus
(luckily so luckily here)   each day a passing
(cross leg uncross) new record   hidden
track: nevermind   nameless overwritten

"This association is purported to reflect, in part, the impact of negative experiences faced by immigrants in the process of assimilation, i.e. acculturative stressors. However, these findings can be explained by high levels of risk for psychiatric disorder among the US-born members of ethnic minority populations, who have both high risk for psychiatric disorders and high levels of acculturation relative to immigrants."— Breslau, Joshua, et. al. "Migration from Mexico to the US and Subsequent Risk for Depressive and Anxiety Disorders: A Cross-National Study."

Arch Gen Psychiatry. 2011 April ; 68(4): 428–433.

INCIDENT: Nothing   an immigrant's
daughter does   is intelligible.   We were
lenient   on her   you understand: the
boys well   they have promise.   Pity.
Bright girl.   Girls with HONOR   don't have
these   kinds of problems. Zero tolerance.
We'll show that   involuntary body. Its spill
from contours.   That language   has no
place   in this class

                 break that   dark horse
still bucking   a tighter bridle don't believe
you   young lady   stealing   or giving it
away   like that   EXPEL   truck driver
border filth   they have no place   in this
palimpsest   CUFFS WHILE WE   LOOK
THROUGH YOUR
nothing an
    immigrant's daughter does   is defensible

first-generation   don't make it the last
you can be anything in America   especially
when you're made   an example

PUNISHMENT: ONE STRIKE.   Or, petrified
lightning. A storm's release   drowned wild
in white sand;   a heat   assimilated
ever-rooting   its permanent

                     shatter[5]

---

[5] Gómez, Francisco C., Ronn Johnson, Qiana Davis, Roberto J. Velásquez. "MMPI—A Performance of African and Mexican American Adolescent First-Time Offenders." August 1, 2000. *Psychological Reports*, Vol 87, Issue 1, pp. 309 – 314.

G.C. WALDREP

Cleeve Abbey Suite

Refectory

kniving the same
extravagant body
the tongue threshed—
the blunt theft
concealed, a calendar
creased
& lactant, only
a man on a ladder
could feast
on this dry island.
Wheat-ghost,
rise into the tremor.
Wheat-reef
even the bees spared,
what byred here
a tractable
ablution, wisp
of the charred depth
the almoner
turns his back upon,
nude geometry
against which now
a single bench
evitates, correcting
for the body's
warmth, its delicate
perlustration.
In pelt after pelt

we find the lock
tended,
lapse upon lapse—

Ghost-Apse

maze & bezel

a scaffold
crossed
with a globe

flag sewn into
raw deed's
oblate garment

it neither
wants nor needs
your muscle

only, not to be
glade
&, dirempt,

the pearl's
external depth

(roofed
with thirst)

a conic section

Roof-Line

scrolled in thirst
& gelded
by our new verticals

the orchard's
single lash
fleering its dense
Bethlehem

a green syllable

helixed
with the long rind's
choral blurt—

observed meridian

of the ear's
doubled rupture

(more datable
in its carbons)

I dreamt
the world-whale
suffered,

that is, to drink

or, straitened,
depth remits its
tined whirr,

its wildest octave

Night Stair

nothing the star allows

a panicked embroidery

let rise
these spruce pavilions

into which the ships
bear
their creased reserves

the whey combed
into its lambent creche

nippling w/ bee-gauze

Slype

vein of door, a late
ripeness
golds forth
twins itself, a mirror
preconceived, & yet
you risk
the tongue's crutch
lapsed effigy
of the bleating
master-pain,
its city glows
with almond-hued
flight
can't you hear
the sun ticking

against the tiles
or, dusk's
paternal lemniscate
against the heel
of the soft
flocks—
tungsten wives
the shallow bay
& you, moist
tenant, briefly hive

shock box

a bag over the head is iconic. if you are thinking only of fashion who are you thinking for? when i was 13 i started writing with both hands at once so i could make something that touched itself in the middle. i became an angel. i put space between the letters of my name and my identity was then entirely composed of light. this is why i swallowed a phone and pulled the cord through my throat and mouth. i'm close to you, vince. when i replace my face with a circular mirror you're inside me still. i am not in love with you, vince. i am convincing you that you are a body in a morgue acting as a patient in a hospital stuffed with doctors. when i was 13 i started writing with both hands at once so i could make something that touched itself in the middle. i became an alchemist. i made pure the gothic deep inside the erotic to compose the world entirely of mirrors. i'm calling you because you are inside of me.

i also need to tell vince that there is a jail built around the house. francesca already knows. i can't tell yet if we are the same person. it has not become clear if my head really is the bag. let's buy compression garments and see if we can squirm ourselves into the shape of each other. i also need to tell vince the jail is actually built around the hospital. they are looking to isolate the contaminant that turns the skin into black striped hosiery, the patterned veils, the eyeleted collars. they are looking to isolate and cure the anti-suckler, the color red. look me in the eye and tell me you don't already feel squeezed. the ball python has a heart, too. how hard have you ever thought about what is inside you? a goat has more than one stomach: an extra chamber to chew what wasn't chewn through and through. ruminant. vince, they can't touch that. vince, that can't touch that. i also need to tell vince the jail is actually built around the morgue.

they is a rhetorical construction. trick, trick. the speaker is the audience. there is a woman walking through the corridors of the mortuary humming something that sounds like bubbles of air bursting on the water's surface. a mirror can redirect a beam of light but it isn't interested in air. something i did not see must have kissed me very softly. did i want help? i do not think i wanted help. when they put my hand in the shock box i was not shocked but i learned what is a shock box and i made one in my mouth. i think we are more afraid of monsters knowing our language than we are of knowing the language of the monster. i made the jailers listen. it is 1979 and i killed mary jane shoes, i killed little girl voices, i killed demurring. i said i am actually all done with jail: i am now the gate.

Bijoux in the Dark

The film was rumored to have disintegrated, but that was not the case. A copy of it existed in the library of the small town where the director had been born and where he was last seen entering a theater that has become a small but enduring monument to his artistry.

According to the descendants of those who first saw the film, some of them many times, the story was not the main reason why they returned over and over again to the theater, to sit in the dark and watch the characters make their way across a silver tundra that was clearly fake, survive innumerable catastrophes that were staged, and, in some cases, under rather preposterous conditions demanded by the machinations of an improbable plot, and—fulfilling what one critic referred to as the classic dénouement—fall in love without their every movement toward each other having been accompanied by music, it was that none of this happened as it had been carefully planned, blocked in, and rehearsed; that accidents of all kinds kept sneaking in, like a three-legged dog that manages to run off with the Sunday ham and not lose the slice of pineapple and maraschino cherry that have been attached to it by the slimmest of means.

Legend has it that the dog made it to a traffic island on the other side of town where it was able to devour the pineapple slice without disturbing either the cherry or the ham, which is a Class A type of unexpected occurrence shooting through the film's darkest crevices, its painted lightning bolts jagging deep into the mineshaft down which we all occasionally tumble, like Alice, once we emerge from the theater and step out onto the busy street—automobiles from another century buzzing by.

The more intrepid members of the audience reported that they made their way to the Empire Diner for a dinner consisting of a small green salad, chicken croquettes, mashed potatoes, and string beans that are never green.

Chocolate pudding provided the right conclusion for some, while others preferred the bread pudding topped with a dollop of crème fraîche. It seems that no one asked for coffee, because they did not want to miss out on their dreams, those little pockets of irresponsibility.

You and I took a different route, and, like the heroes of the film, we ended up facing the prospect of crossing a mesa filled with snow. In the distance was a small farmhouse, smoke curling lazily up from its sturdy chimney.

The camera zoomed in, and the close-up followed.

A man came out on the porch, followed by two small children and a cat. Each of them waved, but the children seemed sad, and the circular motions their hands made was clearly an action that they had repeated many times before. They were methodically trying to wipe clear a window to see what was approaching from the other side. For those in the audience, this moment, where we began hovering in the air, as if we were butterflies or birds floating above the story that was running beneath us, is what we still talk about when the oven is warming up, and our hands sift through the flour as if it is hiding something that that has been misplaced or lost.

Shipboard Entertainment

I suspect that many of us, who are taking this honeymoon cruise for the first time, have already heard that there is a blue cloud swirling through every media outlet, headlined by the report that last Sunday a fleet of UFOs was seen flying across our capital's searchlight skies, but neither puffy pink pundits nor beautifully coiffed, tanned television anchors and their elegantly slim sidekicks have been able to satisfactorily explain how—in the middle of this latest polarizing commotion, its imbalance of flames and fluids—diminutive wayward individuals, such as ourselves, have gained a wide array of new and unlikely talents while sailing in carefully plotted circles: we are able to karate kick the candles that the crew has graciously set up around the perimeter of the beautifully appointed stateroom: we can sing popular songs we have never sung before, and, in some cases, are only now hearing for the first time as the words emerge from our mouths in perfectly tuned order, but if this is—as some among us suspect—an introduction to the collective nightmare that is waiting for us, I think many of us might look forward to it: not all of us, of course—that young couple dancing in the back, for instance, the ones that looked like they just stepped out of a best-selling detective novel, those inky surrogates for our neon desires and midnight fantasies, a string of indulgences that we often try to avoid further stimulating, as they will only lead us deeper into the glittering pleasure dome, that spiral of descent into pandemonium's maze, where we dream of attaining a state of gratification, however temporary, that many claim to forego, choosing instead to embrace life's daily pressures and letdowns, at least that is what the brochure that brought us all here announces, but isn't there a loophole in this narrative and all the others being broadcast, a widening crack that desperadoes—meaning us—use to enter another story closer to the one of their own making, even if it takes place in a deserted underground garage, a mirrored elevator that makes unscheduled stops on unnumbered floors, or a yellow beach bungalow surrounded by unimaginable hostilities, surely you and I—whoever we might be in this imagined life—would have met by now, no matter which puppeteer is directing the action: otherwise we would be working at a golf course, or tending the flowers in a former cemetery, or guarding a wrought iron entrance against the complications that come with sickness and old age, but no, that is not us, because we are chosen to be the ones in the corner of the painting—near where the artist planned to put his signature but didn't, no one knows why—reborn as the gambling younger sister of a crime boss and an apprentice in office lighting systems, or a cryptic ruffian and a smart aleck agent, or a blackballed poet and a debauched vicar—the combinations are as numberless as the stars—or shall we continue on as we were, avoiding all mention of the unprincipled wolf packs prowling the deck of our icebound ship while we wait patiently for the magician's latest act to glue us to our seats.

Acknowledgments

Kanika Agrawal: Alternate versions of this work were published in 2019 in *filling Station* 71, *Foglifter* 4.1, and *Notre Dame Review* 48.

Alejandro Albarrán Polanco (Rachel Galvin, translator): "Confusion" first appeared in *Ruido* (Toluca, Mexico: Bonobos Editores, 2012); "Cowboy" first appeared in *Tengo un pulmón que no es cielo* (La Ciebita, Mexico City: Fondo Editorial Tierra Adentro, 2014. Rachel Galvin's translations of Albarrán's poems have appeared in *Asymptote Journal* (Summer 2017) and in the chapbook *Cowboy & Other Poems* (Ugly Duckling Presse, 2019).

Asmaa Azaizeh (Yasmine Haj, translator): These poems are part of a collection entitled *Don't Believe Me if I Talked to You of War* (Almutawassit, 2019), also published in Dutch and Swedish.

Lisa Marie Basile and Alyssa Morhardt-Goldstein: The excerpts featured here were originally published in *Nympholepsy* (Inside the Castle, 2018). The "Luciana" sections are by Lisa Marie Basile and the "Alraune" sections are by Alyssa Morhardt-Goldstein. Thanks to Tarpaulin Sky for choosing *Nympholepsy* as a finalist for their 2017 Book Prize, and to the *Atlas Review* and *Sporklet*, where portions of the work were previously published.

Anne Boyer: "Death and the Maiden" first appeared in *Black Warrior Review* (43.2).

Bridget Brewer: "Little Skin Bag" was originally published in *The Collagist* 91 (June 2017).

Marty Cain: This excerpt originally appeared in *Dreginald*, and was subsequently published within the full-length *Kids of the Black Hole* (Trembling Pillow Press, 2017).

Seo-Young Chu: A version of this essay first appeared at *Entropy* (entropymag. org).

Tom Comitta: *Airport Novella* was published as a PDF and print-on-demand paperback by Troll Thread (November 2017). Comitta would like to thank Troll Thread editors Joey Yearous-Algozin, Holly Melgard, and Chris Sylvester for supporting and helping to shape this project.

Robert C.L. Crawford: "Forced Center" previously appeared in *Reality Beach* 4 (January 2017).

Devyn Defoe: "The Lovers" was shortlisted for the 2017 White Review Short Story Prize (United States and Canada) and appeared as an online exclusive on the *White Review*'s website (April 2017).

Jaquira Díaz: "Girls, Monsters" appeared in *Tin House*, posted on December 12, 2017. A different version of "Girls, Monsters" appears in *Ordinary Girls* (Algonquin Books, 2019).

Adam Dickinson: These poems were previously published in *Anatomic* (Coach House Books, 2018).

Donald Dunbar: The piece "from *Venus Edamame*" was commissioned by musician and artist Joseph Elm and was first featured on *smoking glue gun* (smokinggluegun.com), with online audio. "Bronze Glitches" and "Thy Shade Shines So" were first published in *Gramma Weekly* and were collected in the book *Safe Word* (Gramma, 2017).

Anaïs Duplan: Individual sections of from "Shigeko, Let's Hitchhike to Japan" were previously published as follows: "Martine Syms, Incense, Sweaters, and Ice, 2017, 1:09:00," "Lawrence Andrews, An I for an I, 1987, 18:41," and "Shigeko Kubota, Video Girls and Video Songs for Navajo Sky, 1973, 31:56" appeared in *Paperbag* 11 (December 2018). "Ephraim Asili, Fluid Frontiers, 2017, 23:04" was published in *Anaïs Duplan: 9 Poems/The Lovers* (Belladonna* chaplet #236, belladonnaseries.org/chaplets/). "Ephraim Asili, Many Thousands Gone, 2014, 7:38" appeared in *The Paris Review* 227 (Winter 2018).

Leah Sophia Dworkin: "The Enormous Radio" was originally published in the *Yalobusha Review* 25 (Summer 2017).

Amal El-Mohtar: "Anabasis" was solicited by Liz Gorinsky and Diana Pho for Tor.com's "Nevertheless, She Persisted" project for International Woman's Day, a series of flash fictions that all include the words "She was warned. She was given an explanation. Nevertheless, she persisted." The story "Anabasis" was provoked by reading a CBC article titled " 'I want to die,' 2-Year-Old Refugee Said during Hours-Long Walk to Manitoba from U.S." (www.cbc.ca/news/canada/manitoba/manitoba-refugees-border-crossing-1.3972374).

Ethan Feuer: "Understory" originally appeared in *Indiana Review* 39.1 (Summer 2017).

Sarah Gallien: "Engendered :: Non[fiction]" was previously published by *Queen Mob's Teahouse* (https://queenmobs.com), posted on October 3, 2017.

Adam Greenberg: These poems and the author's note first appeared in *Witness* XXX.3 (Winter 2017).

Josué Guébo (Todd Fredson, translator): Selections are reproduced from *Think of Lampedusa* (African Poetry Books Series) by permission of the University of Nebraska Press; English translation copyright © 2017 by the Board of Regents of the University of Nebraska. Originally published as *Songe à Lampedusa*, copyright 2014 by Panafrika/Silex/Nouvelles du Sud.

Jane Eaton Hamilton: "Battery" first appeared in *Matrix Magazine* in 2015; was the winner of the 2015 Lit Pop contest, judged by George Saunders; and was a 2015 long-list inclusion for the CBC Canada Writes Creative Nonfiction Prize.

Maria Dahvana Headley: "Memoirs of an Imaginary Country" first appeared in *Boston Review* (Fall 2017).

Kamden Hilliard: "About the Poem" first appeared in *The Destroyer* 4.2. "I Feel Most Black" first appeared in *apt* 6 (2017). "Error 404: Binaries Not Rendered" first appeared in *Sixth Finch* (Winter 2017).

Harmony Holiday: "Crisis Actor" first appeared in *Poetry* (October 2017).

Nasser Hussain: This work first appeared in *SKY WRI TEI NGS* (Coach House Books, 2018). Credit for the maps goes to Matt Stephenson, who is a Senior GIS Specialist at Thurber Engineering Ltd. in Calgary, Alberta, Canada.

Aaron Kent: "Flat Heimurinn" was first published by *Stride* (September 9, 2017). "Injsaður" was first published by *3AM Magazine* (September 28, 2017). "Petal" was first published in *Angry Old Man* 2 (2018).

Alice Sola Kim: "One Hour, Every Seven Years" first appeared in *McSweeney's* 49 ("Cover Stories" issue), and in a "New Voices of Science Fiction" preview (November 12, 2019) hosted by Tachyon Publications (tachyonpublications .com).

Kim Yideum (Ji yoon Lee, Johannes Göransson, and Don Mee Choi, translators): "Construction Contractor" and "The Aria from the Rice Chest" are included in *Poems of Kim Yideum, Kim Haengsook & Kim Min Jeong* (Vagabond Press, 2017).

aris~justine kirby: *Sonnet Infinitéismal n°3 / Matérial Girl n°8* was originally published in full as a chapbook in *Black Warrior Review* 44.1 (Fall/Winter 2017).

Matthias Klein: "Unfurl/ed" first appeared at *Strange Horizons* (strangehorizons.com), posted on August 14, 2017.

Samantha Lamph/Len: This piece was originally published in *Occulum* 2 (December 2017).

Sade LaNay: "as watercolor" and "as sunlight" were previously published in *Black Warrior Review* 42.2 (Spring/Summer 2018) and in the chapbook *self portrait* (Birds of Lace, 2018).

Carlos Lara: Excerpts from *The Green Record* have appeared previously in *Lana Turner: A Journal of Poetry and Opinion*, *Chronopolis*, *NOÖ Weekly*, and *Entropy*. The complete collection was published by Apostrophe Books in 2018.

Lisa Locascio: "Byzantium" previously appeared in *Tin House* (September 12, 2017).

Carole Maso: "Their Green Going" originally appeared in *Conjunctions* 69 with the title "Beauty."

Ben Miller and Dale Williams: This selection from the novel *it all melts down to this* first appeared in *The Offbeat* 17 (Spring 2017). Dale created the images that inspired each chapter. Ben crafted the text and its timeline structure.

Vi Khi Nao: "COLON |KŌLəN|" was first published in Fanzine.

Nathanaël: "Days of Broken Lead" is from *Pasolini's Our* (Nightboat Books, 2018). Reprinted with permission of the author and Nightboat Books. The epigraph by Ingeborg Bachmann is translated by Nathanaël from an existing French translation by Miguel Couffon. All unattributed translations are by Nathanaël.

Em North: "Schrödinger's Ovaries" first appeared in *The Threepenny Review* (Winter 2017).

Alice Notley: "Malorum Sanatio" has been published in a chapbook called *Undo* (above/ground press, 2018).

Danielle Pafunda: "I dwell in the road to the sea everyone travels . . ." first appeared in *the tiny* (September 2017).

Alan C. Pelaez Lopez: "sick in 'America'" first appeared in *Vinyl Poetry and Prose* (November 2017).

Xandria Phillips: "Anarcha and I Negotiate Trauma" and "Edmonia Lewis and I on Academic Leave" first appeared in *Yalobusha Review* (2018).

Olga Ravn (Sherilyn Hellberg, translator): *Celestine* was first published in Danish by Gyldendal (2015). The translation first appeared in *EuropeNow*, posted on March 1, 2017.

Raquel Salas Rivera: Estos son fragmentos de la cinta, publicados originalmente en *Dreginald*. Forman parte del manuscrito *x/ex/exis* que fue publicado en el 2019 por Bilingual Press/Editorial Bilingüe y fue el primer ganador del Premio Ambroggio de la Academia de Poetas Americanos. / These are fragments from the ribbon, originally published in *Dreginald*, and part of the book *x/ex/exis* (Bilingual Press/Editorial Bilingüe, 2019), which was the first winner of the Ambroggio Prize from the Academy of American Poets.

Kit Schluter: These pieces first appeared online in *Black Sun Lit*, then in a book published in Mexico, translated by Mariana Rodríguez: *5 Cartoons/5 caricaturas* (Juan Malasuerte Editores, 2019).

Eric Schmaltz: "Path Dependency" first appeared in *Surfaces* (Invisible Publishing, 2018).

Aurvi Sharma: "Revenge Porn" first appeared in the *Kenyon Review Online* (May/June 2017).

Germán Sierra: "Ecdysis" originally appeared in *minor literature[s]*, posted on February, 28, 2018.

Cedar Sigo: All three poems are included in *Royals* (Wave Books, 2017). "Thrones" was first published in *The Wave Papers* (Wave Books, 2016).

Kyra Simone: "Blue Moon" was originally published in the *Brooklyn Rail* (December/January 2017).

SJ Sindu: "Test Group 4: Womanhood and Other Failures" was first published in *The Offing*, posted on March 6, 2017.

Christopher Soto: "[YSL] HAUTE COUTURE" and "MAYBE THE CUBICLE // IS ANOTHER INCARCERATION" first appeared in *Boston Review* (April 15, 2017).

Joseph Spece: "ODETTE." first appeared in *SHARKPACK Annual* (2018).

Maria Stepanova (Sasha Dugdale, translator): The epic poem "War of the Beasts and the Animals" was first published in English translation in *Modern Poetry in Translation* 3 (2017); the excerpt featured here is included in Sasha Dugdale's translation from Russian of the full-length collection *War of the Beasts and the Animals* (Bloodaxe Books, 2021).

Amital Stern: "FOREIGN BODY EAR" first appeared in *Guernica* magazine (August 2017).

alex terrell: "Black Dog" first appeared in *Black Warrior Review* 44.1 (Fall/ Winter 2017) and was then awarded a PEN/Robert J. Dau Short Story Prize and reprinted in the *PEN America Best Debut Short Stories 2018* anthology (Catapult, 2018).

Ava Tomasula y Garcia: "Videoteca Fin del Mundo" first appeared in *Black Warrior Review* 43.2 (Spring/Summer 2017), was awarded a PEN/Robert J. Dau Short Story Prize, and was then reprinted in the *PEN America Best Debut Short Stories 2018* anthology (Catapult, 2018).

Debbie Urbanski: "On the Problem of Replacement Children" was first published in the *Magazine of Fantasy and Science Fiction* (January/February 2017) as "On the Problem of Replacement Children: Prevention, Coping, and Other Practical Strategies."

Sarah Vap: "Christmas Genital Self-Examination" was first published in *Boston Review*, posted on January 17, 2017, under the title "From Winter: Aphorisms."

Vanessa Angélica Villarreal: "Assimilation Rooms" is included in the book *Beast Meridian* (Noemi Press, 2017).

G.C. Waldrep: "Cleeve Abbey Suite" first appeared in *Conjunctions* 68 (2017).

Candice Wuehle: "shock box" was originally published in *Occulum*, posted on September 25, 2017.

John Yau: "Bijoux in the Dark" and "Shipboard Entertainment" are included in *Bijoux in the Dark* (Letter Machine Editions, 2018).

About the Contributors

KANIKA AGRAWAL is an Indian citizen and longtime "temporary alien" in the United States. She studied biology at MIT, where she came to love restriction enzymes and fluorescent labels, and earned an MFA from Columbia University and a PhD in English from the University of Denver. Her work has appeared in *Black Warrior Review, Foglifter*, and various science fiction and fantasy publications.

ALEJANDRO ALBARRÁN POLANCO was born in Mexico City. His 2018 poetry collection *Algunas personas no son caballos* won the Premio Internacional Manuel Acuña. His other books include *Ruido* (2012), *Tengo un pulmón que no es el cielo* (2014), and *Persona fea y ridícula* (2017). He has received grants from Fondo Nacional para la Cultura y las Artes and Fundación para las Letras Mexicanas, and he is a founding editor of the press Canon Accidental. He is also a musician and conceptual artist whose performances and installations have been featured in numerous art exhibitions. The magazine *La Tempestad* named him the Emerging Writer of 2017.

EMILY ANDERSON is the author of *Little: Novels* (BlazeVOX, 2015), a *Little House on the Prairie* erasure project. As Max Howard, she wrote *Fifteen and Change*, a young adult novel-in-verse (West 44 Books, 2018). Excerpts from her current project, *I Lick Everything at Target*, have been published by *Requited* and by Oscar Presents/Oxeye Press (2016). Emily recently completed a PhD in English at the University at Buffalo–SUNY. She lives in Eau Claire, Wisconsin, where she is an elected city council member.

ASMAA AZAIZEH: A Palestinian poet based in Haifa, she was winner of the Young Writer Award from Al Qattan Foundation for her first volume of poetry, Liwa (Dar Alahliya,2012). Her second poetry collection is entitled *As the Woman From Lod Bore Me* (Dar Alahliya, 2015), and her third collection *Don't Believe Me If I Talk to You of War* was published in Arabic by Almutawassit in Milan, Italy, and in Dutch by Uitgeverij Jurgen Maas. Her poems has been translated into English, German, French, Persian, Swedish, Spanish, and other languages. Asmaa has also worked as an editor of newspapers, a journalist, and a presenter on TV and radio. Currently, she works as the artistic director of the Fattoush book store and Fattoush music bar and gallery.

LISA MARIE BASILE is the founding creative director of the magazine *Luna Luna*. She is most recently the author of *The Magical Writing Grimoire* (Fair Winds Press, 2020), *Light Magic for Dark Times* (Fair Winds Press, 2018), and *Apocryphal* Noctuary Press, 2014), and co-author with f Morhardt-Goldstein o *Nympholepsy* (Inside the Castle, 2018). Her work can be found in the *New York Times, Narratively, Entropy, Best American Poetry, Atlas Review*, and more. Lisa Marie earned a master's degree in writing from The New School and as an undergraduate studied literature and psychology at Pace University.

ANNE BOYER is a poet and essayist from Kansas City. Her books include *The Romance of Happy Workers* (Coffee House Press, 2008), *My Common Heart* (Spooky Girlfriend Press, 2011), *Garments Against Women* (Ahsahta Press, 2015), *A Handbook of Disappointed Fate* (Ugly Duckling Presse, 2018), and *The Undying* (Farrar, Straus and Giroux, 2019), a memoir about cancer and care. Her honors include the 2020 Pulitzer Prize for General Nonfiction, the 2018 Cy Twombly Award for Poetry from the Foundation for Contemporary Arts, a 2018 Whiting Award in nonfiction and poetry, the 2018–2019 Judith E. Wilson poetry fellowship at Cambridge University, and the 2016 CLMP award for *Garments Against Women*. She is an associate professor of liberal arts at the Kansas City Art Institute, where she teaches literature, philosophy, and writing.

BRIDGET BREWER is a queer writer, artist, performer, and educator living in Austin, Texas. She holds an MFA in literary arts from Brown University, and her work is published with *Tarpaulin Sky Magazine, The Collagist, Fanzine*, and *Awst Press*, among others. Currently she serves as a fiction editor with *Nat. Brut* magazine, and facilitates writing workshops for folks in nontraditional spaces around Austin. She also fronts a prairie gothic punkgrass band.

MARTY CAIN is from Vermont. He is the author of the book-length poem *Kids of the Black Hole* (Trembling Pillow Press, 2017) and the chapbook *Four Essays* (Tammy, 2019). Individual works have appeared in *Fence, Tarpaulin Sky, Sink*

Review, and *Tenderloin*. He holds an MFA from the University of Mississippi and is currently a PhD student at Cornell University, where he studies rural poetry communities. With Kina Viola, he edits Garden-Door Press.

DON MEE CHOI was born in Seoul, South Korea, and is the author of *The Morning News Is Exciting* (Action Books, 2010) and *Hardly War* (Wave Books, 2016), and the chapbooks *Petite Manifesto* (Vagabond Press, 2014), *Ahn Hak-sop #4* (The Green Violin, 2018), and *Sky Translation* (Goodmorning Menagerie, 2019), as well as a pamphlet of essays, *Freely Frayed* (Wave Pamphlet 9, 2014). She has received a Whiting Award, Lannan Literary Fellowship, and Lucien Stryk Translation Prize, and was selected for the 2019 DAAD Artists-in-Berlin Program. She has translated several collections of Kim Hyesoon's poetry, including *Poor Love Machine* (Action Books, 2016) and *Autobiography of Death* (New Directions, 2018).

SEO-YOUNG CHU teaches at Queens College, CUNY. "A Refuge for Jae-in Doe: Fugues in the Key of English Major" was previously published in *Entropy* (2017) and included in *Best American Non-Required Reading 2018* (Houghton Mifflin Harcourt, 2018). Other publications include "Free Indirect Suicide," in *The Rumpus* (March 2019); "The DMZ Responds," in *Telos (Fall* 2018); "I, Stereotype: Detained in the Uncanny Valley," in *Techno-Orientalism* (Rutgers University Press, 2015); "Welcome to The Vegas Pyongyang," in *Science Fiction Studies* 39.3 (2012); "Dystopian Surface, Utopian Dream," in *A New Literary History of America* (Harvard University Press, 2009; and *Do Metaphors Dream of Literal Sleep?* (Harvard University Press, 2010). She has one sibling and one beagle nephew ghost.

TOM COMITTA is based in Los Angeles. He is the author of ○ (Ugly Duckling Presse, 2013), *Airport Novella* (Troll Thread, 2017), and *First Thought Worst Thought: Collected Books 2011–2014* (Gauss PDF, 2015, www.gauss-pdf.com /editions), an archive of forty night novels, art books, and poetry collections, which was also installed as a 2015 reading room/exhibition at Royal NoneSuch Gallery in Oakland, California. His writing has appeared in *BOMB*, *The Believer, Fence, New American Writing*, and *The New Concrete* (Hayward Gallery, 2015). Comitta's *The Nature Book*, a collage novel composed entirely of nature descriptions from over three hundred canonical novels, is forthcoming from Coffee House Press..

ROBERT C.L. CRAWFORD's writing has appeared in *Boston Review, Nat. Brut, Flag + Void, Queen Mob's Teahouse, Reality Beach*, and *Powder Keg*, and his essay "Movementalities" in *Prelude* 1 (2015) was cited among *Flavorwire's* Best Literary Criticism of the Year. In 2018 he received his MFA from Columbia University. A founding editor of *Prelude*, he lives in Brooklyn.

DEVYN DEFOE is a writer from California and a recent Stegner Fellow at Stanford University.

JAQUIRA DÍAZ is the author of *Ordinary Girls* (Algonquin Books, 2019), a memoir. Her work has been included in *The Best American Essays*, and she is the recipient of two Pushcart Prizes and fellowships from the *Kenyon Review*, the Wisconsin Institute for Creative Writing, and the MacDowell Colony. She is currently a visiting assistant professor in the MFA program at the University of Wisconsin–Madison. Her work appears in the *Kenyon Review, The Fader, T: The New York Times Style Magazine*, and other publications.

ADAM DICKINSON is the author of four books of poetry. His latest book, *Anatomic* (Coach House Books, 2018), involves the results of chemical and microbial testing on his body. His work has been nominated for the Governor General's Award for Poetry, the Trillium Book Award for Poetry, and the Raymond Souster Award. He was also a finalist for the CBC Poetry Prize and the K.M. Hunter Artist Award in Literature. He has been featured at festivals such as Poetry International in Rotterdam, the Netherlands, and the Oslo International Poetry Festival in Norway. He teaches at Brock University in St. Catharines, Ontario, Canada.

SASHA DUGDALE is a poet, translator, and editor. She has published four collections of poetry, most recently *Joy* (Carcanet, 2017), which was a Poetry Book Society Choice; the collection is named after the long poem "Joy," which won the Forward Prize for Best Single Poem in 2016. As a translator of plays and poetry from Russian, she has worked with theaters across the United Kingdom and United States on new productions of contemporary Russian drama. The former editor of *Modern Poetry in Translation*, her translations of poetry have been shortlisted for the Rossica and Popescu Prizes, and she is co-editor of the international anthology *Centres of Cataclysm* (Bloodaxe, 2016). Her translation of *War of the Beasts and the Animals*, Maria Stepanova's first full-length English-language collection, is being published by Bloodaxe Books in 2021, and her translation of Stepanova's prose work *In Memory of Memory* is forthcoming from New Directions..

DONALD DUNBAR is the author of *Eyelid Lick* (Fence Modern Poets Series prize, 2012) and *Safe Word* (Gramma Poetry, 2017), as well as a number of chapbooks. He lives in Los Angeles, California, and works as a virtual reality designer and developer.

ANAÏS DUPLAN is the author of a full-length poetry collection, *Take This Stallion* (Brooklyn Arts Press, 2016) and a chapbook, *Mount Carmel and the Blood of Parnassus* (Monster House Press, 2017). His poems and essays have been featured in *Hyperallergic*, *Bettering American Poetry*, *THUMP*, and *Complex Magazine*, and on PBS NewsHour and the Academy of American Poets and Poetry Society of America websites. As an arts administrator, who he has facilitated artists' projects in Chicago, Boston, Santa Fe, and Reykjavík. He is founder of the Center for Afrofuturist Studies, a residency program for artists of color in Iowa City, Iowa.

LEAH SOPHIA DWORKIN lives in New York City, where she is working on her first collection of stories, *Hey Whitefish*. Her work has been published in *Fence*, *Juked*, *Hotel*, *Hobart*, *Dostoyevsky Wannabe*, *BOMB*, and elsewhere. Online she goes by frumperella.

AMAL EL-MOHTAR's short fiction has won the Hugo, Nebula, and Locus Awards, and her poetry has won the Rhysling Award three times. Her work has recently appeared in the anthologies *The New Voices of Fantasy* (Tachyon, 2017) and *The Starlit Wood: New Fairy Tales* (Gallery/Saga, 2016), and in magazines such as *Lightspeed* and *Fireside*. She has also published a novella co-written with Max Gladstone, *This Is How You Lose the Time War* (Gallery/Saga, 2019). She writes the "Otherworldly" column for the *New York Times Book Review* and teaches creative writing at the University of Ottawa. Find her online at amalelmohtar.com or on Twitter: @tithenai.

ETHAN FEUER is a writer and designer living in Virginia. His stories have appeared or are forthcoming in the *Indiana Review, Tin House, Electric Lit, DIAGRAM*, and *Smokelong Quarterly*. He holds a BArch from Rice University and an MFA from the University of Virginia, where he was a Poe-Faulkner Fellow and runner-up for the 2017 Henfield Prize. He is the grateful recipient of fellowship support from the Tin House and Tent writing conferences. He is at work on a novel.

448 TODD FREDSON is the author of two poetry collections, *Century Worm* (New Issues Poetry & Prose) and *The Crucifix-Blocks* (Tebot Bach). He has made French-to-English translations of Ivorian poet Tanella Boni's collection *The Future Has an Appointment with the Dawn* (University of Nebraska Press), as well as two books by Ivorian poet Josué Guébo, *Think of Lampedusa* (University of Nebraska Press) and *My country, tonight* (Action Books). He has a PhD in creative writing and literature from the University of Southern California and an MFA from Arizona State University. He is the recipient of Fulbright and NEA Translation fellowships.

SARAH GALLIEN co-founded and edited *alice blue review*. Her work appears in or at *Fanzine, Asimov's Science Fiction Magazine, Wigleaf*, and elsewhere.

RACHEL GALVIN is a poet, translator, and scholar. Her books include *Elevated Threat Level* (Green Lantern Press, 2018), a finalist for the National Poetry Series; *Pulleys & Locomotion* (Black Lawrence Press, 2009); Raymond Queneau's *Hitting the Streets* (Carcanet, 2013), winner of the Scott Moncrieff Prize for translation; *Decals: Complete Early Poetry of Oliverio Girondo*, translated with Harris Feinsod (Open Letter Books, 2018); and *News of War: Civilian Poetry 1936–1945* (Oxford University Press, 2018). Her translation of Alejandro Albarrán Polanco's *Cowboy & Other Poems* was published by Ugly Duckling Presse in 2019. Galvin is a co-founder of Outranspo, an international creative translation collective. She is associate professor at the University of Chicago.

JOHANNES GÖRANSSON is the author of seven books, most recently the memoir *POETRY AGAINST ALL* (Tarpaulin Sky Press, 2019), and translator of several books, most recently Helena Boberg's *From Sense Violence* (Garden-Door Press, 2019) and, with Joyelle McSweeney, Aase Berg's collection of essays *Tsunami from Solaris* (Action Books, 2019). He teaches at the University of Notre Dame and co-edits Action Books.

ADAM GREENBERG holds an MFA in poetry from Brown University. His poetry has appeared in *InTranslation, Columbia Poetry Review, Berkeley Poetry Review,* and *Witness,* among others. His translations of the work of Mexican poet Carla Faesler have appeared in *Chicago Review, Erizo, Asymptote,* and *Anomaly.* He lives in Washington, DC, where he teaches composition.

JOSUÉ GUÉBO is the author of eight collections of poetry, including *Songe* à *Lampedusa,* which won the 2014 Tchicaya U Tam'si Prize for African Poetry. He is a professor at the University of Félix Houphouët-Boigny of Cocody in Abidjan, Côte d'Ivoire. His other books include a collection of short stories as well as two books of scholarship, one that investigates objectivity and artificial intelligence, and another that considers African modernity and the evolving conditions of independence. He is a doctor of the history and philosophy of the sciences.

YASMINE HAJ is a writer, editor, and translator. She completed her master's degree in comparative literature at the University of Toronto, with a focus on modern Arabic literature and French New Wave cinema. She is a co-founder of Dalaala, a collective for translating poetry, fiction, films, and other texts from and into Arabic and English.

JANE EATON HAMILTON is the author of nine books of creative nonfiction, fiction, and poetry. Hamilton's books have been shortlisted for numerous awards, and their memoir *No More Hurt* was a *Sunday Times* bestseller and among the (UK) *Guardian*'s Best Books of the Year. A two-time winner of Canada's CBC Literary Award for fiction, Hamilton has had Notables in BASS and BAE, and their work has appeared in the *Journey Prize, Best Canadian Short Stories,* and *Best Canadian Poetry* and also in publications such as *Salon, The Rumpus, Alaska Quarterly Review,* the *Missouri Review,* the *New York Times,* and *The Sun.*

MARIA DAHUANA HEADLEY is the #1 *New York Times* bestselling author of eight books, most recently *The Mere Wife* (MCD/Farrar, Straus and Giroux, 2018), a contemporary adaptation of *Beowulf*, and a new translation of *Beowulf* for the same publishers. Her Nebula, Shirley Jackson, and World Fantasy Award-shortlisted fiction has been anthologized in many year's best anthologies, including several times in *Best American Science Fiction and Fantasy*. She grew up in rural Idaho on a survivalist sled-dog ranch, and now lives in New York.

SHERILYN HELLBERG is a literary translator and PhD candidate at the University of California–Berkeley, where she is currently writing a dissertation on representations of despair in modern and contemporary women's literature and film. She has published translations of Tove Ditlevsen, Ingvild Lothe, Olga Ravn, and most recently Johanne Bille's *Elastic* (Lolli Editions, 2019). In 2018, she was awarded the American-Scandinavian Foundation's Leif and Inger Sjöberg award for her translation of Caspar Eric's long poem *Nike*.

KAMDEN HILLIARD is a Teaching-Writing Fellow at the Iowa Writers' Workshop. They have published three chapbooks, *Distress Tolerance* (Magic Helicopter Press, 2016) and *Perceived Distance from Impact* (2017, Black Lawrence Press), and *henceforce: a travel poetic* (Omnidawn, 2019). Kam has received support from the Davidson Institute, Callaloo, The UCROSS Foundation, and The NFAA. Their reviews, essays, and poems can be found in *Black Warrior Review*, *Salt Hill*, *West Branch*, *Bennington Review*, and *Prairie Schooner*. Find Kam on the internet at kamdenihilliard.com.

AUA HOFMANN is a writer currently living and working and working in Baton Rouge, Louisiana. She has work published or forthcoming in *Black Warrior Review*, *Fence*, *Anomaly*, *APARTMENT*, and *Grimoire*. Her current project, *leech-book: an anti-grimoire*, is a postgenre work that concerns itself with trans/queer history, medieval magic, and the frustrated desire inherent in encounters with the literary archive. Her website is www.nothnx.com and her twitter is @st_somatic.

HARMONY HOLIDAY is a writer, dancer, archivist, and the author of four collections of poetry: *Negro League Baseball* (Fence Books, 2011), *Go Find Your Father / A Famous Blues* (Ricochet Editions, 2014), *Hollywood Forever* (Fence

Books, 2017), and *A Jazz Funeral for Uncle Tom* (Birds, 2019). She also founded and runs Afrosonics, an archive of jazz and everyday diaspora poetics, and Mythscience, an imprint that reissues work from the archive. She contributed to *S O S*, the selected poems of Amiri Baraka (Grove Press, 2015), transcribing all of his poetry recorded with jazz and primarily existing on out-of-print records. Harmony studied rhetoric at the University of California–Berkeley and taught for the Alvin Ailey American Dance Theater. She received her MFA from Columbia University and has received the Motherwell Prize from Fence Books, a Ruth Lilly Fellowship, and a New York Foundation for the Arts fellowship. She is currently working on a book of poems called *M a a f a*, an accompanying collection of essays and memoir entitled *Reparations: Thieves Who Stole My Blue Days,* and a biography of jazz singer Abbey Lincoln.

NASSER HUSSAIN is currently a lecturer in literature and creative writing at Leeds Beckett University. His first full-length collection of poetry is *boldface* (Burning Eye Press, 2014). His work has appeared in a number of places, most recently in the anthology *Wretched Strangers* (Boiler House Press, 2018) and in the chapbooks *EUN OIA (FOR BOK),* with derek beaulieu's No Press (2018), and *Playing With Playing With Fire,* with Sam Riviere's If a Leaf Falls Press. His current interest is mass transit, and he is exploring the codes, mores, and histories of how we move and are moved. *SKY WRI TEI NGS* is a book of poems written entirely from International Air Transport Association (IATA) airport codes.

OLIVIA INGRAM is a settler academic and poet working on land colonially known as Vancouver, British Columbia. Their work focuses on how the construction, politics, and language of spaces are sculpted by ephemera, gender, colonialism, and geophysical capitalism, and how these are represented in avant-garde poetry and the archive. Her graduate work on Frank O'Hara's *Oranges: 12 Pastorals* was awarded a CGS-SSHRC research grant. Her current work *frequency modulations* is from an ongoing series composed of text found on FM radio stations, aimed at capturing the aural ephemera in a space's contemporary moment.

NEGESTI KAUDO is an essayist rooted in the Midwest. In 2015, she became the youngest recipient (at twenty-two) of the Ohioana Library Association's Walter Rumsey Marvin Grant for unpublished writers under thirty. *For Your Plea-*

sure is a hybrid series, first exhibited in Winter 2017–2018 at the C33 Gallery in Chicago. Her work has been published in *Seneca Review, Fourth Genre, IDK Magazine, NewCity, Vagabond City, Cosmonauts Avenue, Nailed*, and *Mosaic.* She teaches writing at Columbus College of Art & Design and moonlights as a substitute teacher.

AARON KENT is a poet and the publisher of Broken Sleep Books. He is inspired by J. H. Prynne, Godzilla, Haruki Murakami, and his wife and daughter. He gave up black coffee for a couple months, but now is drinking it more than ever.

ALICE SOLA KIM'S writing has appeared in publications such as *The Cut, Tin House, McSweeney's, BuzzFeed Reader*, and *Lightspeed.* She is a winner of a 2016 Whiting Award and has received grants and fellowships from the Elizabeth George Foundation and the MacDowell Colony.

KIM YIDEUM has published six books of poetry, a novel that was translated as *Blood Sisters* (Deep Vellum, 2019), and several collections of essays. She received her PhD for a thesis on Korean feminist poetics, and has received numerous awards for her poetry, including the Kim Daljin Changwon Award (2011), the 22nd Century Literary Award (2015), and the Kim Chunsoo Award (2015). A selection of English translations of her poetry was published as *Cheer Up Femme Fatale* (Action Books, 2016). Two more books in translation have been released in English: *Poems of Kim Yideum, Kim Haengsook & Kim Min Jeong* (Vagabond Press, 2017) and *Hysteria* (Action Books, 2019). She currently teaches at Hanyang University and runs a book cafe, Bookcafe Yideum.

ARIS-JUSTINE KIRBY, or Aristilde Justine Kirby, is "herself, & herself alone." She is Louise Montalescot's daughter. She has chapbooks with Belladonna* (*Daisy & Catherine*, 2017) and *Black Warrior Review* (*Sonnet Infinitéismal n°3 / Matérial Girl n°8*, 2018). She has published poetry with *Vetch, Datableed, Orange Mercury*, and *Best American Experimental Writing 2020* ("Hey, that's here! hell yeah"). She's a candidate for a master of fine arts degree at the Milton Avery Graduate School of the Arts, Bard College. She works at Lil' Deb's

Oasis in Hudson, New York. ("Come have a gay ol' time, on us! It's exactly what you think it is.")

MATTHIAS KLEIN keeps the body of nir childhood cat in the freezer in the hope of one day performing mad science on him. Nir partner insists on keeping the other dead things ne collects in the garage. Nir work has appeared at *Strange Horizons*, *Glittership*, and in the *Brave Boy World* anthology, among others. Find nem probably not being morbid enough on twitter @daystrom-reject.

SAMANTHA LAMPH/LEN is a writer and cat masseuse living in Los Angeles. She is the creator and co-curator of *Memoir Mixtapes*, a literary journal that publishes personal essays and poetry inspired by music. More of her work can be found in *Moonchild Magazine*, *Queen Mob's Teahouse*, *Luna Luna*, *Connotation Press*, and *WAVES: An Anthology of Women's Voices*. Find her online at samanthalamphlen.com or on Twitter @quandoparamucho.

SADE LANAY is the author of *I love you and I'm not dead* (Argos Books, 2019), *Härte* (Downstate Legacies, 2018), *self portrait* (Birds of Lace, 2018), and *Dream Machine* (co•im•press, 2014).

CARLOS LARA is the author of *Like Bismuth When I Enter* (Nightboat, 2020), *The Green Record* (Apostrophe Books, 2018), and the chapbook *God Wave* (Evidence, 2018). He is also the co-author, with Will Alexander, of *The Audiographic As Data* (Oyster Moon, 2016) and the translator of Blanca Varela's *Rough Song* (The Song Cave, 2020). He abides in Los Angeles with his wife and son.

JI YOON LEE'S translations of Kim Yideum's poetry with Don Mee Choi and Johannes Göransson were published in the book *Cheer Up, Femme Fatale* (Action Books, 2015) and shortlisted for the Lucien Stryk Prize. She is also the author of *Foreigner's Folly* (Coconut Books, 2014), *Funsize/Bitesize* (Birds of Lace, 2013), and *IMMA* (Radioactive Moat, 2012). Excerpts from her manuscript *Baby Visa Denied* have appeared in *Fence*. Her translation of Kim Yideum's novel *Blood Sisters* was published in 2019 by Deep Vellum Press. She was born in South Korea, and immigrated alone as a teen to a small town in East Texas. She received her MFA in creative writing from the University of Notre Dame; and to pursue a PhD in creative writing at the University of Houston, she moved back to Texas, the land that keeps pulling her back.

LISA LOCASCIO is the author of *Open Me* (Grove Atlantic, 2018), which was a *New York Times Book Review* Editor's Pick and one of *O Magazine*'s "Ten Titles to Pick Up Now." Her writing has appeared in *The Believer, n+1, Tin House, Electric Literature*, and *Literary Hub*, among many other magazines. She is executive director of the Mendocino Coast Writers' Conference and lives in the Far West, where she is at work on her second book. She gratefully acknowledges *Tin House*, her editor Lance Cleland, and the Mendocino Coast Writers' Conference for giving "Byzantium" space to develop and a home when it was finished.

CAROLE MASO is the author of ten books, including the novels *The Art Lover* (North Point Press, 1990), *AVA* (Dalkey Archive Press, 1993), and *Mother & Child* (Counterpoint Press, 2012); a collection of essays, *Break Every Rule* (Counterpoint, 2000); poems in prose, *Aureole* (Ecco, 1996) and *Beauty Is Convulsive* (Counterpoint, 2019); and a memoir, *The Room Lit by Roses* (Counterpoint, 2002). Professor of literary arts at Brown University, she is the recipient of the 2018 Berlin Prize.

BEN MILLER is the author of *River Bend Chronicle: The Junkification of a Boyhood Idyll Amid the Curious Glory of Urban Iowa* (Lookout Books, 2013). His prose has been featured in *Best American Essays, One Story, Southern Review, Harvard Review, Yale Review, New England Review, AGNI, Raritan, Antioch Review*, and many other journals. He has received creative writing fellowships from the National Endowment for the Arts and the Radcliffe Institute for Advanced Study at Harvard University. Other collaborations with the Brooklyn-based visual artist Dale Williams include the ongoing *Cage Dies Bird Flies* series of text-based works that deploy various media.

ALYSSA MORHARDT-GOLDSTEIN is the co-author, with Lisa-Marie Basile, of *Nympholepsy* (Inside the Castle, 2018) and author of the chapbook *Quiet* (The New School, 2013), winner of The New School University Press contest. She has been finalist and semifinalist for the Tarpaulin Sky Book Prize, and her work can be found in *Sporklet*, *Prick of the Spindle*, *Front Porch*, and others. She is the founder and artistic director of Wildwood Home for the Arts, *SOUND Literary Magazine*, and Diorama, an immersive poetry performance series. She earned her BM in classical vocal performance with a concurrent BA in philosophy and English literature from Mannes Conservatory, and her MFA in poetry from The New School.

UI KHI NAO is the author of *Sheep Machine* (Black Sun Lit, 2018) and *Umbilical Hospital* (Press 1913, 2017); the short story collection *A Brief Alphabet of Torture*, which won FC2's Ronald Sukenick Innovative Fiction Prize in 2016; the novel *Fish in Exile* (Coffee House Press, 2016); and the poetry collection *The Old Philosopher*, which won the Nightboat Books Prize for Poetry in 2014. Her work includes poetry, fiction, film, and cross-genre collaboration. Her stories, poems, and drawings have appeared in *NOON*, *Ploughshares*, *Black Warrior Review*, and *BOMB*, among others. She holds an MFA in fiction from Brown University.

NATHANAËL is the author of more than a score of books written in English or in French, and published in the United States, Québec, and France.

EM NORTH is an ex-physicist, ex-snowboarding instructor, and ex-horse trainer who has lived in ten states in the past eleven years. Her writing has appeared in *The Threepenny Review*, *Catapult*, and elsewhere. She is currently pursuing an MFA in fiction at Johns Hopkins University.

ALICE NOTLEY is the author of numerous books of poetry and has edited and co-edited books by Ted Berrigan and Douglas Oliver. She edited the magazine *Chicago* in the 1970s and co-edited with Oliver the magazines *Scarlet* and *Gare du Nord* in the 1990s. She was the recipient in 2015 of the Poetry Foundation's Ruth Lilly Prize, a lifetime achievement award. Her latest books are *Certain Magical Acts* and *For the Ride,* both from Penguin (2016 and 2020). She lives in Paris, France.

DANIELLE PAFUNDA is the author of nine books, including *Spite* (The Operating System, 2020), *Beshrew* (Dusie Press, 2019), *The Book of Scab* (Ricochet Editions, 2018), and *The Dead Girls Speak in Unison* (Bloof Books, 2017). She teaches at Rochester Institute of Technology.

ALAN PELAEZ LOPEZ is an AfroIndigenous writer and artist from Oaxaca, Mexico. They are the author of *Intergalactic Travels: poems from a fugitive alien* (The Operating System, 2020) and *to love and mourn in the age of displacement* (Nomadic Press, 2020).

JEFFREY PETHYBRIDGE is the author of *Striven, The Bright Treatise* (Noemi Press, 2013). His work appears widely, featured in journals such as *Chicago Review*, *Volt*, *Seattle Review*, *Iowa Review*, *LIT*, and *New American Writing*. He teaches in the Jack Kerouac School of Disembodied Poetics at Naropa University, where he also serves as the managing director of the Summer Writing Program. He's currently at work on a documentary project centered on the torture memos, entitled "Force Drift, an Essay in the Epic." He lives in Denver with the poet Carolina Ebeid and their son Patrick; together they edit the literary zine *Visible Binary*.

XANDRIA PHILLIPS is a poet, educator, visual artist, and the author of *HULL* (Nightboat Books, 2019) and *Reasons for Smoking* (Seattle Review/Paper Hammer, 2018), which won the 2016 *Seattle Review* chapbook contest, judged by Claudia Rankine. They are the poetry editor at Honeysuckle Press and the curator of *Love Letters to Spooks*, a literary space for Black people. Xandria frequently advises *Winter Tangerine*'s New York City workshops hosted by Poets House. Their work has been featured in the *American Poetry Review*, *Beloit Poetry Journal*, *Black Warrior Review*, *Crazyhorse*, and elsewhere. They currently live and breathe in Chicago, Illinois.

OLGA RAVN is one of the leading voices in contemporary Danish literature. She is a graduate of Forfatterskolen, the Danish Academy for Creative Writing. She made her debut with the poetry collection *Jeg æder mig selv som lyng: pigesind* (I Eat Myself Like Heather) (Gyldendal, 2012), for which she received an award from the Danish Arts Foundation. She has since published another poetry collection, *Den hvide rose* [The White Rose) (Gyldendal, 2016), and two novels, *Celestine* (Gyldendal, 2015) and *De ansatte* (The Employees) (Gyldendal, 2018). She is co-founder of the Witches School, a feminist creative writing school.

RAQUEL SALAS RIVERA es un poeta, traductor, y editor. Sus reconocimientos incluyen el nombramiento como Poeta Laureado de la ciudad de Filadelfia, la Beca de Laureado de la Academia de Poetas Americanos, el Premio Nuevas

Voces del Festival de la Palabra de Puerto Rico, el Premio Literario Lambda a una obra de poesía transgénero, y el Premio Ambroggio. También fue semifinalista para el Premio Nacional del Libro del 2018 (EEUU) y el Pen America Open Book Award del 2020. Cuenta con la publicación de cinco poemarios. Su sexto poemario, *antes que isla es volcán / before island is volcano*, es una apuesta imaginativa por un futuro decolonial para Puerto Rico y será publicado por Beacon Press en el 2022. Obtuvo un Doctorado en Literatura Comparada y Teoría Literaria de la Universidad de Pensilvania y actualmente escribe y enseña en Puerto Rico. / RAQUEL SALAS RIVERA is a Puerto Rican poet, translator, and editor. His honors include being named the 2018–19 Poet Laureate of Philadelphia, the Laureate Fellowship from the Academy of American Poets, the New Voices Award from Puerto Rico's Festival de la Palabra, the Lambda Literary Award for Transgender Poetry, and the Ambroggio Prize. He was also longlisted for the 2018 National Book Award and the 2020 Pen America Open Book Award. The author of five full-length poetry books, his sixth book, *antes que isla es volcán / before island is volcano*, is an imaginative leap into Puerto Rico's decolonial future and is forthcoming from Beacon Press in 2022. He holds a Ph.D. in Comparative Literature and Literary Theory at the University of Pennsylvania and now writes and teaches in Puerto Rico.Press, 2020).

KIT SCHLUTER is a poet-translator and book designer living in Mexico City. Among his published and forthcoming translations are books by Amandine André, Anne Kawala, Jaime Saenz, Michel Surya, and Julio Torri, as well as several volumes of stories by Marcel Schwob, including his novella *The Children's Crusade* (Wakefield Press, 2018). A bilingual edition of Kit's book of illustrated stories *5 Cartoons 5 caricaturas*, translated into Spanish by Mariana Rodríguez, was published by Juan Malasuerte Editores (2019). His first book of poems is *Pierrot's Fingernails* (Canarium Books, 2020). Kit edits O'clock Press and co-organizes the poetry reading series "Salón de Belleza" in Aeromoto, a public arts library in Mexico City.

ERIC SCHMALTZ is a poet, an academic, and the author of *Surfaces* (Invisible, 2018). His work has appeared in journals including *Berkeley Poetry Review*, *Jacket2*, *The Capilano Review*, and *Lemon Hound*, and has been exhibited in galleries and art spaces in Toronto, Philadelphia, Buffalo, and Vancouver. In 2018, he guest edited the inaugural issue of *Not Your Best*, which focused on visual poetry and text-art. Eric holds a PhD in English from York University and in 2018–2019 he was a Visiting Postdoctoral Fellow at the University of Pennsylvania.

AURVI SHARMA has received the NYSCA/NYFA Fellowship in Nonfiction and the AWP Kurt Brown Prize as well as awards from Gulf Coast, Prairie Schooner, and Wasafiri. A Bread Loaf–Rona Jaffe Foundation Scholar, she has been awarded fellowships from the MacDowell Colony, Yaddo, Virginia Center for the Creative Arts, Santa Fe Art Institute, *Tin House*, and Sarai. Her essays "Apricots" and "Eleven Stories of Water and Stone" were notables in the *Best American Essays* 2017 and 2016. Her work has also appeared in *Guernica*, *Pleiades*, and *Fourth Genre*, among others. Born and raised in the north Indian hinterlands, Aurvi now lives in New York City, where she is working on a memoir about the Yamuna River and the disobedient women who once occupied its banks.

GERMÁN SIERRA is a neuroscientist and fiction writer. He has published six books of fiction in Spanish—*El Espacio Aparentemente Perdido, La Felicidad no da el Dinero, Efectos Secundarios, Alto Voltaje, Intente usar otras palabras,* and *Standards*. His first book in English is *The Artifact* (Inside the Castle, 2018). Twitter: @german_sierra.

CEDAR SIGO was raised on the Suquamish Reservation in the Pacific Northwest and studied at the Jack Kerouac School of Disembodied Poetics at the Naropa Institute. He is the editor of a collection of writings by Joanne Kyger, *There You Are: Interviews, Journals, and Ephemera,* (Wave Interview Series, 2017), and the author of eight books and pamphlets of poetry, including *Royals* (Wave Books, 2017), *Language Arts* (Wave Books, 2014), *Stranger in Town* (City Lights, 2010), *Expensive Magic* (House Press, 2008), and two editions of *Selected Writings* (Ugly Duckling Presse, 2003 and 2005). He has taught workshops at St. Mary's College, Naropa University, and University Press Books.

KYRA SIMONE is a writer and editor based in Brooklyn. Her work has appeared or is forthcoming in the *Atlas Review, Black Clock, Brooklyn Rail, Conjunctions, F(r)iction, Little Star, Prelude,* and *Vestiges,* among other journals. She is a member of the publishing collective Ugly Duckling Presse and works as an associate editor at Zone Books.

SJ SINDU was born in Sri Lanka and raised in Massachusetts. Sindu's first novel, *Marriage of a Thousand Lies* (Soho Press, 2017), won the Publishing Triangle Edmund White Award for Debut Fiction and was selected by the American Library Association as a Stonewall Honor Book. Also the author of the hybrid fiction and nonfiction chapbook *I Once Met You But You Were Dead* (Split Lip Press, 2017), which won the Turnbuckle Chapbook Contest, and a 2013 Lambda Literary Fellow, Sindu holds a PhD in creative writing from Florida State University. *Blue-Skinned Gods*, Sindu's second novel, is forthcoming from Soho Press in 2021.

CHRISTOPHER SOTO is the author of the chapbook *Sad Girl Poems* (Sibling Rivalry Press, 2016) and the editor of *Nepantla: An Anthology Dedicated to Queer Poets of Color* (Nightboat Books, 2018).

JOSEPH SPECE is editor at Fathom Books. His volumes are *BAD ZOO* (Fathom, 2018) and *Roads* (Cherry Grove, 2013). Public honors in writing include a Ruth Lilly Fellowship; fellowships from the MacDowell Colony, Vermont Studio Center, and the Massachusetts Cultural Council; and the Corrente Prize in Poetry from Columbia University. He lives outside Boston, Massachusetts.

MARIA STEPANOVA is a poet, essayist, and journalist; the author of ten poetry collections and two books of essays. She has been awarded several Russian and international literary awards, including the prestigious Andrey Bely Prize and Joseph Brodsky Fellowship. Her book *Pamyati pamyati*, a cultural history, won Russia's Big Book Prize in 2018, was published in Germany as *Nach dem Gedächtnis* (Suhrkamp, 2018), and is forthcoming in English as *In Memory of Memory*, to be published by New Directions in the US and Fitzcarraldo in the UK. Her most recent collection of poems in English is *War of the Beasts and the Animals* (Bloodaxe Books, 2020), translated by Sasha Dugdale and excerpted in this volume. She is the founder and editor-in-chief of the online, independent, and crowd-sourced journal *Colta.ru*, which covers cultural, social, and political realities in contemporary Russia, with an audience of nearly a million visitors a month.

AMITAL STERN writes film, theater, and hybrid work. Her plays include *Hunger Artist*, performed at the Theatronetto Festival in Tel Aviv, the Jerusalem Fringe Festival, and the Arab-Israeli Theater in Jaffa; *In Waiting*, winner of the Fred Simmons Arts Prize; and *Aliza,* a site-specific work that haunted abandoned buildings in Jerusalem throughout 2017. Her prose has recently appeared in *Guernica* and in a series of installments at Corporeal Clamor, searching for meeting points between body, place and language, women, monsters, and demons. Born and raised in an Orthodox Jewish family in small cities across North America, she now lives in Jerusalem.

ALEX TERRELL writes about the intersection between the mythic and the traumatic. In fiction, she is interested in exploring individuated Black experience, Black bodies, magical realism, Afro-futurism, and how women speak in silent spaces. She is also currently pursuing an MFA at the University of Massachusetts–Amherst.

JIA TOLENTINO is a staff writer at the *New Yorker* and was formerly deputy editor of *Jezebel* and contributing editor at *The Hairpin.* Her first book is a collection of essays, *Trick Mirror: Reflections on Self-Delusion* (Random House, 2019).

AVA TOMASULA Y GARCIA is invested in fights for a redistributive and solidarity economy. She is currently a labor organizer at el Centro de Trabajadores Unidos in Southeast Chicago. She is writing a novel set in the industrial belt of Northern Indiana where her family is from. She wants you to act—now!

DEBBIE URBANSKI is a writer living in Syracuse, New York. Her stories have appeared in *The Sun, Kenyon Review, Nature, Southern Review, Terraform,* and *Best American Science Fiction and Fantasy.*

SARAH VAP is the author of seven books of poetry, poetics, and creative nonfiction. Her book *Viability* (Penguin, 2016) was selected for the National Poetry Series. She is the recipient of a National Endowment of the Arts Fellowship and teaches in the MFA program at Drew University. Her most recent book is *Winter: Effulgences and Devotions* (Noemi Press, 2019).

VANESSA ANGÉLICA VILLARREAL was born in the Rio Grande Valley borderlands to formerly undocumented Mexican immigrants. She is the author of the collection *Beast Meridian* (Akrilica Series, Noemi Press, 2017), which was a Kate Tufts Discovery Award finalist and winner of the John A. Robertson Award for Best First Book of Poetry from the Texas Institute of Letters. Her work has been featured in *BuzzFeed*, *Boston Review*, *The Rumpus*, and *Los Angeles Times*, and on NBC News and the Academy of American Poets online. She is a CantoMundo Fellow, and is currently pursuing her doctorate in English literature and creative writing at the University of Southern California in Los Angeles, where she is raising her son with the help of a loyal dog.

G.C. WALDREP is the author most recently of *feast gently* (Tupelo Press, 2018) and the long poem *Testament* (BOA Editions, 2015). Recent work has appeared in *APR*, *Paris Review*, *New England Review*, *Yale Review*, *Colorado Review*, *Conjunctions*, *New American Writing*, and *Denver Quarterly*. Waldrep lives in Lewisburg, Pennsylvania, where he teaches at Bucknell University and edits the journal *West Branch*. From 2007 to 2018 he served as editor-at-large for the *Kenyon Review*.

DALE WILLIAMS has exhibited his art in the New York City area over the past twenty-five years. He received a 2014 fellowship in Printmaking/Drawing/ Book Arts from the New York Foundation for the Arts. In the summer of 2016, he created a suite of site-specific paintings for "Eutopia" at the Snug Harbor Cultural Center on Staten Island, New York. His most recent one-person show, "America Now Suite," a re-visioning of American history, was held at Gowanus Loft (Brooklyn) in October 2018. His work was also included in the BRIC Biennial III in the winter/spring of 2019.

CANDICE WUEHLE is the author of the full-length collection *BOUND* (Inside the Castle Press, 2018) and the chapbooks *VIBE CHECK* (Garden-door Press, 2017), *EARTH*AIR*FIRE*WATER*ÆTHER* (Grey Books Press, 2015), and *curse words: a guide in 19 steps for aspiring transmographs* (Dancing Girl Press & Studio, 2014). Poems from her collection *Death Industrial Complex* (Action Books , 2020) have appeared in *Black Warrior Review*, *Bennington Review*, *New Delta Review*, and *Fugue*. She is originally from Iowa City, Iowa, and is a graduate of the Iowa Writers' Workshop.

JOHN YAU is a poet, fiction writer, publisher, and critic, whose art and literary reviews are posted regularly on the online magazine *Hyperallergic Weekend*.

His latest books include a selection of essays, *The Wild Children of William Blake* (Autonomedia, 2017); two monographs, *Thomas Nozkowski* (Lund Humphries, 2017) and *Philip Taaffe* (Lund Humphries, 2018); and a book of poetry, *Bijoux in the Dark* (Letter Machine Editions, 2018). He was the recipient of the 2018 Jackson Prize in Poetry. He lives in New York and is professor of critical studies at Mason Gross School of Art (Rutgers University).

Editors

SETH ABRAMSON, an assistant professor of Communication Arts and Sciences at the University of New Hampshire, is the author of fourteen books. His most recent works are the *New York Times* bestsellers *Proof of Collusion* (Simon & Schuster, 2018) and *Proof of Conspiracy* (Macmillan, 2019).

JESSE DAMIANI is Deputy Director of Emerging Technology at Southern New Hampshire University and a *Forbes* contributor. He lives in the Greater Boston Area.

CARMEN MARIA MACHADO is the author of the memoir *In the Dream House* and the short story collection *Her Body and Other Parties*, which was a finalist for the National Book Award. Her essays, fiction, and criticism have appeared in the *New Yorker*, *Granta*, *Tin House*, *Best American Science Fiction & Fantasy*, and elsewhere. She is the Writer in Residence at the University of Pennsylvania and lives in Philadelphia.

JOYELLE MCSWEENEY is the author of ten books: poetry, stories, novels, essays, translations, and plays, including most recently a double-volume of poems, *Toxicon and Arachne* (Nightboat Books, 2020), and a work of decadent ecopoetics, *The Necropastoral: Poetry, Media, Occults* (University of Michigan Poets on Poetry series, 2015). Her debut poetry volume *The Red Bird* inaugurated the Fence Modern Poets Series in 2001, and her verse play *Dead Youth, or, The Leaks* inaugurated the Leslie Scalapino Prize for Innovative Women Performance Artists in 2014. With Johannes Göransson, she co-edits the international press Action Books and teaches at the University of Notre Dame.

MICHAEL MARTIN SHEA is the author of three chapbooks of poetry and hybrid writing: *"Soon"* (Garden-Door Press, 2016), *The Immanent Field* (Essay Press, 2017), and *Comparative Morphologies* (above/ground press, 2018). Individual poems have appeared in *Colorado Review*, *Conjunctions*, *Fence*, *jubilat*, *PEN Poetry Series*, and elsewhere. He is also the translator of Argentine writer Liliana Ponce's chapbook-length work *Diario/Diary* (Ugly Duckling Presse, 2018). He lives in Philadelphia, where he is a doctoral student in Comparative Literature and Literary Theory at the University of Pennsylvania.